Undergraduate Topics in C

T0073460

'Undergraduate Topics in Computer Science' (UTiCS) delivers high-quality instructional content for undergraduates studying in all areas of computing and information science. From core foundational and theoretical material to final-year topics and applications, UTiCS books take a fresh, concise, and modern approach and are ideal for self-study or for a one- or two-semester course. The texts are all authored by established experts in their fields, reviewed by an international advisory board, and contain numerous examples and problems, many of which include fully worked solutions.

The UTiCS concept relies on high-quality, concise books in softback format, and generally a maximum of 275–300 pages. For undergraduate textbooks that are likely to be longer, more expository, Springer continues to offer the highly regarded Texts in Computer Science series, to which we refer potential authors.

James T. Streib · Takako Soma

Guide to Java

A Concise Introduction to Programming

Second Edition

 Springer

James T. Streib
Program in Computer Science
Illinois College
Jacksonville, IL, USA

Takako Soma
Program in Computer Science
Illinois College
Jacksonville, IL, USA

ISSN 1863-7310   ISSN 2197-1781   (electronic)
Undergraduate Topics in Computer Science
ISBN 978-3-031-22841-4   ISBN 978-3-031-22842-1   (eBook)
https://doi.org/10.1007/978-3-031-22842-1

This Springer imprint is published by the registered company Springer Nature Switzerland AG
The registered company address is: Gewerbestrasse 11, 6330 Cham, Switzerland

Preface

James T. Streib[a,1] and Takako Soma[a,2]

[a] Computer Science Program, Illinois College, Jacksonville, IL, USA

[1] Email: james.streib@jtstreib.com.
[2] Email: tsoma@ic.edu.

Purpose

The purpose of this text is to help the reader learn very quickly how to program using the Java programming language. This is accomplished by concentrating on the fundamentals, providing plenty of illustrations and examples, and using visual contour diagrams to illustrate the object-oriented semantics of the language.

Comparison to Other Texts

There are a number of texts on the Java programming language. Some of these texts provide plenty of examples and are very comprehensive, but unfortunately, they sometimes seem to cover too many details, which might make it difficult for a beginning programmer to discern which points are the most relevant. There are also other texts that attempt to provide a shortened introduction to the language, but it seems that these texts might not provide the necessary examples and illustrations and might be better suited for readers who have previous programming experience.

Need

This text attempts to fill the gap between the above two types of books. First, it provides plenty of examples and concentrates primarily on the fundamentals of the Java programming language so that the reader can stay focused on the key concepts. Second, by concentrating on the fundamentals, it allows the text to be more concise and yet still accessible to readers who have no prior programming experience. The result is that the reader can learn the Java programming language very quickly and also have a good foundation to learn more complex topics later.

Features of This Text

This text provides many examples and illustrations. It further has an early introduction to object-oriented programming and uses contour diagrams to illustrate various object-oriented concepts. The contour model was originally developed by John B. Johnson [4]. The model was elaborated on by Organick, Forsythe, and Plummer to illustrate subprograms, parameter passing, and recursion in procedural and functional languages [7]. The model seems quite adaptable to newer programming methodologies such as object-oriented programming as illustrated in a paper by the authors of this text [8]. As discussed in that paper, it was shown that the use of contour diagrams can be an effective tool in helping one learn object-oriented concepts in the Java programming language. By acquiring a good working model of objects, there is less chance of possible misconceptions.

In many places in the text, questions are asked of the reader to help them interact with the material and think about the subject matter just presented. Hopefully the reader will take a few moments to try to answer these questions on their own before proceeding to the answer that follows. To help further reinforce concepts, each chapter has one or more complete programs to illustrate many of the concepts presented and also to help readers learn how to write programs on their own. In addition, for review and practice, there are summaries and exercises provided at the end of each chapter. Further, in the appendices at the end of the text, there are answers to selected exercises and a glossary of important terms. A summary of the features of this text are listed below:

- Stresses the fundamentals.
- Provides many examples and illustrations.
- Has an early introduction to objects.
- Uses contour diagrams to illustrate object-oriented concepts.
- Asks readers questions to help them interact with the material.
- Has one or more complete programs in every chapter.
- Provides chapter summaries.
- Includes exercises at the end of each chapter, with selected answers in an appendix.
- Has a glossary of important terms.

Features New to the Second Edition

The second edition retains all the features of the first edition. In addition to fixing any known errors, any areas that could be clarified have been reworded. Features new to the second edition, include the following:

- Chapter 1 has been reorganized into Chapters 0 and 1. Whereas an experienced programmer can go straight to Chapter 1, it is recommended a new programmer or an experienced programmer who wants a review start with the computer concepts in Chapter 0.
- Chapter 0 contains new topics such as computational thinking and computer ethics.
- Where previously some topics in Chapter 1 were scattered in different sections, they have been consolidated into single sections to help the reader focus on each topic individually.
- Simple graphical user interface (GUI) is introduced in Chapter 1 and used in different sections throughout the text.
- Chapter 11 has been added to include an introduction to bit-wise logic for computer science students taking computer organization in the future or for pre-engineering students to gain exposure to some of the logic capabilities in the C-like languages.
- Chapter 12 introduces parallel processing programming for computer science students who will be taking a course in operating systems in the future.
- Appendix A contains a detailed description of the Java skeleton introduced in Chapter 1 along with additional information on standard output and GUI.
- Additional exercises have been added to various chapters.

Overview of the Chapters

This text first introduces the reader to various computer concepts such as hardware, software, computational thinking, software design, and computer ethics. It then allows the reader to understand a simple program with the appropriate input, processing, and output, followed by an early introduction to objects. It then looks at selection and iteration structures followed by more object-oriented concepts. Next, strings and arrays are examined. This is followed by recursion, inheritance and polymorphism, and elementary files. Then there is an introduction to bit-wise logic and parallel processing. The appendices include information on the Java skeleton, standard output, graphical input/output, exception processing, Javadoc, a glossary, and answers to selected exercises. Lastly, there are references, useful websites and an index. The following provides a brief synopsis of the chapters and appendices:

- Chapter 0 begins with the computer concepts of hardware/software, computational thinking, design, and computer ethics.
- Chapter 1 provides an introduction to variables, input/output, and arithmetic operations.
- Chapter 2 introduces objects and contour diagrams.
- Chapter 3 explains selection structures.
- Chapter 4 shows how iteration structures work.
- Chapter 5 revisits object-oriented concepts.
- Chapter 6 introduces string variables and processing.
- Chapter 7 illustrates arrays and array processing.
- Chapter 8 examines recursion.
- Chapter 9 explores inheritance and polymorphism.
- Chapter 10 discusses elementary files.
- Chapter 11 describes how bit-wise logic works
- Chapter 12 introduces parallel processing programming.
- Appendix A elaborates on the Java skeleton, standard output, and graphical input/output.
- Appendix B discusses elementary exception processing.
- Appendix C presents the basics of Javadoc.
- Appendix D lists a glossary of key terms.
- Appendix E provides answers to selected exercises.

Ordering of the Chapters

Typically, there are three ways objects can be introduced to the beginning programmer:

- Objects first.
- Objects last.
- Objects interleaved.

This text takes the latter approach where objects are discussed in Chapters 2, 5, and 9. However, recognizing that some readers and instructors might want to use one of the first two approaches, this text can be read using alternative orders. For example, should an objects first approach want to be taken, after reading Chapter 1, Chapters 2 and 5 can be read next, followed by Chapters 3 and 4. Should an object later approach want to be used, Chapters 3 and 4 can be read prior to Chapters 2 and 5.

To help facilitate these alternative approaches, starting with Chapter 3, the Complete Program sections at the end of each chapter have examples with and without using objects. Note that Chapter 9 requires an understanding of arrays, which is covered in Chapter 7, and it can be read after completing that chapter.

Scope

As mentioned previously, this text concentrates on the fundamentals of the Java programming language such as input/output, object-oriented programming, arithmetic and logic instructions, control structures, strings, arrays including elementary sorting and searching, recursion, files, bit-wise logic, and parallel processing programming. As a result, it might not cover all the details that are found in some other texts, and if necessary, these topics can be supplemented by the instructor or reader, or covered in a subsequent text and/or second semester course.

Audience

This text is intended primarily for readers who have not had any previous programming experience; however, this does not preclude its use by others who have programmed previously. It can serve as a text in an introductory programming course, as an introduction to a second language in a practicum course, as a supplement in a course on the concepts of programming languages, or as a self-study guide in either academe or industry. Although no prior programming is assumed, it is recommended that readers have the equivalent of an introduction to functions course that includes trigonometry which will help with problem solving and understanding the examples presented in the text.

Acknowledgments

In addition to the reviewers of the first edition, the authors would like to thank Mark E. Bollman of Albion College and James W. Chaffee of the University of Iowa for their continued work on this edition. Also, the authors would like to acknowledge the students of Illinois College who have read and used various sections of the first edition in the classroom. On a personal note, James Streib would like to thank his wife Kimberly A. Streib and son Daniel M. Streib. Takako Soma would like to thank her family and friends, near and far.

   Note that Java is a registered trademark of Oracle and/or its affiliates and that Windows is a registered trademark of Microsoft Corporation in the United States and/or other countries.

Feedback

The possibility of errors exist in any text, therefore any corrections, comments, or suggestions are welcome and can be sent to the authors via the e-mail addresses below. In addition to copies of the complete programs presented in the text, any significant corrections can be found at the website below.

Website: http://www.jtstreib.com/GuideJavaProgramming.html

Illinois College
Jacksonville, IL, USA
October 1, 2022

James T. Streib
james.streib@jtstreib.com
Takako Soma
tsoma@ic.edu

Contents

SPRINGER NATURE

00892037778

PACKING LIST

Springer Nature Customer Service Center LLC
200 Hudson Street, Suite 503
Jersey City, New Jersey 07331-1218
customerservice@springernature.com
www.springernature.com

FEI# 26-2544201
GST# 836145300
QST# 1218563852

Please quote with queries >	Delivery No:	Customer Account No:	Purchase Order No:	Date	Pages
	00892037778		COM2065470	2/15/2023	1 / 1

Bill To:

BAKER & TAYLOR BOOKS
LORRI VICKERY ACCOUNTS PAYABLE DEPT
2550 W TYVOLA RD
CHARLOTTE, NC 28217

Ship To:

BAKER & TAYLOR BOOKS
COMMERCE SERVICE CENTER
251 MT OLIVE CHURCH ROAD
COMMERCE, GA 305991100

TelePhone 8154722444

Quantity	Product No.	Description	List Price	Discount	Amount
1	9783031228414	Streib/Soma, Guide to Java (Undergraduat	$59.99		59.99

Total Units	1
Total Books Weight - lb.	1.77
Delivery Method	B & T UPS Collect PICKUP

THIS IS NOT AN INVOICE

End User Purchase Order:

COM2065470

This enclosed Packing Slip provides a list of all products contained in this shipment. The invoice for this shipment will be sent to the billing address listed on the top of this form. Please refer to the delivery number listed on this form in your correspondence with Customer Service to expedite the processing of your query.

Thank you for your order!

Questions regarding this order?
> **Tel: 800 - SPRINGERNATURE (777-4643)**
> 24 hours a day, 7 days a week
> Email:customerservice@springernature.com

> **US Returns to:** Springer Nature Returns Dept | 1550 Heil Quaker Blvd Suite 200 | LaVergne, TN 37086
> **Canadian returns to:** c/o Georgetown Terminal Warehouse | 34 Armstrong Ave. | Georgetown | Ontario L7G 4R9

General terms and conditions of payment can be found at www.springer.com/policy.

Springer

natureresearch

BMC

J.B.METZLER

palgrave
macmillan

Apress

SCIENTIFIC
AMERICAN

macmillan
education

Springer Healthcare

Springer Medizin

Adis

0

Introduction to Computing Concepts

James T. Streib[a*] and Takako Soma[a]

[a] Computer Science Program, Illinois College, Jacksonville, IL, USA

Abstract

In addition to an introduction to hardware and software concepts, including the concept of compiling, interpreting, and executing a program, there is an introduction to computational thinking, software design, and computer ethics.

Keywords

Hardware, Software, Computational Thinking, Software Design, Computer Ethics.

0.1 Introduction

Although this chapter is labeled as Chapter 0, that does not diminish its importance. The reason for such a numbering is to allow readers with a previous introduction to computing concepts and programming to proceed onto Chapter 1. However, for readers with no prior introduction or for those who would like a refresher, this chapter provides an important overview of hardware, software, computational thinking, software design, and computer ethics.

0.2 Overview of Hardware and Software

0.2.1 Hardware

As many readers may already know from using application software such as a word processor, a computer system is composed of two major parts: *hardware* and *software*. Since this book is primarily about writing software, this section on hardware is understandably brief. The hardware is the physical computer that includes five basic components: the central processing unit (*CPU*), the random-access memory (*RAM*) or just *memory* for short, input (typically a keyboard), output (typically a monitor), and *storage* (often a disk) as shown in Fig. 0.1.

J. T. Streib and T. Soma, *Guide to Java*, Undergraduate Topics in Computer Science,
https://doi.org/10.1007/978-3-031-22842-1_0

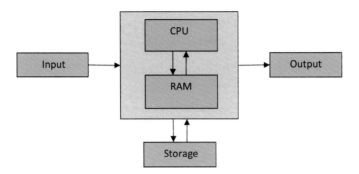

Fig. 0.1 Computer hardware

0.2.2 Software

In order for computer hardware to perform, it is necessary that it has software. Essentially, software (often called a program) is the set of instructions that tells the computer what to do and when to do it. A program is typically loaded from storage into the computer's RAM for subsequent execution in the computer's CPU. As the program executes or runs, it will typically ask the user to input data which will also be stored in RAM. The program will then process the data, and various results will be output to the monitor. This Input, Process, Output sequence is sometimes abbreviated as *IPO*.

The only type of instruction a computer can actually understand is low-level *machine language*, where different types of CPUs can have different machine languages. Machine language is made up of ones and zeros, which makes programming in machine language very tedious and error-prone. An alternative to using machine language is *assembly language* which is also a low-level language that uses *mnemonics* (or abbreviations) and is easier to use than ones and zeros [10].

However, if the only language that the computer can directly understand is machine language, how does the computer understand assembly language? The answer is that the assembly language is translated into machine language by another program called an *assembler* (see Fig. 0.2). Note that there is a one-to-one correspondence between assembly language and machine language, and for every assembly language instruction, there is typically only one machine language instruction. However, even though assembly language is easier to program in than machine language, different types of CPUs can also have different types of assembly languages, so the assembly language of one machine can be different from that of another machine and needs a seperate assembler.

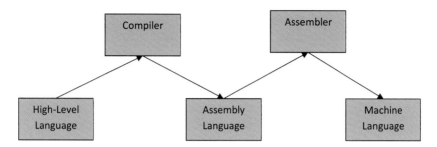

Fig. 0.2 Assemblers and compilers

0.2.3 History and Java

The solution to making programming easier and allow programs to be used on different machines is through the use of high-level languages which are more English-like and math-like. One of the first high-level programming languages was FORTRAN (FORmula TRANslation), which was developed in the early 1950s to help solve mathematical problems. There have been a number of high-level languages developed since that time to meet the needs of many different users. Some of these include COBOL (COmmon Business Oriented Language) developed in the 1950s for the business world, BASIC (Beginners All-purpose Symbolic Instruction Code) developed in the 1960s for beginning programmers, Pascal in the 1970s previously used for teaching computer science students, C in the 1970s for systems programming, and C++ in the 1980s for Object-Oriented Programming (OOP).

Java is also an OOP language that was developed at Sun MicroSystems (which is now a subsidiary of Oracle Corporation) and was released in 1995. OOP is a programming methodology that makes it more convenient to reuse software and will be discussed further in Chaps. 2 , 5 , and 9 .

Although no prior programming experience is necessary to learn Java in this text, programmers with experience in C or C++ will recognize a number of similarities between Java and these languages. Conversely, programmers learning Java first will also notice a number of similarities should they subsequently learn C or C++. The reason for this similarity between these languages is that both Java and C++ are based on C. Since Java does not contain some of the features of C++ (such as operator overloading and multiple inheritance, where overloading and inheritance will be discussed in Chaps. 5 and 9), it is an easier language to learn.

0.2.4 High-level Translation

If high-level languages are easier to learn and use, how can they be implemented on a computer that can only understand machine language? Similar to assembly language needing an assembler, the program needed to translate a high-level language to a low-level language is a *compiler* or an *interpreter*. Although there is a one-to-one correspondence between assembly language and machine language, there is a one-to-many correspondence between a high-level language and a low-level language. This means that for one high-level language instruction, there can be many low-level assembly or machine language instructions. Even though different CPUs need different compilers or interpreters to convert a particular high-level language into the appropriate machine language, compilers and interpreters allow the same high-level language to be used on different CPUs.

The difference between a compiler and an interpreter is that a compiler will translate the high-level language instructions for the entire program to the corresponding machine language for subsequent execution, whereas an interpreter will translate and then execute each instruction one at a time. Further, a compiler might translate directly to machine language, or it might translate the high-level language to assembly language, and then let an assembler convert the assembly language program to machine language as shown in Fig. 0.2. Once the machine language is created, it is subsequently loaded into the computer's RAM and executed by the CPU.

As mentioned above, an interpreter works slightly differently than a compiler. Instead of converting an entire high-level program into machine language all at once and then executing the machine language, an interpreter converts one line of the high-level program to machine language and then immediately executes the machine language instructions before proceeding on with the converting and executing of the next high-level instruction (see Fig. 0.3). The result is that compiler-generated code executes faster than interpreted code because the program does not need to be converted each time it is executed. However, interpreters might be more convenient in an educational or development environment because of the many modifications that are made to a program which require a program to be converted each time a change is made.

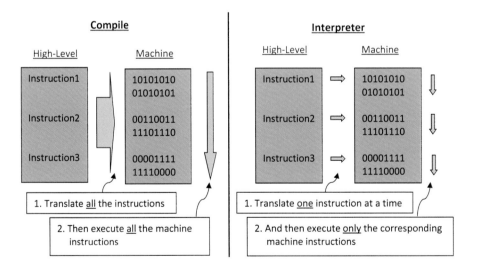

Fig. 0.3 Compilers and interpreters

Java is somewhat unique in that it uses both a compiler and an interpreter to convert the high-level instructions to machine language. A compiler is used to convert the Java instructions into an intermediate-level language known as *bytecode*, and then the bytecode is converted into machine language using an interpreter.

Since the intent of Java was for portability on the World Wide Web, the advantage of using both a compiler and an interpreter is that most of the translation process can be done by the compiler, and when bytecode is sent to different types of machines, it can be translated by an interpreter into the machine language of the particular type of machine that the code needs to be run on (see Fig. 0.4).

Note that just as there can be a one-to-many relationship between high-level and low-level instructions, there can be a one-to-many relationship between Java and bytecode. However, unlike the one-to-one relationship between assembly language and machine language, there can also be a one-to-many relationship between bytecode and machine language, depending on the machine for which the bytecode is being interpreted.

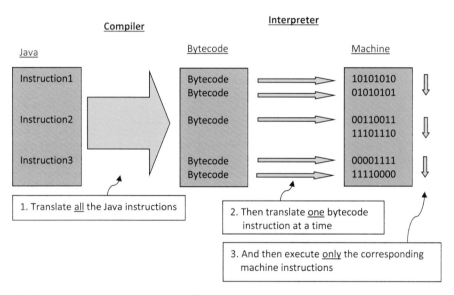

Fig. 0.4 Java instructions, bytecode, and machine language

0.3 Introduction to Computational Thinking

According to Wing, "Computational thinking is using concepts from computer science to solve problems and design systems" [12]. As can be seen in the following chapters, in order to write a good program, a number of techniques need to be used, including decomposition, pattern recognition, abstraction, algorithms, and logical thinking. *Decomposition* is used to break down problems into smaller sections, which makes complex problems more manageable. *Pattern recognition* is the process of finding similarities to previously solved problems. Then, the same solution or a slightly modified solution can be used to solve new problems. *Abstraction* is the filtering out of unnecessary information. In other words, taking a step back from the specific details and focusing on the big picture allows one to create a more generic solution. *Algorithms* are step-by-step instructions to solve a problem. It is important to create a plan, an algorithm, for the solution when solving a problem. *Logical thinking* is deductive inference of new information on existing information. Computational thinking is a problem-solving process that involves a number of core principles from computer science as mentioned above.

But how can these principles be used in non-programming context, for example, solving the Tower of Hanoi game? The Tower of Hanoi game consists of three pegs, and initially one of the non-centered pegs contains several rings stacked in order of descending diameter from bottom to top. The goal is to move the stack of rings to another non-centered peg as shown in the Fig. 0.5.

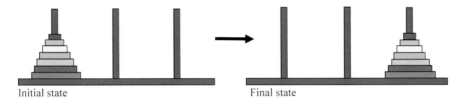

Initial state   Final state

Fig. 0.5 Tower of Hanoi game

During the process, only one ring can be moved at a time which means only a top ring is removed among the towers at any given time. **Consequently,** several rings cannot be moved at once. Another rule is that a bigger ring cannot be placed on the top of a smaller one. At the start of the game, the only ring that can be moved is the smallest ring and it may be placed on one of the two pegs. Next, there are two rings that can be moved. There is no good reason to move the smallest one back to the original stack or to another peg. So, the next move should be moving the second smallest ring. As it cannot be stacked on the top of the smallest one, naturally it goes on the other peg. By understanding the rules, logical thinking is used to determine the next step. When making a move, do not be distracted by color of the rings or pegs, nor the sounds they make, but focus on the rings. This is simplifying the problem using abstraction. As in Fig. 0.6 after successive moves, there is a point where the largest ring is on one peg and rest of the rings are stacked on another peg in order the largest to the smallest from the bottom to the top. Realize that during the moves, a ring can be placed on the top of any ring that is bigger than itself, not merely the next larger ring.

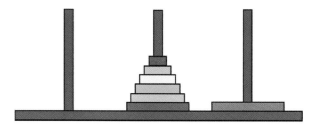

Fig 0.6 The largest ring in the final position

Now the task is to move the stack that has one smaller number of rings. During the process there will be a situation where the second largest ring is on the top of the largest one and the rest of the rings are stacked in correct order on another peg as shown in Fig. 0.7.

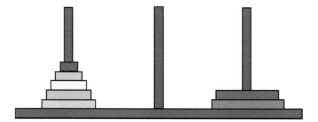

Fig 0.7 The largest and the second largest rings in the final position

Notice that every time the largest ring of the particular stack is placed in the final position, the next problem is to solve the same problem with one less number of rings, which means the task to solve the Tower of Hanoi game is divided into smaller problems using decomposition. Also realize that the same technique can be used to solve the problem with different sizes by seeing the pattern. Making a plan of where to moving a ring is step-by-step procedure, which is an algorithm.

Computer scientists naturally use computational thinking when writing programs, however, as can be seen in the Tower of Hanoi example, it also allows non-computer scientists to benefit from a computational approach to problem-solving. Many disciplines have been influenced by computational thinking in some way, including statistics, biology, engineering, and economics. As computational thinking can be applied in everyday life, currently there is an initiative to introduce computational thinking skills to primary and secondary school children as well as reinforcing them at the college level.

0.4 Essentials of Software Design

0.4.1 Syntax, Semantics, and Errors

During the process of translating a language to machine language, the translator catches certain types of errors. Before looking at the various types of errors, a distinction should be made between the *syntax* and the *semantics* of a program. Simply stated, the syntax is the grammar of the language, and the semantics is the meaning or what each instruction does. To explain further, syntax is the spelling of the individual words, where the semicolons go, and so on. If mistakes are made, a compiler will detect what are known as *syntax errors*, generate messages to the programmer, and the program will not be compiled or executed. Although syntax is very important, there is a tendency for first-time programmers to spend too much time learning syntax to avoid syntax errors. However, there must be equal time spent on semantics to ensure that the program does what the programmer intended it to do.

Even though there might not be any syntax errors, there can be what are called *execution errors* or *run-time errors*, such as division by zero. When these types of errors occur, the appropriate error messages are generated and execution stops. Even worse, there can also be *logic errors*, which are mistakes in the logic of the program so that the program does not do what was intended. The unfortunate aspect of logic errors is that they do not produce any error messages which can make them extremely difficult to find and fix.

0.4.2 Design Methodology

When writing a program for the first time, there is a tendency to want to just start keying the program into the computer and get it to work. As a result, many beginning programmers focus primarily on the syntax of their program because they want to avoid getting syntax errors. Initially this method of just typing in a program appears to work fairly well when programs are small at the beginning of a class and in the text. However, as problems get more complex and they become more difficult to solve, the programs written this way will tend to have not only more syntax errors but complicated logic errors which are more difficult to correct since no error messages are provided.

As an analogy, an individual might be able to build a small storage shed by just sawing and nailing some lumber together without worrying about the overall design of the project. However, with a larger project such as a house, apartment building, or office building, that methodology would not be sufficient. Instead, there are many other people who must be consulted, including the original customer who wants the building built, the architects who work with the customer, the contractors, and the carpenters. The same holds true in the world of programming where a programmer and/or systems analyst works with others such as customers, users, and managers.

What are needed are various strategies and tools to help write programs correctly to minimize logic errors. Just as in the above example where blueprints and plans are used by the architect, there are techniques that can be used by analysts, software engineers, and programmers. Although the complete process for developing software might not be needed initially with smaller programs, it does not hurt to practice the various techniques on smaller programs to gain familiarity, so that when one advances to more difficult projects, one is comfortable with many of the techniques. Although the following techniques are used primarily with non-object-oriented programs, they can be augmented with object-oriented design techniques introduced in chapter 2 and used in larger programs.

There are many different methodologies and number of stages within the various methodologies for solving problems that can be found in different texts, but upon closer examination, they are all rather similar. They tend to include at least four stages, and they are usually comparable to the following:

1. Analysis
2. Design
3. Implementation
4. Maintenance

0.4.2.1 Analysis

The analysis stage is where the needs of the user or customer are first determined. Questions concerning the form and quantity of the input, the type of processing that needs to be done, the storage requirements of data, and the type of output needed are asked and clarified at this stage. This would be similar to a customer in a construction project trying to determine what type of building should be built. In a first semester programming class, this stage may or may not be included. Sometimes a professor might have already completed the analysis stage and included what is needed in the programming assignment. However, at other times, they might require this stage and a number of questions will need to be asked by the student. This might be especially true when working on a team project in a software design or senior capstone course.

0.4.2.2 Design

The design stage is where a project begins to take shape. It is similar to the architect creating a set of blueprints and models for the user to examine, because changes are much easier to make on paper or with the model than once the construction of the building has started. Various tools such as pseudocode and Unified Modeling Langue (UML) diagrams (discussed shortly) are used by systems analysts, software engineers, and programmers to help design the program. Again, it is much easier to make changes during the design phase than after the programming has begun.

0.4.2.3 Implementaion

The implementation stage is where the code is actually written, entered, compiled, and syntax errors are corrected. Once the code is free of syntax errors, it is thoroughly tested. This includes testing various components of the program to be sure each section is working properly. If not, the code needs to be debugged to correct any logic errors. In addition to the various components, the entire program needs to be tested to ensure that all the components work together as planned. Sometimes errors are a result of not following the design, whereas other times, it is not necessarily the code but rather the design itself that has the error, in which case one has to go back and correct the error in the design. The result is that the stages above do not necessarily need to be rigorously adhered to, but rather when at a stage one may need to return to a previous stage for clarification or to fix a possible error.

Although it is tempting to jump directly to the implementation stage, this tendency should be avoided. It is important to take the time to properly design the *algorithm* first before starting to key in a program. An algorithm is a step-by-step sequence of instructions, not necessarily implemented on a computer. Once an algorithm is implemented in a specific language, it is then a program. By taking the time to design a well-thought-out algorithm, there will be fewer logic errors in the program. Although it might seem to take longer to include the design stage, the savings will be more than made up for in less time spent fixing logic errors later.

0.4.2.4 Maintenance

The maintenance stage is where all the modifications and updates take place. In an industrial strength program, more time is spent in the maintenance phase than all of the three preceding stages. This is because once a program is up and running, there can be numerous changes that need to be made over the lifetime of a program. This is another reason why a program should be designed well in order to facilitate modifications later in the life of a program. Unfortunately, beginning programmers do not often experience this stage of a program, because once the concepts are learned from one programming assignment, the program is often not used again and another program is assigned to introduce the next set of concepts. However, in some upper-level courses, the assignments get longer, existing programs might be modified and reused, and students get to have some experience with the maintenance stage of programs. Regardless, it helps even beginning students to design well-thought-out programs to gain practice in the event that a professor decides it might be easier to modify an existing program rather than having to design a new program from scratch, as done in the real world.

0.4.3 Tools and Techniques

0.4.3.1 Pseudocode

One technique that can help during the design stage is the use of *pseudocode*. Pseudocode is a combination of English and a programming language. Since it is not a programming language, this is the reason for its name as "pseudo" code. The advantage of using pseudocode is that one can concentrate on the logic of an algorithm and not worry about the syntax of a particular programming language. In fact, well-written pseudocode should be understood by any programmer regardless of the programming language that they use, and they should be able to convert the pseudocode into their particular programming language. However, there can be many different versions and levels of detail that can be included in pseudocode, so it is best to check with one's instructor or company for any preferences or standards that are employed. As a simple example, consider the following pseudocode on the left compared to the Java statement on the right:

Calculate the area of a rectangle   areaRec = height * width;

At this time it is not nececessary to understand the Java code on the right. However, note that the verbal description on the left is much easier to understand than the detailed Java code. As a result, one does not need to concentrate on the intricate syntax, but rather the semantics. As an alternative, notice the more specific pseudocode on the left.

areaRec ← height x width   `areaRec = height * width;`

Both the pseudocode and the Java code are known as assignment statements as will be discussed in the next chapter. Note that an arrow is used in the pseudocode instead of an equal sign in the Java code to indicate an assignment statement. This helps illustrate the direction of assignment, since some languages use symbols other than an equal sign to illustrate assignment. Also notice that a mathematical symbol is used instead of an asterisk to illustrate multiplication. Lastly, a semicolon is not used since not all other languages use them to terminate statements.

The result is that the pseudocode in the second example is more specific than the first example which helps with the translation to Java, but it is also more generic than the Java statement which helps in the translation to other languages as well. Again, these are just two samples of pseudocode, so be sure to check your local guidelines and requirements which should be used. In this text, when pseudocode is used, it will be written with as much detail as possible so as not to be ambiguous and to help with the translation into Java.

0.4.3.2 OOP and UML

Since the term object has been used previously, what is an object? In the past, programs were often written with large sections of code that were not very helpful to reuse when another program needed to be written.

It can help with the understanding of the idea of objects to think of an automobile. An automobile has many different parts such as steering mechanisms, transmissions, brakes, etc. Instead of designing the transmission as unique to only one type of auto, a generic plan for a transmission can be designed first. Then particular versions of the transmission could be built to be put into different types of automobiles. The plans for the transmission can be thought of as a class and the differing versions of the transmission as instances of that class, or in other words, objects. This way a whole new design for a transmission does not need to be created for each type of auto, but rather just a different variation. The same applies to software, where a whole new complete design does not need to be created but just a different version of the original class. Although this is just a brief glimpse of objects, this same idea can be applied to software and a more complete discussion will be presented in Chapter 2.

Unified Modeling Language (UML) is a visual method used to help contruct a program using classes and objects. One might ask since Java is an Object Oriented (OO) language and UML is helpful in creating an OO program, why would one need pseuodocode? The answer is because each class and instance of a class or object contains code, pseudocode can help with the design of the class. So whereas UML helps with the creating of classes and objects, pseudocode helps with the creation of code within classes and objects. UML will be discussed further in Section 2.10.

0.4.3.3 Debugging

Even when all attempts to write a logically correct program are followed, the possibility of logic errors still exists. The process of finding and fixing logic errors is known as *debugging*. When trying to debug a program, a programmer should not start to randomly alter code in the hope that the error might be fixed. Although this might work occasionally with smaller programs, it rarely works as programs become larger and more complex. Instead, one should look for patterns in the output in an attempt to isolate the problem. Further, one needs to carefully check the program by walking through the code to ensure that it is doing what was originally intended.

To assist in this process many Integrated Development Environments (IDEs), which are used to enter, edit, compile, and execute a program, sometimes include debuggers that can trace the contents of various memory locations to help locate a logic error. However, do not rely on the debugger alone to help correct the problem, but rather use it as a tool to assist in tracing the logic of the program. If a debugger is not available, well-placed output statements at critical points in the program can help in the debugging process. In the end, it is the programmer reading the code carefully to see what the code is actually doing, rather than what one thinks it is doing, that will ultimately fix logic errors in a program. [9]

0.5 A Brief Look at Computer Ethics

As one is just learning to write code in a programming language, there is a tendency to be preoccupied with getting programs to work correctly. However, at the same time when acquiring a lot of technical knowledge, it is also important to learn what is needed to enter the computing profession. This includes, but is not limited to knowledge of various ethical issues concerning property, privacy, and responsibility.

Initially one might not think this is important since they are just a beginner and not working for a major company. Although this may not seem initially significant, these issues become increasingly even more important as one rapidly gains new knowledge, even during a course of a semester.

For example, when beginning programmers are working on their own individual programming assignments in a classroom environment, they will often be turned in for a grade. Assuming it is not a group programming assignment, each student's program is considered to be their own property whether it is on paper or on a file in a computer. If one student has access to another student's program, then this could be a concern of intellectual property rights.

In another example, one might have the opportunity to work in the Information Technology (IT) department at the school, college, or university. This might entail working on another student's, staff member's, or faculty member's computer. In doing so, one might have access to programs and files that have sensitive information which would concern the privacy of others.

Also, consider the possibility that after completing a year or two of coursework, one might have the opportunity to work on an internship writing programs for a company. Then the programs are no longer merely submitted for a grade but are integral to the operation of that company. Mistakes are no longer just points taken off for a grade, but could have an impact on financial matters and affect people's lives. The result is that the testing and correct operation of a program is imperative and is the responsibility of the programmers.

The field that includes these instances and other related issues is known as ethics. Entire stand-alone courses are offered, typically from the philosophy department, and corresponding books have been written that address the many theories and the application of those theories to specific instances. In addition, these ethical theories have been applied to paticular areas such as business ethics, medical ethics, environmental ethics as well as computer ethics. With respect to the latter, many colleges offer separate courses in computer ethics that may be given as an elective or may be required for a major in computer science.

Since entire books have also been written on the field of computer ethics it would not be possible to discuss all the theories here. Fortunately, various professional organizations in many different fields provide codes of ethics. The same is true in the field of computing where the Institute of Electrical and Electronics Engineers (IEEE) Computer Society[3] and the Association of Computing Machinery (ACM) [1] have each developed a Code of Ethics. These codes help provide guidance when confronting various ethical situations within the world of computing.

These codes are provided by their respective organizations and are available online. The reader is encouraged to look at least one of these codes as possibly indicated by one's instructor. It might also prove interesting to look at both codes to see the similarities and possible differences between them.

After examining a code of ethics such as the ACM Code of Ethics, there are some exercises at the end of the chapter based on the discussion at the beginning of this section that can serve either as a discussion in the classroom or as an essay question in a homework assignment. Although it is beyond the scope of this text to examine the theories and codes in any detail, there are a number of texts that examine theories and issues in more detail such as "Ethics in Computing: A Concise Module" by Joseph Migga Kizza. [5]

0.6 Summary
- Machine language and assembly language are low-level languages, where the former uses ones and zeros and the latter uses mnemonics.
- High-level languages are more English-like, where C, C++, and Java are examples of high-level languages.
- Compilers convert the entire high-level language program into machine language before executing the machine language program, whereas interpreters convert a high-level language program one instruction at a time and then execute only the corresponding machine language instructions before converting the next high-level instruction.
- Java is a hybrid system, where the Java instructions are converted into an intermediate language called bytecode using a compiler and then the bytecode is converted into machine language using an interpreter.
- Computational thinking is a problem-solving process that includes decomposition, pattern recognition, abstraction, algorithms, and logical thinking. The above are skills that you can apply in life in general.

- Even if one is just beginning in the field of computing, it is important to understand professional obligations.
- Three important areas of computer ethics include but are not limited to property, privacy, and responsibility,
- Two prominent professional Codes of Ethics are provided by the IEEE Computer Society and the ACM.

0.7 Exercises (Items Marked with an * Have Solutions in Appendix _E_)

1. A River Crossing puzzle involves a famer crossing a river with a wolf, a goat, and a cabbage on the way home. After the famer bought them at the market, he rented a boat to cross the river. The farmer could take only one of his purchases with him, the wolf, the goat, or the cabbage, when taking the boat. If a wolf, a goat, and cabbage are left unattended together, the wolf would eat the goat, or the goat would eat the cabbage. The farmer's challenge is to bring himself and his purchases to the other side of the river, leaving each purchase intact. After solving the problem discuss how the computational thinking concepts, decomposition, pattern recognition, abstraction, algorithm, and logical thinking, were used to come up with the answer.

2. Sudoku is a number-placement puzzle. In original Sudoku, the objective is to fill a 9×9 grid with numbers so that each column, each row, and each of the nine 3×3 sub-grids contain all the numbers from 1 to 9. Discuss how the computational thinking concepts, decomposition, pattern recognition, abstraction, algorithm, and logical thinking, could be used to solve the puzzle.

3. Compare the two codes of ethics mentioned previously in Section 0.5. Identify one or more elements that are similar. If possible, identify one element that appears in one code but does not seem to appear in the other.

4. Using one of the code of ethics such as the ACM Code of Ethics, or the code assigned by the instructor, analyze the following scenarios as to the proper course of action. *Be sure* to indicate which element in the code applies.

   a. A student in a first-year course has asked a fellow student for assistance with their programming assignment. After starting to look over the program for the potential error, the student seeking assistance says "This is sure taking a lot of time. Might it be easier to just send me a copy of the file containing your program and I can just change the name at the top?" According to the code of ethics selected or assigned, what should the student who is providing the assistance do? What alternatives are there?

   b. A student is working in the Information Technology department and has been asked to work on a faculty members personal computer to install a new version of a software package. In the process, the student sees the spreadsheet containing the grades for the professor's classes. Thinking that it will cause no harm, the student worker decides to look up a grade of a friend in the spreadsheet. According to the code of ethics selected or assigned, should the student worker do this? Is it causing any harm?

c. An intern at a local company is having difficulty with a small section of code being worked on which is a part of a much larger project. When testing the section of code, the intern realizes that it works over 99% of the time and rarely fails. Since the intern is afraid of losing the internship, the possibility of a failure happening is very small and the code is an insignificant part of the much larger project, the intern submits the code as being complete. Based on the code of ethics selected or assigned, should the intern submit the code as complete? What alternatives are there?

1

Input/Output, Variables, and Arithmetic

James T. Streib[a*] and Takako Soma[a]

[a] Computer Science Program, Illinois College, Jacksonville, IL, USA

Abstract

This chapter provides an initial skeleton program from which to create subsequent programs. An introduction to variables, constants, assignment statements, arithmetic operations, and simple input/output using the keyboard and monitor is also provided. Further, there is a discussion concerning comments and a simple complete program is included at the end of the chapter.

Keywords

Input/Output, Variables, Assignment Statement, Arithmetic, Comments.

1.1 Introduction

This section introduces the reader to the basics of the Java programming language and helps get the first program up and running as quickly as possible. To that end, the explanation of some of the more complicated aspects of a Java program are deferred until later. Many of the OOP (Object-Oriented Programming) concepts are only briefly introduced, but will be discussed more thoroughly in Chapters 2, 5, and 9. For those who want a more detailed discussion and elaboration of some of the concepts presented in this chapter, it can be found in Appendix A. However, note that for some of the sections of Appendix A, it helps to have read at least Chapters 2, 5, and possibly 9, or have had previous OOP programming experience.

1.2 Java Skeleton

Probably the best way to understand a programming language is to start right away with a sample program. Although the following program does not do anything, it will serve as a skeleton to add instructions to in the future and provide a starting point to understand the basic layout of a Java program. At first the program in Fig. 1.1 might look a bit intimidating, but with various explanations and with time it will become more understandable. For now, a few of the words and symbols will be explained here and the rest will be discussed elsewhere in the text.

```
class Skeleton {
    public static void main(String[] args) {

        // body of main program

    }
}
```

Fig. 1.1 Java skeleton program

The first line in the program begins with the reserved word `class`. A *reserved word* is one that has a special meaning in a program and cannot have its meaning changed by the programmer nor can it be used for other purposes. As briefly discussed in Chapter 0, a class is a definition of a group of objects. Although classes and objects will be discussed further in Chap. 2 , for now think of a class as a blueprint for a house and the houses built from the blueprint as objects.

The word `Skeleton` following the reserved word `class`, is the name of the class that is provided by the programmer. This name is known as an *identifier* and the rules for identifiers will be discussed in Section 1.4. Note that usually class names begin with a capital letter. The entire definition of the class, `Skeleton`, should be placed between the first opening brace and the last closing brace, { }.

This class has one method definition starting on the second line. A *method* is like a function in mathematics which are sent values via arguments and can return a single value. Typically, the body of the method is indented to improve the readability of the program.

The word `main` is the name of the method. When a program is run, the system will search for the `main` method and start executing instructions in the `main` method. For now, the rest of the words in this line will be discussed later throughout the text and in Appendix A. The definition of the `main` method also starts with an opening brace and ends with a closing brace. Inside the braces, a sequence of instructions would be placed. For now, the method does not have any instructions and only contains a comment line.

Comments will not be compiled and executed when the program is run. They are used to make programs easier for other programmers to understand. Comments can start with `//` symbols and continue to the end of the line as shown in Figure 1.1, or be placed between `/*` and `*/` symbols. The `//` symbols are used for a single-line comment, and `/*` and `*/` are used when the comments run over multiple lines. Comments are discussed more thoroughly in Section 1.9, The above program should compile without any syntax errors and run without any execution errors, except unfortunately it does not do anything.

1.3 "Hello World!"

Unless a program performs some type of output, it is not particularly useful and it is difficult to know whether the program has run. Output can be of many forms including output to a screen, a printer, or a disk. In this section, only output to a screen will be considered. Although there are several ways to output data to the screen, this section will examine the simplest of them to get started.

1.3.1 Text-based Output

One of the more common first programs written when learning a new language is the infamous "Hello World!" program. The advantage of this program is to make sure that one is writing a program correctly and using the compiler properly. This program can be written as shown in Fig. 1.2.

```
class Output {
    public static void main(String[] args) {
        System.out.println("Hello World!");
    }
}
```

Fig. 1.2 Hello World!

The program looks very similar to the original `Skeleton` program in Fig. 1.1, except that the class name has been changed from `Skeleton` to `Output` and the comment line has been replaced with the `System.out.println("Hello World!");` statement. This statement outputs the string contained within the double quotation marks to the monitor. Java uses `System.out` to refer to the standard output device which by default is the monitor. To perform output, one simply uses the `println` method to display a primitive value or a string to the monitor. The `println` method is part of the Java Application Programming Interface (*API*) which is a predefined set of classes that can be used in any Java program. The classes and methods in the Java API provide a variety of fundamental services that are not part of the language itself.

The method name `println` is often pronounced as "print line," even though it is not spelled that way. The `print` portion of `println` causes the information in the parentheses to be output to the computer screen, and then the `ln` portion of `println` causes the cursor on the screen to move down to the next line. In this case, the only information in the parentheses is the string `"Hello World!"`. Following the closing parenthesis, the statement is terminated with a semicolon.

Go ahead and try typing in this program on your computer using the *IDE* (Integrated Development Environment) installed in your lab, home computer, or place of employment and then compile and execute the program. Provided there are no syntax errors, the output should appear similar to the following, where the underscore represents the ending location of the cursor on the screen:

```
Hello World!
_
```

Notice that the quotation marks are not output to the screen and the cursor appears on the next line. Also note that the cursor might not appear on the screen, since there is no input yet, but in this example, it serves to illustrate where any subsequent input or output would appear.

1.3.2 GUI-based Output

Text-based output is simple and easy to implement while learning concepts of a programming language and testing programs. However, when an application is written for customers, a Graphical User Interface (*GUI*) is a user-friendly way of displaying output.

Simple GUI based output to display a message dialog box can be accomplished by using the showMessageDialog method as shown in Fig. 1.3.

```
import javax.swing.*;

class MsgBoxOutput   {
    public static void main(String[] args) {
        JOptionPane.showMessageDialog(null, "Hello World!");
        System.exit(0);
    }
}
```

Fig. 1.3 Message Dialog Box

The JOptionPane.showMessageDialog indicates that the showMessageDialog method is defined in the standard class JOptionPane. The method passes two arguments where the first argument, null, causes the dialog box to appear in the center of the screen. The second argument is the message to be displayed in the dialog box.

   Note that since the JOptionPane class is not automatically available to Java programs, the import javax.swing.* statement is added at the beginning of the program. All the predefined classes and methods in the Java Aplication Program Interface (API) are organized into packages, and the import statement identifies those packages that are not automatically available.

   Also, notice that the last statement System.exit(0) causes the program to stop executing since a program with JOptionPane does not automatically stop when the end of the main method is reached. When the program above is executed a dialog box shown below appears on the screen.

When the user clicks the OK button, the dialog box will close. Both types of output, text-based and GUI-based, will be used throughout the text, with text-based used more frequently due to its simplicity.

1.4 Variables and Constants

One of the things that often needs to be added to the skeleton are data members. Another name is a memory location so that data can be stored. Yet another name is a *variable* since the contents of the memory location can vary, just as a variable in mathematics.

In order to understand variables and how data is stored in memory, it is oftentimes very helpful to draw a picture of the memory location. A memory location can be thought of as a mailbox that has two main parts. One part is the contents, which includes the letters that are inside the mailbox, and the other is the address of the mailbox as shown in Fig. 1.4.

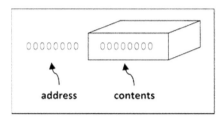

Fig. 1.4 Representation of memory

The address of the mailbox is usually a number, like the address of a memory location in a computer. At the machine language level, the address is in ones and zeros, just like the machine language instructions mentioned in Chapter 0. However, using numbers to represent the address of a memory location can be quite confusing, especially if there are hundreds of memory locations in a program. Instead, it is helpful to use characters to form names, called *symbolic addressing*, to make it easier to remember what data is stored in what memory location as shown in Fig. 1.5. In this example, the name number is used to describe the contents of the corresponding memory location. This is one of the primary advantages of using assembly language over machine language, and this is also true of all high-level languages including Java.

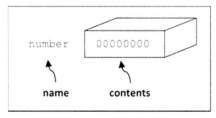

Fig. 1.5 Using names for memory locations

Instead of a three-dimensional representation of a mailbox to represent a memory location, it is much easier to draw a two-dimensional representation. Further, instead of using ones and zeros to represent the contents of the memory location, it is easier to use the decimal number system to represent values as follows:

number   0

Although not as crucial in high-level languages (like Java) as it is in low-level languages (machine and assembly languages), it is important to remember that a memory location has two features: its address and its contents. In Java, the programmer is typically concerned about its contents.

Given the above representation of variables, how are they actually created or declared? When a variable is declared, there are two things that must be done. First, a variable needs to be given a name so that it can be referred to by various instructions in the program, and second, the type of data that will be stored in the memory location needs to be indicated. The reason for this is that although all the data is stored as ones and zeros as discussed above, different types of data are stored using different combinations of ones and zeros. A single one or zero is called a binary digit (abbreviated as a *bit*), and a group of 8 bits is called a *byte*. Typically, the more bytes that make up a memory location, the larger the number that can be stored in the location. Although how the data is actually stored is beyond the scope of this text, Table 1.1 shows some of the types of data, the size, and the range of values that can be stored for each type.

Table 1.1 Data types

Type	Size	Range
byte	1 byte	−128 to 127
short	2 bytes	−32,768 to 32,767
Int	4 bytes	−2,147,483,648 to 2,147,483,647
long	8 bytes	−9,223,372,036,854,775,808 to 9,223,372,036,854,775,807
float	4 bytes	$-3.40282347 \times 10^{38}$ to 3.4028347×10^{38}
double	8 bytes	$-1.79769313486231570 \times 10^{308}$ to $1.79769313486231570 \times 10^{308}$
char	2 bytes	one character
String	2 or more bytes	one or more characters

Typically, the types int, double, char, and String are the ones that are used the most frequently. For example, should one want to declare a variable named number and have it store an integer, it would be declared as follows:

```
int number;
```

First the type is indicated, in this case int for integer, and then the identifier or name of the variable number is given, followed by a semicolon. An identifier or the name of the variable can be almost anything except for a reserved word as discussed in Section 1.2, but there are certain rules that need to be followed as well as some suggestions that should be followed. The length of the variable name can be from 1 to any number of characters long. Further, the variable name can be composed of letters, numbers, underscores _, and dollar signs $, but must begin with a letter. Also, the variable name is case sensitive, meaning that cat, Cat, and CAT are separate variable names and correspond to separate memory locations.

Typically, a variable name should not be too long, because they can be difficult to read, but by the same token, they should not be too short either, for it could become difficult to remember what it represents. For example, if the letter n were used instead of number, then it might not be clear whether n stood for name, number, or numeral. Exceptions to this are for variables from a mathematical expression. For example, the variables x, y, and z are commonly used to represent the points of a Cartesian coordinate system, and i, j, or k are used for loop control variables as will be discussed in Chap. 4 . Although most of the time this text will avoid the use of shorter names, on occasion shorter names might be used to save space or for the sake of simplicity to concentrate on other aspects of a code segment. If a variable is too long, it can be difficult to read as in the following: numberofcatsanddogs. Common practice in Java is not to capitalize the first letter of a variable but to capitalize the first letter in all subsequent words, as in numberOfCatsAndDogs. Notice that it is a little easier to read that way. Also on occasion, abbreviations can be used such as num instead of number, but be sure to use good ones. Further, this text will occasionally show some of the more commonly used abreviations.

Variables of other types can be declared as well, such as a variable of type float or double. Although numbers of type float take up less space in the computer's memory, they are less precise and can sometimes cause inaccuracy in calculations. Even though they take up more memory, this text will use double variables to alleviate some possible problems later. For example, should one want to declare a variable to hold a double precision value, it would be declared as follows:

```
double average;
```

Further it could contain a value and would look like the following:

$$average \quad \boxed{0.0}$$

Notice that instead of showing the number zero as an integer, it is represented as a real number with a decimal point, to indicate its type as a double.

All of the types given in Table 1.1, other than the String type, are known as primitive data types, meaning that when they are declared, the memory needed to store the associated data is allocated at that time. However, a String data type is a reference data type. When a variable of type String is declared, the memory allocated is not used to store the data, but rather only to store a reference to the data. String data types are unique in that although they are technically objects, they can be used syntactically as if they were primitive data types.

The first part of this text will use strings in a very limited capacity. An understanding of strings is much easier once one has had an introduction to objects and practice with objects, so a full description of how string objects are created and manipulated is presented in Chap. 6 . However, for now, this text will represent strings "as if" they are primitive data types, and the following shows a character primitive data type and a simplified view of the string data type. For example, a character and string could be declared as follows:

```
char initial; String name;
```

and would be represented with values as follows, respectively:

initial 'T'   name "John"

Note that the `char` data type is represented using single quotation marks and that the `String` is represented using double quotation marks. Although a character could be represented as a `String` of length one, it is usually better to use the `char` data type. Further, there are also ways to extract a single `char` type from a `String` data type. Again, a full description will be deferred until Chap. 6 .

In contrast to variables, a constant can be declared so that its value cannot be changed. Although not nearly as useful as variables, constants have their place in a program when a value does not need to be changed, nor should be changed. For example, if an integer `N` needs to remain a 7, then it could be declared as follows, where the use of the reserved word `final` indicates that `N` is a constant:

```
final int N = 7;
```

Typically, constant names are declared as all capital letters to help other programmers distinguish them from variables. In another example, suppose a number like `PI` needs only two digits after the decimal point, then it could be declared as follows:

```
final double PI = 3.14;
```

Although the use of a constant might not be readily apparent at this time, their use will become clearer in subsequent examples after discussing assignment statements in the next section.

1.5 Assignment Statements

In the previous section, all the drawings of the memory locations had values in them. How did those values get there? By default, Java technically initializes all `int` variables to 0 and `double` variables to 0.0. Also, `char` variables are initialized to the empty character indicated by two single quotation marks `''` and `String` variables are initialized to `null` as will be discussed further in Chap. 6 . Although this can be helpful in some instances, in many other languages variables do not have a default value. The variables contain whatever was in that memory location from the last time it was used which could be interpreted as junk to another program, cause logic errors, and be difficult to debug. Variables with unknown initial values are said to be indeterminate. As a result, many programmers do not use Java's default values and assume instead that the initial values of variables are indeterminate, which will also be the assumption of this text. So instead of initially showing an integer variable with the number 0 in it, this text will show the variable as indeterminate with a dashed line in it as shown below:

number ---

Does this mean that all variables need to be initialized to some value? Not necessarily. As will be seen, only those variables that need an initial value for subsequent processing should be initialized. Initializing a variable to a value when it does not need to be initialized could be confusing to other programmers reading the code, as will be discussed later in this chapter and in Chap. 4 on iteration structures.

So, if a variable is assumed not to be initialized, how does one initialize a variable to a value such as 0 or any other value for that matter, such as 5? After a variable is declared, it can be given a value in an assignment statement using an assignment symbol. The assignment symbol is the equal sign. However, when one first starts to use the equal sign, one must remember that it does not mean that the variable on the left is "equal to" the value on the right, but rather that the value on the right is copied into or assigned to the variable on the left. Again, this is best shown by way of an example:

```
int number;
number = 5;
```

After the variable number is declared as type int, the second statement indicates that the integer 5 is assigned or copied into the variable number and the memory location would then appear as follows where green indicates a change:

number   5

Again, the assignment statement is not really saying that number is equal to 5 or equals 5, but rather that the variable number is assigned a 5 or takes on the value of 5. Although it is tempting to say that number equals 5 and even though most people will understand what is meant, try to avoid saying it, and there will be less difficulty in the future as shown in Sect. 1.8 on arithmetic statements.

Note that it is possible to combine the previous two statements into one statement as shown below. It looks similar to the definition of a constant in the previous section but without the word final in the statement:

```
int number = 5;
```

The above syntax is perfectly legal and saves a line when writing a program. However, when first learning a language, it helps to reinforce the distinction between the declaration of a variable and the assignment of a value to a variable. Of course, if one's instructor does not mind the above shortcut or if one is studying this text on their own and likes the shortcut, then go ahead and use it. However, this text will use the previous two-line method at least for the next few chapters to help reinforce the distinction between the declaration of a variable and the assignment of a value to a variable.

Continuing, what if one wanted to take the contents of number, and copy it into another memory location named answer? For example, consider the following code segment:

```
int number, answer;
number = 5;
answer = number;
```

After both number and answer have been declared in the first line, the variable number is then assigned the value 5 in the second line and answer will still be indeterminate. The memory locations would look as follows:

number [5]   answer [---]

The third line then takes a copy of the contents of `number` and places it into the memory location `answer` as shown below:

number [5]   answer [5]

Note that the assignment statement does not remove the 5 from `number` and put it into `answer`, but rather it takes a copy of the 5 and puts it into `answer`. The original 5 in `number` does not disappear. Why does it copy and not move it? The reason is because it is actually faster for the computer to copy it and not take the time to delete the original. This is a fundamental concept in most computer languages and will become more important in the writing of subsequent programs.

Again, the important point to notice is that the copying of values is from right to left, not left to right. This sometimes causes confusion among beginning programmers, possibly because they are used to reading from left to right. The reason why Java and many previous languages go from right to left is because they are mimicking some of the assembly languages on many machines. Ideally it would be nice if languages used an arrow to show how values are copied as shown below:

```
answer ← number;
```

However, most keyboards do not have an arrow character, so an equal sign was used. Just be very careful to remember that values are copied from right to left and there should not be any problems.

Assigning variables of type `double` is similar to the above and will not be shown here; however, a couple of points need to be made concerning assigning variables of different types. For example, what would happen if a variable of type `int` was assigned to a variable of type `double` as shown below?

```
int number;
double result;
number = 5;
result = number;
```

As before, the contents of the memory locations after the assignment of 5 to `number` would be as follows:

number [5]   result [---]

Then when the next assignment statement is executed, the `int` value of 5 would be copied, converted to a `double` value of `5.0`, and assigned to `result` as follows:

number   5   result   5.0

Would the value in `number` be converted to a `5.0`? The answer is no, as shown above, because only the variable to the left of the assignment symbol is altered by an assignment statement. The 5 in `number` is not converted, but rather when it is copied, it is converted to the proper type so that it can be assigned to `result`.

If an `int` value can be stored in a variable of type `double`, is the reverse true? The answer is no, because, for example, how could the number `5.7` be stored as an integer without the fractional part? A way around this problem is to use a typecast operator. A typecast operator allows a value of one type to be converted to another type. In the case below, the typecast operator `(int)` converts the `double` value in `number` to type `int` so it can be assigned to `result`. As before, the value in `number` would not change and would still contain a `5.7`. However, what happens to the fractional part? The result is that it is truncated and a 5 is stored in `result`:

```
double number;
int result;
number = 5.7;
result = (int) number;
```

What if the value needed to be rounded instead? Fortunately, Java has the `Math` class which contains a method named `round`. As mentioned previously, a method is somewhat like a function in mathematics. The name of the class, `Math`, is followed by a period and the name of the method, `round`. Parentheses are placed after the method name and contain the argument, `number`, which is sent to the method. The code segment from above is rewritten below:

```
double number;
int result;
number = 5.7;
result = (int) Math.round(number);
```

Unfortunately, when the `round` method is sent a value of type `double`, it returns a value of type `long`, but the typecast operator `(int)` can again be used to convert the value of type `long` to type `int`. Since `number` initially contains `5.7`, the variable `result` would contain a 6. Again, the value in `number` would not change and would still contain a `5.7`.

number   5.7   result   6

Of course, if the precision of the type `double` is needed, the better solution would be to change the type of `result` to `double` to preserve the fractional part of `number`. The round method is one of the many methods available in the Math class which is discussed in more detail in Sect. 1.8 on arithmetic statements.

1.6 Output

1.6.1 Text-based

Recall from Section 1.3 that the following:

```
System.out.println("Hello World!");
```

output the following:

```
Hello World!
_
```

where the cursor appeared on the next line. However, what if one wanted to split the string so that it appears on two separate lines? This can be accomplished by using two separate System.out.println statements as follows:

```
System.out.println("Hello");
System.out.println("World!");
```

As one might suspect, the output would appear as follows:

```
Hello
World!
_
```

The string "Hello" is output and the cursor moves down to the next line. Then, the string "World!" is output, and again the cursor moves down to the next line in preparation for the subsequent line to be output.

In another example, what if one wanted to output the following with a blank line between the two words and the cursor at the bottom?

```
Hello

World!
_
```

The following code segment would accomplish this task:

```
System.out.println("Hello");
System.out.println();
System.out.println("World!");
```

The first statement outputs the word Hello and moves the cursor down to the second line. The second statement does not output anything, so the ln of the System.out.println statement causes the cursor to move down to the third line and the blank line to appear on output. Lastly, the word World! is output and the cursor moves down to the fourth line. Note that usually a System.out.println() indicates that a blank line will be output, but there are exceptions that are discussed further in Appendix A.

Although the above is useful for outputting strings and vertically formatting output, how does one output integers and real numbers? Combining the information learned in the previous two sections, one can then have a program as shown in Fig. 1.6.

```
class Output {
    public static void main(String[] args) {
        int num;
        num = 5;
        System.out.println(num);
    }
}
```

Fig. 1.6 Outputting an int

This program declares the variable num to be of type int, assigns the value 5 to num, and then outputs the contents of the variable num. Note that the variable num is not enclosed in quotation marks, so the word num is not output, but rather the contents of the variable num are output. Unfortunately, only the integer 5 would be output to the screen which would not be very useful. Instead, it is helpful to output some other information for the user to identify and understand the information on the screen.

The output statement in the program in Fig. 1.6 can be modified to include the string "The number is " followed by a plus sign prior to the variable num as shown in Fig. 1.7. A plus sign between two strings or between a string and any other type of data means concatenation. In other words, the string "The number is " and the contents of num are output as if they are one string. It should be noted that one needs to be careful should only two integers be separated by a plus sign, because then it would mean addition as will be discussed in Sect.1.8. However, provided a string or a concatenated string appears to the left, then the item to the right of the plus sign will be concatenated instead of added. Note that there is a space within the quotes at the end of the string so that the contents of the variable num are separated from the word is in the string. The result is that the output of this program would appear as follows:

```
The number is 5
```

—

```
class Output {
    public static void main(String[] args) {
        int num;
        num = 5;
        System.out.println("The number is " + num);
    }
}
```

Fig. 1.7 Outputting an int with description of output

What happens if one outputs a number of type `double` using the same format shown in Fig. 1.7? For example, Fig.1.8 outputs the contents of the variable `num` of type `double`.

```
class Output {
    public static void main(String[] args) {
        double num;
        num = 1.0 / 3.0;
        System.out.println("The number is " + num);
    }
}
```

Fig. 1.8 Outputting a `double` precision number without formatting

As will be discussed further in Sect.1.8, the / means division and `num` will take on the value of one third. When the above program is compiled and executed, the screen displays

`The number is 0.3333333333333333`

Although using high precision is necessary during computation, it may not be needed when a number of type `double` is displayed. How can one limit the number of digits after the decimal point in a floating-point number? A predefined method in the Java API called `printf` can be used. The general syntax of the `printf` method is as follows:

`printf(control string, expr, expr, …)`

where `control string` is a string that may consist of substrings and format specifiers and an `expr` represents a variable, expression, or constant value. A format specifier indicates how an `expr` should be displayed. A specifier `%d` is used for a decimal integer, `%f` for a floating-point number, `%c` for a character, and `%s` for a string. For numbers, the total width and precision can be indicated in a specifier. For example, the specifier `%10d` outputs an integer value with a width of at least 10. The specifier `%10.2f` outputs a floating-point number with a width of at least 10 including a decimal point and two digits after the decimal point. The width of character and string values can also be indicated. For example, the specifier `%3c` outputs a single character and adds two spaces before it, and `%10s` outputs a string with a width at least 10 characters. If there is more than one `expr` to be output, they must match the specifiers within the control string in order, number, and type. Using the formatting information described above, the program in Fig. 1.8 can be rewritten as in Fig. 1.9.

```
class Output {
    public static void main(String[] args) {
        double num;
        num = 1.0 / 3.0;
        System.out.printf("The number is %4.2f", num);
        System.out.println();
    }
}
```

Fig. 1.9 Formatting a `double` precision number

The floating-point number stored in the variable num will be output with two digits after the decimal point. Since a space is included before the specifier in the string after the word is, there will be a space between is and the number as shown below:

```
The number is 0.33
```

Also notice that since the printf method does not move the cursor to the next line. A System.out.println(); statement needs to be added at the end of the program in order to have the same effect as the program in Fig.1.8.

Some characters cannot be simply included between double quotes for output. In order to output a double quotation mark, a back slash in front of the double quotation marks needs to be used, \". The following statement

```
System.out.println("He said \"Hello\".");
```

will output

```
He said "Hello".
```

Similarly, a backslash can be output by placing an extra backslash in front of one as shown below:

```
System.out.println("How to output a backslash, \\");
```

This will produce an output of

```
How to output backslash, \
```

1.6.2 GUI-Based

When using GUI-based output and if multiple lines of text need to be displayed in a message box, the control character \n, which stands for "newline", can be used to separate the lines as in

```
JOptionPane.showMessageDialog(null, "Hello\nWorld!");
```

which results in the dialog box shown below:

As can be seen, Hello, and World! are output on separate lines. The \n can also be used in a string with text-based output, which works similarly to the ln portion of a println statement. Since there is no choice with message boxes, it will be used in GUI-based output and the ln will be used more often in text-based output.

The output of integers in message boxes is fairly easy, where the variable name needs to be placed in the parameter list. If one wants to identify the integer being output to the user, then just as with text-based output, the identifying string is concatenated with the integer using the + sign. Likewise, the output of double precision numbers can be formatted as with text-based output. The program in Figure 1.10 is the same as Figure 1.9 except GUI-based output is used:

```
import javax.swing.*;
public class MsgBoxOutput {
    public static void main(String[] args) {
        double num;
        num = 1.0 / 3.0;
        JOptionPane.showMessageDialog(null, "The number is "
                            + String.format("%4.2f", num));
    }
}
```

Fig. 1.10 Outputting a `double` precision number using GUI

The `format` method defined in the `String` class in `String.format("%4.2f", num)` will return a formatted number and display it in a dialog box. Note that the format method does not alter the contents of `num`.

1.7 Input

1.7.1 Text-based

The ability to declare variables, assign values to them, and output strings and variables is very important but does not allow for many useful programs. As it stands, anytime one wants to change the output of a program, one has to edit the program and recompile it before executing the program. What is needed is a way to input data into a program. As with output, input can come from a variety of sources such as the keyboard, mouse, or a disk and this section will deal with the simplest form of input from the keyboard.

As in the last section, it is best to start with a simple example based on the previous program in Fig. 1.7 and modified as shown in Fig. 1,11. Although the description of the first few lines of the following program might be a little complicated due to the nature of input in Java, the actual statements that perform the input are less complicated as will be seen shortly.

Remember when the `System.out.println` and `System.out.printf` statements were used for output, the `java.lang` package including the `System` class was not imported at the beginning of the program. This is because the `java.lang` package, which includes the `System` and `Math` classes, is used extensively, and is automatically imported into all Java programs.

```
import java.util.*;
class InputOutput {
   public static void main(String[] args) {
      int num;

      Scanner scanner;
      scanner = new Scanner(System.in);

      num = scanner.nextInt();

      System.out.println("The integer is " + num);
   }
}
```

Fig. 1.11 Program to input an integer

Similar to GUI-based output, notice the addition of the `import` statement in the first line. The `import` statement is added in order to use a predefined method for input, but instead of the `swing` package, the `util` package is used for text-based input.

In order for input to work properly, one needs a place to store the data entered. The first statement in the body of the main method declares the variable `num` as type `int`. The next statement is the declaration of the variable `scanner` of type `Scanner` as shown below:

`Scanner scanner;`

`Scanner` is not a primitive data type like `int` or `double`, but rather it is a class. As discussed briefly in Section 0.4.3.2 and will be discussed further in Chap. 2 , a class can be thought of as the set of blueprints for a building. Notice that the class name begins with an upper-case `S`, whereas the variable name begins with a lower-case `s`. Continuing, the following statement

`scanner = new Scanner(System.in);`

creates a new instance of the `Scanner` class, or in other words a `Scanner` object. This can be thought of as how an individual building might be constructed from a set of blueprints. Java uses `System.in` to refer to the standard input device, which is the keyboard. Unlike output, input is not directly supported in Java; however, the `Scanner` class can be used to create an object to get input from the keyboard. The above statement then assigns a reference to the new object to the variable `scanner`. Again, although this might be a little confusing at this point, the important thing is be sure to include the `import` statement and the above two statements in any program that needs to input data.

The next statement below shows how the `Scanner` object is used to scan the input for the next integer. The method `nextInt` will make the system wait until an integer is entered from the keyboard, and then the integer input is assigned to the variable `num`:

```
num = scanner.nextInt();
```

The last statement in the program is the same as before where the value of `num` is output to the computer screen. However, if one were to enter, compile, and run this program as given, the result might be a little confusing. The reason is that there would only be a blinking cursor on the screen as the system is waiting for input and there would be no indication of what should be input without having to look at the program. To solve this problem, it is usually best to provide a *prompt* to let the user know what should be input. A prompt is just an output of a message to the user to help them understand what is expected to be input. The program in Fig. 1.12 includes a prompt just prior to the input.

```
import java.util.*;
class InputOutput {
    public static void main(String[] args) {
        int num;

        Scanner scanner;
        scanner = new Scanner(System.in);

        System.out.print("Enter an integer: ");
        num = scanner.nextInt();

        System.out.println("The integer is " + num);
    }
}
```

Fig. 1.12 Prompting a user to input a number

As can be seen, the prompt is nothing more than the output of a string to indicate what the program is expecting in terms of input. Instead of using a `System.out.println();` notice that a `System.out.print();` without the `ln` is used which causes the cursor to stay on the same line for subsequent input. Further, a prompt should be formatted well such as including a space after the colon so that the cursor is separated from the prompt. After entering the data and when the user presses the Enter key, the cursor then moves to the next line.

Furthermore, a prompt should be *user-friendly*. A user-friendly prompt is one that clearly describes what the user should input, as in the case above where it asks for an integer. A user-friendly prompt can be polite such as "Please enter a number: ", but typically a prompt should avoid the use of first-person words like "I" and "you", as in "I would like you to...", since the computer is a machine, not a human.

Now would be a good time to enter, compile, and run the program in Fig. 1.12 to see how it works. The results should be similar to the following:

```
Enter an integer: 5
The integer is 5
─
```

In addition to `nextInt`, the method `nextDouble` reads a number of type `double`, the method next reads a word of type String that ends prior to a space, and the method nextLine reads an entire line of text of type String, including all the spaces until the user presses the **Enter** or **Return** key. All of these methods work similarly to the method nextInt.

1.7.2 GUI-based

A GUI input dialog box can be created by using the showInputDialog method that is also defined in the JOptionPane class. The following code shows how the showInputDialog method can be invoked:

JOptionPane.showInputDialog(null,"What is your first name?");

As with the showMessageDialog method, it sends a JFrame object and a String object as arguments. As before, the null value causes the dialog box to appear in the center of the screen. The second argument is a message displayed above a text field in the dialog box. The text field is an area in which the user can type a single line of input from the keyboard. When the statement is executed, a dialog box will appear and a user can enter text in the text field as in Figure 1.13.

Fig. 1.13 An input dialog box asking the first name

When the **OK** or **Cancel** button is clicked, or the **Enter** key is pressed, which is an alternative to pressing the **OK** button, the dialog box will disappear. However, it does not do anything more and the value entered in the text field is gone. In order to save the value the user entered, a String variable needs to be declared, and in this case it is called firstName. Then the value returned from the method has to be assigned to a variable both as shown below:

String firstName;
firstName = JOptionPane.showInputDialog(null,
          "What is your first name?");

Now, if the user enters Maya in the text field and clicks the **OK** button or presses the enter key, a reference to the String object with the value "Maya" will be assigned to the String variable firstName . If the user clicks the **OK** button or presses the enter key without entering anything in the text field, firstName will reference the object of the String type with an empty string. If the user clicks the **Cancel** button regardless of what was entered in the text field, firstName will contain the value null.

The following program demonstrates how to use both types of dialog boxes. Notice the import javax.swing.*; statement, which is not only needed for GUI-based output, but GUI-based input as well. The program uses an input dialog box to ask a user to enter their first name and displays a greeting in a message dialog box:

```java
import javax.swing.*;
class MsgBoxName {
   public static void main(String[] args) {
      String firstName;
      firstName = JOptionPane.showInputDialog(null,
               "What is your first name?");
      JOptionPane.showMessageDialog(null, "Hello, "
         + firstName + "!\nHow are you?");
      System.exit(0);
   }
}
```

When the above program is executed, the input dialog box in Fig. 1.13 again appears. If the user enters Maya and clicks the OK button, the message dialog box in Fig. 1.14 will be displayed.

Fig. 1.14 Message Dialog Box

Unlike the Scanner class for text-based input that supports different input methods for specific data types, such as nextInt and nextDouble , the JOptionPane accepts only string input. Even if the user enters numeric data, the showInputDialog method always returns the user's input as a String . For example, if the user enters the number 18 into an input dialog box, the showInputDialog method will return the String value "18" . This can be a problem if the input is used later in mathematical calculations because mathematical computations cannot be performed on strings. In such a case, a conversion from a string to a number needs to be performed. Here is an example of how to accomplish this using the Integer.parseInt method:

```java
String str;
int age;

str = JOptionPane.showInputDialog(null,
      "How old are you?");
age = Integer.parseInt(str);
```

When the above code executes and after the user enters 18 , the dialog box would look as shown in Fig. 1.15.

Fig. 1.15 An input dialog box containing the value entered

When the user clicks the OK button, the dialog box disappears and the String variable str will hold the String value "18". It will then be converted to an integer and assigned to the int variable age . If the user enters a string that cannot be converted to a type int, for example, 18.0 or the word eighteen, a NumberFormatException error will result (the topic of exceptions will be covered in Appendix B). Table 1.2 lists common methods to convert the string input to numerical data values.

Table 1.2 Methods for converting strings to numbers

Methods	Description
Byte.parseByte	Convert a String to a byte
Double.parseDouble	Convert a String to a double
Float.parseFloat	Convert a String to a float
Integer.parseInt	Convert a String to a int
Long.parseLong	Convert a String to a long
Short.parseShort	Convert a String to a short

1.8 Arithmetic Statements

The ability to input data, copy data from one memory location to another, and output data is fundamental to almost every computer program. However, unless there is the capability to manipulate and process data to convert it into information that can be output and used, the power of the computer has hardly been tapped. One of the first things computers were used for and continue to be used for is arithmetic computation, which is the subject of this section.

1.8.1 Binary Operators

The four basic operations of arithmetic, addition, subtraction, multiplication, and division can be accomplished in Java by the use of the binary operators +, -, *, and /, respectively. The word binary in this case does not mean the binary number system, but rather that these operators have two operands (such as variables and constants) that are manipulated by the operators. As before, the best way to illustrate this is through an example. Consider the following code segment:

```
int num1, num2, sum;
num1 = 5;
num2 = 7;
sum = num1 + num2;
```

After the variables of num1 and num2 have been assigned the values 5 and 7, respectively, the contents of the memory locations would appear as follows:

What occurs next is that the expression on the right side of the last assignment statement is evaluated. The contents of num1 are brought into the CPU, and then the contents of num2 are added to it in the CPU. Once the expression on the right side of the assignment symbol has been evaluated, the result of the expression in the CPU is then copied into the variable to the left of the assignment symbol. As in Sect.1.5, the copying goes from right to left, so the expression is always on the right side of the equal sign and there can only be one variable on the left side. The results of this evaluation and assignment can be seen below:

| num1 | 5 | | num2 | 7 | | sum | 12 |

Of course the values for num1 and num2 in the above segment could have been input from the keyboard, and the result in sum could be output to the screen, but for now simple assignment statements are used to initialize num1 and num2, and the value of sum is not output to keep the segment simple. The examples following will use this same pattern; however, a complete program using input and output will be shown in Sect. 1.10.

Similar equations can be made using subtraction, multiplication, and division, and examples incorporating these operators will follow later in this section. Still, a few comments need to be made about mixing variables of different types. As shown above, when two variables of the same type are used, the result is of that type. However, should one or both of these operands be of type double, then the result will also be of type double. For example, if num1 is of type int and num2 is of type double, then the result of the expression would be of type double. Of course, if the result of the expression is of type double, then it could not be assigned to the variable sum of type int. Either the round method would need to be used or the type of sum would need to be changed to double.

There is also a unique aspect to the division operation depending on the types of its operands. As with the other operators, if either or both of the operands are of type double, then the result of the division is also of type double. So, for example, 7.0 divided by 2 would be 3.5. If both operands are of type int, the result will of course be of type int. Although this does not pose a problem with the other arithmetic operators, the result of division when performing arithmetic often has a fractional component, and one would write it as 3½, 3.5, or possibly 3 with a remainder of 1. However, if the result of the division operation in Java is of type `int`, the fractional part is discarded and the result is simply 3. Although one does not get the fractional part with integer division, what if one wanted to determine the remainder? That can be done with the mod operator which is represented by the percent sign, `%`. To illustrate, consider the following code segment, where all variables are of type `int`:

```
int num1, num2, quotient, remainder;
num1 = 7;
num2 = 2;
quotient = num1 / num2;
remainder = num1 % num2;
```

Gven the initial values, upon completion of the segment, the respective memory locations would contain the following:

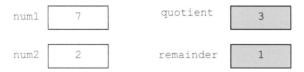

1.8.2 Precedence

Although it is relatively easy to create some simple instructions that contain only one operator, what about expressions with more than one operator? In that case, an awareness of the precedence of the various operators is needed. The precedence in Java is the same as in mathematics, on a scientific calculator, or in a spreadsheet application program. First, the multiplication and division operators have precedence over addition and subtraction. For example, given the following code segment, what are the contents in `answer`?

```
int answer, x, y, z;
x = 2;
y = 3;
z = 4;
answer = x + y * z;
```

Unfortunately if one guessed 20, that would be wrong. Remember that multiplication has precedence over addition so the result of the multiplication of y and z, which contain 3 and 4, would be 12, plus the contents of x, which is 2, would be 14.

However, what if one wanted to perform the addition first? As in arithmetic, one can always use parentheses to override the precedence of the operators, so that

```
answer = (x + y) * z;
```

would result in `answer` containing a 20. If there are more than one set of parentheses, then the innermost nested ones are evaluated first, and if the parentheses are not nested, the parentheses are evaluated from left to right. In fact, if there is a tie of any sort, such as two addition symbols, or an addition symbol and a subtraction symbol, the order is also from left to right.

Given all this information, what would be the answers in the following segment?

```
int answer1, answer2, x, y, z;
x = 3;
y = 4;
z = 5;
answer1 = x - y + 6 / z;
answer2 = (x * (y + 2)) % 2 - 1;
```

First, note that there are some constants in the mathematical expressions on the right side of the assignment statement and this is perfectly acceptable. In the first expression, the 6 / z is evaluated first and the result would be 1. After that, which operation is performed second? Since there is a tie in the precedence between the subtraction and the addition, and the subtraction is on the left, it is performed first, where 3 minus 4 is -1. Lastly, the 1 from the division is added to the -1 from the subtraction, so the answer is 0.

In the second expression, which operation is performed first? Since there are nested parentheses, the y + 2 is performed first with an answer of 6. Then the 3 in x is multiplied by the 6 for a value of 18. Then the 18 is divided by 2, where the remainder is 0, and lastly the 1 is subtracted from the 0 for a final answer of -1.

When trying to evaluate expressions, it is sometimes helpful to draw a line underneath each of the sub-expressions to help one remember which parts of the expression have been evaluated and remember their respective values. For example, the first expression above would appear as follows:

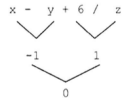

Since parentheses override the order of precedence, why can't one just use parentheses all of the time and avoid having to remember the order of precedence? One could do that, but the resulting expressions would have an inordinate number of parentheses and they could be quite difficult to read. Further, since the precedence rules in most languages are fairly similar and most programmers use parentheses sparingly, it is to one's advantage to learn and use them correctly. For further practice, see the exercises at the end of this chapter.

1.8.3 Unary Operators

Just as there are binary operators that have two operands, there also exist unary operators that have only one operand. The two most common are the plus sign and the minus sign, where the latter is used more frequently as in the following example:

```
z = -x + y;
```

The thing to remember about unary operators is that they have a higher priority than binary operators. So in the above statement, the negative of the value contained in x is added with the value in y and the result placed in the variable z. Should one want to negate the entire quantity, then parentheses would need to be used as in the following example, where the values in x and y are added together first, then negated, and the result placed in z.

```
z = -(x + y);
```

1.8.4 Incrementing

There are of course other arithmetic expressions to be learned, including how the contents of a variable can be incremented or decremented by 1 or more. There are a couple of ways to do this, and the method that is applicable in most programming languages will be examined first. One way is to first get the contents of a variable, add or subtract 1, and then copy the new number back to the variable as follows:

```
int x, y;
x = 0;
y = 0;
x = x + 1;
y = y - 1;
```

At first the fourth and fifth statements above might appear unusual to the beginning programmer. The fourth statement seems to be saying that x is equal to x + 1, which would be impossible in algebra. How could a value in x be equal to itself plus 1? The answer is that it cannot. The reason why this might look unusual is that one might be mistaking the equal sign in Java as an equal sign in algebra, which it is not. If one recalls from Sect.1.5, the equal sign in Java is the assignment symbol which takes a copy of the result on the right side and places it in the variable on the left.

In this case, the value in x, which is a 0 as shown above, plus a 1 is 1, and that is the value placed into x. So prior to execution of the fourth statement, the value in x is a 0, and after the execution of the fourth statement, the value in x is a 1. The same sort of process occurs with the statement using subtraction where the final value in y would be a -1. Also note that since both variables appear on the right side of the assignment symbol, they must be initialized to some value and should not be indeterminate. At first these statements might be a little confusing, but with time they become second nature. Statements like these are often used to increment and decrement variables that are used as counters and will be discussed in detail in Chap. 4 .

Since these operations are fairly commonplace, the languages C, C++, and Java have shortcuts for these as follows:

```
++x;        or        x++;
--y;        or        y--;
```

These operators are very convenient. The operators on the left side work the same way as those on the right when they are used as standalone statements. The style on the right is seen more often and will be used again extensively in Chap. 4 . However, when used as part of a larger expression, the two styles have entirely different meanings. For example, consider the following two statements:

$$a = ++x; \quad b = y++;$$

If x and y originally contain a 2, their respective memory locations would initially appear as follows:

At first it might seem that all four variables would contain a 3, but that would be incorrect. When the ++ (or --) appears prior to a variable, the increment is performed before the assignment or any other operation that might be in the expression. On the other hand, if the ++ (or again --) appears after the variable, then any other operations are performed first, including the assignment operation. The result is that in the example on the left, the value of x is incremented by 1, which makes x contain a 3, and then the new value of x would be assigned to a, which would then also contain a 3. In the example on the right, the value in the variable y, which is a 2, is first assigned to b . Then the value in y would be incremented to 3 and the value in b would still be a 2 as shown below:

Using the more simple initial approach such as $x = x + 1;$ is common in almost all languages, so this text will tend to use this initially to help reinforce how an expression like this works. However, as mentioned above, standalone operators, the ++ and -- can be fairly useful and easy to use, and this text will use them more frequently in <u>Chap. 4</u> . Further, when these operators are used in more complicated expressions, their use becomes much more difficult to understand, and it is for this reason that this text will tend to avoid the use of the ++ or -- operators in this fashion. However, be aware that intermediate and advanced texts often use these operators more frequently in complicated expressions, so one needs to know how they work and also be careful when reading code containing them.

1.8.5 Summing

As shown at the beginning of this section, when two variables are added together, the sum is often stored in a third variable. However, similar to counting, when a constant such as a 1 is added to a variable in the process of trying to find a total, one variable is added to another variable. For example, consider the following segment:

```
int total, num;
total = 0;
```

```
num = 5;
total = total + num;
```

where the initial contents of the respective memory locations would appear as follows:

As with previously incrementing by 1, it might look a little odd to see the variable `total` on both sides of the equal sign. Again the equal sign does not mean equality but assignment, where the expression on the right is evaluated first and the results are then stored in the variable on the left. Also, since the variable `total` appears on both sides of the assignment symbol, it needs to be initialized with a value prior to the statement. After the 0 and 5 are added together, the results are then placed back into `total` as follows:

Just as with the increment operation, the ability to find a total also has a shortcut. This shortcut is as follows and has the same effect as the instruction above.

```
total += num;
```

Similar shortcuts can also be used with the subtraction, multiplication, and division operators, but are used less frequently than addition. As with the previous shortcuts, this is only possible in languages like C, C++, and Java and does not appear in all languages. Likewise, since they do not appear in all languages and do not illustrate as readily how values can be totaled, this text will tend not to use these shortcuts as often.

1.8.6 Arithmetic Functions

Although all the basic arithmetic operation are available in the Java programming language, there are a number of other functions that would be helpful to have available. In addition to the constants `PI` and `E` for π and e, respectively, many extra functions are in the `Math` class. Including the `round` method previously introduced in Sect.1.5, some of the other methods include square root, the power function, and the trigonometric functions. These methods along with some others are shown in Table1.3.

Table 1.3 Various methods in the `Math` class

Method	Function Performed	Arguments	Value Returned
cos(x)	cosine	double (in radians)	double
pow(x,y)	x to the power of y	double	double
round(x)	round	float (or double)	int (or long)
sin(x)	sine	double (in radians)	double
sqrt(x)	square root	double	double
tan(x)	tangent	double (in radians)	double
toDegrees(x)	convert radians to degrees	double	double
toRadians(x)	convert degrees to radians	double	double

```
int x, y;
double z, power, sqRoot, sine, cosine;
x = 2;
y = 3;
z = Math.PI;
power = Math.pow(x,y);
sqRoot = Math.sqrt(y + 1);
sine = Math.sin(z);
cosine = Math.cos(z);
```

Fig. 1.16 Sample Math class constants and methods

To illustrate a few of these functions, examine the program segment in Figure 1.16. The methods should be fairly straightforward given their descriptive names and the reader's requisite mathematical background. After execution of the segment, the answers stored in the variables power, sqRoot, sine, and cosine would be 8.0, 2.0, 0.0, and −1.0, respectively. Note that the value in z is in terms of PI, because the trigonometric functions work with radians instead of degrees. If the initial value in z was in degrees, the method toRadians could be used.

1.9 Comments

Although comments were discussed briefly in Sect. 1.2, there are few more items that should be discussed. As mentioned previously, comments are either preceded by two slashes //, and the remainder of the line is considered a comment by the compiler, or a comment can begin with a slash and an asterisk /* and end with an asterisk and a slash */ allowing a comment to extend over multiple lines in a program. Single-line comments are helpful in explaining an individual line or multiple lines of code. Although a single-line comment can be placed off to the right-hand side of the statement it is describing, it can sometimes get crowded once code is indented as shown in Chaps. 3 and 4. As a result, this text will usually place comments just prior to a line of code or code segment being documented. For example, the following comment helps the reader of the program understand what the subsequent statement accomplishes:

```
// calculate the area of a rectangle
areaRect = base * height;
```

Multiple-line comments are also helpful to create what are called headings at the beginning of programs and methods in class definitions. The format of these headings can vary in different computer courses and companies, so be sure to determine your local requirements. An example of one such heading might be as follows:

```
/* name: your name
class : cs 1xx
prog : one
date : mm/dd/yyyy
*/
```

Once filled with the corresponding information, this heading identifies the author of the program, which class it was written for, the program number, and the date written. As can be seen, comments are good for documenting what various sections of code do in a program and identify who wrote a program, among other things. Having comments within a program explaining what a program does is known as internal documentation, whereas having explanations that appear in manuals (whether online or in physical manuals) is known as external documentation. Internal documentation tends to be more specific and is helpful to programmers, whereas external documentation tends to be more general and is useful to users, customers, and managers who may not understand programming.

Although at first some of the simpler programs will not appear to need comments, it becomes imperative to include comments as programs become larger and more complex. If the original programmer is on vacation or is no longer with a company, documentation is essential to help other programmers understand how the program works. Although many of the programs written in a first programming course might not be too complex, it is helpful to include comments to gain practice in good commenting techniques. To that end, the complete programs at the end of each chapter will include comments to help the reader understand the program and learn some commenting techniques.

Another way to document a program is by using Javadoc. This technique is very useful with larger programs that have many classes and methods, and an introduction is presented in Appendix C. Again, many computer science departments and computer science professors have different documentation standards, as do many different companies. Although they share some commonalities, there can also be a number of differences. Find out what your professor's or company standards are and be sure to follow them closely.

1.10 Complete Program: Implementing a Simple Program

Combining all the material from this chapter, one can now write a simple program to prompt for and input various numbers, perform a wide variety of calculations, and output answers as needed. In this section, a program that calculates two roots of a quadratic equation $ax^2 + bx + c = 0$ will be developed and implemented. As might be recalled from mathematics, the following is the definition of the two roots:

$$r_1 = \frac{-b + \sqrt{b^2 - 4ac}}{2a}$$

and

$$r_2 = \frac{-b - \sqrt{b^2 - 4ac}}{2a}$$

Problem statement: Write a program to calculate the two roots of a quadratic equation. Assume that $a \neq 0$ and the relationship $b^2 \geq 4ac$ holds, so there will be real number solutions for x.

Once a problem statement has been given, the requirements can be determined by analyzing the problem. The program will:

- Prompt a user to enter values for a, b, and c
- Compute the two roots
- Display the two roots

During the design stage, pseudocode can be used to outline the program. It lists the steps that need to be taken to accomplish the task. At this point, one does not need to be concerned with the details of the implementation, such as the name of the class or the parameters in the `main` method. The following is the pseudocode for a program calculating two roots of a quadratic equation:

> declare a, b, c, root1, root2
>
> input (a)
> input (b)
> input (c)
> $\text{root1} \leftarrow \left(-b + \sqrt{b^2 - 4ac}\right) / (2a)$
>
> $\text{root2} \leftarrow \left(-b - \sqrt{b^2 - 4ac}\right) / (2a)$
>
> output (root1, root2)

Observe in the formulas for the roots that the expression in the square root is called the discriminant and is used in calculating both roots. Therefore, the square root of discriminant can be calculated prior to the computation of `root1` and `root2`, so that it does not need to be calculated twice. The augmented pseudocode is

> declare a, b, c, root1, root2, sqrtDiscr
>
> input (a)
> input (b)
> input (c)
> $\text{sqrtDiscr} \leftarrow \sqrt{b^2 - 4ac}$
> root1 ← (-b + sqrtDiscr)/(2a)
> root2 ← (-b − sqrtDiscr)/(2a)
>
> output (root1, root2)

After the design phase comes the implementation phase. Consider the following program that is derived from the pseudocode above:

```
// A program to calculate two roots of a quadratic equation.
// Assume that a <> 0 and the relationship b^2 >= 4ac holds,
// so there will be real number solutions for x.

import java.util.*;

class QuadEq {
   public static void main(String[] args) {

      // declaration and initialization of variables
      double a, b, c, root1, root2, sqrtDiscr;
      Scanner scanner;
      scanner = new Scanner(System.in);

      // input a, b, and c
      System.out.print("Enter a: ");
```

```
a = scanner.nextDouble();
System.out.print("Enter b: ");
b = scanner.nextDouble();
System.out.print("Enter c: ");
c = scanner.nextDouble();

// compute the square root of discriminant
sqrtDiscr = Math.sqrt(Math.pow(b,2) - 4*a*c);

// compute the two roots
root1 = (-b + sqrtDiscr) / (2*a);
root2 = (-b - sqrtDiscr) / (2*a);

// output the two roots
System.out.println();
System.out.println("Two roots of the equation, " + a
                + "*x*x + " + b + "*x + " + c + " = 0, are");
System.out.printf("%.2f and %.2f.", root1, root2);
  }
}
```

Observe the formula for the discriminant for `root1` and `root2` . The methods `sqrt` and `pow` are defined in the `Math` class and are used to calculate the square root of the discriminant and the number b raised to the power of 2. All the parentheses are necessary to obtain the answer, which is accurate to at least two decimal places. In the output section of the program, `println` is called at the beginning in order to have a blank line between the input and output. The specifiers for `root1` and `root2` do not include the width to avoid any extra space before the roots are output since an extra space is included in the string. Given the above program, sample input and output are shown below:

```
Enter a: 2.0
Enter b: -5.0
Enter c: -3.0
Two roots of the equation, 2.0*x*x + -5.0*x + -3.0 = 0, are
3.00 and -0.50.
```

1.11 Summary

- `System.out.print` leaves the cursor on the same line, whereas `System.out.println` moves the cursor to the next line.
- Just because there are no arguments in a `System.out.println`, it does not mean a blank line is output. A blank line is output with a `System.out.println` when there is no preceding `System.out.print` statement.
- A Graphical User Interface (GUI) can be used for user-friendly input and output with dialog boxes.
- Remember that multiplication and division have a higher precedence than addition and subtraction and that unary operators have an even higher precedence.
- Parentheses can override any operator precedence, where the innermost nested parentheses have the highest precedence. It is also good practice not to use unnecessary parentheses.

- Whenever there is a tie at any level of precedence, the operators or parentheses are evaluated from left to right.
- The ++ or -- operators are an easy shortcut when used as standalone statements. However, great care must be taken when they are used in assignment statements or with other operators. In that case, if the ++ or -- precede a variable, it is performed first, but if they appear after the operand, they are performed last.

1.12 Exercises (Items Marked with an * Have Solutions in Appendix E)

1. Indicate whether the following statements are syntactically correct or incorrect. If incorrect, indicate what is wrong with the statement:

   A. `integer num1, num2;`
   *B. `double num3;`
   C. `7.8 = num3;` Assume that a variable `num3` has been declared correctly.
   *D. `int j;`
   `    j = 5.5;`

2. Assume the following declaration and initialization of variables:

   ```
   int i, j;
   double d;
   i = 1;
   j = 5;
   d = 2.34;
   ```

   Determine the value for each of the following expressions, or explain why it is not a valid expression:

   *A. `i / j;`
   B. `j + d;`
   C. `Math.pow(j);`
   D. `i - j * d`
   E. `i + d * (j * 3 - 2) / 4`

3. Assuming the following declaration and initialization of variables,

   ```
   int i;
   double d;
   i = 3;
   d = 2.34;
   ```

   Determine the value assigned to the variable in each of the following assignment statements, or explain why it is not a valid assignment statement:

   A. `i = d;`
   *B. `d = i + d;`
   C. `d = Math.pow(5, Math.sqrt(Math.pow(i, 2)));`

4. Implement each of the following statements in the Java language:

   A. Declare a variable `weight` of type `double`.

*B. Declare a constant EULER_NUMBER of type `double` and assign it the value
     `2.7182`.

5. Given the following Java program, what will be output to the screen? Be sure to line
    everything up properly. Use an underscore to represent a blank and the words `blank`
    `line` to represent a blank line:

```
class OutputTest {
    public static void main (String[] args) {
        System.out.println ("alpha ");
        System.out.println ();
        System.out.print (" beta");
        System.out.println (" gamma");
    }
}
```

*6. Write code to output the following pattern:

```
* *        * *
* *        * *
   * * * *
   * * * *
   * * * *
   * * * *
* *        * *
* *        * *
```

7. After the following statements are executed, what is stored in `value1`, `value2`,
    and `value3`?

```
int value1 = 5;
int value2 = 9;
int value3 = 4;
value1 = value2;
value2 = value3;
value3 = value1;
```

8. Write an equivalent Java assignment statement for each of these mathematical
    expressions.

A. $v = \dfrac{49x^{15}}{y+z}$

*B. $s = r\pi\sqrt{r^2 + h^2}$

C. $a = \dfrac{\sin g}{c}$

9. Write a complete program to prompt for and input a number, and then compute 2 to the power of the number that was input. The form of the input and output can be found below, and as always be careful with the vertical and horizontal spacing.

Input and Output:

```
Enter the number: 4.0

Two to the power of 4.0 is 16.0.
```

10. Repeat the previous exercise using dialog boxes. Examples of input and output dialog boxes are shown below:

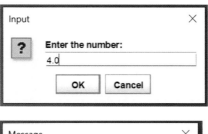

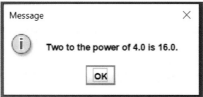

11. Rewrite the complete program in Sect. 1.10 using dialog boxes for input and output.

2

Objects: An Introduction

James T. Streib[a*] and Takako Soma[a]

[a] Computer Science Program, Illinois College, Jacksonville, IL, USA

Abstract

This chapter introduces classes and objects. Public and private data members along with value-returning methods and void methods with parameters are discussed. How objects are created and how methods are invoked are illustrated using contour diagrams. Contours help the reader have a better understanding of object-oriented concepts by providing visual representation of objects. Constructors are introduced along with multiple objects and classes. Lastly, UML (Unified Modeling Language) class diagrams are illustrated and a complete program implementing a simple class and client program is provided.

Keywords

Memory Location; Class Number; Void Method; Main Program.

2.1 Introduction

Having written a complete Java program in the proceeding chapter, one should have a basic understanding of how a program works. However, as programs get larger, they can become very difficult to modify. It would be similar to trying to write a paper or book as just one long paragraph without any chapters, sections, or paragraphs. To help make a program easier to read, modify, and maintain, it can be broken up into sections much like a book is divided up into chapters. Further, if a section of a book needed to be referred to many times, instead of repeating that section over and over again, it could possibly be placed in an appendix, and then the appendix can be referred to as necessary. Similarly, if a section of a program needs to be used again, the program can be broken up into subprograms. Instead of having to rewrite the code, a program can just call the same subprogram repetitively, thus saving time rewriting the code and saving memory as well.

However, what if the repeated code is only slightly different from the code that has been previously written? One could rewrite the code again with only slight modifications, but the chance for making mistakes would increase. There would also be time wasted rewriting existing code and memory wasted to store the code.

Instead of the above scenario, the programming methodology called object-oriented programming (OOP) could be used. OOP allows programmers to identify the common memory locations and code and then create what is known as a *class*. Then as variations of the class are needed, they can be made based on the original class. This allows for the reuse of a software that has been initially created in the original class, and the new classes are just variations on the theme of the original class.

A class is essentially a definition of an object or group of objects. For example, in the real world, the drawings, plans, or blueprints for a house are a definition for a single house or a group of houses. Although blueprints could be drawn up for a single custom-built

J. T. Streib and T. Soma, *Guide to Java*, Undergraduate Topics in Computer Science,
https://doi.org/10.1007/978-3-031-22842-1_2

house, many times there might be a set of master blueprints for a group of houses. A subdivision could be built with houses that are all very similar but have various subtle differences so that they do not all look the same. For example, some houses might be built with different color siding, with windows in different locations, with one or two car garages, and so on. The reason for doing this is to keep the cost of the individual houses reasonable. Should a major change in the blueprint need to be made for all the houses, then only the master blueprints would need to be changed. However, if a change only needs to be made to some of the houses, such as only to those houses that have fireplaces, then only the individual supplement that contains the plans for fireplaces would need to be changed. This idea is called *inheritance* and will be explored further in Chap. 9 . However, before learning more about that topic, the fundamentals of object-oriented programming must be discussed first.

2.2 Classes and Objects

In object-oriented terminology, the master blueprint would be called the class definition, and an actual house would be an *instance* of that class or what is known as an *object* as shown in Fig. 2.1. This can be a source of confusion for some beginning programmers which sometimes use the words class and object interchangeably. However, if one keeps the distinction between the plans or blueprints as the class and the individual houses as instances of the class or the objects themselves, it makes the learning of object-oriented programming easier in the long run.

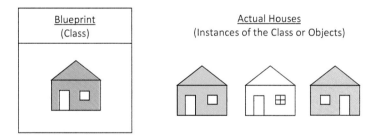

Fig. 2.1 Classes and objects using blueprints and houses

   Although a class can be placed in the same file right before or after the class that contains the main program, it is often placed into a separate file. This eventually helps when there are a number of different classes and when there is more than one programmer working on a project. However, this text will show classes immediately after the main program in order to save space.

   As with the initial skeleton of the main program in Chap. 0, the introduction of classes will also start with an empty class called Number as shown below:

```
class Number {

}
```

As can be seen, a class is somewhat similar to the main program except it is much simpler. As before, the word `class` is a reserved word, `Number` is the name of the class, and the opening and closing braces indicate the body of the class.

2.3 Public and Private Data Members

As before, an empty class is not very useful until code is added to it. Two of the most important items in a class definition are its data members and methods. A *data member* is similar to the declaration of a variable in the previous chapter. An important difference is that data members need to be declared using the access modifiers: `public` or `private`. A *public* data member is one that can be seen and used by an object of the class in which it was declared but can also be used outside the object, such as the main program. A *private* data member is one that can only be seen or used within an object of the class and cannot be used externally, such as by the main program. As shown below, the variable or data member x is declared as `private`, and the data members y and z are declared as `public`.

```
class Number {
    private int x;
    public int y, z;
}
```

At first, one might be tempted to declare all data members as `public` to allow for easy access from the calling program. However, this would be in contradiction with why one creates a class in the first place. One of the important aspects of OOP is *data encapsulation*. This means that the data in an instance of a class is encapsulated within the object and not directly accessible from the outside world. For example, in an automobile there are various parts which are inaccessible when one is driving, such as the fuel tank. However, through a gauge on the dashboard, one can tell whether there is fuel in the fuel tank. This is similar to public and private data members, where in many instances one does not want the main program having direct access to the data members. So although it is possible to declare data members as `public`, they will most often be declared as `private`.

If a data member is not directly accessible when it is declared as `private`, how does one gain access to it? The answer is through a *method*, specifically a `public` method which can indirectly allow access to `private` data members. Although methods are sometimes declared as `private`, for now most of the methods will be declared as `public`. If a method is just accessing and examining the contents of a data member, it is known as an *accessor*. Should a method alter a data member, it is known as a *mutator*. An accessor method is often used to get the contents of a data member and a mutator is often used to set the contents of a data member. In particular, an accessor method is known as a value-returning method, and a mutator is known as a `void` method, as discussed in the next two sections.

2.4 Value-Returning Methods

First, consider a method that returns the contents of a private integer data member x as follows:

```
public int getX() {
   return x;
}
```

The word `public` means that the method can be accessed from the main program. If the data member is `private`, then the method invoked from the main program to access the data member is declared as `public`. (How the method is invoked will be discussed in Section 2.6.) The word `int` is the type of the value that will be returned to the main program. The name of the method is `getX` and it is used in the main program to invoke the method. Inside the opening and closing parentheses `()` is known as a *parameter* list and is used for sending information to the method. Since this method is an accessor and not a mutator, there is no information being sent to the method, so the parameter list is empty. The opening and closing braces `{ }` indicate the body of the method that contains the instructions, just as in the main program. The `return` instruction followed by the variable x indicates what value will be returned to the main program. Although there can be more than one `return` statement in a method, it is a good programming practice to include only one `return` statement, and typically as the last statement in the method, as will be discussed later in Chap. 3 . Returning to the automobile example, the `getX` accessor method is somewhat like the fuel gauge on the dash panel of a car that displays the amount of fuel in the fuel tank.

2.5 `void` Methods and Parameters

As an example of a void method, consider the following:

```
public void setX(int  a)  {
   x = a;
}
```

As with the value-returning method, the void method is also `public` so it can be invoked from the main program. The word `void` indicates that the method will not return a value. Similarly, `setX` is the name of the method that will be used when invoking the method from the main program as will be discussed Section 2.6.

Unlike the previous method, this method has a *parameter* (sometimes called a *formal parameter*) between the parentheses. Notice that it looks similar to a variable declaration, and in a sense, it is like a variable declaration with a type and a variable name. However, what is unique about a parameter is that it can accept a value from the calling program. This is accomplished through an invoking statement, where there is another variable or constant called an *argument* (sometimes called an *actual parameter*) and the value of the argument is passed to the parameter. This is not unlike how the value on the right side of an assignment symbol = is copied into the variable on the left side. This copying of a value from an argument to a parameter is known as pass-by-value, or in other words this type of parameter is known as a *value parameter*. A value parameter provides one-way communication from the main program to the method. Other programming languages have additional parameter passing mechanisms that provide two-way communication, but Java has only value parameters, which makes the task of learning parameters a little easier. A visual example of how this works will be demonstrated in Section 2.7 on contour diagrams. Lastly, the only statement in the method is x = a; which is a simple assignment statement that takes a copy of the contents in the parameter a and copies it into the data member x, as discussed in Chap. 1 .

A question that might be asked is where is a good place for the data member x to be declared, since it does not appear in either of the two methods? If the variable is used by only one of the two methods, it should be declared locally in that method, but if the value in the variable is needed in both methods, it should be declared as a data member in the class. If a variable is declared in a method, it is sometimes referred to as a *local* variable since only that method has access to it. However, if a variable is declared as a data member, it is sometimes referred to as a *global* variable since it is accessible by all the methods in the object. In this example, since the variable x is used by both methods, it is declared as a data member so that both methods have access to it. To illustrate a complete class using both the data member x and the two previous methods, the class definition of Number is shown in Fig. 2.2.

```
class Number {

    // Data Member
    private int x;

    // Methods
    public void setX(int a) {
        x = a;
    }
    public int getX() {
        return x;
    }

}
```

Fig. 2.2 Number class

Unlike the previous skeleton, the new class Number contains the private data member x. Note, the order of the methods is irrelevant. Sometimes the methods are put in alphabetical order, but this text will typically list the mutators first followed by the accessors, and then order them alphabetically within each group. The use of comments and line spacing helps with the readability of the class, although they will sometimes be omitted to save space in this text.

2.6 Creating Objects and Invoking Methods

Given the discussion of classes and methods in the previous sections, how are instances of classes created and the methods invoked? The best way is to show an example of a complete main program. Using the skeleton program from Chap. 1 with the appropriate code added, consider the program in Fig. 2.3.

```
class Invoke {
   public static void main(String[] args) {

      int y, z;
      Number num;

      y = 5;
      num = new Number();

      num.setX(y);
      z = num.getX();

      System.out.println("The integer is: " + z);

   }

}
```

Fig. 2.3 Invoking program

Note that there are two variables named y and z declared as type int, but there is also a variable named num that is declared as type Number. Just like different variables can be declared as primitive data types, variables can also be declared as a type of a class. Similar to the primitive types, the contents of the class variables are initially indeterminate. In order to create a new instance of a class, in other words a new object, the new operator must be used, and then a reference to the new object is typically placed into a variable. The statement num = new Number(); performs these two tasks. First, a new object is created via the new Number() section of the statement. Then a reference to that new object is placed in the variable num through the assignment symbol =. It is important to remember that simply declaring a variable is not sufficient to create an object, but rather after the variable is declared, a new object must be created and then assigned to the variable. A shorter way of doing this is as follows:

```
Number num = new Number();
```

Although this technique might occasionally be used later in the text to save space, for now the two statements as shown below will be used to reinforce the concepts of variable declaration, object creation, and the assignment of references to variables.

```
Number num;
num = new Number();
```

This also reinforces the idea concerning the separate declaration and assignment of variables presented in Chap. 1 . If one's instructor prefers using a single statement or if one is reading this text independently and wants to use just one statement, then of course do so.

To invoke a method depends on what sort of method it is: void or value-returning? In the program in Fig. 2.3 the statement

```
num.setX(y);
```

illustrates how to invoke a void method. Since setX is a method accessable in the object, it follows the period after the variable num. Since a `void` method is used as an mutator, the variable y is the argument and the value in it is sent to the corresponding parameter in the method which in this case is the variable x. After the method has been executed, the instruction immediately following the invocation is executed.

The statement immediating following shows how a value-returning method is invoked. The statement

```
z = num.getX();
```

again shows that the method `getX` is placed immediately after the period. Note that the argument list does not contain anything between the parentheses, Although it is possible to send information to a value-returning method, this is typically not done because a value-returning main purpose is to serve as an assessor. Since it is returning a value, the value could be output or be used as part of an equation, but typically the value needs to be stored some place. In this case the value being returned, in this case the value in x, is assigned to the variable z.

This section shows the syntax needed to create an object and invoke methods, but how does it work? In other words, what are its semantics? The next section will illustrate the semantics of creating objects and invoking methods using contour diagrams.

2.7 Contour Diagrams

As indicated in the preface, contour diagrams are a very useful mechanism to visualize how objects, data members, methods, and parameters work. By building a good working visual model of objects, there will be less of chance having misconceptions as to how objects work. By building a solid foundation of the fundamental concepts, it makes it easier to understand more complex ideas in the future.

The purpose of using contours is to not only show the data members, similar to the variables that were drawn in _Chap. 1_, but also to show the _scope_ of where the data members are accessible. The scope of a local variable is the method where it is declared, and the scope of data member is all of the methods in the object.

Although not required, it is also helpful to include the type of the variable in the contour to avoid confusion among the many different types of variables. In addition to the variables, contours can also show how parameters are represented in the methods. Lastly, contours show the dynamic or changing nature of a program as it executes.

As before, it is helpful to start with an example. The program from Fig. 2.3 is combined with the class from Fig. 2.2 to create Fig. 2.4 with each line numbered in a comment to the right for convenience in the description that follows. The contour diagram in Fig. 2.5 shows the state of execution just _prior_ to the execution of Line 5 in the main program.

```
class Invoke {                                              // Line 1
    public static void main(String[] args) {               // Line 2
        int y, z;                                           // Line 3
        Number num;                                         // Line 4
        y = 5;                                              // Line 5
        num = new Number();                                 // Line 6
        num.setX(y);                                        // Line 7
        z = num.getX();                                     // Line 8
        System.out.println("The integer is: " + z);        // Line 9
    }                                                       // Line 10
}                                                           // Line 11
class Number {                                              // Line 12
    private int x;                                          // Line 13
    public void setX(int a) {                               // Line 14
        x = a;                                              // Line 15
    }                                                       // Line 16
    public int getX() {                                     // Line 17
        return x;                                           // Line 18
    }                                                       // Line 19
}                                                           // Line 20
```

Fig. 2.4 Invoking program and Number class

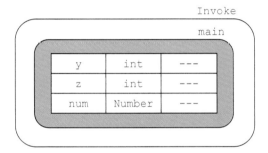

Fig. 2.5 State of execution just prior to Line 5

The outer contour represents the class Invoke, and the inner contour around the boxes shows the scope of the variables in the main program. Although the contours do not indicate much presently, the use of the contours will become clear shortly. Further, note that although technically the Invoke contour should be drawn for each of the following figures, it is not very useful at this time and will not be drawn for the rest of this chapter in order to simplify the drawings. However, it will be reintroduced and discussed further in Chap. 5 .

Continuing, the first column of boxes on the left indicates the names of the variables, and the boxes in the middle indicate the types of the variables, where y and z are of type int, and num is of type Number. Lastly, the boxes on the right indicate the current contents of the variables. Note that the state of execution is just prior to line 5, not after its execution. While technically y and z are initialized by the system to 0, this text will continue to assume that the variables do not contain an initial value and are indeterminate as discussed in Chap. 1 .

Although rather simplistic here, once Line 5 is executed, the contents of variable y now contain the value 5. Figure 2.6 shows the state of execution just prior to the execution of Line 6 and also does not show the outer contour for the `Invoke` class.

main

y	int	5
z	int	---
num	Number	---

Fig. 2.6 State of execution just prior to Line 6

However, when `num=new Number();` in Line 6 is executed, things start to get interesting. Just like the `Invoke` contour was drawn in Fig. 2.5, when a new instance of the `Number` class is created, a new corresponding contour is also created. Although as mentioned previously the contour for `Invoke` is not very useful at this time, the contour for `Number` is necessary for the following discussion. Note that there is one data member in the class and it is shown within the `Number` contour. Once the instance is created, a reference to the object is assigned to the variable `num`. This reference is illustrated as an arrow in the contour diagram, where the arrow points to the new contour and the end of the arrow is placed in the variable `num`. Figure 2.7 shows the state of execution just prior to Line 7 in main.

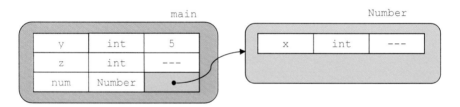

Fig. 2.7 State of execution just prior to Line 7

The next line to be executed is `num.setX(y);` in Line 7, which invokes the method `setX`. Prior to having the flow of control go from Line 7 to Line 15 in the `setX` method, a number of things need to occur. Just like when a new object is created and a corresponding contour is drawn, the same holds true when a method is invoked. Since the method is part of the instance of the class `Number`, this is where the corresponding contour appears. A convenient way of remembering this is that whenever there is a period, or what is often just called a dot, in the invocation of a method, then one needs to follow the reference or arrow to the corresponding contour. With the instruction `num.setX(y);` one just starts with the variable `num`, then follows the arrow to the `Number` contour, and then within the Number contour creates another contour for the setX method as shown in Fig. 2.8 which illustrates the state of execution just prior to Line 15 in setX.

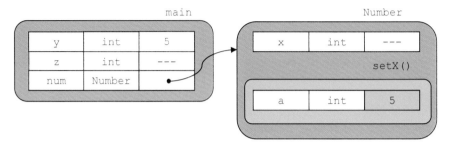

Fig. 2.8 State of execution just prior to Line 15

Note that the contour setX has a memory location associated with it for the parameter a. As mentioned in Sect. 2.5, a parameter is essentially a variable that takes on the value of the corresponding argument. Since the value contained in the variable y which is used as an argument in the main program is a 5, then the corresponding parameter takes on a copy of that same value, similar to an assignment statement. This also illustrates why parameters in Java are called value parameters, because they merely take on the value of the corresponding argument. Note that an argument and the corresponding parameter can have the same name or different names. In this example, the argument y and parameter a have different names, illustrating that the two do not have to be the same. Then when Line 15 is executed, Fig. 2.9 shows the state of execution just prior to Line 16 in setX.

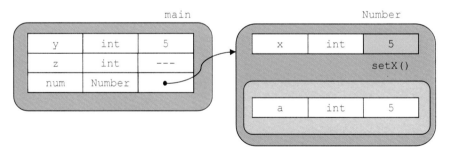

Fig. 2.9 State of execution just prior to Line 16

Note that Line 15 is the assignment statement x = a; where the contents of the parameter a will be copied into the variable x. However, notice that the parameter a is inside the contour for setX and the variable x is in the contour for the object or instance of Number. Is it okay for the contents of a to be assigned to x? The answer is yes. The reason is that when executing a statement that contains a variable, the system first looks for the variable within the innermost contour for the variable. If it is found, it uses that variable or parameter. If it is not, then the system looks at the variables contained within the next most encompassing contour diagram. If the variable is found, it is used. However, if the variable is not found, then a syntax error will be generated during compilation time. It is very important to note that although the system will look at any encompassing contour, it cannot look into another contour. In other words, it will look outside of a contour, but it cannot look into another contour.

Another way of looking at this is to say that the scope of the variable a includes only the method setX; however, the scope of the variable x includes both the object num and the method setX. The word scope is just a way of expressing in which objects and methods a variable is accessible. Problems can occur when there are two variables of the same name, and examples will be illustrated later in _Chap. 5_, but for now this text will use different variable names to avoid this difficulty.

Although Line 16 is not an instruction, it does represent the end of method setX. When the method is done executing, control is transferred back to the main program. Since setX is a void method, control is transferred back to the line just after the one that invoked the method. The result is that Fig. 2.10 represents the state of execution just prior to Line 8 in the main program.

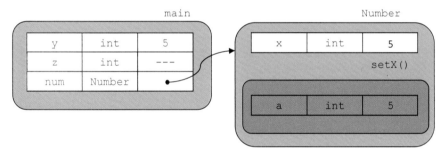

Fig. 2.10 State of execution just prior to Line 8

Note that the contour for the setX method is shaded as light red. The reason for this is to indicate the contour is deallocated, where the memory locations associated with the method are no longer accessible. Although the contour can and is often simply erased as shown in Fig. 2.11, it is sometimes helpful to show the contour as shaded prior to erasing it so that the contents of the memory locations can still be seen by others. Although shading a contour might be difficult when drawing a contour by hand, an alternative is to just very lightly cross it out while still allowing its contents to be seen.

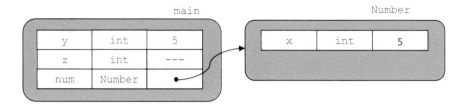

Fig. 2.11 State of execution just prior to Line 8 (alternative)

So what happens when z=num.getX(); in Line 8 is executed? Similar but somewhat different to the invoking of the void method setX, the value-returning method getX is invoked, and the state of execution just prior to Line 18 is shown in Fig. 2.12.

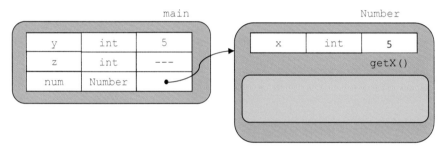

Fig. 2.12 State of execution just prior to Line 18

Note that there are no memory locations allocated in the contour for getX. The reason for this is that there are no parameters in the parameter list, nor are there any local variables declared within the method, as will be discussed later. As a result, no memory locations are allocated within the contour. So what happens when the return x; statement is executed? Since there is no variable declared by the name x in the getX contour, the system looks outside the contour to see the variable x in the Number contour. The number 5 in the variable x is the value returned to the main program. Since this is a value-returning method, control does not return back to the line after the line that invoked the method, but rather control is returned back to the same line from which it was invoked, so that the value returned can be assigned to a variable or possibly output. When the return is executed, control is transferred back to Line 8, where the number 5 is assigned to the variable z in the main program.

Figure 2.13 shows the state of execution just prior to Line 9 with the contour for getX shaded as discussed previously. Alternatively, the contour for getX does not need to be shaded nor drawn as shown in Fig. 2.14.

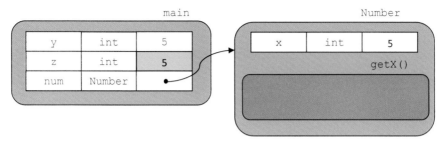

Fig. 2.13 State of execution just prior to Line 9

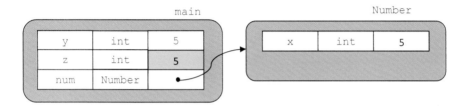

Fig. 2.14 State of execution just prior to Line 9 (alternative)

Since Line 9 is just a print statement and does not contribute to the understanding of objects, the state of execution after Line 9 is not shown here. Although almost every contour was drawn to illustrate the intricate details in the preceding example, this will not always be the case. In the future, some of the more simplistic contours might be skipped, but should they be needed they will be drawn in order to explain a particular concept, as in the next section on constructors.

2.8 Constructors

When a new object is created, it is sometimes nice to have the various private data members initialized to specific values. This is convenient and allows variables to have default values in case a programmer forgets to initialize them. The mechanism needed to accomplish this task is known as a *constructor*. A constructor is a special method that is automatically invoked once at the time an object is created via the `new` instruction. It looks similar to other methods, but instead of having its own unique name as determined by the programmer, it has the same name as the class. Although this can be confusing at first, it helps to remember that when a new object of a class like `Number` is created, the method that serves as the constructor for the class has the same name, `Number`, and does not have a return type. Again, it is best to show an example. In this case the constructor initializes the data member `x` to the default value `0`, again assuming that the initial value of variables is indeterminate as discussed in Chap. 1 .

```
public Number() {
    x = 0;
}
```

Including the above constructor, the previous class would look as shown in Fig. 2.15, where typically constructors are located after the data members but prior to all the other methods.

```
class Number {

    // Data Member
    private int x;

    // Constructor
    public Number() {
        x = 0;
    }

    // Methods
    public void setX(int a) {
        x = a;
    }

    public int getX() {
        return x;
    }

}
```

Fig. 2.15 The Number class with a constructor

Using the first 11 lines of the main program in Fig. 2.4 and replacing lines 12 through 20 with the code from Fig. 2.15, the program in Fig. 2.16 is the revised one from Fig. 2.4 that now incorporates a constructor. Instead of walking through the entire program as was done in the last section, only the first few lines of the program will be executed to illustrate how a constructor works.

```
class Invoke {                                              // Line 1
    public static void main(String[] args) {               // Line 2
        int y, z;                                          // Line 3
        Number num;                                        // Line 4
        y = 5;                                             // Line 5
        num = new Number();                                // Line 6
        num.setX(y);                                       // Line 7
        z = num.getX();                                    // Line 8
        System.out.println("The integer is: " + z);        // Line 9
    }                                                      // Line 10
}                                                          // Line 11
class Number {                                              // Line 12
    private int x;                                         // Line 13

    public Number() {                                      // Line 14
        x = 0;                                             // Line 15
    }                                                      // Line 16
    public void setX(int a) {                              // Line 17
        x = a;                                             // Line 18
    }                                                      // Line 19
    public int getX() {                                    // Line 20
        return x;                                          // Line 21
    }                                                      // Line 22
}                                                          // Line 23
```

Fig. 2.16 Invoking program and Number class with a constructor

After executing Line 5, the contour in Fig. 2.17 shows the state of execution just prior to the execution of Line 6 in the main program. If the contour looks familiar, it is because it is the same contour that appeared previously in Fig. 2.6.

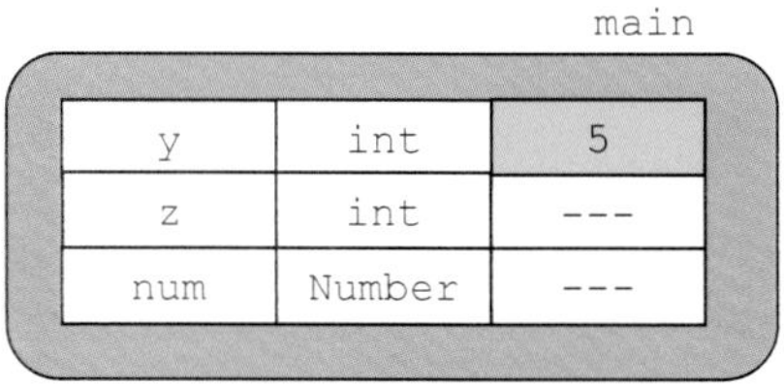

Fig. 2.17 State of execution just prior to Line 6

However, what happens when Line 6 is executed is different from the previous program. As before a contour is created for an instance of the Number class which contains the variable x. Recall from the discussion above that a constructor is automatically executed when a new instance of an object is created. As a result, a contour is also created for the constructor as shown in Fig. 2.18 which shows the state of execution just prior to Line 15 in the constructor for the class Number.

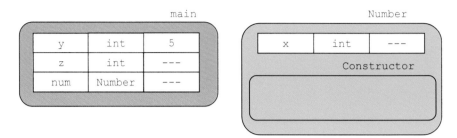

Fig. 2.18 State of execution just prior to Line 15

Notice that the contour is empty, since there are no local variables or parameters as was the case previously with the getX() method. Also note that there is no arrow pointing to the contour either. That is because while the constructor is executing, the reference to the object has not yet been assigned to the variable num.

After Line 15 is executed, the state of execution looks as shown in Fig. 2.19. Notice that the variable x has been initialized to 0 . Since there is not a variable named x in the constructor, the system looks outside to find the variable x in the class Number, similar to the setX method as discussed previously. Once Line 16 is finished, the contour for the constructor is deallocated and shaded in light red. The flow of control then returns back to Line 6 in the main program, and the reference to the object is assigned to the variable num as shown in Fig. 2.20.

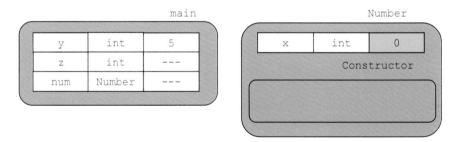

Fig. 2.19 State of execution just prior to Line 16

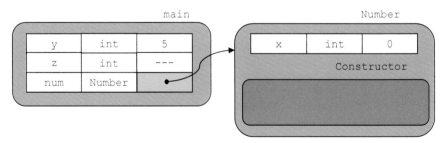

Fig. 2.20 State of execution just prior to Line 7

The program then continues to execute Line 7 just as it did previously, where the only difference is that the variable x has been initialized to the number 0 instead of being indeterminate. Although the initialization could have been accomplished by invoking the setX method with a parameter of 0, the advantage of using a constructor is that a programmer does not need to explicitly invoke a method and does not run the risk of forgetting to do so, which under some circumstances might cause a logic error. Although this is a simple example, as programs become more complicated, the role of a constructor will become more important. When one begins to learn more about data structures in later courses, the role of the constructor as just a mere initializer will diminish, and it takes on roles more befitting of its namesake as a constructor. For now, it is a good practice to use constructors when possible to gain more familiarity and become more comfortable with their use and function.

2.9 Multiple Objects and Classes

Is it possible to have more than one instance of a class or more than one class? The answer is yes and this section will address some of the issues with multiple objects and classes. For example, if one wanted to have two instances of the preceding Number class, the program could be written as in Fig. 2.21. In the interest of simplifying the contours, the number of variables has been reduced in this example. For example, instead of using local variables as arguments as done in the previous section, constants are used as arguments in Lines 6 and 7. Also, note that the values returned from getX are not stored in variables, but rather just simply output as shown in Lines 8 and 9. Again, these shortcuts are not generally encouraged, but they do save some space in the contour diagrams and hopefully help the reader see the points currently under consideration more clearly.

```
class Invoke {                                          // Line 1
   public static void main(String[] args) {             // Line 2
      Number num1, num2                                 // Line 3
      num1 = new Number();                              // Line 4
      num2 = new Number();                              // Line 5
      num1.setX(5);                                     // Line 6
      num2.setX(7);                                     // Line 7
      System.out.println("Num1 = " + num1.getX());      // Line 8
      System.out.println("Num2 = " + num2.getX());      // Line 9
   }                                                    // Line 10
}                                                       // Line 11
class Number {                                          // Line 12
   private int x;                                       // Line 13
   public Number() {                                    // Line 14
      x = 0;                                            // Line 15
   }                                                    // Line 16
   public void setX(int a) {                            // Line 17
      x = a;                                            // Line 18
   }                                                    // Line 19
   public int getX() {                                  // Line 20
      return x;                                         // Line 21
   }                                                    // Line 22
}                                                       // Line 23
```

Fig. 2.21 Program to create multiple instances of the same class

Notice that there are now two variables of type `Number` on Line 3. As before, it is helpful to use contour diagrams to assist in the understanding of the code. In this case, only the first part of the code will be executed, and the remainder of the code is left as an exercise at the end of the chapter. Figure 2.22 shows the state of execution after Line 5 but just prior to Line 6.

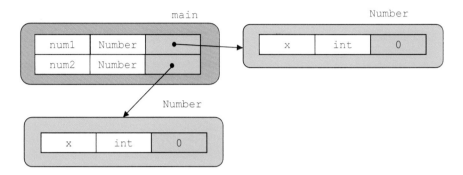

Fig. 2.22 State of execution after creating two instances prior to Line 6

Note that after the constructor has been invoked twice, there are now two instances of the class `Number`. There are also two variables with the same name, `x`, but does this cause any problems during the execution of the program? The answer is no, because each variable `x` is in a different instance of the `Number` class, where one of the variables is in the object referenced by `num1` and the other by `num2`. Upon completion of Line 6, Fig. 2.23 shows the state of execution after the execution of Line 18, but prior to the execution of Line 19 in the `setX` method.

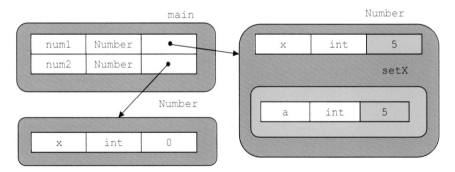

Fig. 2.23 State of execution just prior to Line 19

As before, the contents of the parameter `a` have been placed in the data member `x`. However, is there any confusion as to where the `setX` method contour should appear? No there is not; since the method call was `num1.setX(5);` the system knows to execute the setX method in the contour referenced by num1. As discussed previously in Sect. 2.7, an easy way of reading the code num1.setX(5); is to first go to the variable name in the contour, in this case num1, and when there is a dot after the variable name in the code, follow the corresponding reference or arrow to the appropriate contour. In other words, a dot in the line of code refers to a reference or arrow in the contour diagram. After following the reference to the corresponding contour diagram, the contour for the method setX is created. This also reinforces that it is very important to create the initial object contour and corresponding reference correctly when the new instruction is first executed, because all subsequent code is dependent upon it.

Although the creation of two instances of the same class is fairly straightforward, one must be careful when manipulating the two instances. For example, what if one wanted to take a copy of the integer 5 in the variable x in num1 and put it in the variable x in num2? At first it would seem to be a simple assignment operation from Chap. 1 , for example, a = b; to copy an integer from the variable b into the variable a. However, when dealing with objects, the results might not be what one expects. For example, what if one wrote the code num2 = num1? The contents of num1 would be copied into num2, but remember, what exactly is in num1? It is not the integer 5, but rather a reference to the corresponding object that contains the integer 5. What is copied is not the integer 5, but rather the result would be that num2 points to the same object as num1 and the previous object that num2 referenced would be deallocated as shown in Fig. 2.24.

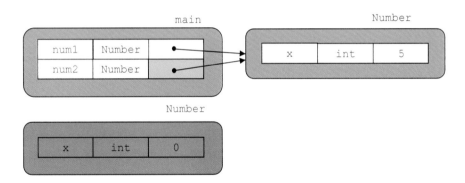

Fig. 2.24 Results of num2 = num1;

Given that the simple assignment statement above does not accomplish the intended task, how then could the integer 5 be copied from the x in num1 to the x in num2? Although another technique will be shown later in Chap. 5 , for now a temporary variable temp could be used, and the contents of x in num1 could be retrieved using the method getX. Then the corresponding x in num2 could be set with the method setX as shown in the following code segment:

```
int temp;
temp = num1.getX();
num2.setX(temp);
```

Alternatively, the temporary variable might not be used, and the getX method could be used as a parameter for the setX method as shown in the following shortened segment:

```
num2.setX(num1.getX());
```

Here the getX method is invoked first, and then the results returned are used as a parameter to be sent to the setX method. Although the above shortcut works well, for now this text will occasionally use a temporary variable to help make the code a little easier to read.

Just as it is possible to have multiple instances of a single class, it is also possible to have multiple instances of multiple classes. To elaborate further on the Number class and make it a little more interesting, suppose there is a class defined that has methods to calculate the area of a square and another class has methods to define and calculate the area of a rectangle. Although it could be argued that a square is just a special case of a rectangle, for now they will be defined as two separate classes, and this will pave the way to help explain the concept of inheritance later in Chap. 9 .

The class Square will need a method to set the length of the sides and another to calculate the area of the square. Although the method that calculates the area could also return the area (see Sect. 2.11 for the alternative technique), for now an accessor method will be used to return the area of the square, and all three methods are shown in Fig. 2.25.

```
class Square {

    // Data Members
    private int side, area;

    // Constructor
    public Square() {
        side = 0;
        area = 0;
    }

    // Methods
    public void setSide(int s) {
        side = s;
    }
    public void calcArea() {
        area = side * side;
    }
    public int getArea() {
        return area;
    }

}
```

Fig. 2.25 Square class

Note that instead of a single data member as in the previous example, there are now two private data members, one for the side and one for the area. Except for the different variable names, note the constructor, setSide, and getArea methods are similar to the constructor, setX, and getX methods in the previous example. The only real difference is the inclusion of the calcArea method which calculates the area of the square, and it is implemented as a void method.

The Rectangle class can be implemented similar to the Square class. The major difference between these two classes is that with a rectangle, it is possible to have the two sides be of different lengths, so there needs to be two variables instead of just one to represent the sides, in this case, sideX and sideY as shown in Fig. 2.26.

```
class Rectangle {

    // Data Members
    private int sideX, sideY, area;

    // Constructor
    public Rectangle() {
        sideX = 0;
        sideY = 0;
        area = 0;
    }

    // Methods
    public void setSide(int sX, int sY) {
        sideX = sX;
        sideY = sY;
    }
    public void calcArea() {
        area = sideX * sideY;
    }
    public int getArea() {
        return area;
    }
}
```

Fig. 2.26 Rectangle class

Notice the use of three variables in the bodies of the constructor and the calcArea method. Also, since the setSide method is modifying more than one side, the body of that method is also changed, but more importantly, the setSide method has two parameters instead of just one. Lastly, the getArea method remains unchanged.

Both classes can now be implemented and used with a main program as illustrated in Fig. 2.27. As with the last program and again not generally encouraged, in order to help save space in the contours, note that in Lines 7 and 8 constants are used as arguments and in Lines 11 and 12 the get methods are located in the println statements.

```
class Multiple   {                                          // Line 1
   public static void main(String[] args) {                 // Line 2
      Square square;                                         // Line 3
      Rectangle rect;                                        // Line 4
      square = new Square();                                 // Line 5
      rect = new Rectangle();                                // Line 6
```

```
      square.setSide(2);                                  // Line 7
      rect.setSide(3, 4);                                 // Line 8
      square.calcArea();                                  // Line 9
      rect.calcArea();                                    // Line 10
      System.out.println("Square = " + square.getArea()); // Line 11
      System.out.println("Rectangle = " + rect.getArea());// Line 12
   }                                                      // Line 13
}                                                         // Line 14
class Square {                                            // Line 15
   private int side, area;                                // Line 16
   public Square() {                                      // Line 17
      side = 0;                                           // Line 18
      area = 0;                                           // Line 19
   }                                                      // Line 20
   public void setSide(int s) {                           // Line 21
      side = s;                                           // Line 22
   }                                                      // Line 23
   public void calcArea() {                               // Line 24
      area = side * side;                                 // Line 25
   }                                                      // Line 26
   public int getArea() {                                 // Line 27
      return area;                                        // Line 28
   }                                                      // Line 29
}                                                         // Line 30
class Rectangle {                                         // Line 31
   private int sideX, sideY, area;                        // Line 32
   public Rectangle() {                                   // Line 33
      sideX = 0;                                          // Line 34
      sideY = 0;                                          // Line 35
      area = 0;                                           // Line 36
   }                                                      // Line 37
   public void setSide(int sX, int sY) {                  // Line 38
      sideX = sX;                                         // Line 39
      sideY = sY;                                         // Line 40
   }                                                      // Line 41
   public void calcArea() {                               // Line 42
      area = sideX * sideY;                               // Line 43
   }                                                      // Line 44
   public int getArea() {                                 // Line 45
      return area;                                        // Line 46
   }                                                      // Line 47
}                                                         // Line 48
```

Fig. 2.27 The main program along with the Square and Rectangle classes

As before, in order to see the difference between instances of multiple classes, it is helpful to walk through the contour diagrams, at least part of the way. The contour in Fig. 2.28 illustrates the state of execution after Line 6 and before the execution of Line 7 in the main program.

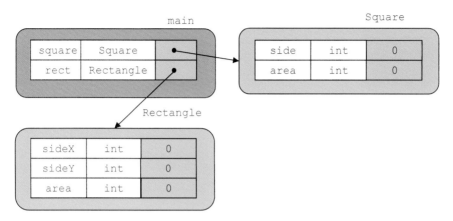

Fig. 2.28 State of execution just prior to Line 7

Previously in Fig. 2.22, the two object contours were identical because they were two instances of the *same* class. However, here in Fig. 2.28 the two object contours are different because they are instances of *different* classes. After executing Line 7, Fig. 2.29 shows the state of execution just prior to Line 23 in the setSide method.

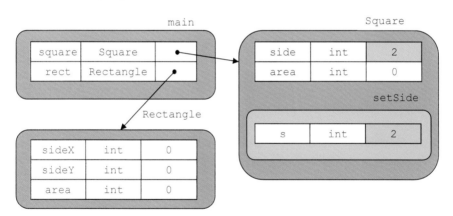

Fig. 2.29 State of execution prior to Line 23

Is there any confusion as to where the setSide method contour appears? No, since the method call was square.setSide(2); the system knows to execute the setSide method in the Square class because square is of type Square. Although somewhat different, this is similar to the previous example in Fig. 2.23 where there were two variables of the same name, but in that example there were two instances of the same class. In this case, there are two methods of the same name, but they are in two different classes. As before, an easy way of reading the code and the contour diagram is to go to the variable name, in this case `square`, and when there is a dot after the variable name in the code, follow the corresponding reference or arrow to the appropriate contour and then create the method contour in the corresponding object contour.

After returning to Line 8 in the main program, the `rect.setSide(3,4);` statement is executed, and control is transferred to Line 39 in the corresponding `setSide` method in the `Rectangle` class. Figure 2.30 then shows the state of execution just prior to Line 41.

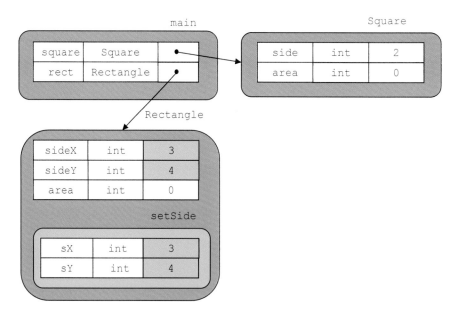

Fig. 2.30 State of execution just prior to Line 41

Note that this time the `setSide` method contour appears in the `Rectangle` class contour, and there are two parameters instead of one. Later it will be seen that there can be several methods within a class with the same name; however, they can be distinguished by having a different number, type, or order of the types of parameters. This concept is called *method overloading* and will be discussed in detail in Chap. 5. In the current example, although there are two methods that have the same name, it is not a problem because the two methods are in different classes. As with the previous example, the completion of the contours is left as an exercise at the end of the chapter.

2.10 Unified Modeling Language (UML) Class Diagrams

Whereas contours are helpful in examining how a specific object works, when an application becomes larger and includes several classes, it is helpful to get a better picture of the relationship among the various classes using Unified Modeling Language (*UML*) diagrams. UML diagrams can also help one not only see relationships between classes but also see the relationships among the objects of different classes. UML is a language specifying a graphical notation for describing software designs in an object-oriented style. It gives one an overall view of a complex system more effectively than a Java program which may provide too much detail. Again, whereas contour diagrams are helpful when trying to understand the execution of a program, UML diagrams are helpful when trying to design a program. The class definitions and objects discussed in the previous sections can be illustrated using UML class diagrams. Figure 2.31 shows how the `Number` class in Fig. 2.16 can be displayed using UML class diagram notation.

Number
x: int
Number()
setX(a: int)
getX(): int

Fig. 2.31 UML class diagram of `Number` class

In the UML class diagram, both data members and methods are included. A class is displayed as a box that includes three sections: The top section gives the class name, the middle section includes the data members for individual objects of the class, and the bottom section includes methods that can be applied to objects. In this example, the middle section represents the data member `x`, and the type of the data member is specified by placing a colon : followed by the name of the type. The methods in the `Number` class include the constructor `Number`, along with the two methods, a mutator `setX` and an accessor `getX`. Methods are denoted as the following format:

`methodName(parameterName: parameterType): returnType`

Notice that if there is no information being sent to the method, the inside of the parentheses will be empty, and if the method does not return a value, the `returnType` will not be included. In Fig. 2.31, the type of the return value is specified after the colon, similar to the type of data members. The parameter list `(a: int)` for the method `setX` indicates that information is sent to the method and the value of `a`, which is of type `int`, is assigned to the data member. By having an empty parameter list in the parentheses, the `getX` method does not accept any information and returns a value of type `int` which is the value stored in the data member `x`.

Similar to contour diagrams, but not as detailed, UML notation can also be used to illustrate objects graphically. In the main method of Fig. 2.16, an object named `num` is instantiated from the class `Number`. Then the value 5 is assigned to the data member of the object `num` through a mutator method. UML notation for the object after Line 7 is executed is shown in Fig. 2.32.

Fig. 2.32 UML notation for object num of the Number class

In the diagram, the top section gives the object name followed by the class name after the colon, all of which is underlined. The bottom section lists the data members. In this example, the variable x contains the value 5.

2.11 Complete Program: Implementing a Simple Class and Client Program

Combining all the material from this chapter, one can now define a simple class and use an instance of a class in a client program. A client program is a program that creates objects of existing clases and uses methods defined for the objects. Thus the program that implements the main method is the client program. In this section, a program to calculate the area of a circle will be developed.

Problem Statement: Write a program to calculate the area of a circle.

Once a problem statement is given, the requirements can be established by analyzing the problem. The program will:

- Accept a radius from the user
- Compute the area of the circle using the given radius
- Display the area

Next, some further issues can be considered. Since the area of more than one circle may need to be calculated, a class describing a circle should be defined separately from the main program. In the definition of a circle, only the value of the radius which is the main characteristic of a circle should be kept. In some circumstances where a calculation is very complex, it might be better to calculate the result just once and invoke a method to get the result each time it is needed, thus saving compute time. But since the calculation for the area of the circle is not very complex, it can be computed at any time using the value of the radius, and it does not need to be stored in the object.

Having addressed some of the issues, the design of the application can proceed. The definition of the Circle class in UML notation is shown in Fig. 2.33.

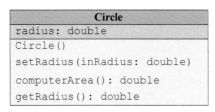

Fig. 2.33 UML class diagram of the Circle class

According to the diagram, a Circle object has a data member radius of type double which is a property that characterizes a circle shown in the middle section. The behavior of an object is defined by the methods in the bottom section. The first method is a constructor which creates a new object and performs the initialization of the data members when a new object is created. Each circle can assign a value of radius by performing the setRadius method, invoke the computeArea method to return its area, and return the value of radius using the getRadius method.

After the design phase comes the implementation phase. Figure 2.34 contains the code defining the class for a Circle object.

```
// definition of Circle class

class Circle {
    // data member
    private double radius;

    // constructor
    public Circle() {
        radius = 0.0;
    }

    // mutator method
    public void setRadius(double inRadius) {
        radius = inRadius;
    }

    // method to calculate the area of the circle
    public double computeArea() {
        return Math.PI * Math.pow(radius,2);
    }

    // accessor method
    public double getRadius() {
        return radius;
    }
}
```

Fig. 2.34 Circle class

A client program to test the functionality of the Circle class is given in Fig. 2.35.

```
// a program to calculate the area of a circle

import java.util.*;                                     // Line 1

class CalcAreaCircle {                                  // Line 2
   public static void main(String[] args) {             // Line 3

      // declaration and initialization of variables
      double radius;                                    // Line 4
      Circle circle;                                    // Line 5
      Scanner scanner;                                  // Line 6
      circle = new Circle();                            // Line 7
      scanner = new Scanner(System.in);                 // Line 8

      // input radius
      System.out.print("Enter the radius: ");           // Line 9
      radius = scanner.nextDouble();                    // Line 10
      circle.setRadius(radius);                         // Line 11

      // compute and output the area of the circle
      System.out.println();                             // Line 12
      System.out.print("The area of the circle with
                        a radius of");                  // Line 13
      System.out.printf(" %.2f cm is %.2f", radius,
                        circle.computeArea());          // Line 14
      System.out.println(" square cm.");                // Line 15
   }
}
```

Fig. 2.35 A client program for `Circle` class

When the above program is compiled and executed using the sample input of 2.0, the output of the program looks like this:

```
Enter the radius: 2.0
The area of the circle with a radius of 2.00 cm is 12.57 square cm.
```

In this example, an object `circle` was instantiated from the class `Circle`, and the user provided `2.0` for the value of the `radius` of the circle. The UML notation for the object, `circle`, is shown in Fig. 2.36.

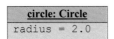

Fig. 2.36 UML notation for the object, `circle`, of the `Circle` class

As before, the top section contains the object name `circle` followed by the class name `Circle` after the colon, all of which is underlined. The bottom section lists the data member `radius` of the object `circle`. In this example, the variable `radius` has a value `2.0`.

2.12 Summary

- Remember that a class is like a definition, whereas an instance of a class is an object.
- Private data members and methods can only be accessed internally within an object of a class, whereas public data members and methods can be accessed both internally and externally.
- A value-returning method is used to return a value back to the invoking statement.
- It is best to use only one return statement in a value-returning method and also to place the return statement as the last statement in the method.
- A `void` method is usually used to set values in an object.
- Arguments in an invoking statement are used to send values to a method, and the corresponding parameters are used to receive values within the method.
- Each time an object is created or a method is invoked, a corresponding contour should be drawn.
- The `new` instruction creates a new instance of a class, and the reference to the new instance is often assigned to a variable.
- A constructor is automatically invoked when the `new` instruction is executed and is often used to initialize data members. Remember that a constructor has the same name as the name of the class and does not have a return type.

2.13 Exercises (Items Marked with an * Have Solutions in Appendix E)

1. Indicate whether the following statements using the `Circle` class in Fig. 2.34 in Sect. 2.11 are syntactically correct or incorrect. If incorrect, indicate what is wrong with the statement:

   *A.   `Circle circle = new circle();`
   B.   `Circle circle`
        `Circle = new Circle(5);`
   *C.   `circle.getRadius();` assume that an object `circle` has been declared and created correctly.
   D.   `circle.setRadius("two");` assume that an object `circle` has been declared and created correctly.
   E.   `circle.setRadius();` assume that an object `circle` has been declared and created correctly.

2. Draw contour diagrams to show the state of execution prior to the following line numbers of the `CalcAreaCircle` class in Fig. 2.35 in Sect. 2.11.

   A. Line 8
   B. Line 12 (assume an input value of 2.0)

3. Draw contour diagrams to show the state of execution prior to Line 8 of the `Invoke` class in Fig. 2.21 in Sect. 2.9.

4. Answer the questions A–D about the following declaration of class `Circle`:

```
class Circle {
   private double radius;

   public Circle() {
      radius = 0.0;
   }
   public double getRadius() {
      return radius;
   }

   public void setRadius(double inputRadius) {
      radius = inputRadius;
   }

   public double computeCircumference() {
      return 2*Math.PI*radius;
   }

   public double computeArea() {
      return Math.PI*Math.pow(radius,2);
   }
}
```

*A. Declare and create a variable of type `Circle` called `innerCircle`.
 B. Write a statement using the `setRadius` method to change the value of `innerCircle`'s data member, `radius` to `10.0`.
*C. Write a statement using the `getRadius` method to output the value of `innerCircle`'s data member, `radius`, preceded by the phrase `"The value of radius is "`.
 D. Write a statement using the `computeCircumference` method to output the value of `innerCircle`'s circumference, preceded by the phrase `"The value of the circumference is "`.

5. Draw contour diagrams to show the state of execution prior to Line 11 of the class `Multiple` shown in Fig. 2.27 in Sect. 2.9.

6. Write a complete program to calculate the volumes of a cone and a hollow cylinder. The shape of a hollow cylinder is shown below, where r is the radius of the inner cylinder and R is the radius of the outer cylinder:

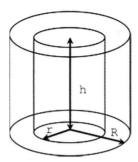

First, draw a UML diagram similar to Fig. 2.31 for a class named Cone as described below and then write the code to implement the Cone class.

*A. The Cone class has two private data members, radius and height, of type double.

B. Write code for a constructor to set the data members to default values of 0.0.

C. Write code for the accessor methods, getRadius and getHeight, that return the value of the appropriate data member.

*D. Write code for the mutator methods, setRadius and setHeight, that each have one formal parameter which is stored as the value of the data member.

E. Write a method named computeVolume to compute the volume of a cone and return the computed volume to the client. The formula to find the volume of a cone is $\frac{1}{3}\pi r^2 h$.

Second, draw a UML diagram similar to Fig. 2.31 for a class named HollowCylinder as described below and then write the code to implement the HollowCylinder class.

F. The HollowCylinder class has three private data members, innerRadius, outerRadius, and height, of type double.

G. Write code for a constructor to set the data members to 0.0.

H. Write code for the accessor methods, getInnerRadius, getOuterRadius, and getHeight, that return the value of the appropriate data member.

I. Write code for the mutator methods, setInnerRadius, setOuterRadius, and setHeight, that each have one formal parameter which is stored as the value of the data member.

J. Write a method named computeVolume to compute the volume of a hollow cylinder and return the computed volume to the client. The formula to find the volume of a hollow cylinder is $\pi h(R^2 - r^2)$.

Third, write a client program to test the Cone and HollowCylinder class as defined above. Name this class CalcVolume. The main method should perform the following tasks:

K. Allow the user to enter a radius of the cone.

L. Allow the user to enter a height of the cone.

M. Declare and create a `Cone` object setting the data members to the values entered by the user.

N. Allow the user to enter an inner radius of the hollow cylinder.

O. Allow the user to enter an outer radius of the hollow cylinder.

P. Allow the user to enter a height of the hollow cylinder.

Q. Declare and create a `HollowCylinder` object setting the data members to the values entered by the user.

R. Output the phrase `"The volume of the cone with a radius of XX cm and a height of XX cm is XX cubic cm."`, where the `XX`s are the input values and the value returned from the method.

S. Output the phrase `"The volume of the hollow cylinder with an inner radius of XX cm, an outer radius of XX cm, and a height of XX cm is XX cubic cm."`, where the `XX`s are the input values and the value returned from the method.

Here is some sample input and output:

```
Input for the cone
Enter the radius: 2.0
Enter the height: 3.0
Input for the hollow cylinder
Enter the inner radius: 2.0
Enter the outer radius: 4.0
Enter the height: 3.0
The volume of the cone with a radius of 2.00 cm and
a height of 3.00 cm is 12.57 cubic cm.
The volume of the hollow cylinder with an inner radius
of 2.00 cm, an outer radius of 4.00 cm, and
a height of 3.00 cm is 113.10 cubic cm.
```

Finally, draw a UML diagram similar to Fig. 2.32 for the objects created in the `main` method.

3

Selection Structures

James T. Streib[a*] and Takako Soma[a]

[a] Computer Science Program, Illinois College, Jacksonville, IL, USA

Abstract

Selection structures are explained in this chapter using flowcharts, pseudocode, and the corresponding Java code. The if-then, if-then-else, and nested if structures, including if-then-else-if and if-then-if structures, are introduced. The dangling-else problem is also discussed. Logical operators are presented followed by the introduction of the case structure. Two complete programs are provided: one with objects and one without.

Keywords

If Statement, Logical Operator;Truth Table; Switch Statement; Break Statement.

3.1 Introduction

Chapter 1 showed how to perform input, arithmetic, and output, which are fundamental to many subsequent programs. Chapter 2 introduced elementary object-oriented programming, which allows programs to be designed using objects and methods. Although invoking a method causes a program to branch to another subprogram and this alters the flow of control, the order in which the methods are executed can be determined by examining the code to see the order in which they are invoked. In other words, each time the program is executed, it would have the same order of execution regardless of what was input. What gives software some of its power is the ability to alter the flow of control of a program, so that during different executions of the program with different input, it will behave in a different fashion. This ability is a result of a program being able to use control structures.

The word "structure" is a generic description of statements regardless of the programming language, whereas "statements" are the individual instructions which can vary from language to language. Control structures can alter the flow of control of a program and can be classified as two main groups, selection structures and iteration structures. Selection structures, sometimes also called decision structures, allow the program to take two or more different paths based on different conditions, whereas iteration structures, sometimes called repetition structures, allow a program to repeat a part of the code many times. In this chapter, various forms of the selection structures will be examined along with the associated Java statements.

3.2 If-Then Structure

The most basic of the selection structures is the if-then structure. If a particular condition is true, the **then** portion of the structure is executed; otherwise the **then** portion of the structure is not executed. It is very similar to natural languages, where one might say "If it is hot today, then I'll buy ice cream." If it was actually hot later in the day, then one would

J. T. Streib and T. Soma, *Guide to Java*, Undergraduate Topics in Computer Science, https://doi.org/10.1007/978-3-031-22842-1_3

buy ice cream; otherwise one would not buy ice cream. Before looking at specific Java code for this example, it is helpful to look at a visual representation using a *flowchart*. There are many different types of flowcharts, where Fig. 3.1 shows the type of flowchart that will be used in this text.

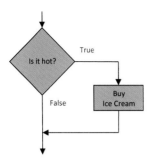

Fig. 3.1 Flowchart representing an if-then structure

In Fig. 3.1, the diamond shape represents a selection structure and the arrows represent the flow of control. The arrow at the top represents entrance into the selection structure. The statement inside the diamond is a question and its results are either true or false. The two labeled arrows exiting the diamond represent the flow of control should the condition be true or false. The true branch is known as the **then** branch which contains a rectangle representing a statement, and there are no statements in the false branch. The rectangles can be used to hold various statements such as input, output, and assignment statements. In this example, the question is asked "Is it hot?", and if the answer is true, the **then** or true branch is taken and one would "Buy Ice Cream." Should the answer to the question be false, the false branch is taken and one does not buy ice cream.

However, the example shown in Fig. 3.1 is not very precise for writing a program. It is not clear what is classified as hot, so it might be better to specify a particular temperature. To make it easier to write a program, it would be best to use a variable such as temp for temperature, where temp would first need to be input. It could then be tested in an if-then structure. For example, if it is 90° Fahrenheit or above, the message "Buy Ice Cream" could be output. Although not necessary now, but for convenience later, a message indicating "End of Program" can also be output as shown in Fig. 3.2.

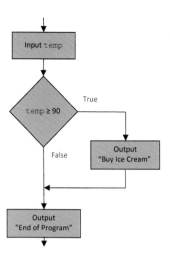

Fig. 3.2 Flowchart using the variable `temp`

Specifically, the flowchart in Fig. 3.2 first inputs the value of `temp`. Next it tests if the value in `temp` is greater than or equal to 90. If it is true, it outputs the message "Buy Ice Cream", and if it is false, it does not output the message "Buy Ice Cream". In either case, the flow of control continues on to the end of the if-then structure and the message "End of Program" is output.

The comparison between `temp` and 90 is known as a conditional expression, and the greater than or equal to symbol is known as a relational operator and it could be any of the relational operators that one has previously learned in mathematics. For example, one could also say `temp` "greater than" 89, where 90 would still output the message "Buy Ice Cream", and a `temp` "equal to" 89 would not. However, what if the variable `temp` was of type `double`? Then, a `temp` of 89.5 would cause the message "Buy Ice Cream" to be output, and this might not be what was intended. As a result, it is a good idea not to change what is given and to implement what was originally intended.

Although flowcharts are good for visually depicting the logic of a program, sometimes they are cumbersome to draw. As an alternative to flowcharts, pseudocode can be used to create the logic for a program as discussed previously in Chap. 1. The above flowchart could be implemented in pseudocode as follows:

```
input temp
if temp ≥ 90 then
    output "Buy Ice Cream"
output "End of Program"
```

After **temp** is input, the word **if** indicates an if-then structure. The condition appears between the words **if** and **then** and the word **then** is optional. If the condition is true, the statement immediately following the **if** statement is executed, and execution proceeds to the statement following. Note that the true section of the structure is indented to visually indicate the **then** section. If the condition is false, control branches or jumps over the indented **then** section and the last statement is executed.

Given the above flowchart and pseudocode, how could they be implemented in Java? The code would look as shown below:

```
System.out.print("Enter a temperature: ");
temp=scanner.nextInt();
if(temp >= 90)
   System.out.println("Buy Ice Cream");
System.out.println("End of Program");
```

The input and output statements should look familiar from Chap. 1. What is new and different is the if-then statement. Note that there are parentheses around the conditional expression and the word `then` does not appear in the code. Although the word `then` does not and should not appear in Java, the true section of an if-then statement is still referred to as the **then** section. Also, just like the pseudocode, it is a good idea to indent the true or **then** section, but be aware that indenting the code does not affect the flow of control in the program. It is done as a courtesy for other programmers to help improve the readability and maintainability of the code.

Lastly, note that the $\geq$ symbol has been replaced with the $>=$ symbols. This is because the mathematical symbol $\geq$ does not exist in the Java programming language and the $>=$ symbols need to be used instead. As one might suspect, some of the other mathematical symbols do not exist in Java as well as indicated in Table 3.1.

Table 3.1 Relational symbols

Mathematical symbol	Java symbol
>	>
$\geq$	>=
<	<
$\leq$	<=
=	==
$\neq$	!=

In addition to the "less than or equal to" symbols, notice the "equal to" symbol. Instead of a "single" equal sign, it is represented in Java as a "double" equal sign. The reason for this is to distinguish the check for equality $==$ from the assignment symbol $=$. This is a common mistake for beginning Java programmers to use the wrong symbol, so extra care must be taken when writing a conditional expression in a control structure. Although not as problematic as the "equal to" symbol, notice that the "not equal to" symbol is $!=$.

To illustrate a complete program that can be keyed into the computer to test the current if-then statement, see Fig. 3.3. This program can also be modified to test subsequent selection statements introduced in this chapter.

```
import java.util.*;
class Selection {
   public static void main(String[] args) {
      int temp;
      Scanner scanner;
      scanner = new Scanner(System.in);
      System.out.print("Enter a temperature: ");
      temp=scanner.nextInt();
      if(temp >= 90)
         System.out.println("Buy Ice Cream");
      System.out.println("End of Program");
   }
}
```

Fig. 3.3 Complete program using the if-then statement

It should further be pointed out that syntactically there can be only one statement in the then section of an `if` statement in Java. But if there can be only one statement in Java, how can more than one statement be placed in the then section? Taking a minute to think about it, a way this problem can be solved has already been presented in Chap. 2 . Yes, multiple statements could be placed in a method and then an invoke statement could be placed in the then section. However, if a method was not being used to solve this problem, how could more than one statement be put into the then section?

With flowcharts and pseudocode, there are no restrictions to using only one statement as there is in Java. In a flowchart, additional boxes can be placed in the then branch and each box represents a new statement. For example, in addition to the message "Buy Ice Cream", the message "Buy Lemonade" could be added as shown in Fig. 3.4.

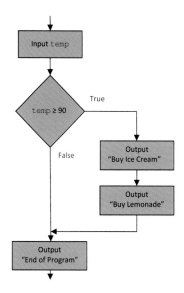

Fig. 3.4 Flowchart with two statements in the then section

In pseudocode, if more than one statement is needed in the **then** section, it is simply inserted and indented to visually indicate to the reader that the additional statements are part of the **then** section and do not belong after the **then** section, such as in the following:

```
input temp
if temp ≥ 90 then
    output "Buy Ice Cream"
    output "Buy Lemonade"
output "End of Program"
```

However, if one attempted to write the above pseudocode in Java as follows, there would be a logic error:

```
// *** Caution: Incorrectly Implemented Code ***
System.out.print("Enter a temperature: ");
temp=scanner.nextInt();
if(temp >= 90)
   System.out.println("Buy Ice Cream");
   System.out.println("Buy Lemonade");
System.out.println("End of Program");
```

Although this might look correct, it is sometimes a common error made by beginning programmers. By merely moving the "Buy Lemonade" statement to the left as shown below, there is no change in the logic of the segment, and the true flow of control is made more obvious, where the "Buy Lemonade" message is output regardless of the temperature:

```
// *** Caution: Incorrectly Implemented Code ***
System.out.print("Enter a temperature: ");
temp=scanner.nextInt();
if(temp >= 90)
   System.out.println("Buy Ice Cream");
System.out.println("Buy Lemonade"); // <--- Unindented
System.out.println("End of Program");
```

As stated previously, the indentation of the code does not affect the flow of control of the program in Java. So how does one indicate that there is more than one line of code in the **then** section? The answer is through the use of a compound statement. A compound statement is indicated by the use of opening and closing braces, { and }. For example, the above pseudocode would be correctly implemented as follows:

```
// *** Correctly Implemented Code ***
System.out.print("Enter a temperature: ");
temp=scanner.nextInt();
if(temp >= 90) {
   System.out.println("Buy Ice Cream");
   System.out.println("Buy Lemonade");
}
System.out.println("End of Program");
```

The compiler sees the compound statement which allows more than one statement to be in the **then** section. Although syntactically to the compiler there is still only one statement, specifically the compound statement, there are now logically two statements in the **then** section. Notice that the opening brace appears just after the closing parentheses of the conditional expression and the closing brace lines up with the if statement. Although there are a number of other styles, this text will use the style shown above. However, should one's instructor or place of employment use a different style, be sure to follow it.

3.3 If-Then-Else Structure

The if-then structure is helpful when there is something that needs to be done in addition to the normal flow of control. However, what if one wanted to have a program do one thing in one case and another thing in an alternative case. Using a new example, assume that if the number of credit hours input, using the variable credits, is 120 or greater, the program should output the message "Graduate"; otherwise the program should output "Does not graduate".

Is it possible to solve this problem using only if-then structures? The answer is yes, by using two if-then structures in the pseudocode that follows:

    if credits ≥ 120 then
        output "Graduate"
    if credits < 120 then
        output "Does not graduate"

Although this solution works, the problem with this method is that it has to ask two questions. For example, if the number of credit hours is equal to 120, then the message

"Graduates" would be output. However, even though the message has already been output, the code still needs to check to see if the number of credit hours is less than 120 and branch around the output "Does not graduate" message. It should be clear that if one of the options is true, the other one is false, so there is no need to check the opposite condition. This can be accomplished with the use of the if-then-else structure. An example of the flowchart for this scenario is as shown in Fig. 3.5.

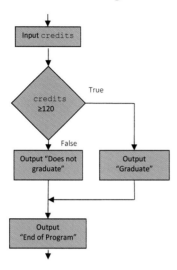

Fig. 3.5 If-then-else structure

Note that unlike the flowchart in the previous section, the false section is no longer empty. Instead, it contains a box to output the message "Does not graduate". The false section of the flowchart is also called the **else** section. The pseudocode for this flowchart is shown below:

```
input credits
if credits ≥ 120 then
    output "Graduate"
else
    output "Does not graduate"
output "End of Program"
```

Notice that the word **else** lines up with the word **if** and that the **else** section of the pseudocode lines up with the **then** section. The Java code to implement the pseudocode is as follows:

```
System.out.print("Enter the credit hours: ");
credits=scanner.nextInt();
if(credits >= 120)
   System.out.println("Graduate");
else
   System.out.println("Does not graduate");
System.out.println("End of Program");
```

As with the pseudocode, notice that the word `if` and the word `else` line up and the **then** and **else** sections line up. What if there needs to be more than one statement in either the **then** or **else** sections? As before with the if-then statement, a compound statement must be used.

It is possible to reverse the above **then** and **else** sections, but one needs to be cautious and reverse the conditional expression correctly. What is the opposite of greater than or equal to? Be careful, it is not less than or equal to. If one used less than or equal to, then those students who had exactly 120 credit hours would be listed as not graduating, much to their dismay! Instead, the opposite of greater than or equal to is simply less than as shown below:

```
System.out.print("Enter the credit hours: ");
credits=scanner.nextInt();
if(credits < 120)
    System.out.println("Does not graduate");
else
    System.out.println("Graduates");
System.out.println("End of Program");
```

Although the above code performs identically to the previous code, why should one be chosen over the other? Unless there is a compelling reason to do otherwise, such as the original description is unduly confusing, it is usually better to write the code to follow the original specifications as given. However, if either way is acceptable, then code is often written to have the most common occurrence in the **then** section and the exception in the **else** section. In the above example, most seniors will more than likely have 120 credit hours or more at graduation, so using the original code segment is probably the best choice.

When writing if-then structures, it is important to write them so that they not only work correctly but they are also efficient in terms of memory utilization. For example, consider the following code segment:

```
if(a > 0) {
    b = b + 1;
    a = a - b;
    c = c + a;
}
else {
    b = b + 1;
    a = a + b;
    c = c + a;
}
```

Note that the first and last statements in both the **then** and **else** sections are the same. The only statement that is different between the two is the middle statement in each segment. Given that the other statements are the same, why are they duplicated in the **then** and **else** sections? The answer is that they should not be and they can be moved. Not only are they taking up more memory, they also present a possible problem when someone attempts to modify the code, where a programmer might accidently modify a statement in one section and fail to modify the other statement in the other section which might lead to a subsequent logic error. Although this does not appear to present as much of problem here in a small code segment, it could be much more serious in larger code segments.

If the duplicate statements are to be consolidated and moved, where should they be relocated? By examining the above code segment, the variable b modified in the first statement in each segment is used by the second statement, so it should be moved prior to the if statement. Similarly, the variable a used in the last statement is modified by the middle statement, so it should be relocated after the if-then-else statement. In other words, care must be used to ensure that the logic is not altered when moving statements to optimize an if-then-else statement or any code segment for that matter. Below is the modified code segment that clearly is less cluttered without the braces, uses less memory, and would be easier to modify in the future. The result is that once one has written code that works correctly, be sure to take the time to ensure that it is also a well-written code.

```
b = b + 1;
if(a > 0)
    a = a - b;
else
    a - a + b;
c = c + a;
```

Note further that it is also possible to write an if-then structure as an if-then-else with either an empty **else** section or an empty **then** section. In both cases, leaving an empty **else** or **then** section in Java requires a semicolon in either section, which might lead subsequent programmers to wonder what might have been accidently left out. Unless there is intent to fill in the empty section in the immediate future, it is best to just write the code simply as an if-then. If code is written with an empty **else** section, the **else** section should be removed. In the case of an empty **then** section, it is usually best to carefully reverse the conditional expression and again write the code as an if-then.

3.4 Nested If Structures

If there is only one selection, the if-then is the best choice, and should there be two selections, the if-then-else structure is the obvious choice. But what if there are three or more choices? Sure, a series of if-then structures could be used, but although this "works," it is a very inefficient solution as discussed in the previous section. Instead, a series of if-then-else structures could be nested. There are two ways if-then-else structures can be nested: the subsequent if-then-else statements could be nested in the **else** section or in the **then** section of the previous if-then-else. The first form of nesting is called an if-then-else-if structure and the second is called an if-then-if structure. Note that there are no Java statements that correspond to each of these two structures, but rather they can be created fairly easily from a pair of if-then-else statements. Of the two, the former tends to be used more often and will be discussed first.

3.4.1 If-Then-Else-If Structure

As mentioned above, an if-then-else-if structure is created when an if-then-else is nested in the else section of an if-then-else. Using a new example, assume that the temperature is input in degrees Celsius and messages are to be output as to whether water is in the form of steam, water, or ice. At 100° or greater, water is in the form of steam, and at 0° or less, it is in the form of ice; otherwise it is in its liquid state. As before, it is helpful to view the structure in the form of a flowchart as shown in Fig. 3.6.

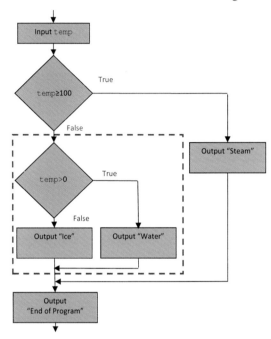

Fig. 3.6 Nested if-then-else-if structure

Notice that the second if statement appears in the else section of the first statement. The dotted lines are not part of the flowchart, but rather are included to help one see that the inner if-then-else is contained in the else section of the outer if-then-else. If the first condition is true, the message "Steam" is output and no further testing is necessary. If the first condition is false, then further testing occurs in the nested if-then-else structure. Given the flowchart in Fig. 3.6, the corresponding pseudocode would appear as follows:

```
input temp
if temp ≥ 100 then
    output "Steam"
else
    if temp > 0 then
        output "Water"
    else
        output "Ice"
output "End of Program"
```

As with the flowchart, the dashed lines are not part of the pseudocode. Rather, they are included to allow one to see how the inner if-then-else structure is nested in the else portion of the outer if-then-else structure. In particular, note that the nested `if` and `else` line up with the output statement in the then section of the outer if-then-else structure. Again, if the first condition is true, the then section is executed and no further testing occurs, but if the first condition is false, the nested if is executed.

As would be expected, the Java code looks very similar:

```
System.out.print("Enter the temperature: ");
temp=scanner.nextInt();
if(temp >= 100)
    System.out.println("Steam");
else
    if(temp > 0)
        System.out.println("Water");
    else
        System.out.println("Ice");
System.out.println("End of Program");
```

The dashed lines are not included in the Java code so that one can concentrate on the indentation and the syntax. As with the pseudocode, note how the inner `if` and `else` line up with the `System.out.println` statement in the then section of the outer `if` statement.

Since there appears to be more than one statement in the else section of the outer if-then-else structure, does there need to be a pair of braces, { and }, in that section? In other words, does a compound statement need to be used? The answer is no, because an if-then-else statement is syntactically considered to be a single statement. Although it would not cause a syntax error to include the braces, it could cause some programmers to wonder if a second statement was forgotten and not included. Some instructors might not care whether the extra pair of braces is included, but this text will omit them to help the reader get used to this programming style.

Does it matter which test is first? If all the groups are equal, then the answer is no. However, if one of the groups occurs more frequently, then it would be best to put it first so that fewer tests would need to be done. This is especially true when an `if` statement is inside an iteration structure as will be seen in Chap. 4. What if the middle section occurs more often? This could prove to be a problem at this point, but it will be discussed further in Sect. 3.5 on logical operators.

3.4.2 If-Then-If Structure

Since it is possible to nest an if-then-else structure in the else section of an outer if-then-else structure, is it possible to nest an if-then-else structure in the then section of an outer if-then-else structure? The answer is yes, and this type of structure is called an if-then-if structure. Again, there is no Java statement called an if-then-if, but rather this name merely indicates what section the subsequent if-the-else is nested. The flowchart for an if-then-if that implements the example from the previous section is shown in Fig. 3.7.

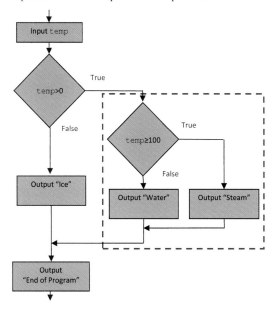

Fig. 3.7 Nested if-then-if structure

As before, the dashed lines are not part of the flowchart but help indicate how the if-then-else is nested in the then section of the outer if-then-else. In particular, notice how the relational expression in the first if is changed from ≥100 to >0. The reason for this is because previously when the temp was at 100 or greater, the then section would be executed and the message "Steam" would be output. However, with the if-then-if structure, the then section now contains a nested if and has two groups that need to be further subdivided. The relational expression in the outer if structure is changed to >0, so when temp is zero or less than zero, execution proceeds to the else section. As discussed previously in Sect. 3.2, be careful to write the relational expression properly, otherwise a logic error could occur. After checking for a temperature greater than zero, the nested if checks whether the temperature is greater than or equal to 100, and if so the message "Steam" is output, otherwise the message "Water" is output. As before, the pseudocode for the nested if-then-if can be found below:

```
input temp
if temp > 0 then
    if temp ≥ 100 then
      output "Steam"
    else
      output "Water"
else
    output "Ice"
output "End of Program"
```

Notice the nested if-then-else in the **then** section of the outer if-then-else and note the level of indentation. As should be expected, the Java code follows. Again pay attention to the indentation and the absence of braces:

```
System.out.print("Enter the temperature: ");
temp=scanner.nextInt();
if(temp > 0)
    if(temp >= 100)
        System.out.println("Steam");
    else
        System.out.println("Water");
else
    System.out.println("Ice");
System.out.println("End of Program");
```

Since the if-then-else-if and the if-then-if structures can perform the same tasks, which is the better choice? In one sense it depends on the circumstances. If the original specifications are written in such a fashion to make it easier to implement with one or the other structure, then the most appropriate structure should be used. However, often the original specifications are written in a way that is easier to communicate to other users and programmers, and this tends to be in an if-then-else-if fashion. For example, assume there were an equal number of different denominations of coins and someone wanted to move all of the one cent pieces. Ordinarily a person would not try to remove all the other coins to leave only the one cent coins, but instead it would be easier to merely remove the one cent coins. If there were subsequent coins to be removed, such as the five cent pieces, they would be the next to be removed and so on.

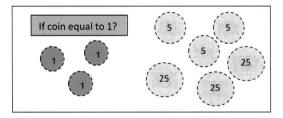

This is similar to the previous example, where instead of checking for temperatures above freezing and then checking for temperatures that produce steam or water, it is more natural to check for the temperatures that are greater than or equal to 100°. In other words, the if-then-else-if structure is often chosen over the if-then-if structure because that is the way people often speak and tend to write specifications. Further, it is helpful to have the program written similar to the specifications to assist other programmers who might be maintaining and modifying the program in the future. There is yet another reason why the if-then-else structure is used more often than the if-then-if as discussed in the next section.

3.4.3 Dangling Else Problem

The if-then-if structure also suffers from an occasional problem due to the nature of the Java syntax. For example, assume that one wanted to modify the previous temperature example to implement the flowchart in Fig. 3.8 which only the messages for "Steam" and "Ice" are to be output.

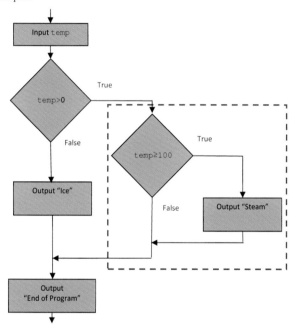

Fig. 3.8 "Ice" or "Steam" flowchart

The flowchart can also be implemented as shown in the following pseudocode:

```
input temp
if temp > 0 then
    if temp ≥ 100 then
        output "Steam"
else
    output "Ice"
output "End of Program"
```

In both cases, what is intended is that if the temperature is greater than or equal to 100, then the first and second **if** statements are true and the message "Steam" is output. If the temperature is 0 or less than 0, the first **if** is false and the message "Ice" is output. However, if the temperature is greater than 0 or less than 100, then the first **if** statement would be true, and the second **if** would be false, and since there is no code in the **else** section of the second **if**, no message is output. It would appear that the code for the above could be implemented as follows:

```
// *** Caution: Incorrectly Implemented Code ***
System.out.print("Enter the temperature: ");
temp=scanner.nextInt();
if(temp > 0)
   if(temp >= 100)
      System.out.println("Steam");
else
   System.out.println("Ice");
System.out.println("End of Program");
```

However, what appears to be correctly implemented code is not accurately implementing the logic from the flowchart and pseudocode. If the pseudocode follows from the flowchart, and the code follows from the pseudocode, how can this be? The problem is that the pseudocode is relying on indentation to indicate which parts belong in the **then** and **else** sections, but recall from Sect. 3.2 that indentation does not affect the flow of control in Java or in most languages for that matter. This is known as the "dangling else" problem. It might not be clear which `if` statement the `else` statement is paired. If the above code segment has the `else` and the subsequent `System.out.println` indented, note that the code presents itself entirely differently:

```
// *** Caution: Incorrectly Implemented Code ***
System.out.print("Enter the temperature: ");
temp=scanner.nextInt();
if(temp > 0)
   if(temp >= 100)
      System.out.println("Steam");
   else       // Indented ---->
      System.out.println("Ice");            // Indented ---->
System.out.println("End of Program");
```

Instead of the `else` appearing to belong to the outer `if`, it now seems to belong to the inner `if` statement. If indenting doesn't affect the flow of control, which of the above two code segments is correct? The answer is neither, but the second one more accurately represents the flow of control, because an `else` is always matched with the closest `if` statement. The result is that the flowchart for the above code segment is as shown in Fig. 3.9.

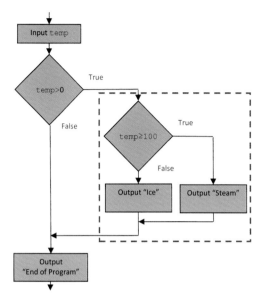

Fig. 3.9 Flowchart representing the "Dangling Else" problem

If `temp` is less than or equal to 0, then nothing is output, and if the temperature is greater than 0, but less than 100, then the message "Ice" is output, which is clearly incorrect. Although indenting is a useful way of indicating flow of control in pseudocode, it is only useful in illustrating the flow of control in Java when it is done properly. If indenting will not help correct the above problem, what can be done to correct the code? There are a couple of solutions. One is to include braces to force the `else` to match up with the outer `if` instead of the inner `if` as shown below:

```
// *** Correctly Implemented Code ***
System.out.print("Enter the temperature: ");
temp=scanner.nextInt();
if(temp > 0) {
   if(temp >= 100)
      System.out.println("Steam");
}
else
   System.out.println("Ice");
System.out.println("End of Program");
```

Note that in addition to the braces, the `else` is moved to the left to line up with the outer `if` to improve readability. But doesn't the inclusion of braces contradict the suggestion from Sect. 3.2 to not use braces for a single statement and use them only when they are necessary? No, not in this case, because although the if-then structure in Java is only a single statement, the braces are necessary in this case to force the `else` to match with the proper `if` statement.

In fact, some might suggest that braces should always be used to avoid a special case such as this. However, it seems somewhat counterintuitive to use braces everywhere for only a single potential error, since too many braces might clutter up a program and hurt the overall readability. There is another solution and that is to generally avoid the use of the if-then-if structure and instead primarily use the if-then-else-if structure, which does not suffer from this problem, as shown below:

```
// *** Correctly Implemented Code ***
System.out.print("Enter the temperature: ");
temp=scanner.nextInt();
if(temp >= 100)
   System.out.println("Steam");
else
   if(temp <= 0)
      System.out.println("Ice");
System.out.println("End of Program");
```

Again, does this mean one should never use the if-then-if structure? No, as mentioned previously use the if-then-if structure only when the nature of the problem lends itself to its usage and use extra caution to ensure that the code written actually implements the intended logic. Further, an example of the use of the if-then-if structure is shown in the next two sections.

However, it might appear that the initial cause of the above problem results from the indentation used in the previous pseudocode. Does this mean that one should not rely on indentation when writing pseudocode and braces should be used to help indicate nesting? The answer is largely left up to the individual, the instructor of a class, or the standards in a company. As long as one is aware of the potential problem, indentation can be used in pseudocode to indicate the flow of control. Also, if one wants to ensure that a mistake does not occur in writing subsequent Java from the pseudocode, then the inclusion of braces in the above instance would provide extra insurance that the pseudocode is not accidently implemented incorrectly. However, this text will not use braces in pseudocode to save space and help the reader better understand the potential problems.

3.5 Logical Operators

Although nested `if` statements are very useful in the circumstances discussed in the previous section, there are techniques that can make them even more useful. For example, assume that the only message needed to be output was the opposite of the example presented in the previous section. If the temperature is greater than 0° and less than 100°, only the message "Water" needs to be output. This could be done with either an if-then-if structure or an if-then-else-if structure, where the former is shown below:

```
System.out.print("Enter the temperature: ");
temp=scanner.nextInt();
if(temp > 0)
   if(temp < 100)
      System.out.println("Water");
System.out.println("End of Program");
```

However, does the use of an if-then-if above go against the suggestion in the previous section to use the if-then-else-if? No not really, because this is one of those cases that lend itself better to the use of the if-then-if. The use of an if-then-else-if would result in an empty then section which should be avoided as discussed in Sect. 3.3 and as shown below:

```
System.out.printl("Enter the temperature: ");
temp=scanner.nextInt();
if(temp >= 100);
else
   if(temp > 0)
      System.out.println("Water");
System.out.println("End of Program");
```

Note the semicolon at the end of the first if statement indicating an empty then section, which can be quite confusing. Clearly in this instance the if-then-if structure is a better solution than the if-then-else-if structure. However, by using logic there is an even better solution to this problem, and before presenting the solution, it is best to look over the fundamentals of logic operations.

Logical operators are also known as Boolean operators, which are named after George Boole (1815–1864) an English-born mathematician and logician. The results of Boolean operations are the values true or false which can be stored in variables of type boolean as shown below:

```
boolean flag;
flag = true;
```

Further, any relational or logic operation can be assigned to a boolean variable, and that variable can be used subsequently in an if statement. Although not used as often, it is sometimes helpful to have a relation in one part of a program, set a boolean variable (often called a flag and coded as flag), and then test the flag later in another part of the program. The result is that both of the following code segments are equivalent:

```
if(x == 0)
   System.out.println("x equals 0");
flag = x == 0;
if(flag)
   System.out.println("x equals 0");
```

Although at first the assignment statement of the second segment might look a little strange, if one thinks about it for a minute, the comparison of x == 0 results in either true or false. The true or false is then assigned to the boolean variable flag. Lastly, when the if statement is executed, should the value in flag be true, the then portion of the if is executed. Otherwise the value in flag is false, the then portion is skipped, and any statement that might follow is executed. In the second instance, does the variable flag need to be compared to the Boolean values of true or false? The answer is no, because the variable `flag` is of type `boolean` and already contains either the value `true` or `false`, so the comparison is unnecessary. Although the first example is more common, again the second is useful to set a flag in one part of a program and test it in another part of a program.

Continuing, there are three fundamental logic operations called and, or, and not. The first of these three has a value of true when both conditions are true. For example, a graduation requirement for a major in computer science might include that a student takes both a course in calculus and discrete mathematics. If one takes one course but not the other, or takes neither course, then the major will not be complete. This can be represented in the form of a truth table, where all the possible combinations of the two courses are listed on the left side and the result of the and operation is listed on the right in Table 3.2. The variables c and d are used to represent the calculus and discrete mathematics courses, respectively, and the letters T and F are used to represent the values true and false, respectively. Note that result is true only when both c and d are true.

Table 3.2 Truth table for the and operation

c	d	c and d
F	F	F
F	T	F
T	F	F
T	T	T

As an example of the or operation, suppose that in order to complete a major in computer science a student must take one of two electives, such as a course in artificial intelligence or a course in computer graphics. If a student takes one course or the other, then the student has fulfilled the requirement. But what if both courses are taken? In the case of the or operation under consideration here, known as an inclusive-or, the results are true when one or the other, or both are true. The result is that a student would have also fulfilled the requirement if both courses were taken. On the other hand, an exclusive-or is true when only one or the other is true, but not both. Although some other languages have both types of or operators, Java only has the inclusive-or as illustrated in the truth table in Table 3.3, where the letter a represents artificial intelligence and the letter c represents computer graphics. As can be seen, if either a or c is true, or both are true, the result is true. If neither is true, the result is false.

Table 3.3 Truth table for the or operation

a	c	a or c
F	F	F
F	T	T
T	F	T
T	T	T

The last of the logic operators is the not operator, which when applied to something that is true initially, the result is false and vice versa. For example, if one has taken an introduction to computer science course, then the result is true, but if one has not taken the course, the result is false. In Table 3.4 the letter c represents the introduction to computer science course. Since there is only one variable, there are only two entries in the truth table. In fact, to determine the number of entries needed in a truth table, just count the number of variables in the expression and raise 2 to that power. For example, if there were three variables in a logical expression, how many entries would be needed? The answer is 2 raised to the 3rd power which is equal to 8.

Table 3.4 Truth table for the not operation

c	not c
F	T
T	F

In Java the and, or, and not operations are represented using the &&, ||, and ! symbols, as shown in Table 3.5.

Table 3.5 Logic operations and Java symbols

Logic operation	Java symbol
And	&&
Or	||
Not	!

Using this information, how can the if-then-if structure presented at the beginning of this section be simplified? Instead of checking first whether `temp` is greater than 0 and subsequently checking whether `temp` is less than 100, it would make sense to use the and operation. Although it would be nice to use a range such as $0 < temp < 100$ as done in mathematics, note that this would cause a syntax error in Java. Instead, the relation must be written with two separate comparisons each using the variable `temp` as in `temp > 0 && temp < 100`. The previous if-then-if structure can now be written as follows:

```
System.out.print("Enter the temperature: ");
temp=scanner.nextInt();
if(temp > 0 && temp < 100)
   System.out.println("Water");
System.out.println("End of Program");
```

Could the above if statement been written as `if(temp >= 1 && temp <= 99)`? Given that the variable `temp` is of type `int` in the past couple of examples, the answer is yes. However, what if the variable `temp` was a `double`? Then, a temperature such as 0.5° would not be output as "Water," which would be incorrect. Again as discussed previously in Sect. 3.3, it is usually better to write a program with the proper endpoints and relations even when programming with integers to help prevent a possible future logic error should a program be modified later.

Although the basic operations of logic are fairly simple, expressions can become quite complex as the number of operations increase, so extra care must be taken when creating Boolean expressions. For example, suppose someone had originally coded the following `if` statement with an empty then section to check for a correct battery voltage in order for a system to operate correctly. Further, suppose that one wanted to convert the if-else structure to an if-then structure, how could that be accomplished?

```
if(voltage < 10.5 || voltage > 14.0);
else
   System.out.println("Correct Voltage");
```

The message needs to be moved from the `else` section to the **then** section. In other words the message should be output when the condition is true, not when it is false. The simple way to convert the condition is to simply add a **not** operator in front of the conditional expression and remember to remove the semicolon from the end of the `if` statement as follows:

```
if(!(voltage < 10.5 || voltage > 14.0))
   System.out.println("Correct Voltage");
```

However, one must be careful with the **not**, because just as arithmetic operators have precedence rules, so to do logical operators. The **not** operator has the highest priority, the **and** operator has the second highest priority, and the **or** operator has the lowest priority. Further, just as with arithmetic operators, when there is a tie between two operators, the order is from left to right, and parentheses can be used to override any precedence rules where the expression in the innermost nested parentheses is evaluated first. The order of precedence for logical operators is summarized in Table 3.6.

Table 3.6 Logical operator precedence

Operator	Precedence
innermost nested ()	Highest
!	
&&	
||	
Tie – left to right	Lowest

As a result, note that when the **not** is added, there are a set of parentheses around the original logical operator and its operands from the previous `if` statement, because without them the result would be different. A truth table is a convenient way to prove that the two are different. To simplify the above relations, the Boolean variables **a** and **b** are used in the truth table below:

a	b	!a	!a || b	a||b	!(a||b)
F	F	T	T	F	T
F	T	T	T	T	F
T	F	F	F	T	F
T	T	F	T	T	F

≠

Notice that the intermediate columns are shown to help ensure that there are no mistakes, or if one is made, it is easy to see where it occurred. Further, note that the arrow pointing to the two columns shows that !a || b is not equal to !(a || b). Specifically, the values in the second and fourth line down are not equal, and although the other two are correct, it takes only one instance to prove that they are not equal. Further, something like this might be difficult to catch when testing a program. If these particular instances are not tested, a program could subsequently have a logic error and no error message would be generated.

Returning to the if statement, what if one didn't want to have the not symbol in the if statement. Could it be rewritten without the ! symbol? The answer is yes, but again one must be careful when changing a logical expression. Similar to what can be done in arithmetic with a minus sign, the not symbol can be distributed over the terms in the parentheses. Although similar, it is different than arithmetic and De Morgan's laws must be used, which were formulated by Augustus De Morgan (1806–1871), a British mathematician and logician. Simply stated, if a not is distributed over either an and operator or an or operator, the operands must be complemented. Further, the operators must be changed to an or operator or an and operator, respectively. To help understand these laws better, they are listed in Table 3.7.

Table 3.7 De Morgan's laws

not (a and b)	=	not a or not b
not (a or b)	=	not a and not b

To show that the laws are indeed correct, a truth table can be used to prove that they are equal using the techniques shown above, and this is left as an exercise at the end of the chapter. To show how De Morgan's laws can be used in Java in the previous if statement, first the ! symbol is distributed over the operands and then the || operator is changed to an && operator as shown below:

```
if(!(voltage < 10.5) && !(voltage > 14.0))
    System.out.println("Correct Voltage");
```

Since there are now two not symbols, the relations can be changed to their opposites, thus eliminating the need for the two not symbols. Of course, one has to be careful to reverse the relationals correctly as has been discussed previously. The final if statement without the ! symbols is shown below:

```
if(voltage >= 10.5 && voltage <= 14.0)
    System.out.println("Correct Voltage");
```

Given some of the potential problems above, if a code segment can be written without using logical operators, then generally it is better to do so to avoid the added complexity and the potential for errors. When creating nested if structures, it is helpful not to have the first if contain a logical operator and instead rewrite the if structure to use a simple expression first. For example, in a code segment concerning temperatures, instead of starting with the water range and using an and operator, it is better to start with the steam or ice range which do not require a logical operator.

Another potential complexity often occurs when some beginning programmers feel compelled to include a logical operator on subsequent if statements. However, this is often unnecessary as shown previously in the temperature example where the first `if` checks for temperatures of 100° and above. Since the higher temperatures have already been removed by the first `if` statement, it is not necessary to include the logical operators in the subsequent `if` statement to check whether the temperatures are below 100°. As a general rule, if the logical operators are necessary or they help to reduce the number of `if` statements, then they should be included. However, if the code can be written without the use of logical operators, it is best not to include them. An example of when to use or not use logical operators can be found at the beginning of the next section.

As one writes logical operators with conditional expressions as operands, care must also be taken which conditional expression comes first. For example, the following code segment checks to make sure that `i` is not equal to 0 and that the results of the division operation are positive before outputting a message. What would happen if both `i` and `total` contained a 0?

```
if(i != 0 && total / i >= 0 )
   System.out.println("The average is positive");
```

Since `i` is equal to 0, the result of the first operand is false. However, does it matter what the results of the second operand are? Since false `&&` false is false and false `&&` true is also false, there is no need to check the second operand. This averts the division by zero error and the **then** portion of the `if` statement would not be executed. This is known as a *short circuit*, where if the first operand of an `&&` operation is false, there is no need to check the second operand.

So given the above, what would happen if the operands were reversed as follows and the value `i` and `total` were still 0?

```
if(total / i >= 0 && i != 0)
   System.out.println("The average is positive");
```

At first, it seems to be okay because the `if` statement is still checking to see if `i` is not equal to 0. However, although both tests are included in the `if` statement, recall from the discussion above that the operand on the left is evaluated first. Further if `i` was not equal to 0, there would not be a problem, but in the instance where `i` is equal to 0, there would be a division by zero error before the comparison of `i` to 0 in the second operand.

A similar problem can occur with the `||` operator, where if the first operand is true, there is no need to check the second operand. The reason this occurs with both the `&&` and `||` operators is the result of the underlying machine language generated by the compiler and the interpreter. For a further explanation, see *Guide to Assembly Language: A Concise Introduction* [10]. Although this short circuit evaluation of statements can be helpful in some instances, it can cause a problem if one is not careful with the order of the operands. So when writing logical operators, in addition to being careful with the precedence of logical operators and De Morgan's laws, one should also be careful with the order of the operands.

3.6 Case Structure

As can be imagined, if the number of nested `if` statements becomes too deep, the resulting code might be difficult to read and maintain. For example, consider when a student's quiz score is input and a message is output indicating how well the student performed as implemented in the following code segment:

```
System.out.print("Enter a quiz score: ");
score=scanner.nextInt();
if(score == 9 || score == 10)
    System.out.println("Very Good");
else
    if(score == 8)
        System.out.println("Good");
    else
        if(score == 7)
            System.out.println("Fair");
        else
            if(score == 6)
                System.out.println("Poor");
            else
                if(score >= 0 && score <= 5)
                    System.out.println("Very Poor");
                else
                    System.out.println("Invalid quiz score");
System.out.println("End of Program");
```

Notice the use of an or operation in the first `if` statement to test for a score of either 9 or 10 and the output of the message "Very Good". Note that an and operator could have been used instead as in `if(score >= 9 && score <= 10)`, but since the range is only two integers, it is probably better represented using an or operator. However, with the last `if` statement above, it is easier to use the and operator to test for the range of numbers instead of listing out each of the possibilities. Lastly, notice that if the `score` does not fall between 0 and 10 inclusive, then a message is output indicating that it is an invalid quiz score.

Although the above code segment works, what if there were more levels of scores to check and corresponding messages to be output? The level of indentation could become quite ungainly and the code might become more difficult to read and modify. Luckily, most languages have what is known as a case structure to help with these situations. In Java this structure is known as the `switch` statement. A `switch` statement is like a multi-way `if` statement. The contents of a simple variable or the result of an expression causes the flow of control to branch to one of the many particular cases, and the corresponding code is then executed. The above nested if-then-else-if structure can be implemented using a `switch` statement as follows:

```
System.out.print("Enter a quiz score: ");
score=scanner.nextInt();

switch(score) {
    case 10:
    case 9:   System.out.println("Very Good");
              break;
    case 8:   System.out.println("Good");
              break;
    case 7:   System.out.println("Fair");
              break;
    case 6:   System.out.println("Poor");
              break;
    case 5:
    case 4:
    case 3:
    case 2:
    case 1:
    case 0:   System.out.println("Very Poor");
              break;
    default: System.out.println("Invalid quiz score");
}
System.out.println("End of Program");
```

The first thing to be aware of is that the variable `score` cannot be of type `double` or `float`. Although it is possible to use typecast operators with these types, in these instances the use of nested if structures might be a better choice. This is one of the drawbacks of the `switch` statement, where typically only variables or expressions of type `int` and `char` can be used. The second thing to note in the `switch` statement is that the variable `score` is not part of a relational expression (using >, >=, etc.) as it can be in an `if` statement. Instead, the contents of the variable `score` are compared with each of the `case` statements that follow. If a match is found, then control is transferred to the corresponding `case` statement, and the code that follows is executed. For example, if the value in the variable `score` is a 10, then control is transferred to `case 10:` and the code that follows is executed. As mentioned above, an expression can be used instead of a variable, and an example of this follows later.

Syntactically, there is one set of braces which indicate the beginning and end of the entire `switch` statement; however, note that there are no braces in each of the individual `case` sections even when there is more than one statement. The reason for this is that at the end of each case section, a `break` statement is included. The use of the `break` statement causes the flow of control to be transferred to the end of the `switch` statement. Without it, the flow of control would fall through to the code that follows the next `case` statement. Although it is legal to write code that does not use a `break` statement, the need to do so is very rare and is considered to be of poor programming style. Doing so usually makes code difficult to debug or modify and should be avoided.

The last section of the `switch` statement is the `default` statement, which is executed when a matching `case` is not found. Although a `default` can be placed anywhere within the switch statement, it is typically placed at the end of the switch statement. It should be noted that switch statements are not required to have a default statement. However, if a switch statement does not have a default statement and the particular value is not found in the cases given, then nothing will be executed in the switch statement, and in the previous example, nothing would be output. Although this might be what was intended, a value that is not part of the data to be processed might cause a logic error later on in the program. As a result, default statements are usually included as a precautionary measure.

Notice that the default case does not have a break statement. If there were no default statement, then the last case section would not need to have a break statement either. The reason is that upon completion of executing the code in the last case or default, the flow of control will simply fall through to the next statement following the switch statement. Although a break statement could be included, it is not necessary and will not be included in this text.

With respect to indenting, there are a number of styles that can be followed, but typically the individual case statements are indented three spaces, and the code in each section is lined up after the colons. Again, should one's instructor or place of employment have a different style, be sure to follow that style.

Also, note that each of the individual possible values of the variable score has its own case statement. Unfortunately a relation cannot be used in the case statements and this is another of the switch statement's drawbacks. However, there are on occasion a few ways around this limitation as will be seen later.

For example, instead of having quiz scores of 10 through 0, what if the variable score was used to hold an exam score from 100 through 0, where a score of 100 through 90 inclusive was to output a message "Very Good", 89 through 80 was to output the message "Good", and so on? For a nested if structure, the solution is fairly simple. Instead of just checking for one or two integers as in the previous nested if structure, it could be modified to check for a range of integers using an **and** logical operator as in the following segment:

```
System.out.print("Enter an exam score: ");
score=scanner.nextInt();
if(score >= 90 && score <= 100)
   System.out.println("Very Good");
else
   if(score >= 80 && score < 90)
      System.out.println("Good");
   else
      if(score >= 70 && score < 80)
         System.out.println("Fair");
      else
         if(score >= 60 && score < 70)
            System.out.println("Poor");
         else
            if(score >= 0 && score < 60)
               System.out.println("Very Poor");
            else
               System.out.println("Invalid exam score");
System.out.println("End of Program");
```

Note that each if statement has an && to check for a range of values. However, wasn't it suggested in Sect. 3.5 to avoid this? Yes it was, but in previous examples, such as the temperature example, there were no upper and lower bounds, but in this case there are the bounds of 0 and 100. Although it appears necessary to include a range in each if statement in this example, is there a way that it could be rewritten to avoid having to include an **and** operator in every if statement? The answer is yes, where an extra if statement can be placed prior to the other if statements. This can be written as an if-then-else-if structure starting with if (score < 0 || score > 100) and with the error message at the beginning, or it can be coded as an if-then-if, which allows for the error message to be written at the end. To reflect the preferred order of the switch statement, the latter if structure is chosen as shown in the following segment:

```
System.out.print("Enter an exam score: ");
score=scanner.nextInt();
if(score >= 0 && score <= 100)
    if(score >= 90)
        System.out.println("Very Good");
    else
        if(score >= 80)
            System.out.println("Good");
        else
            if(score >= 70)
                System.out.println("Fair");
            else
                if(score >= 60)
                    System.out.println("Good");
                else
                    System.out.println("Very Poor");
else
    System.out.println("Invalid exam score");
System.out.println("End of Program");
```

Note the use of De Morgan's rules in the first if statement where the || is replaced with an && and the relations are reversed. With an if statement checking the range of the scores added at the beginning, there is no longer a need to have an **and** operator in each of the subsequent if statements, which simplifies the code. Also, the extra if at the beginning makes it so the last if statement checking for the range from 0 to 59 can be eliminated, since after all the previous if statements, the only scores left would be in that range. Although an if-then-if is used as the outer if, the last nested if has its own else statement and therefore the problem of a dangling else is avoided.

As can be seen, the exam score problem can be implemented relatively easily using nested if statements, but how could this be implemented using a switch statement? Does there need to be a separate case for each of the 101 possibilities? Without using an arithmetic expression, the answer would be yes. However, since the messages output are based upon exam scores in multiples of 10, if one thinks about it for a minute, there is a solution to this problem. What if each number is divided by 10? For example, if the score 98 is divided by 10, then the answer appears to be 9.8. But wasn't it said previously that the switch statement can't be used with floating point numbers? The answer is yes.

However, recall that an integer divided by an integer is an integer, so the answer above would be just 9, not 9.8. Since each division results in an integer, the control can be transferred to the appropriate `case`. As another example, what if the value in `score` is a 70 or 79? Then, 70/10 is 7 and 79/10 is also 7, so in both cases a message of "Fair" could be output.

But what about values that fall outside the range, such as −10 and 110? When divided by 10, they result in −1 and 11, respectively, and would be caught by the `default` statement. However, what about numbers like −1 and 101? When divided by 10, they would result in 0 and 10, respectively, so clearly this would not work. The solution is similar to the preceding nested **if** structure as shown below:

```
System.out.print("Enter an exam score: ");
score=scanner.nextInt();
if(score >= 0 && score <= 100)
    switch(score/10) {
        case 10:
        case 9:  System.out.println("Very Good");
                 break;
        case 8:  System.out.println("Good");
                 break;
        case 7:  System.out.println("Fair");
                 break;
        case 6:  System.out.println("Poor");
                 break;
        case 5:
        case 4:
        case 3:
        case 2:
        case 1:
        case 0:  System.out.println("Very Poor");
    }
else
    System.out.println("Invalid exam score");
System.out.println("End of Program");
```

Notice that there are no braces around the `switch` statement in the **then** section of the if-then-else statement because it is syntactically only one statement. Since the value in `score` is being divided by 10, will the value in `score` be altered? No, because as discussed in _Chap. 1_ , the variable `score` is not being assigned a new value. Also notice that there is no `default` statement because the error message is part of the **else** section of the if-then-else statement. Lastly, note that since `case 0:` is the last statement, the `break` statement is not included prior to the closing brace of the `switch` statement.

Given that it appears that the `switch` statement can solve this problem, when should the `switch` statement be used instead of nested `if` statements? Granted the above solution was helpful in this instance, because each of the message categories were multiples of 10. If other problems are multiple of other particular values, then the `switch` statement can be just as useful. However, if each of the categories are not of the same multiple, then the `switch` statement might not be as useful and nested `if` statements are probably a better solution to the problem.

In general, if statements can work in all instances and the switch statement has various limitations. If there are only one or two alternatives, then the if-then or if-then-else structures are probably the best choice, because using the switch statement could be considered overkill. Likewise, if there are only three or possibly four alternatives, then the if-then-else-if will be used by this text to give the reader practice with using nested if statements. If the problem has five or more of alternatives, then the switch statement can be the better choice. However, if the number of cases for each alternative are too numerous, then nested if statements might again provide the best solution.

3.7 Complete Programs: Implementing Selection Structures

The first program in this section is a simple program that does not include objects, whereas the second program incorporates objects to help reinforce concepts learned in Chap. 2 .

3.7.1 Simple Program

Hurricanes are classified into five categories by the US National Oceanic and Atmospheric Administration (NOAA) based on the speed of the wind as shown below:

Category	Wind speed (mph)
1	74–95
2	96–110
3	111–130
4	131–155
5	Over 155

In this section a program using selection structures which will categorize a hurricane will be developed. As in the past two chapters, this program will be developed step by step. First, the problem that will be solved is:

Problem Statement: Write a program to classify a hurricane.

Once a problem statement is given, the requirements can be established by analyzing the problem. The program will:

- Accept the wind speed of a hurricane from a user
- Determine the category of the hurricane
- Display the category of the hurricane

Because of the nature of the problem, a selection structure will be used. Since there are five alternatives, five separate if statements could be used to check the range of the wind speed. Assuming the wind speed is stored in the variable windSpeed, a possible solution is shown below:

```
if(windSpeed >= 74 && windSpeed <= 95)
   System.out.println("The hurricane is category 1.");
if(windSpeed >= 96 && windSpeed <= 110)
   System.out.println("The hurricane is category 2.");
if(windSpeed >= 111 && windSpeed <= 130)
   System.out.println("The hurricane is category 3.");
if(windSpeed >= 131 && windSpeed <= 155)
   System.out.println("The hurricane is category 4.");
```

```
if(windSpeed > 155)
    System.out.println("The hurricane is category 5.");
```

Is this a good design? The answer is no, because all five conditions will be checked every time the program is run as was discussed in Sect. 3.3. This means a nested if structure would be a better choice. How can the conditions be nested? Here is one solution:

```
if(windSpeed >= 74 && windSpeed <= 95)
    System.out.println("The hurricane is category 1.");
else
    if(windSpeed >= 96 && windSpeed <= 110)
        System.out.println("The hurricane is category 2.");
    else
        if(windSpeed >= 111 && windSpeed <= 130)
            System.out.println("The hurricane is category 3.");
        else
            if(windSpeed >= 131 && windSpeed <= 155)
                System.out.println("The hurricane is category 4.");
            else
                if(windSpeed > 155)
                    System.out.println("The hurricane is category 5.");
```

Is this a good design? It is better than the first solution because whenever the condition becomes true, the rest of the conditions will not be checked. However, it is always a good idea to reduce the number of logical operators. The complete code shown below will check the wind speed in reverse order so that a logical operator is not required in the first if statement nor in the subsequent if statements:

```
// a program to classify a hurricane

import java.util.*;
class ClassifyHurricane {
  public static void main(String[] args) {

    // declaration and initialization of variables
    int windSpeed;
    Scanner scanner;
    scanner = new Scanner(System.in);

    // input a wind speed
    System.out.print("Enter the wind speed (mph): ");
    windSpeed = scanner.nextInt();

    // determine the category of the hurricane
    if(windSpeed > 155)
      System.out.println("The hurricane is category 5.");
    else
      if(windSpeed >= 131)
        System.out.println("The hurricane is category 4.");
      else
        if(windSpeed >= 111)
          System.out.println("The hurricane is category 3.");
        else
          if(windSpeed >= 96)
            System.out.println("The hurricane is category 2.");
          else
            if(windSpeed >= 74)
              System.out.println("The hurricane is category 1.");
            else
              if(windSpeed >= 0)
                System.out.println("Not a hurricane.");
              else
                System.out.println("Invalid wind speed.");
  }
}
```

Notice that the code is indented only two spaces instead of three to help conserve space. Although three spaces is preferred, when using a number other than three, be sure to be consistent. When the above program is compiled and executed using the sample input of 125, the output of the program looks like this:

```
Enter the wind speed (mph): 125
The hurricane is category 3.
```

The first two conditions returned false, and since the third condition was true, it found the hurricane was category 3. The flow of control skipped the rest of the conditions in the nested selection structure and reached the end of the program. The program also checks for an invalid wind speed, which is any negative value. When the program is executed with −50 as a wind speed, the output looks as shown below:

```
Enter the wind speed (mph): -50
Invalid wind speed.
```

3.7.2 Program with Objects

How can the concept of objects, discussed in Chap. 2 , be incorporated into the program in the previous section? If an object for a hurricane is created, information about a particular hurricane such as a wind speed and a category can be stored inside of the object, and two hurricanes can be compared. Figure 3.10 contains the code defining the class for a Hurricane object.

```
// definition of Hurricane class

class Hurricane {
    // data members
    private int windSpeed;
    private int category;

    // constructor
    public Hurricane() {
        category = 0;
        windSpeed = 0;
    }

    // mutator methods
    public void setWindSpeed(int inWindSpeed) {
        windSpeed = inWindSpeed;
    }

    public void setCategory() {
        if(windSpeed > 155)
            category = 5;
        else
            if(windSpeed >= 131)
                category = 4;
            else
                if(windSpeed >= 111)
                    category = 3;
                else
                    if(windSpeed >= 96)
                        category = 2;
                    else
                        if(windSpeed >= 74)
                            category = 1;
    }

    // accesor methods
    public int getWindSpeed() {
        return windSpeed;
    }

    public int getCategory() {
        return category;
    }
}
```

Fig. 3.10 Hurricane class

Notice the `setCategory` method uses the value of `windSpeed` which is stored in the object to determine the category of the hurricane. As a result, the `setCategory` method does not require any parameters. In the main program shown in Fig. 3.11, two hurricane objects are created. After a user enters the wind speed of both hurricanes, the program determines the categories and outputs them. Then, it compares the categories of the two hurricanes.

```java
// a program to classify and compare hurricanes

import java.util.*;
class Hurricanes {
   public static void main(String[] args) {

      // declaration and initialization of variables
      Hurricane hurricane1, hurricane2;
      int windSpeed;
      Scanner scanner;
      hurricane1 = new Hurricane();
      hurricane2 = new Hurricane();
      scanner = new Scanner(System.in);

      // input wind speeds and set both windSpeed and category
      System.out.print("Enter the wind speed (hurricane1): ");
      windSpeed = scanner.nextInt();
      hurricane1.setWindSpeed(windSpeed);
      hurricane1.setCategory();
      System.out.print("Enter the wind speed (hurricane2): ");
      windSpeed = scanner.nextInt();
      hurricane2.setWindSpeed(windSpeed);
      hurricane2.setCategory();

      // output the categories of the hurricanes
      System.out.println("Hurricane1 is category " +
                         hurricane1.getCategory());
      System.out.println("Hurricane2 is category " +
                         hurricane2.getCategory());

      // compare two hurricanes
      if(hurricane1.getCategory() > hurricane2.getCategory())
         System.out.print("Hurricane1 is stronger.");
      else
         if(hurricane1.getCategory() < hurricane2.getCategory())
            System.out.print("Hurricane2 is stronger.");
         else
            System.out.print("Hurricane1 and 2 are the same.");
   }
}
```

Fig. 3.11 A client program for `Hurricane` class

The stronger hurricane can be found by comparing the categories of the two hurricanes. Since the value of the category is stored in each object, it can be retrieved by using an accessor, the getCategory method. When the above program is compiled and executed using the sample input of 100 and 160, the output of the program looks as given below:

```
Enter the wind speed (hurricane1): 100
Enter the wind speed (hurricane2): 160
Hurricane1 is category 2.
Hurricane2 is category 5.
Hurricane2 is stronger.
```

3.8 Summary

- The then and else sections of an if statement can syntactically contain only one statement. Should more than one statement need to be included, use a compound statement by putting two or more statements in braces. If there is only one statement in the then or else section, braces are not needed and should not be used.
- Empty then or else sections should be avoided in if-then-else statements and the code should be rewritten as an if-then.
- When nesting if statements, the if-then-else-if structure tends to be used more often than the if-then-if structure. When using the if-then-if structure, be careful to avoid the dangling else problem.
- Logical operator precedence from highest to lowest is () – innermost nested first, !, &&, ||, and in a tie – left to right.
- De Morgan's laws are not (a and b) = not a or not b and not (a or b) = not a and not b.
- The switch statement works well with integer and character data but is not as useful with floating point or double precision data.
- Generally, be sure to include a break statement after every case section, except for the last one, unless there is a default statement at the end.
- Although a default statement is not required in a switch statement, it is usually a good idea to include one at the end and it does not need a break statement.
- Should there be only one or two alternatives, use an if-then or if-then-else statement respectively and avoid the use of a switch statement. If there are three or four alternatives, a switch could be used, but in this text nested if statements will be used. Lastly, if there are five or more alternatives, a switch statement should be used if possible.

3.9 Exercises (Items Marked with an * Have Solutions in Appendix E)

1. Given the code segment below, indicate the output for the following initial values of y:

```
int x = 50;
if(y > 10)
    x = 30;
if(y < 20)
    x = 40;
System.out.println(x);
```

*A. What is the output if the integer variable y contains 10?
 B. What is the output if the integer variable y contains 15?
 C. What is the output if the integer variable y contains 30?

2. Given the code segment below, indicate the output for the following initial values of x and y:

```
int z = 0;
if (x >= 100)
    if (y < 0)
        z = 25;
    else
        z = 50;
else
    if (y < 0)
        z = 75;
    else
        z = 100;
System.out.println(z);
```

A. What is the output if the integer variable x contains 10 and y contains −15?
*B. What is the output if the integer variable x contains 100 and y contains 20?
C. What is the output if the integer variable x contains 200 and y contains −100?

3. Given the code segment below, indicate the output for the following initial values of x, y, and z:

```
int w = 0;
if (x > 0 && y > 0)
    if (z == 0)
        w = w + 1;
    else
        if (z == - 1)
            w = w + 2;
        else
            w = w + 3;
else
    if (x > 0)
        w = w + 4;
    else
        w = w + 5;
System.out.println(w);
```

  A. What is the output if the integer variable x contains 1, y contains 0, and z contains 2?

  B. What is the output if the integer variable x contains 0, y contains 1, and z contains −1?

 *C. What is the output if the integer variable x contains 1, y contains 2, and z contains 1?

4. Declare a Boolean variable, isEligible, and assign it a value of false.

5. Evaluate each Boolean expression as true or false. Show intermediate steps. Assume int num1 = 5, int num2 = -2, int num3 = 0, boolean flag1 = true, and boolean flag2 = false .

```
*A. num1 > num2 || flag2
 B. num1 < num2 && num3 >= 0
*C. num2 < 0 || flag1 && flag2
 D. (num2 < 0 || flag1) && flag2
*E. (num2 < 0 || !flag1) && flag2
 F. num1 != 0 && num2 != 0 && num3 != 0
```

6. Using a truth table, show that the first De Morgan's law discussed in Sect. 3.5 is correct.

7. Using a truth table, show that the second De Morgan's law discussed in Sect. 3.5 is correct.

*8. Write a code segment to ask a user to enter a number between 1 and 4, and print the name of the class (First-Year, Sophomore, Junior, and Senior) corresponding to the number. Use a case structure.

*9. Repeat the previous exercise using a selection structure instead of a case structure.

10. Repeat the previous exercise using dialog boxes for input ajnd output.

11. Write a code segment to ask a user to enter a number between 1 and 12, and print the name of the month corresponding to the number. Use a selection structure.

12. Repeat the previous exercise using a case structure instead of a selection structure.

13. Repeat the previous exercise using dialog boxes for input ajnd output.

14. In Sect. 3.5 it was mentioned that a mathematical expression like $0 < temp < 100$ would cause a syntax error if used as a condition in an if-then structure in a Java program. Explain why.

15. The dew point temperature is a good indicator of how humid it feels during a hot day. The US National Weather Service (NWS) summarizes the human perception of humidity using the dew point temperatures shown in the table below.

Dew point temperature (°F)	Human perception
75 or higher	Extremely uncomfortable
70–74	Very humid
65–69	Somewhat uncomfortable
60–64	OK
55–59	Comfortable
50–54	Very comfortable
49 or lower	A bit dry

Write a complete program using a selection structure to output how a person feels for a given dew point temperature. The program should perform the following tasks:

    a.   Allow the user to enter a dew point temperature.
    b.   Determine the human perception for a given dew point temperature.
    c.   Output the corresponding phrase from the table.

Here is some sample input and output:

```
Enter a dew point temperature (F): 55
Comfortable
Enter a dew point temperature (F): 30
A bit dry
Enter a dew point temperature (F): 90
Extremely uncomfortable
Enter a dew point temperature (F): 65
Somewhat uncomfortable
```

16. Repeat the previous exercise using a case structure instead of a selection structure.
17. Repeat the previous exercise using dialog boxes for input ajnd output.
18. Write a complete program to compare the temperatures of three different cities and find the hottest city. First, implement a class called `Thermometer` as described below:

    A.   `Thermometer` has one private data member, `temperature` of type double.
    B.   Write code for a constructor to set a data member to the default value of `0.0`.
    C.   Write code for an accessor method, `getTemperature`, which returns the value of the appropriate data member.
    D.   Write code for a mutator method, `setTemperature`, which has one formal parameter, and store it as the value of the data member.

Then, write a client program to test the `Thermometer` class defined above. Call this class `Temperatures`. The `main` method should perform the following tasks:

    E.   Allow the user to enter the temperatures of three cities.
    F.   Declare and create three `Thermometer` objects setting the instance data member to the values entered by the user.
    G.   If `city1` is the hottest city among the three cities, output a phrase like `"City1 is the hottest city."`

Here is some sample input and output:

```
Enter the temperature of city1: 93.4
Enter the temperature of city2: 76.1
Enter the temperature of city3: 85.8
City1 is the hottest city.
Enter the temperature of city1: 76.5
Enter the temperature of city2: 85.2
Enter the temperature of city3: 66.9
City2 is the hottest city.
```

4

Iteration Structures

James T. Streib[a*] and Takako Soma[a]

[a] Computer Science Program, Illinois College, Jacksonville, IL, USA

Abstract

This chapter shows how iterations structures work using flowcharts, pseudocode and Java. It includes pretest indefinite loop structures, both count and sentinel controlled `while` loops. The posttest indefinite `do-while` loop and the definite iteration `for` loop are also discussed. Nested loops and potential problems are examined, and complete programs both with and without objects are included.

Keywords

Loop Structure; Loop Control Variable (LCV); Pre-test Loop; Post-test Loop, Sentinel Controlled Loop.

4.1 Introduction

Selection structures were discussed in Chap. 3 , which allows a program to follow one of two or more paths. Iteration structures, sometimes called repetition structures, allow a program to repeat a section of code many times. It is this capability to repeat or loop that gives the computer the ability to perform a task over and over again.

In creating any type of loop, it will generally have three parts: initialization, test, and change. When performing a repetitive task, one typically does not think about the particular steps of the repetition, but taking a moment to think about the process, one can recognize these three components. For example, if a student needs to do a number of homework problems for a mathematics class, they might count each of the problems, starting with the number one. This can be seen as the initialization phase which is performed just once. As the student starts to do the first problem, they might look at their notes to see how many problems they need to do, where in this example the student might need to do ten problems. Noticing that the count one has not passed the number ten, the student realizes the assigned homework is not completed. This is known as the test phase. As the student finishes the first problem, the student then counts to the next number, two, and this act of counting is the change phase of the repetitive process. The student again compares the count to the number of problems to be completed. This process of counting and comparing is the repetitive process of change and test. The process continues until the student has finished the tenth problem and the iterative process stops. Although this detailed analysis is much more than what a person does when performing a repetitive task, it is what the computer needs to do to perform a loop.

In particular, this chapter will examine indefinite and definite loop structures. The first type of loop iterates an unknown number of times, whereas the second type of loop structure loops a fixed number of times. The first of these two loops can be divided into what are known as pretest and posttest loop structures, where the first has the test or conditional expression at the beginning of the loop and the second has the conditional expression at the end of the loop. Since the pretest indefinite loop structure is probably the most versatile, it is discussed first.

4.2 Pretest Indefinite Loop Structure

A pretest indefinite loop structure is a loop that has the test or conditional expression at the beginning of the loop and can iterate an indefinite number of times. An indefinite loop structure can also be made to loop a fixed number of times, and this is one of the reasons it is a very useful loop structure. The pretest indefinite loop structure in Java is known as a while loop. The while loop can generically be represented in a flowchart as shown in Fig. 4.1.

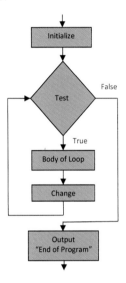

Fig. 4.1 Generic while loop

At first glance, the flowchart of the while loop might appear similar to the flowchart for the if structure presented in the last chapter. The reason for this might be because of the diamond-shaped conditional expression near the top of the flowchart, but upon closer examination, one should be able to see a number of differences. The first box is for the initialization of a variable which occurs just once. That is followed by the diamond-shaped box where the test of the variable occurs. Note that like the if structure, there is a true and a false branch, but instead of the true branch going off to the right, it is pointing downward. Further, note that the two branches do not meet together at the bottom, but instead the false branch goes to the box with the "End of Program" message and the true branch ultimately ends up going back to the test. It is the true branch that forms the actual loop. The first section in the loop is known as the body of the loop. It is here that any task or tasks that need to be performed repetitively can be placed. This can be any sort of input, processing, or output that needs to be performed. The body of the loop can also include nested if structures or even nested loops as will be shown later in this chapter. Lastly, the change to the variable occurs before the flow of control loops back to the test. Although the change can occur anywhere in the loop, it is best to be consistent in its placement, and for now it is the last thing that is done in the loop.

4.2.1 Count-Controlled Indefinite Iteration Structure

Although the generic flowchart is fine for understanding the basic layout and concept of a loop, it is helpful to see exactly how the loop performs. In the next flowchart, the initialize, test, and change are replaced with more specific statements. In this case, the loop is known as a count-controlled loop and the variable controlling the loop is sometimes called the Loop Control Variable (*LCV*). In this example, the LCV will be the variable i as shown in Fig. 4.2.

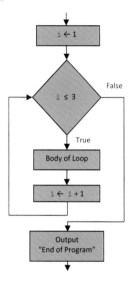

Fig. 4.2 Count-controlled while loop

To understand the loop, the best thing to do is walk through the logic. First, the variable i in the flowchart is initialized to 1. Then, the variable i is tested to see if it is less than or equal to 3, which is true. The body of the loop is executed for the first time and the value of i is incremented by 1, so that the value of i is equal to 2. The flow of control is returned back to the test, where i is less than or equal to 3. The body of the loop is executed for the second time, and the value of i is incremented to 3. The value is tested again and i is still less than or equal to 3, so the body of the loop is executed for the third time and the value of i is incremented to 4. The next time the value is tested, it is no longer less than or equal to 3, so the false branch is taken and the message "End of Program" is output. In the end, the final value of i is 4 and the body of the loop was executed three times.

As in the previous chapter on if structures, it is nice to examine the pseudocode equivalent of the while structure as seen below:

```
i ← 1
while i ≤ 3 do
   //body of loop
   i ← i + 1
output "End of Program"
```

First, note that the while is written as while i ≤ 3 do, where while-do is a common way to describe the while loop structure. Of course, if one wanted to write it as while (i ≤ 3) to make the pseudocode look a liitle more like the Java language as will be seen shortly, that is okay. However, it is recommended that whatever style of pseudocode is chosen, it should be consistent. As with if structures, note that the body of the loop, including the increment, is indented approximately three spaces. Lastly, note that the output statement is not in the loop so it is not indented.

As one might suspect, the Java syntax is similar to the pseudocode as shown below:

```
i = 1;
while(i <= 3) {
   // body of loop
   i = i + 1;
}
System.out.println("End of Program");
```

The first line is the initialization, the second line is the test with the conditional expression in parentheses like an if statement, and the increment of the variable i is inside the compound statement. Note that the statement i++ could be used instead as shown in Chap. 1 , and this style is often used in loops. Notice that braces are being used around the comment concerning the body of the loop and also the increment. Are these braces required in this particular code segment? At first the answer might seem to be yes, because there appear to be two statements in the loop. However, recall from Chap. 1 that comments are ignored by the compiler, so technically there is only one statement in the loop and the answer to the question is no. Why then are there braces included in the above segment? The reason is that in addition to the increment, there are usually other statements in the body of the loop. It is uncommon to see only one statement in a while loop, so braces are included in the above example in anticipation of more statements being added later.

What if the user wanted to loop a different number of times other than three? That would require the user to modify and recompile the program, but many users do not have knowledge of programming. To expand upon the above, the value 3 could be changed to an integer variable n, and the value for n could be prompted for and input from the user as shown below:

```
System.out.print("Enter the number of times to loop: ");
n = scanner.nextInt();
i = 1;
while(i <= n) {
   // body of loop
   i = i + 1;
}
System.out.println("End of Program");
```

If the user entered the value 3, the loop would still iterate three times as it did before. Further, the user now has the option to enter any other number for the value of n which allows the loop to have more versatility. However, what if the user entered a value of 0 instead? One other important thing about a while loop is that it is known as a pretest loop, meaning that the test is at the beginning of the loop. In this particular case, the variable i is initialized to 1 and then the comparison would be performed. Since the 1 in the variable i is not less than or equal to the 0 in the variable n, the result would be false and the body of the loop would not be executed. This is one of the important features about a pretest loop because the body of the loop might be executed anywhere from zero to many times. This is a reason why the while loop is one of the more versatile loops as will be seen below.

As an example of how the while loop structure can be used to solve a problem in the Java language, consider a user who wants to add a series of numbers. If there are a relatively small fixed number of integers to be added, then a loop might not be necessary. Consider the following code segment that would add three numbers entered by the user:

```
int num1, num2, num3, total;
System.out.print("Enter an integer to be summed: ");
num1 = scanner.nextInt();
System.out.print("Enter an integer to be summed: ");
num2 = scanner.nextInt();
System.out.print("Enter an integer to be summed: ");
num3 = scanner.nextInt();
total = num1 + num2 + num3;
System.out.println("The total is " + total);
```

Although the above works, what if there were a large number of integers to be added, say 1,000? The number of variables, prompts, and inputs would be overwhelming when writing the code, and the program would also take up a lot of memory. Returning to the example above where only three numbers need to be added, the number of variables used to store the input could be reduced to one. This would make the task a little easier, but more importantly it paves the way to see how the problem could be solved using a loop.

Using only a single variable num instead of three variables, the first integer could be prompted for, input, and placed into the variable total. The second integer could be input into the variable num and added to the variable total. The same would occur with the third integer and then the sum in total is output.

```
int num, total;
System.out.print("Enter an integer to be summed: ");
total = scanner.nextInt();
┌ System.out.print("Enter an integer to be summed: ");
│ num = scanner.nextInt();
└ total = total + num;
┌ System.out.print("Enter an integer to be summed: ");
│ num = scanner.nextInt();
└ total = total + num;
System.out.println("The total is " + total);
```

In the code above, the three prompts and inputs look the same, but the assigning of the first integer input into `total` makes it different from the subsequent assignment statements. The last two groups of statements indicated by the brackets could be placed in a loop, but the first group could not be placed in the loop. It would be convenient if there did not need to be this exception, so instead of assigning the first value input into `total`, the variable `total` could be initialized to zero; thus, the first value input into `num` could be added to the variable `total` just as all the other integers.

```
int num, total;
total = 0;
┌ System.out.print("Enter an integer to be summed: ");
│ num = scanner.nextInt();
└ total = total + num;
┌ System.out.print("Enter an integer to be summed: ");
│ num = scanner.nextInt();
└ total = total + num;
┌ System.out.print("Enter an integer to be summed: ");
│ num = scanner.nextInt();
└ total = total + num;
System.out.println("The total is " + total);
```

The first group is no longer a special case, so it can also be put into a loop that iterates three times. The body of the loop would contain a prompt and input for the integer `num` followed by the variable `num` added to the variable `total`. However, to allow for the first time `num` is added, the variable `total` would need to be initialized to zero prior to the loop. Then each time through the loop, the current value in `num` could be added to the previous value in the variable `total`. The first time through the loop, the value in `num` would be added to the zero in `total`, the second time to the previous value in `total`, and so on until the loop terminates, and the final value in the variable `total` is the sum of all the integers input.

```
int num, total, i;
total = 0;
i = 1;
while(i <= 3) {
    System.out.print("Enter an integer to be summed: ");
    num = scanner.nextInt();
    total = total + num;
    i = i + 1;
}
System.out.println("The total is " + total);
```

Notice that the basic loop is the same as the loop presented earlier, with the initialization, test, and change of the variable `i`. Also note that the variable `total` is initialized to zero so that the integers input can be summed. Lastly, notice that three statements from the previous code segment are no longer written three times, but rather only once, because the loop will iterate three times and accomplish the same task.

How does one know what belongs inside the loop and what belongs outside the loop? If outside the loop, does it belong before or after the loop? By looking for patterns on a smaller number of items, one should be able to see those items that need to be repeated and those items that need to be executed only once. In the above example, the variables for counting and the total need to be initialized only once, and they should be placed prior to the loop. Since the output of the total needs to occur only once, it should be placed outside and after the loop. Further, since there are three integers to be prompted for, input, and summed, that code should be placed inside the loop. An advantage of the above code segment is that if just three values were being input or 1,000 values were being input, the only thing that would need to be changed is the number 3 in the while statement. This version of the code is much easier to write than straight line code and also takes up less memory.

The previous code segment is a significant step forward by utilizing the power of the computer to perform repetitive tasks; however, it can be improved. As it is currently written, if the user wants to input and sum four integers instead of three, the user would have to edit and recompile the program. Since most users are not programmers, is there a way to make this program easier to use? The answer is yes. As before, a prompt and input can be placed prior to the loop to allow the user to input the number of integers to be summed as shown below:

```
int num, total, i, n;
total = 0;
i = 1;
System.out.print("Enter the # of integers to be summed: ");
n = scanner.nextInt();
while(i <= n) {
    System.out.print("Enter an integer to be summed: ");
    num = scanner.nextInt();
    total = total + num;
    i = i + 1;
}
System.out.println("The total is " + total);
```

Notice the prompt and input of the variable n prior to the while statement, and also notice that the number 3 in the while statement has been changed to the variable n. Again, this makes the program much more useful since it does not require the user to make changes to the program. For example, if the user started the program and then decided that they did not want to sum any integers, the user could just enter the number 0, and since the while loop is a pretest loop, the user would never be prompted to input any integers. Further, since total was initialized to 0, the message indicating a total of 0 would be output also.

There are of course other tasks that could be added to the above program. For example, what if the user wanted to find the average of the integers entered, how would this be written? Since total needs to be divided by the number of items, one thought is to use the value in the variable i. However, its final value is one more than the number of items entered. If three items were input and since it was initialized with a 1, it would contain the number 4 at the end of the loop. That value could be decremented by one to make it the correct number, but why use the counter when the variable n contains the number of items which was originally entered by the user? The answer is that the use of the variable n is the better choice as shown in the following code segment:

```
int num, total, i, n;
double average;

total = 0;
i = 1;
System.out.print("Enter the # of integers to be summed & averaged: ");
n = scanner.nextInt();
while(i <= n) {
    System.out.print("Enter an integer to be summed & averaged: ");
    num = scanner.nextInt();
    total = total + num;
    i = i + 1;
}
average = total / n;
System.out.println("The total is " + total);
System.out.println("The average is " + average);
```

First, notice that average is declared as type double. Also, note that the calculation of the average is outside the loop at the end of the segment because the average only needs to be calculated once. Offhand, the above segment appears to be fairly good. However, there are a few problems with it. If the program was executed using a 3 for the first prompt and then using the three integers 5, 7, and 8 for the values to be summed and averaged, what would the answer be? Using a calculator one would say 6.666..., but is this the answer that the program would generate? The answer is no because the program would output the answer 6.0, which is incorrect. The variable average is type double so that is not the problem. However, look carefully at the division on the right side of the assignment symbol. Recall from Chap. 1, an integer divided by an integer is an integer, which in this case is 6. The assignment of the integer to a variable of type double causes the 6 to be changed to 6.0, which is the number that is output. How can this be corrected? The answer from Chap. 1 is to use a (double) typecast operator on one of the variables involved in the division which will force the answer to be of type double. Also, it would help to format the output so that it would not be a repeating decimal.

There is another problem with the previous code segment that might not be as readily apparent. What would happen if the user entered a 0 for the number of items to be summed and averaged? As discussed previously, the user would not be prompted for integers to be entered. The problem occurs after the loop in the division statement. The value in n would be a 0 which would cause an execution error, or in other words a run-time error. How could this problem be solved? An if statement could be included so that division would not occur unless the value in n is positive. Should the average message still be output? That would depend on the original specifications. In this case it would not hurt to still output the message, but it would probably be a good idea to ensure that the variable average contained the value 0. The updated program with all of the above changes can be seen below:

```
int num, total, i, n;
double average;
total = 0;
i = 1;
System.out.print("Enter the # of integers to be summed & averaged: ");
n = scanner.nextInt();
while(i <= n) {
    System.out.print("Enter an integer to be summed & averaged: ");
    num = scanner.nextInt();
    total = total + num;
    i = i + 1;
}
if(n > 0)
    average = (double) total / n;
else
    average = 0.0;
System.out.println("The total is " + total);
System.out.printf("The average is %.1f" + average);
System.out.println();
```

Although typically users will not enter a negative number or the number 0 as the number of items to be summed, programmers need to write programs that work correctly under such circumstances. The old adage "If something can go wrong, it will" applies to software development as well. As a result, these sorts of possibilities should also be addressed in the design and specifications of programs so that they will be taken care of properly when a program is written. This sort of programming is known as *robust* programming and will be discussed at various points throughout the text. However, at other times it will not be included when introducing a new concept and to save space. When encountering an assignment or specifications for a programming project that lack robustness, it is always advisable to check with the user or the instructor when in a classroom setting.

4.2.2 Sentinel Controlled Loop

The use of a prompt in the previous program to indicate how many integers will be entered is better than having the number "hard coded" into the program. A disadvantage with the previous loop structure is that it requires the user to know in advance how many integers will be entered prior to running the program. If the user miscounts the number of integers, the program will not work correctly. For example, if the user overcounts the number of integers, then the user will have one or more extra prompts to enter data and the average will be off, which is unacceptable. If the user undercounts the number of integers, then the user will have leftover data and again the average will be off. In these cases the only real alternative is for the user to restart the program from the beginning. Although this is not much of a problem for a small data set, it is clearly impractical for a large number of data items.

Instead of having the user count all the data items prior to running the program, wouldn't it be useful to have the program do the counting for the user? This can be accomplished using a sentinel controlled loop, or what is sometimes called an End of Data (*EOD*) loop, which is usually implemented using a while loop. The idea is that the user continues to enter data until a sentinel value or end of data indicator is entered indicating that the end of data has been reached. The key is that the sentinel or EOD indicator must be a value that is different from the other data values. Using the above example, if only nonnegative integers were entered, then a negative integer such as -1 could be used as a sentinel. The main disadvantage of this method is that sometimes there is not an acceptable value that can serve as a sentinel, but in those instances where a sentinel is available, the sentinel controlled loop is better than the previous count-controlled loop. Although a count is not necessary to control the loop anymore, a count can be added to the program to help calculate the average as will be seen later.

As always, it is helpful to begin with an example as shown in the following code segment:

```
System.out.print("Enter a non-negative integer or -1 to stop: ");
num = scanner.nextInt();
while(num != -1) {
  // body of loop
  System.out.print("Enter a non-negative integer or -1 to stop: ");
  num = scanner.nextInt();
}
System.out.println("End of Program");
```

The first thing to notice is that the variable i is no longer controlling the loop. Since the while loop does not need a counter, it is called an indefinite loop structure. Whereas in the previous section one could tell how many times the loop would iterate merely by looking at it, such as looping 3 times or in some cases n times, here the number of times is not readily apparent and the code could loop indefinitely.

At first this loop might appear a little confusing because the value num is prompted for and input in two places, once outside prior to the loop and another time inside at the end of the loop. However, if one takes a little time to think about the loop, it is not as confusing as it looks. First, the prompt and input outside prior to the loop is sometimes called a *priming read*. This can be thought of as the initialization section of the loop. The test portion of the loop includes the comparison of the value input into the variable num to the sentinel value of -1. If the value input is equal to the sentinel, then the loop is not executed, otherwise the data can be processed in the body of the loop. The second prompt and input is the change portion of the loop, where all subsequent values are input. Again, if a subsequent value input is not equal to the sentinel, the value is processed, otherwise the loop terminates.

A disadvantage to the above loop is that as written, only a value of -1 will terminate the loop. What would happen if the user input a -2? As can be seen, all other negative values would be processed in the body of the loop, which might not be what was intended. Instead, the prompt and test could be rewritten to include all negative numbers as sentinel values as shown below:

```
System.out.print("Enter a non-negative integer ");
System.out.print("or a negative integer to stop: ");
num = scanner.nextInt();
while(num >= 0) {
   // body of loop
   System.out.print("Enter a non-negative integer ");
   System.out.print("or a negative integer to stop: ");
   num = scanner.nextInt();
}
System.out.println("End of Program");
```

Note that due to the length of the prompts, they are split into separate print statements and that the `while` statement now checks to see if `num` is greater than or equal to 0. Again, as long as the sentinel value is not part of the data to be processed, the sentinel controlled loop can prove to be a nice alternative to count-controlled loops. To help illustrate the usefulness of this loop, the following code segment shows how it can be used to implement the calculation of `total` in the example from the previous section:

```
int num, total;
total = 0;
System.out.print("Enter a non-negative integer to be summed ");
System.out.print("or a negative integer to stop: ");
num = scanner.nextInt();
while(num >= 0) {
   total = total + num;
   System.out.print("Enter a non-negative integer to be summed ");
   System.out.print("or a negative integer to stop: ");
   num = scanner.nextInt();
}
System.out.println("The total is " + total);
```

As before, the value of `total` should be initialized to 0 prior to the loop. Notice that adding `num` to `total` is the first line in the body of the loop. Is this correct? At first this might look a little strange, but it is correct. Remember that the priming read will input the first value to be summed. Also, sometimes beginning programmers think there should be an `if` statement before adding `num` to `total` because they think that the sentinel value might be included in the `total`. However, an `if` statement is not necessary because the `while` loop is a pretest loop, and if a sentinel value is input, the loop would terminate.

Can this loop be further expanded to include the calculation of the average as done previously? Yes, but a count will need to be added to the loop so that the `total` can be divided by the number of integers that are input as shown below:

```
int num, total, i;
i = 1;
total = 0;
System.out.print("Enter a non-negative integer to be summed ");
System.out.print("or a negative integer to stop: ");
num = scanner.nextInt();
while(num >= 0) {
   i = i + 1;
   total = total + num;
   System.out.print("Enter a non-negative integer to be summed ");
   System.out.print("or a negative integer to stop: ");
   num = scanner.nextInt();
}
if(i-1 > 0)
   average = (double) total / (i - 1);
else
   average = 0.0;
System.out.println("The total is " + total);
System.out.printf("The average is %.1f" + average);
System.out.println();
```

First notice that the value of i is initialized to 1 as has been done previously, and again it is incremented at the beginning of the loop prior to when total is calculated. Although the increment could be placed elsewhere, it is usually a good idea to keep all calculations together for ease of reading and modification of the code. Another thing to notice is that the variable i does not appear in the parentheses of the while statement. This again is because it is a sentinel controlled loop and not a count-controlled loop. Further, note the i-1 in the if statement, because the final value in i is one more than the number of times the loop was executed. Also notice that the total is divided by (i - 1), because without the parentheses the division would be incorrect. However, instead of using i - 1 twice, it might be more convenient to subtract 1 from i and then use just i as shown in the code segment below:

```
i = i - 1;
if(i > 0)
   average = (double) total / i;
else
   average = 0.0;
```

Although this method works, there is a more convenient way of solving this problem. Even though individuals tend to start counting from the number 1, it is often more helpful to have programs start counting from the number 0. By starting the count from 0, the final value in i will no longer be off by 1 at the end of the segment. This will become even more apparent in Chap. 7 on arrays, because an array actually starts at location 0. The following code segment reflects this change:

```
int num, total, i;
i = 0;
total = 0;
System.out.print("Enter a non-negative integer to be summed ");
System.out.print("or a negative integer to stop: ");
num = scanner.nextInt();
while(num >= 0) {
    i = i + 1;
    total = total + num;
    System.out.print("Enter a non-negative integer to be summed ");
    System.out.print("or a negative integer to stop: ");
    num = scanner.nextInt();
}
if(i > 0)
    average = (double) total / i;
else
    average = 0.0;
System.out.println("The total is " + total);
System.out.printf("The average is %.1f" + average);
System.out.println();
```

So far the count-controlled loop and the sentinel controlled loop have been introduced separately. Is it possible to combine both in one loop? Given the information presented in Sect. 3.5 on logic operations, the answer is yes. For example, what if one wanted to have a sentinel controlled loop that would accept up to a maximum of 10 numbers? In other words, the user could keep entering data until a sentinel value was entered, but if a sentinel value was not entered, the loop would stop after 10 numbers had been entered. The result is that the tests for the sentinel value and the count would need to occur in the while statement. Looking at a portion of the previous program, an && operator could be added to the while statement so that the body of the loop is executed only when both the value in num is not equal to a sentinel value and the count is less than 10.

```
int num, total, i;
i = 0;
total = 0;
System.out.print("Enter a non-negative integer to be summed ");
System.out.print("or a negative integer to stop: ");
num = scanner.nextInt();
while(num >= 0 && i < 10) {
    i = i + 1;
    total = total + num;
    System.out.print("Enter a non-negative integer to be summed ");
    System.out.print("or a negative integer to stop: ");
    num = scanner.nextInt();
}
System.out.println("The total is " + total);
```

Note that the test for i is less than 10 instead of less than or equal to 10. This is because the variable i now begins at 0 instead of 1. If the value in num is greater than or equal to 0 and the count is less than 10, then the body of the loop is executed. However, if either the value in num is a sentinel value or the value in i is 10 or greater, then the loop will not be executed.

What if there isn't an acceptable value that can be used as a sentinel value? Another possibility is to repeatedly prompt the user and ask if there is any data to be entered. A prompt asking the user to enter a Y or N, for yes or no, respectively, could be output using a sentinel controlled loop. Then, if there is more data, the user could be prompted to input data for each iteration through the loop as shown below:

```
int num, total, i;
char answer;
total = 0;
System.out.print("Is there data to be entered, Y or N? ");
answer = scanner.nextChar();
while(answer == 'Y' || answer == 'y') {
   System.out.print("Enter a non-negative integer to be summed: ");
   num=scanner.nextInt();
   total = total + num;
   System.out.print("Is there more data to be entered, Y or N? ");
   answer = scanner.nextChar();
}
System.out.println("The total is " + total);
```

Note that the `while` loop checks for either an uppercase Y or a lowercase y to make it convenient for the user. Also, notice that if the user does not respond with either Y or y, it is assumed that the user entered either N or n and the loop terminates. Further, the prompts for more data can be different as necessary, as shown by the inclusion of the word `more` in the last prompt above. The disadvantage to this program segment is that the user has to enter a character each time before entering the actual data to be processed, but if a suitable sentinel value cannot be found, then this might be the only alternative.

4.3 Posttest Indefinite Loop Structure

In addition to the pretest indefinite loop structure of the previous section, Java also has a posttest indefinite loop structure called the do-while structure. Whereas a pretest loop has its test at the beginning and the body of the loop may be executed zero to many times, the posttest loop structure has its test at the end of the loop and the body of the loop will be executed one to many times. In other words, regardless of the result of the test, the body of the posttest loop will be executed at least once. As before, looking at the flowchart is a good place to start as shown in Fig. 4.3.

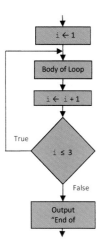

Fig. 4.3 Count-controlled do-while loop

It is easy to notice that the test condition is now located at the end of the loop instead of the beginning, thus showing it is a posttest loop structure. The body of the loop is executed while the condition is true, and when it is false, the flow of control falls through to the next statement. The above flowchart can be written in pseudocode as follows:

```
i ← 1
do
    //body of loop
    i ← i + 1
while i ≤ 3
output "End of Program"
```

As with previous pseudocode, the indenting indicates the body of the loop. As should be suspected, the Java code looks similar as follows:

```
i = 1;
do {
    // body of loop
    i = i + 1;
} while(i <= 3);
System.out.println("End of Program");
```

Notice the use of a compound statement, the { }, which is not optional within the do-while statement. Even if there is only one statement between the words do and while, a compound statement must be included. However, since the body of a do-while almost always has more than one statement, it is unlikely that one would forget to include the braces. Modifying the above code segment to prompt the user to enter the number of times to loop, similar to the last section, results in the code segment below:

```
System.out.print("Enter the number of times to loop: ");
n = scanner.nextInt();
i = 1;
do {
   // body of loop
   i = i + 1;
} while(i <= n);
System.out.println("End of Program");
```

How many times would the body of the loop be executed in the above code segment if
the user entered a value of 0 for n? The answer is one. Unlike the answer of zero for the
pretest loop structure, the body of the loop is executed at least once with a posttest loop
structure, because the comparison is at the end after the body of the loop has been executed.
If one did not want the above code to iterate once in the event that someone entered a value
of 0 for n, how would the code need to be modified? If one thinks about it, an if statement
would need to be added at the beginning of the body of the loop or just prior to the loop to
check for a value of zero or a negative number. Of these two choices, the if would be
better placed outside the loop so that it does not need to be checked through each iteration
of the loop and is executed only once prior to the loop as shown below:

```
System.out.print("Enter the number of times to loop: ");
n = scanner.nextInt();
if(n >= 1) {
   i = 1;
   do {
      // body of loop
      i = i + 1;
   } while(i <= n);
}
System.out.println("End of Program");
```

Although the above code segment solves the problem of iterating once through the loop
when the value of n is 0 or negative, it does appear a little cumbersome with the use of
both an if and a do-while statement. The above code segment can be easily implemented
using a simple while loop as presented in the previous section and repeated below:

```
System.out.print("Enter the number of times to loop: ");
n = scanner.nextInt();
i = 1;
while(i <= n) {
   // body of loop
   i = i + 1;
}
System.out.println("End of Program");
```

Clearly, the second example above using only the while loop is simpler than the
previous example using an if and do-while statements. This is not to say that the many
examples in the previous section and other problems cannot be implemented using the do-
while and an if statements (see the exercises at the end of the chapter). Rather it is

oftentimes simpler to use just the `while` statement instead. It is for this reason that the `while` statement tends to be used more often than the do-while statement.

Although in most cases having the test at the beginning is more convenient, there are some special cases where the do-while can be quite useful. For example, assume that for input a user has to input an integer between 0 and 10, inclusive. If the user enters a number outside the range, then the user needs to be re-prompted to input the number again. At first this might seem to be a good application for the `if` statement, but what if the user continues to enter the wrong number? A single `if` statement would allow the user only one chance to reenter a correct number. Instead, a loop would be a better choice. The problem could be solved using a `while` loop, but since the user has to be prompted at least once, the do-while might be a good choice as seen below:

```
do {
   System.out.print("Enter a number between 0 and 10, inclusive: ");
   number = scanner.nextInt();
} while(number < 0 || number > 10);
```

The above loop provides a simple way to give a user multiple attempts to correct a problem with the input data. However, a disadvantage of the above loop is that the user might continue on indefinitely entering the wrong number. A solution is that a counter could be added so that after a certain number of attempts, the loop stops. Then, an `if` statement after the loop could check the number of attempts and either use a default value or exit the program.

Another disadvantage of the above code segment is that the subsequent message output is the same as the first one, so the user might not understand what they did incorrectly. If a more detailed message is needed, an `if` could be added to the body of the loop to check a flag and offer a different message.

```
firstAttempt=true;
do {
   if(firstAttempt)
      firstAttempt=false;
   else
      System.out.println(number + " is an incorrect number");
   System.out.print("Enter a number between 0 and 10, inclusive: ");
   number = scanner.nextInt();
} while(number < 0 || number > 10);
```

Note the `firstAttempt` flag is set to `true` prior to the loop in order to indicate the first attempt, and once in the loop, the flag is set to `false` to indicate subsequent attempts. In the case of a subsequent attempt, a message is output to the user indicating what was input so that they might see what was incorrect. Notice that regardless of whether it was the first attempt or a subsequent attempt, a number needs to be prompted for and input, so the prompt and input statements come after the `if` statement. However, the use of the flag and `if` statement might seem a little clumsy, so possibly a `while` loop could be used instead. The advantage here is that the message in the body of the loop could be different than the initial message used in the priming read as follows:

```
System.out.print("Enter a number between 0 and 10, inclusive: ");
number = scanner.nextInt();
while(number < 0 || number > 10) {
   System.out.print(number + " is an incorrect number, try again");
   System.out.print("Enter a number between 0 and 10, inclusive: ");
   number = scanner.nextInt();
}
```

As suggested previously, a count could also be added so that after a certain number of attempts, the loop would stop. Again in this case, the pretest loop seems to be a little more appropriate than the posttest loop. In any event, a programmer should analyze the requirements and specifications of the program to be written and use the type of loop that best suits the task at hand.

4.4 Definite Iteration Loop Structure

As discussed in Sect. 4.2.1, the `while` loop can be used as a count-controlled loop. Since loops often need to iterate a fixed number of times, most languages include what is known as a definite iteration loop structure or what is sometimes called a fixed iteration loop structure. In Java, this is called a `for` loop, and like the `while` loop, it is a pretest loop.

The `for` loop has a flowchart similar to the one shown previously in Fig. 4.2. However, instead of having the initialization and test as separate statements as they are in the `while` loop, they are included as part of the `for` loop statement. To help illustrate this in flowchart form, the diamond that has only the test portion of a `while` loop can be replaced with a rectangle that contains all three parts typically present in a loop (Fig. 4.4).

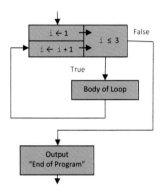

Fig. 4.4 Definite iteration loop flowchart

Notice that the initialization, test, and change are all located in one rectangle signifying that all three operations are written in the same statement. The optional internal arrows illustrate how the flow of control occurs within the statement. Notice that the order of operations is the same as with the previous flowchart for the `while` statement. The initialization is done just once prior to the loop. The test is done prior to the body of the loop and the change occurs after the body of the loop.

The pseudocode for the `for` loop can be written as follows:

```
for i ← 1 to 3 incremented by 1 do
    //body of loop
output "End of Program"
```

In the **for** loop, the initialization is indicated as i←1, the **to** 3 is the test, and the change is the **incremented by** 1. Note that the use of the word **do** is optional and the body of the loop is indented. As before, the Java code template follows:

```
for(i=1; i<=3; i++)
    // body of loop
System.out.println("End of Program");
```

After the `for` in the parentheses are the initialization `i=1`, the test `i<=3`, and the change or increment `i++`, all separated by semicolons. Note that the increment is using the shortcut `i++` which is common in a `for` statement. Also notice that there are no braces in this example around the body of the loop, because if there is only one statement, they are unnecessary. Since the change or increment of the variable `i` is in the `for` statement itself, it is not uncommon that there might be only one statement in the body of a `for` loop. However, if there is more than one statement in the body of the loop, the use of a compound statement is necessary. In the above example, it is assumed that the variable `i` is declared elsewhere, but it is also possible to declare the variable `i` within the `for` statement itself by preceding the initialization of `i` with the word `int` as in `for(int i=1; i<=3; i++)`. This is also a fairly common practice and will be used on many occasions in the future.

Note that it is possible to have more than one statement in each of the three sections that are separated by semicolons within the parenthesis and each statement would be separated by commas. This gives the `for` statement quite a bit of flexibility, but this can become quite confusing and is considered by some to be poor programming practice. Since anything that can be done with a `for` loop can also be done by the `while` loop, should such a complex `for` loop need to be written, the programmer is usually better off writing the loop as a `while` loop. That being said, when should the `for` loop be used instead of a `while` loop? Since the `for` loop is typically thought of as a fixed iteration structure, it is in those situations where a fixed number of tasks need to be done that the `for` loop should be used.

As an example of using the `for` loop, assume that Java did not contain the `pow` function in the `Math` class. How could the power function be implemented using iteration? As before, whenever trying to solve a problem using iteration, it helps to write down an example using specific values to see if a pattern can be found, followed by a more general solution. For example, when trying to calculate x^n, where x is the number 2 and n is an integer greater than or equal to zero, then the following is a list of possible results:

$$2^0 = 1$$
$$2^1 = 1 * 2 = 2$$
$$2^2 = 1 * 2 * 2 = 4$$
$$2^3 = 1 * 2 * 2 * 2 = 8$$
.
.
.
$$2^n = 1 * 2 * 2 * 2 * \ldots * 2 \ (n \text{ times})$$

Further, if x is considered to be a positive nonzero integer in this example, then the above can be rewritten more generally as follows:

$$x^0 = 1$$
$$x^1 = 1 * x$$
$$x^2 = 1 * x * x$$
$$x^3 = 1 * x * x * x$$
.
.
.
$$x^n = 1 * x * x * x * \dots * x \text{ (n times)}$$

As stated above, when solving a problem, it is helpful to try and see if there is a pattern present. In the above example, it can be seen that 2^0 and x^0 are defined to be 1, so that might be a good starting point for initialization. Further, note that for any value of n, there appears to be that number of multiplications present. For example, 2^3 is 2 multiplied by itself 3 times. This might be useful in the test part of the loop where the loop might need to iterate n times. Further, since the loop will iterate a fixed number of times, this would be a good fit for the `for` loop. Using this information, the loop skeleton from above can be modified to solve the problem.

First, four variables will need to be declared, the loop control variable i, variables for both x and n, and a variable for the result which could be named `answer` as shown below:

```
int i,x,n,answer;
```

The values for x and n would need to be prompted for and input from the user as in the following:

```
System.out.print("Enter a value for x: ");
x = scanner.nextInt();
System.out.print("Enter a value for n: ");
n = scanner.nextInt();
```

Next, if the loop needs to loop n times, then instead of having the relational expression compare the loop control variable i to 3 as was done previously, couldn't it instead be compared to n? The answer is yes, where the loop would not iterate 3 times, but rather n times. Also note that the answer for x^0 is 1. Further, each line in the definition for x^n begins with the number 1, so this might be a good initial value for the variable `answer`. The result is that the following code segment could implement the power function:

```
int i,x,n,answer;
System.out.print("Enter a value for x: ");
x = scanner.nextInt();
System.out.print("Enter a value for n: ");
n = scanner.nextInt();
answer = 1;
for(i=1; i<=n; i++)
    answer = answer * x;
System.out.println(x + " raised to the " + n + " power = " +
answer);
```

Notice that `answer` is initialized to 1, that the loop iterates n times, and that each time through the loop `answer` is multiplied by x. Also note that there is only one statement in the body of the `for` loop so a compound statement is not used. What would happen if 0 or a negative value were entered for the value of n? The result would be that the initial value 1 in the variable i would not be less than or equal to the value 0 in n. Since the `for` loop is a pretest loop structure, the loop would not iterate, and the initial value 1 in `answer` would be output. Could this problem have been solved using a count-controlled `while` loop? Yes, but since the loop needs to iterate a fixed number of times, the `for` loop is the better choice. As will be seen later, the `for` loop will be especially useful with arrays in Chap. 7.

4.5 Nested Iteration Structures

As seen in Sect. 4.3, iteration structures can be nested within selection structures, and the reverse can also occur. Further, iteration structures can also be nested within other iteration structures, and when using nested loops, they require some special considerations. To start, consider the following nested while loops:

```
int i,j;
i = 1;
while(i <= 3) {
   j = 1;
   while(j <= 2) {
      System.out.println("i = " + i + " j = " + j);
      j = j + 1;
   }
   i = i + 1;
}
System.out.println("End of Program");
```

First, notice that the loop control variable for the outer loop is the variable i and the loop control variable for the inner loop is the variable j. Although it is okay to reuse the same variable when the loops are not nested, if the same variable is used in a nested loop, it might cause what is known as an infinite loop as discussed in the next section. Given the above code segment, how many times will the inner `println` output its message? The answer is six times. If the outer loop iterates 3 times and the inner loop iterates 2 times, then one can multiply the number of times each loop iterates to get the answer, where 3 times 2 is 6. The output of the above code segment can be seen below:

```
i = 1 j = 1
i = 1 j = 2
i = 2 j = 1
i = 2 j = 2
i = 3 j = 1
i = 3 j = 2
End of Program
```

Note that the variable j counts to 2 and then starts over again when the value of i changes. It is often said in a description of this behavior that the value of the inner loop control variable varies more rapidly than the outer loop control variable which varies more slowly. Looking at another segment, how many times would the message generated by the inner println be output in the following example?

```
int n,count;
System.out.print("Enter a value for n: ");
n = scanner.nextInt();
count = 0;
for(int i=1; i<=n; i++)
   for(int j=1; j<=n; j++)
      System.out.println("count = " + count++);
System.out.println("End of Program");
```

Although one might answer that it depends on the value in n, one can still give answer in terms of n. Given the previous example where the number of times the body of the loop was executed was equal to the number of times iterated by the outer loop times the inner loop, the same principle applies here. The outer loop is n and the inner loop is n, so n times n equals n^2. As a particular example, if the value of n was 6, then the body of the inner loop would execute 36 times.

First, note that the variables i and j are declared in the for statements. Second, notice that there are no compound statements in either for loop in the above code segment. The reason is that the inner for loop has just one statement in the body of its loop and the inner for loop is just one statement in the body of the outer for loop so braces are unnecessary. Lastly, note the use of count++ which increments the value of count after it has been output.

At present, the need for nested loops is not as great, but later in <u>Chap. 7</u> nested loops will be important when data needs to be sorted, for example, in ascending order. Nested loops will also be important when dealing with what are known as two-dimensional arrays.

4.6 Potential Problems

There are a number of problems that can occur with loops, some of which have already been alluded to earlier in this chapter. For example, if the relation in the test section of a loop is incorrect, the loop might iterate more or less times than was originally intended. The best way to check for this is try going through the code segment using a small enough number so that it is easy to walk through the segment but a big enough number so that any pattern in the code can be observed. A good number to test with is the number 3 as has been used frequently in this chapter.

Just as it is important to check that the final number is correct, it is also important to ensure that the initial value is correct. For example, switching from the number 1 to the number 0 as the initial value usually requires a change in the relation in the test as discussed in Sect. 4.2.

Other considerations are to be sure that the loop control variable is initialized in the first place. If one forgets to initialize it, then the value in the loop control variable would be indeterminate and the loop would iterate an unknown number of times. Probably a more serious problem is when one forgets to include a change in the body of a loop. Even though the loop control variable has been initialized properly and tested correctly, if there is no change in the loop, one has what is called an *infinite loop*, meaning the loop never stops. This can make it seem that the computer is "locked up" and not responding, or the program might ask for input or messages are output without stopping.

Other concerns happen when incrementing the loop control variable by a value other than 1, such as counting by 2 and testing for only a particular value instead of a range of values as in the following code segment:

```
i = 0;
while(i != 3) {
   // body of loop
   i = i + 2;
}
System.out.println("End of Program");
```

Notice that the value of i starts with the number 0, then is incremented to 2, and then 4, so the value in i is never equal to the number 3. Although it is okay to increment by values other than 1, it is important that the comparison is in a range of numbers such as <=3 and that the loop iterates the expected number of times.

One might have noticed that the loop control variables used have always been integers. A variable of type char can also be used as will be shown in the next section. Although real numbers can be used, sometimes the computer cannot represent real numbers accurately. For example, the number 0.1 cannot be represented exactly on a computer, because it is a repeating fraction in the binary number system (base 2) and is less than 0.1. If one wrote a program such as the following and added the value of 0.1, ten times, the result would not be equal to 1.0:

```
double i;
i = 0.0;
while(i < 1.0) {
   // body of loop
   i = i + 0.1;
}
System.out.println("End of Program");
```

Instead of looping ten times as might be expected, the above program actually iterates eleven times. Again, real numbers can be used, but it is generally not good practice.

As said previously, when writing loops, or any code for that matter, it is important to check programs carefully with smaller data sets and to also test the program thoroughly with actual data on the computer to help avoid the possibility of logic errors.

4.7 Complete Programs: Implementing Iteration Structures

As in Chap. 3 , the first example does not use objects and the second example includes objects.

4.7.1 Simple Program

Using iteration structures and selection structures, one can write programs that are more complex and robust. Suppose that a program needs to be developed to find an average and the highest test scores in a course. This program will:

- Allow a user to enter student exam scores assuming a score is an integer value between 0 and 100
- Compute the average and find the highest score
- Display the average and the highest score

Since there will be more than one score that needs to be processed, instead of storing each score in different variables, a loop will be used to input them. What kind of loop should be used? Because most likely every class has a different number of students, the number of iterations will not be known in advance. The program could ask the user to enter the number of students before the loop and use a `while` loop or a `for` loop. On the other hand, since the range of scores is given, a sentinel value can be easily identified in order to use a sentinel loop. It is not a good idea to use a do-while loop, because there may be no scores to be processed. Using a sentinel of -1, a pretest indefinite sentinel controlled loop structure will be used here. When no score is entered, there is no reason to compute an average, find the highest score, or display them. Therefore, in that case the message, "No scores were entered." will be output. Finding the average of numbers using a loop was discussed in Sect. 4.2, but what about finding the highest score? Since all of the scores are not saved, the highest value cannot be determined after the loop is terminated by looking at all the data at once. Then, how can the highest score be found as the scores are input? The answer is to keep the highest score among the scores entered so far. Assuming all the variables are declared appropriately, the following code finds the highest value entered:

```
// priming read
System.out.print("Enter a score or -1 to stop: ");
score = scanner.nextInt();
highestScore = score;
// loop to enter scores
while(score != -1) {
   if(highestScore < score)
      highestScore = score;
   System.out.print("Enter a score or -1 to stop: ");
   score = scanner.nextInt();
}
```

Notice that the first score input is used to initialize the variable `highestScore` which keeps the highest value up to that point. If the first score is not -1, then in the loop the score is checked against the highest score. At this point, only one test score has been entered; therefore, the values of `score` and `highestScore` are the same, meaning the condition of the `if` statement is `false`. If the second value entered is not equal to -1, the body of the loop will be executed again. The second input is compared with the value of highestScore, which has the first value input at this point. If the condition is false, it means the first value input is greater than the second. If the condition is true, it means the most recent value input is greater than the highest one so far, so highestScore needs to be updated. This process is repeated until the user enters a sentinel value of −1. At the end, the value of highestScore is the largest value of all the scores input. The complete program is shown below:

```java
// a program to find average and maximum of scores

import java.util.*;

class Scores {
    public static void main(String[] args) {

        // declaration and initialization of variables
        int score, highestScore, count;
        double sum;
        Scanner scanner;
        highestScore = 0;
        count = 0;
        sum = 0.0;
        scanner = new Scanner(System.in);

        // priming read
        System.out.print("Enter a score or -1 to stop: ");
        score = scanner.nextInt();
        if(score == -1)
            System.out.println("No scores were entered.");
        else {
            // loop to enter scores
            highestScore = score;
            while(score != -1) {
                if(highestScore < score)
                    highestScore = score;
                count++;
                sum += score;
                System.out.print("Enter a score or -1 to stop: ");
                score = scanner.nextInt();
            }

            // compute and output the average and the highest score
            System.out.println();
            System.out.printf("Average score is %.2f.", sum/count);
            System.out.println();
            System.out.println("The high score is " +
                                highestScore + ".");
        }
    }
}
```

First, notice the prompt and input prior to the loop which is the priming read. It is necessary to determine whether to enter the loop or not by checking the first input value against the sentinel. The prompt and input in the loop determine if the loop should continue to iterate. As was discussed in Sect. 4.6, it is important to make sure that the loop will eventually terminate to avoid an infinite loop. In this program a sentinel value of -1 will stop the loop. If there are no scores and the user enters -1 at the very beginning, the program will not execute the body of the loop in the else section of the if-then-else, thus ensuring that division by 0 will not occur for the calculation of the average. With the input value of -1 the output is as follows:

```
Enter a score or -1 to stop: -1
No scores were entered.
```

With values other than -1, the variable `count` is incremented by 1 inside the loop body to keep track of the number of scores and is used to find the average. Notice that `sum`, which has the total of all the scores, is declared as type `double`. Although `score` is of type `int`, by declaring `sum` as type `double`, the result of the calculation `sum/count` to find the average will be of type `double` since it is a `double` divided by an `int`. An example of the output with three scores is shown below:

```
Enter a score or -1 to stop: 88
Enter a score or -1 to stop: 97
Enter a score or -1 to stop: 65
Enter a score or -1 to stop: -1
Average score is 83.33.
The high score is 97.
```

4.7.2 Program with Objects

Next consider an example that involves objects. An object that keeps a distribution of scores for a particular exam is useful to figure out how many students made a grade of A, B, C, D, or F. The `Grades` class defines data members, a constructor, and three methods, `enterGrade`, `getNumStudents`, and `getPercent`. The definition of the `Grades` class is shown below and the actual implementation of the three methods is discussed shortly:

```
// definition of Grades class

class Grades {
    // data members
    private int numA, numB, numC, numD, numF, count;

    // constructor
    public Grades() {
        numA = 0;
        numB = 0;
        numC = 0;
        numD = 0;
        numF = 0;
        count = 0;
    }

    // methods
    public void enterGrade(int score) {
        // See Figure 4.5
    }

    public int getNumStudents(char grade) {
        // See Figure 4.6
    }

    public double getPercent(char grade) {
        // See Figure 4.7
    }
}
```

Since the cutoff for the grade of A is 90, scores between 90 and 100 will receive a grade of A. Scores between 80 and 89 will result in a grade of B because the cutoff for the grade of B is 80, and so on. If the score is outside the range of 0–100, it is simply ignored in the enterGrade method. For example, what happens if the score is 95? Since it is a valid input inside the range of 0–100, the count is incremented by 1 to keep track of the number of scores entered. Then, it will increment the counter for the A group by 1. The enterGrade method shown in Fig. 4.5 is used to distribute the scores entered by the instructor into the correct grade group.

```
public void enterGrade(int score) {
    if(score >= 0 && score <= 100) {
        count++;
        if(score < 60)
            numF++;
        else
            if(score < 70)
                numD++;
            else
                if(score < 80)
                    numC++;
                else
                    if(score < 90)
                        numB++;
                    else
                        numA++;
    }
}
```

Fig. 4.5 Implementation of `enterGrade` method

The `getNumStudents` method in Fig. 4.6 returns the number of scores assigned to a particular grade and is implemented using a `switch` statement. It takes a grade (A, B, etc.) in a variable of type `char` as a parameter and returns a value of type `int`.

```
public int getNumStudents(char grade) {
    int numStudents;
    switch(grade) {
        case 'A': numStudents = numA;
                  break;
        case 'B': numStudents = numB;
                  break;
        case 'C': numStudents = numC;
                  break;
        case 'D': numStudents = numD;
                  break;
        case 'F': numStudents = numF;
                  break;
        default:  numStudents = -1;
    }
    return numStudents;
}
```

Fig. 4.6 Implementation of `getNumStudents` method

The `getPercent` method in Fig. 4.7 finds the percentage of scores assigned to a designated grade level and is also implemented using a `switch` statement. It takes a `char` value and returns a value of type `double`. Notice that the value 100.0 of type `double` is multiplied by the number of scores for the particular grade which is a value of type `int`, to make the result of type `double`. The result is divided by a value of type `int` stored in `count`, which results in the percentage of type `double`. If an invalid character is passed as a parameter, the value of −1, which represents an invalid value, is returned.

```
public double getPercent(char grade) {
    double percent;
    switch(grade) {
        case 'A': percent = 100.0*numA/count;
                  break;
        case 'B': percent = 100.0*numB/count;
                  break;
        case 'C': percent = 100.0*numC/count;
                  break;
        case 'D': percent = 100.0*numD/count;
                  break;
        case 'F': percent = 100.0*numF/count;
                  break;
        default:  percent = -1;
    }
    return percent;
}
```

Fig. 4.7 Implementation of getPercent method

Like the previous Scores program, the client program using a Grades object outputs the message "No scores were entered. ", if there were no scores as shown below:

```
Enter a score or -1 to stop: -1
No scores were entered.
```

An example of the output with eight scores is shown below:

```
Enter a score or -1 to stop: 97
Enter a score or -1 to stop: 88
Enter a score or -1 to stop: 65
Enter a score or -1 to stop: 40
Enter a score or -1 to stop: 58
Enter a score or -1 to stop: 69
Enter a score or -1 to stop: 80
Enter a score or -1 to stop: 81
Enter a score or -1 to stop: -1
```

Grade	Distribution	Percent(%)
A	1	12.5
B	3	37.5
C	0	0.0
D	2	25.0
F	2	25.0

The client program will create an object of the Grade class named class1 and each score is processed as it is entered. The exam scores are input using a while loop since the number of scores is indefinite. The result is output using a for loop because the number

of lines is known. The table displays the distribution and percent for each grade. The
complete client program is shown below:

```
// a program to find the distribution of the grades

import java.util.*;

class ClassGrades {
   public static void main(String[] args) {

      // declaration and initialization of variables
      Grades class1;
      int score;
      char letter;
      Scanner scanner;
      class1 = new Grades();
      scanner = new Scanner(System.in);

      // priming read
      System.out.print("Enter a score or -1 to stop: ");
      score = scanner.nextInt();

      if(score == -1)
         System.out.println("No scores were entered.");
      else {
         // loop to enter scores
         while(score != -1) {
            class1.enterGrade(score);
            System.out.print("Enter a score or -1 to stop: ");
            score = scanner.nextInt();
         }

         // print distribution and percent
         System.out.println();
         System.out.println("Grade      Distribution      Percent(%)");
         for(letter='A'; letter<'E'; letter++) {
            System.out.printf("%3c          %6d             %7.1f",
               letter, class1.getNumStudents(letter),
               class1.getPercent(letter));
            System.out.println();
         }
         System.out.printf("%3c          %6d             %7.1f",
            'F',class1.getNumStudents('F'),class1.getPercent('F'));
         System.out.println();
      }
   }
}
```

The first line of the table contains column titles that are printed prior to the for loop.
The second through fifth lines output the grade, distribution, and percent for grades for A,
B, C, and D using a for loop. Notice that the char variable' letter is used as a loop
control variable in the for loop. It is initialized to "A" at the beginning of the for loop,
and when it is incremented by one, the value of letter is updated to the next character
in alphabetical order such as A to B, and B to C. Because there is a gap between D and F,

the information for the grade of F needs to be printed outside the `for` loop at the end. Control characters, `c`, `d`, and `f`, are used in the control string of the first `printf` statement to output the variables of type `char`, `int`, and `double`, respectively, in order to format the table as described in Chap. 1 .

4.8 Summary

- The `while` loop and the do-while loop are known as indefinite iteration loop structures.
- The `for` loop is known as a definite or fixed iteration loop structure.
- The do-while loop is a posttest loop structure and can iterate one to many times.
- The `while` loop and the `for` loop are pretest loops which can iterate zero to many times.
- The do-while loop must always use a compound statement in the body of the loop whether there are one or many statements.
- The body of the `for` and `while` loops only need to use a compound statement when there is more than one statement in the body of the loop. If there is only one statement, the compound statement is unnecessary.
- When nesting loops, be sure to use a different loop control variable for each loop.

4.9 Exercises (Items Marked with an * Have Solutions in Appendix E)

1. Identify the syntax errors in the following code segment:

```
int sum, i;
sum = 0;
i = 0;
while (i >= 0); {
   sum = sum + i;
   i = i + 2;
}
```

*2. Identify the syntax errors in the following code segment:

```
int product;
product = 1;
for (i=1, i <= n, i++)
    product = product * i;
```

*3. Determine the output from the following code segment:

```
int sum;
int count;
sum = 0;
count = 1;
while (sum < 10) {
    sum = sum + count;
    count++;
    System.out.println("sum = " + sum);
    System.out.println("count = " + count);
}
System.out.println("sum = " + sum);
System.out.println("count = " + count);
```

4. Determine the output from the following code segment:

```
int sum = 2;
int number = 3;
do {
    sum = sum + number;
    number++;
    System.out.println("sum = " + sum);
    System.out.println("number = " + number);
} while (sum < 3*number);
System.out.println("sum = " + sum);
System.out.println("number = " + number);
```

5. Determine the output from the following code segment:

```
int outer = 1;
while (outer < 4) {
    int inner = 1;
    while (inner <= outer) {
        System.out.println("outer is "+outer+" inner is "+inner);
        inner+=3;
    }
    outer+=2;
    System.out.println("outer is "+outer+" inner is "+inner);
}
```

*6. Determine the output from the following code segment:

```
int i, j;
for (i=1; i<=5; i++) {
    for (j=1; j<=5-i; j++)
        System.out.print(" ");
    for (j=1; j<=2*i; j++)
        System.out.print("*");
    System.out.println();
}
```

7. Rewrite the following `for` loop as a

    A.   `while` loop
  *B.   do-while loop

```
int total, count;
total = 0;
for (count = 1; count <= 40; count+=3)
    total += count;
```

8. Assuming n is input, rewrite the following `while` loop as a(n)

 *A. `for` loop
  B. `if` statement and a do-while loop

```
int total, count, n;
total = 0;
count = 0;
n = 5;
while (count < n) {
    total += count;
    count++;
}
```

9. A store is having a sale and items are either 30, 50, or 70 % off. Assuming all the items priced between $5.00 and $50.00 are on sale, output the following table using nested loops. Using correct formatting, make sure that the output is exactly as shown below:

Original Price	30% off	50% off	70% off
$ 5.00	$ 3.50	$ 2.50	$ 1.50
$10.00	$ 7.00	$ 5.00	$ 3.00
$15.00	$10.50	$ 7.50	$ 4.50
$20.00	$14.00	$10.00	$ 6.00
$25.00	$17.50	$12.50	$ 7.50
$30.00	$21.00	$15.00	$ 9.00
$35.00	$24.50	$17.50	$10.50
$40.00	$28.00	$20.00	$12.00
$45.00	$31.50	$22.50	$13.50
$50.00	$35.00	$25.00	$15.00

10. Repeat Exercise 15 in _Chap. 3_ to allow the user to enter temperatures for any number of cities using the best iteration structure.

11. Repeat Exercise 15 in Chap. 3 to allow the user to find the hottest city for any number of sets of 3 cities. Use input, message, and confirmation dialog boxes. Confirmation dialog boxes are discussed in Appendix A.6. Three input dialog boxes are used to input temperature of three different cities. Then, a message dialog box displays the hottest city. After that a confirmation dialog box should appear to see if the user would like to continue. Use the best iteration structure.

12. The Fibonacci sequence is the series of numbers which can be found by adding up the two numbers before it as shown below:

   0, 1, 1, 2, 3, 5, 8, 13, 21, 34, ...

   Write a complete program to compute the Fibonacci number for an integer.

13. Repeat Exercise 12 to allow the user to repeat finding the Fibonacci number for an integer. Use input, message, and confirmation dialog boxes. Confirmation dialog boxes are discussed in Appendix A.6. An input dialog box is used to input an integer. Then, a message dialog box displays the Fibonacci number for the integer. After that a confirmation dialog box should appear to see if the user would like to continue. Use the best iteration structure.

14. Given two numbers, the largest divisor among all the integers that divide the two numbers is known as the greatest common divisor. For example, the positive divisors of 36 are 1, 2, 3, 4, 6, 9, 12, 18, and 36, and the positive divisors of 8 are 1, 2, 4, and 8. Thus, the common divisors of 36 and 8 are 1, 2, and 4. It follows that the greatest common divisor of 36 and 8 is 4. Write a complete program to compute the greatest common divisor of two integers.

15. The product of the first 5 integer is 120. Identify the problem with the following code segment and discuss how to fix it.

```
int answer, count, number;
count = 0;
answer = 0;
number = 1;
while(count <= 5) {
    answer = answer * number;
    count++;
    number++;
}
```

5

Objects: Revisited

James T. Streib[a*] and Takako Soma[a]

[a] Computer Science Program, Illinois College, Jacksonville, IL, USA

Abstract

Objects are revisited in this chapter. The sending and returning an object to and from a method is illustrated using contours. Overloaded constructors and methods are discussed and the reserved word this is introduced. Local, instance, and class constants and variables along with class methods are shown using contour diagrams. Two complete programs, one with focus on overloaded methods and another with class data members and methods are included.

Keywords

Passing Objects, Overloading, Class Data Members, Reserved Word this, Contour Diagram.

Having learned in the previous two chapters about selection and iteration structures, both of which allow for more complex programs, it is time to return to the topic of objects that was introduced in Chap. 2 . Objects allow programs to be created in a more modular way that makes complex programs easier to understand. In this chapter, topics such as passing objects to and from a method, constructor and method overloading, class data members and methods, and the use of the reserved word this will be discussed. At first, this chapter will use only simple objects to illustrate these concepts so that the details can more readily be understood and then more complex examples will be included in the complete programs at the end of the chapter.

5.1 Sending an Object to a Method

So far all that has been discussed is how primitive data types can be sent to a method. However, data is often more complex than just a simple data type, so it would be helpful to have a way to send not just an item or two but rather an entire object to a method. For example, consider a method to determine the length of a line segment. It would need to be sent the two endpoints of the line, each consisting of x and y coordinates, which would require four arguments to be sent to the method. Since each point has two coordinates, this would lend itself to the creation of a simple class. Although in Java there is a Point class in the java.awt package, a point is a simple enough concept to help explain the sending of an object to a method that this text will define its own class for a point. Whereas the Java class Point uses integers, the class defined here will use double precision numbers and will be called PointD. Consider the preliminary definition of the class in Fig. 5.1.

```
class PointD {
    private double x, y;
    public PointD() {
        x = 0.0;
        y = 0.0;
    }
    public void setX(double xp) {
        x = xp;
    }
    public void setY(double yp) {
        y = yp;
    }
    public double getX() {
        return x;
    }
    public double getY() {
        return y;
    }
}
```

Fig. 5.1 Preliminary definition of PointD class

The PointD class definition is fairly simple with the usual get and set methods. However, what will make it more interesting is the introduction of a method which allows an invocation to send an object of type PointD. For this example, assume the existence of a method called distance which will calculate the distance between two points. Since the method will be defined within the PointD class, it can be invoked by an object of type PointD and also use an argument of type PointD. Assuming the existence of two points p1 and p2 of type PointD, the method could be invoked as dist=p1.distance(p2);. What would such a method look like? Recall from algebra that the distance formula is

$$\text{dist} = \sqrt{(x_1 - x_2)^2 + (y_1 - y_2)^2}$$

Then the code for the method could be as follows:

```
public double distance(PointD p) {
    double dist;
    dist = Math.sqrt(Math.pow(x-p.getX(),2)
            + Math.pow(y-p.getY(),2));
    return dist;
}
```

First, notice that the method returns a value of type double. Second, note that the parameter is not of type double but rather of type PointD. Lastly, although the local variable dist is not required to be declared as local, it makes the subsequent contour diagram easier to follow when illustrating how objects are passed. Using all the information above and combined into a complete program, it could appear as shown below:

```
class Example {                                              // Line 1
   public static void main(String[] args) {                  // Line 2
      double dist;                                            // Line 3
      PointD p1, p2;                                          // Line 4
      p1=new PointD();                                        // Line 5
      p2=new PointD();                                        // Line 6
      p1.setX(4.0);                                           // Line 7
      p1.setY(4.0);                                           // Line 8
      p2.setX(8.0);                                           // Line 9
      p2.setY(7.0);                                           // Line 10
      dist = p1.distance(p2);                                 // Line 11
      System.out.print("The distance between (");             // Line 12
      System.out.print(p1.getX() + "," + p1.getY());          // Line 13
      System.out.print(") and (" + p2.getX() + ",");          // Line 14
      System.out.println(p2.getY() + ") is " + dist);         // Line 15
   }                                                          // Line 16
}                                                             // Line 17

class PointD {                                               // Line 18
   private double x, y;                                       // Line 19
   public PointD() {                                          // Line 20
      x = 0.0;                                                // Line 21
      y = 0.0;                                                // Line 22
   }                                                          // Line 23
   public void setX(double xp) {                              // Line 24
      x = xp;                                                 // Line 25
   }                                                          // Line 26
   public void setY(double yp) {                              // Line 27
      y = yp;                                                 // Line 28
   }                                                          // Line 29
   public double getX() {                                     // Line 30
      return x;                                               // Line 31
   }                                                          // Line 32
   public double getY() {                                     // Line 33
      return y;                                               // Line 34
   }                                                          // Line 35
   public double distance(PointD p) {                         // Line 36
      double dist;                                            // Line 37
      dist=Math.sqrt(Math.pow(x-p.getX(),2)                   // Line 38
          + Math.pow(y-p.getY(),2));                          // Line 39
      return dist;                                            // Line 40
   }                                                          // Line 41
}                                                             // Line 42
```

Utilizing contour diagrams, the passing of objects can easily be illustrated. Note that some steps will be skipped since many of them were discussed thoroughly in Chap. 2. The state of execution prior to Line 11 in the main program would be as shown in Fig. 5.2.

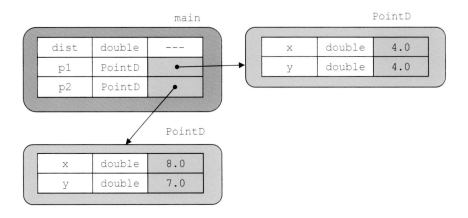

Fig. 5.2 State of execution prior to Line 11

Since the method `distance` is invoked from `p1`, the contour for the method appears in the contour referenced by `p1` as shown in Fig. 5.3, indicating the state of execution just prior to Line 40 in the `distance` method.

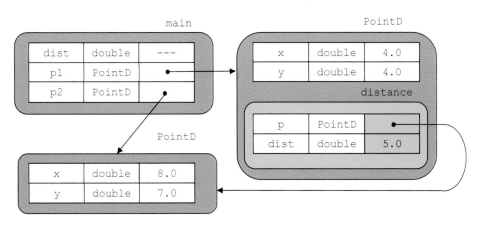

Fig. 5.3 State of execution prior to Line 40

In addition to the local variable `dist`, the method also contains a memory location for the parameter `p`. Note that when passing an object to a method via a parameter, the parameter does not contain the entire object. Rather, since the argument `p2` has a reference to an object, the parameter `p` contains a copy of the reference to that same object. Although a straight arrow could have been drawn directly to the object, it would have covered up some of the information within the contour, so in this example, it is drawn around the contour diagram for the sake of neatness. However, in the future the arrows may be drawn over parts of contours in order to save space. Note that both the argument p2 and the parameter p are pointing to the same contour. When the calculation for the dist is performed, the references to x and y are to the ones globally accessible within the object pointed to by p1, whereas the getX and getY methods access the variables in the object referenced by p.

5.2 Returning an Object from a Method

If an object can be passed to a method, can an object be returned from a method? The answer is yes, as will be demonstrated in the example that follows. Whereas the previous example returned the dist of type double, this example will determine the midpoint of a line. The equations to determine the midpoint are as follows:

$$midx = \frac{x_1 + x_2}{2} \quad midy = \frac{y_1 + y_2}{2}$$

Since the midpoint consists of x and y coordinates, this lends itself to the creation of a method to return an object of type PointD. The method midPoint below implements the equations above:

```
public PointD midPoint(PointD p) {
    PointD mid;
    mid = new PointD();
    mid.setX( (x+p.getX()) / 2 );
    mid.setY( (y+p.getY()) / 2 );
    return mid;
}
```

Notice that in addition to the parameter, the return type is also of type PointD. The method also creates an instance of type PointD and assigns the reference to the variable mid which is also declared of type PointD. The method then calculates the midpoint and sets the x and y coordinates in mid prior to the return of the object to the invoking program.

This method can be added to class PointD, and in Fig. 5.4, it replaces the previous method distance in order to save space.

```
class Example {                                              // Line 1
    public static void main(String[] args) {                 // Line 2
        PointD middle;                                       // Line 3
        PointD p1, p2;                                       // Line 4
        p1=new PointD();                                     // Line 5
        p2=new PointD();                                     // Line 6
        p1.setX(4.0);                                        // Line 7
        p1.setY(4.0);                                        // Line 8
        p2.setX(8.0);                                        // Line 9
        p2.setY(7.0);                                        // Line 10
        middle = p1.midPoint(p2);                            // Line 11
        System.out.print("The mid-point between (");         // Line 12
        System.out.print(p1.getX() + "," + p1.getY());       // Line 13
        System.out.print(") and (" + p2.getX() + ",");       // Line 14
        System.out.print(p2.getY()+") is (" + middle.getX()); // Line 15
        System.out.println("," + middle.getY() + ")");       // Line 16
    }                                                        // Line 17
}                                                            // Line 18

class PointD {                                               // Line 19
    private double x, y;                                     // Line 20
    public PointD() {                                        // Line 21
        x = 0.0;                                             // Line 22
        y = 0.0;                                             // Line 23
    }                                                        // Line 24
    public void setX(double xp) {                            // Line 25
        x = xp;                                              // Line 26
    }                                                        // Line 27
    public void setY(double yp) {                            // Line 28
        y = yp;                                              // Line 29
    }                                                        // Line 30
    public double getX() {                                   // Line 31
        return x;                                            // Line 32
    }                                                        // Line 33
    public double getY() {                                   // Line 34
        return y;                                            // Line 35
    }                                                        // Line 36

    public PointD midPoint(PointD p) {                       // Line 37
        PointD mid;                                          // Line 38
        mid = new PointD();                                  // Line 39
        mid.setX( (x+p.getX()) / 2 );                        // Line 40
        mid.setY( (y+p.getY()) / 2 );                        // Line 41
        return mid;                                          // Line 42
    }                                                        // Line 43
}                                                            // Line 44
```

Fig. 5.4 Complete program returning an object from a method

Prior to the execution of Line 11, the contour diagram would look similar to Fig. 5.2 in the previous example, except the variable dist of type double would be replaced with the variable middle of type PointD. After invoking the midPoint method, the contour diagrams would appear similar to the ones shown in Fig. 5.3 in the previous section, except that in addition to the variable middle appearing in the main program, the distance contour would be replaced with the midPoint contour and the variable dist in the contour would be replaced with the variable mid of type PointD which would be indeterminate. However, once the body of the method midPoint is executed, that is when the significant differences can be seen when a new object is created in Line 39. Figure 5.5 illustrates this by showing the state of execution prior to the return statement in Line 42.

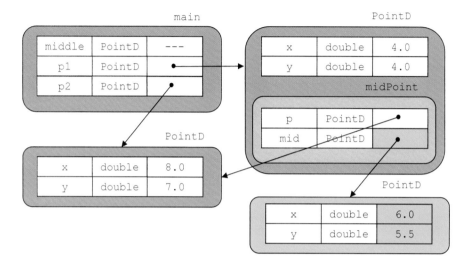

Fig. 5.5 Contour just prior to the execution of the return statement in Line 42

Notice that in addition to the contour referenced by the parameter p, there is another contour referenced by the local variable mid that contains the coordinates of the midpoint. As with the passing of a reference to an object via a parameter, the entire contour will not be returned to the main program, but rather only the reference to the contour will be returned as illustrated in Fig. 5.6 which shows the state of execution prior to Line 12.

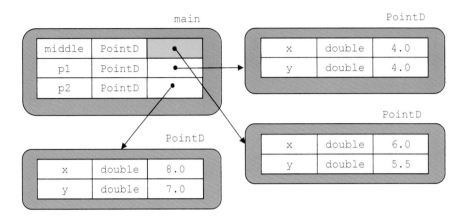

Fig. 5.6 Contour after returning to the main program prior to Line 12

Notice that the contour for the method `midPoint` no longer exists after returning to the main program. However, the value in `mid` was returned back to the invoking statement on Line 11 and assigned to the variable `middle`, which now contains the reference to the object containing the midpoint values. When the output statements refer to the `getX` and `getY` methods of the appropriate objects, the correct values will be output.

5.3 Overloaded Constructors and Methods

This section looks at overloaded and default constructors, as well as overloaded methods.

5.3.1 Overloaded Constructors

The constructor in the previous example initializes the variables x and y to 0.0 as a default value. In addition, a constructor could have been created to initialize the instance variables to the values wanted by a programmer as shown in the following:

```
public PointD(double xp, double yp) {
    x = xp;
    y = yp;
}
```

A programmer could then initialize x and y via the constructor when the object was created as shown below:

```
p1 = new PointD(4.0,4.0);
```

The advantage of this method is that a programmer does not need to invoke the `setX` and `setY` methods to initialize the variables in the object. Does this mean that the set methods could be deleted from the class definitions? If the values in the variables did not need to change, then yes the set methods could be deleted. However, what if after initializing the variables, their values needed to be changed later in the program? Then of course the set methods would need to be retained in the class definition.

Given the previous constructor and the new constructor above, which of the two is better and which one should be included in the class definition? The answer depends on what needs to be done. For example, if the values are going to be changed often, then the first constructor and the set methods are the best choice, but if the values are going to be set just once, then the second constructor is probably the better choice.

However, when the class is written, it might not be known which type of constructor would be the best one to include. Wouldn't it be nice to include both constructors and allow the programmer a choice? But further, could this cause a syntax error by having two constructors with the same name? The answer to the first question is yes and the answer to the second question is no. The reason why this would not cause an error is because even though the name of the constructor is the same, the number of parameters is different because the first constructor does not have any parameters and the second one has two parameters. This is known as *overloading*. In other words, even though constructors have the same name, they can differ by the number of parameters, the types of the parameters, or the order of the different types of parameters. When used carefully, overloading can be a very useful technique.

Using the knowledge gained from Sect. 5.1, it is also possible to pass an object to a constructor. For example, if an object was already created and a copy of that object was needed, then that object could be passed via a parameter to another constructor to create the copy. Such a constructor would look as shown below:

```
public PointD(PointD p) {
    x = p.getX();
    y = p.getY();
}
```

Notice that instead of two parameters of type `double`, there is now only one parameter of type `PointD`. In the body of the constructor, the coordinates are retrieved from the object sent using the `getX` and `getY` methods and placed into the x and y variables of the current object. The result is that if one wanted to create two objects with the same set of coordinates; instead of writing the following code:

```
p1 = new PointD(1.0,1.0);
p2 = new PointD(1.0,1.0);
```

one would merely need to write the following:

```
p1 = new PointD(1.0,1.0);
p2 = new PointD(p1);
```

Given the two new constructors, the original `PointD` class could be rewritten as follows:

```
class PointD {
   private double x, y;
   public PointD() {
      x = 0.0;
      y = 0.0;
   }
   public PointD(double xp, double yp) {
      x = xp;
      y = yp;
   }
   public PointD(PointD p) {
      x = p.getX();
      y = p.getY();
   }
   public void setX(double xp) {
      x = xp;
   }
   public void setY(double yp) {
      y = yp;
   }
   public double getX() {
      return x;
   }
   public double getY() {
      return y;
   }
}
```

Using this new class, a programmer could create three different instances of the PointD class as follows:

```
PointD p1, p2, p3;
p1 = new PointD();
p2 = new PointD(1.0,1.0);
p3 = new PointD(p2);
```

Notice that the objects are being created using three different constructors. The only difference is the number of arguments. Further, since the first constructor ensures that coordinates referenced by p1 will be initialized to 0.0, the second constructor initializes the variables referenced by p2 via the arguments, and the third constructor makes a copy of the previous object which will be referenced by p3, the set methods do not need to be called. However, if the values in the points need to be changed later, the set methods are still there if necessary.

5.3.2 Default Constructors

Note that if a constructor is not included in a class by the programmer, the system will generate a *default constructor*. Should the programmer include a constructor without any parameters, then this constructor overrides the default constructor generated by the system.

Although a bit confusing, this constructor provided by the programmer is also sometimes called a default constructor since it overrides the system default constructor. However, if one writes only the two new constructors above, and a default constructor is not included by the programmer, then the system will not generate a default constructor. In such a case, were one to code a `p1=new PointD();` statement, a syntax error would occur. The result is if one wants to override the system default constructor, it is a good idea to override it with a programmer-defined default constructor to avoid a possible syntax error. Even if overloading is not being used in the class, it is generally best for a programmer to include a default constructor and not rely on the system default constructor.

5.3.3 Overloaded Methods

Just as constructors can be overloaded, so can methods. As with constructors, the name of the method can be the same, but the number of parameters, the types of the parameters, or the order of the different types of parameters must be different. For example, take the `distance` method from Sect. 5.1 which requires one parameter as shown again below:

```
public double distance(PointD p) {
    double dist;
    dist=Math.sqrt(Math.pow(x-p.getX(),2)
        + Math.pow(y-p.getY(),2));
    return dist;
}
```

What if another method was needed to determine the distance of a point from the origin? Certainly one could invoke the method above by having one of the two points as the origin using the new constructors introduced in this section as follows:

```
PointD p1, p2;
p1=new PointD();
p2=new PointD(3.0,4.0);
dist = p2.distance(p1);
```

In this example, the default constructor initializes the coordinates of `p1` to `0.0`, and the second constructor initializes the coordinates of `p2` to `3.0` and `4.0`. But the assumption could be that the distance will be calculated from the origin, and it would be convenient not to need it as a parameter in the distance method. Such a method would look as follows:

```
public double distance() {
    double dist;
    dist = Math.sqrt(Math.pow(x,2)+ Math.pow(y,2));
    return dist;
}
```

Instead of invoking the previous method with the `dist = p2.distance(p1);` statement, it could be invoked using the new method as follows:

```
dist = p2.distance();
```

Again, the name of the method is the same, but the number of parameters is different. As mentioned earlier, it is also possible to have the same number of parameters but different types of parameters or a different order of the different types of the parameters.

For example, assume a method of the Student class was to be sent two parameters: one for the number of credit hours and another to indicate whether the student has graduated. In the main program below, notice that in one case, an integer is in the first argument position and in the second case a Boolean value is the first argument position. Would this cause a problem?

```
class Example {
    public static void main(String[] args) {
        Student student1, student2;
        student1 = new Student();
        student2 = new Student();
        student1.setInformation(119,false);
        student2.setInformation(true,120);
    }
}

class Student {
    private int creditHours;
    private boolean graduation;
    public Student() {
        creditHours=0;
        graduation=false;
    }
    public void setInformation(int credits, boolean grad) {
        creditHours=credits;
        graduation=grad;
    }
    public void setInformation(boolean grad, int credits) {
        creditHours=credits;
        graduation=grad;
    }
}
```

If there were only one method named setInformation, the answer would be yes. However, notice the setInformation method is overloaded. The parameters are reversed in the second method so that the order of the arguments in the calling program does not matter. Thus, if a programmer accidently puts the arguments in the wrong order, there is no error. As stated previously, overloading can sometimes be helpful if used carefully and not excessively.

5.4 Use of the Reserved Word this

In looking at portion of the original PointD class from Fig. 5.1 shown below, the parameter names in the constructor and in the two set methods are listed as xp and yp.

```
class PointD {
   private double x, y;
   public PointD(double xp, double yp) {
      x = xp;
      y = yp;
   }
   public void setX(double xp) {
      x = xp;
   }
   public void setY(double yp) {
      y = yp;
   }
}
```

What would happen if the names of the variables xp and yp were changed to x and y, respectively? What would x and y refer to, the data members or the parameters?

```
/** Caution: Incorrectly Implemented Code **/

class PointD {
   private double x, y;
   public PointD(double x, double y) {
      x = x;
      y = y;
   }
   public void setX(double x) {
      x = x;
   }
   public void setY(double y) {
      y = y;
   }
}
```

The answer to the second question is that the parameters and local variables declared in a method take precedence over any globally declared variables in the object. The answer to the first question is that the contents of the parameters x and y would merely be assigned back into the memory locations associated with the parameter. The result is that the private data members would not contain the new values sent from the invoking program, and this is probably not what was intended.

Is it possible to use the same variable names for both the parameters and the instance data members? The answer is yes. In any particular instance, the reserved word this can be used to refer to the instance. Java uses this as a self-referencing pointer to refer to the current object. Using the reserved word this, the previous class can be rewritten as shown below:

```
class PointD {
   private double x, y;
   public PointD(double x, double y) {
      this.x = x;
      this.y = y;
   }
```

```
public void setX(double x) {
    this.x = x;
}
public void setY(double y) {
    this.y = y;
}
}
```

So, for example, consider the shortened skeleton of the program presented at the beginning of this chapter that uses only the setX and getX methods shown below:

```
class Example {                                            // Line 1
    public static void main(String[] args) {               // Line 2
        PointD p1;                                         // Line 3
        p1=new PointD();                                   // Line 4
        p1.setX(4.0);                                      // Line 5
        System.out.print("x equals " + p1.getX());         // Line 6
    }                                                      // Line 7
}                                                          // Line 8

class PointD {                                             // Line 9
    private double x, y;                                   // Line 10
    public PointD() {                                      // Line 11
        x = 0.0;                                           // Line 12
        y = 0.0;                                           // Line 13
    }                                                      // Line 14
    public void setX(double x) {                           // Line 15
        this.x = x;                                        // Line 16
    }                                                      // Line 17
    public double getX() {                                 // Line 18
        return x;                                          // Line 19
    }                                                      // Line 20
}                                                          // line 21
```

In the setX method, x refers to the parameter, and the value in x is assigned to this.x which is the data member x in the object. In a sense, this is a pointer to the current object as illustrated in the contour in Fig. 5.7 showing the state of execution just prior to Line 17.

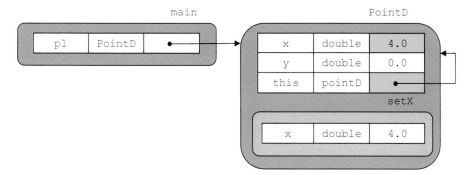

Fig. 5.7 State of execution prior to Line 17

Notice the arrow pointing back to the object `PointD`. It illustrates the word `this` and shows how the data member x is referenced. Although the example in Fig. 5.7 includes the cell for `this` and a self-referencing arrow, it tends to clutter up the contour diagrams, so in general it will not be included because its existence is understood. Notice that the constructor and the `getX` do not use the reserved word `this` on Lines 12, 13, and 19. In this case the word `this` is not necessary. Although one could still include the word `this`, it can be distracting to use it when it is not needed. As a result, this text will not use the word `this` unless it is necessary.

The reserved word `this` can also be used in situations beyond just referring to variables. It can refer to constructors and methods as well. For example, consider the three constructors presented in the previous section and relisted below using the reserved word `this` in the second constructor:

```
class PointD {
    private double x, y;
    public PointD() {
        x = 0.0;
        y = 0.0;
    }
    public PointD(double x, double y) {
        this.x = x;
        this.y = y;
    }
    public PointD(PointD p) {
        x = p.getX();
        y = p.getY();
    }
}
```

In one sense, the first constructor is just a special case of the second constructor, so it could be defined in terms of the second constructor. In other words, it could invoke the second constructor with the values `0.0` for the x and y coordinates. But how could it invoke the second constructor? Again, since it is the current object that needs to be referenced, the reserved word `this` could be used as shown below:

```
public PointD() {
   this(0.0,0.0);
}
```

Even the third constructor could be written to invoke the second constructor as:

```
public PointD(PointD p) {
   this(p.getX(),p.getY());
}
```

Since an object of type `PointD` is being passed to the constructor, the methods `getX` and `getY` can be invoked to retrieve the values in `x` and `y`, which in turn can be sent as arguments to the second constructor. In order to invoke the second constructor, it is referred to using `this`.

The advantage of the above technique is that if later a change needs to be made to the constructors, it might not need to be made to all three constructors, but possibly only one of them. This reduces the possibility of introducing unintended errors into the program, and the result of the modifications introduced in this section can be seen below:

```
class PointD {
    private double x, y;
    public PointD() {
        this(0.0,0.0);
    }
    public PointD(double x, double y) {
        this.x = x;
        this.y = y;
    }
    public PointD(PointD p) {
        this(p.getX(),p.getY());
    }
}
```

As with variables and constructors, it is possible to use the word `this` when referring to methods in the same object. For example, suppose that a method needed to access another method such as the previous `distance` method within the same class. It could be invoked as `this.distance()`. Although the method can be invoked using the reserved word `this`, there is no need to do so. As a result, the use of the word `this` prior to the invoking of a method should be avoided.

5.5 Class Constants, Variables, and Methods

This section will discuss how constants, variables, and methods can be declared not only within a method and in each instance of a class but also how they can be declared in the class itself. First, it looks at constants, then variables, and lastly methods.

5.5.1 Local, Instance, and Class Constants

If a constant needs to be used only within a single method, then it can be declared within that method. However, if several methods in the same class use the same constant, it could be declared within each method but that could take up more space. If that constant needs to be changed, then it will need to be changed in more than one location. Although there already exists the `Math.PI` constant discussed in Sect. 1.7, consider for example, the following program which includes the user-defined constant `PI`:

```
class Example {                                              // Line 1
    public static void main(String[] args) {                 // Line 2
        double radius;                                       // Line 3
        Circle c;                                            // Line 4
        c = new Circle();                                    // Line 5
        radius = 3.0;                                        // Line 6
        c.setRadius(radius);                                 // Line 7
        System.out.print("A circle of radius " + radius);    // Line 8
        System.out.print(" has a circumference of ");        // Line 9
        System.out.printf("%5.2f",c.circumference());        // Line 10
        System.out.printf(" and area %5.2f",c.area());       // Line 11
        System.out.println();                                // Line 12
    }                                                        // Line 13
}                                                            // Line 14

class Circle {                                               // Line 15
    private double r;                                        // Line 16
    public Circle() {                                        // Line 17
        r=0.0;                                               // Line 18
    }                                                        // Line 19
    public void setRadius(double r) {                        // Line 20
        this.r=r;                                            // Line 21
    }                                                        // Line 22
    public double circumference() {                          // Line 23
        final double PI=3.14;                                // Line 24
        double c;                                            // Line 25
        c = 2 * PI * r;                                      // Line 26
        return c;                                            // Line 27
    }                                                        // Line 28
    public double area() {                                   // Line 29
        final double PI=3.14;                                // Line 30
        double a;                                            // Line 31
        a= PI * r * r;                                       // Line 32
        return a;                                            // Line 33
    }                                                        // Line 34
}                                                            // Line 35
```

In addition to the existence of the local variables `c` and `a` to help with understanding the contour diagrams, notice that both methods have their own locally declared constant `PI` at Lines 24 and 30. When each method is executed, its own copy of the constant is allocated. The contour diagram in Fig. 5.8 illustrates that each method has its own copy and shows the state of execution prior to Line 33.

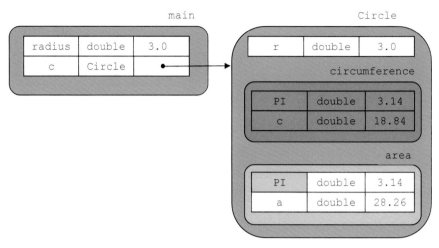

Fig. 5.8 State of execution prior to Line 33

Even though one contour is deallocated (indicated by the light red contour) before the next one is invoked, it still had to allocate the constant. While this is only a minor problem now, any local constants can take up much more space in a recursive algorithm as will be discussed in Chap. 8 . Since there is a potential for wasted memory, it would be better if the constant were not associated with each method, but rather with the object as illustrated in the following section showing the Circle class:

```
class Circle {                                  // Line 15
   private final double PI = 3.14;              // Line 16
   private double r;                            // Line 17
   public Circle() {                            // Line 18
      r = 0.0;                                  // Line 19
   }                                            // Line 20
   public void setRadius(double r) {            // Line 21
      this.r = r;                               // Line 22
   }                                            // Line 23
   public double circumference() {              // Line 24
      double c;                                 // Line 25
      c = 2 * PI * r;                           // Line 26
      return c;                                 // Line 27
   }                                            // Line 28
   public double area() {                       // Line 29
      double a;                                 // Line 30
      a = PI * r * r;                           // Line 31
      return a;                                 // Line 32
   }                                            // Line 33
}                                               // Line 34
```

Only the class is shown here because the main program has not changed and again the local variables in the method remain to help with the contour diagrams. Notice that the declaration of the constant is no longer within each method, but rather in the class at Line 16. An immediate obvious advantage is that should the constant need to be changed, it needs only to be changed in one location. The contour diagram representing the state of execution prior to Line 32 is shown in Fig. 5.9.

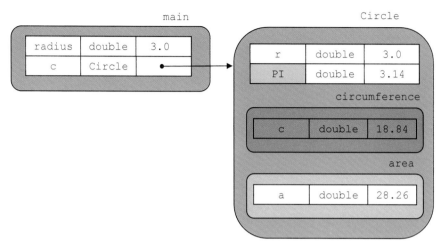

Fig. 5.9 State of execution prior to Line 32

Note that the constant PI no longer appears in each of the methods, but rather is located in an instance of the Circle class. The advantage to declaring the constant in the class as opposed to each individual method is that the constant only needs to be allocated once.

However, what if more than one object was declared? Then there would be one constant allocated within each of the objects. Consider the following modification to the main program that declares and allocates two objects:

```
double radius1, radius2;    // Line 3
Circle c1,c2;               // Line 4
c1 = new Circle();          // Line 5
c2 = new Circle();          // Line 6
radius1 = 3.0;              // Line 7
radius2 = 4.0               // Line 8
c1.setRadius(radius1);      // Line 9
c2.setRadius(radius2);      // Line 10
```

Using the same Circle class as before, without invoking any of the methods except for the constructor, note the state of execution just prior to Line 9 in the main program in Fig. 5.10.

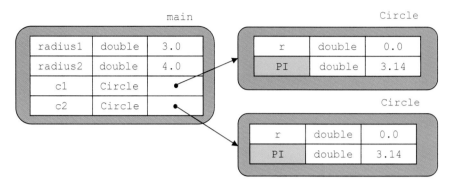

Fig. 5.10 State of execution prior to Line 9

Notice that the constant `PI` appears in both instances of the `Circle` class. Just like with the methods when the constant was moved from the individual methods, wouldn't it be nice if the constant could be moved so that it would be accessible by both objects? This can be accomplished by using what is known as a class constant. Showing the new complete program below, a class constant is created by using the reserved word `static` as shown in Line 24 below:

```
class Example {                                         // Line 1
   public static void main(String[] args) {             // Line 2
      double radius1, radius2;                           // Line 3
      Circle c1,c2;                                      // Line 4
      c1 = new Circle();                                 // Line 5
      c2 = new Circle();                                 // Line 6
      radius1 = 3.0;                                     // Line 7
      radius2 = 4.0;                                     // Line 8
      c1.setRadius(radius1);                             // Line 9
      c2.setRadius(radius2);                             // Line 10
      System.out.print("A circle of radius " + radius1); // Line 11
      System.out.print(" has a circumference of ");      // Line 12
      System.out.printf("%5.2f",c1.circumference());     // Line 13
      System.out.printf(" and area %5.2f",c1.area());    // Line 14
      System.out.println();                              // Line 15
      System.out.print("A circle of radius " + radius2); // Line 16
      System.out.print(" has a circumference of ");      // Line 17
      System.out.printf("%5.2f",c2.circumference());     // Line 18
      System.out.printf(" and area %5.2f",c2.area());    // Line 19
      System.out.println();                              // Line 20
   }                                                     // Line 21
}                                                        // Line 22

class Circle {                                           // Line 23
   private static final double PI = 3.14;                // Line 24
   private double r;                                     // Line 25
   public Circle() {                                     // Line 26
      r = 0.0;                                           // Line 27
   }                                                     // Line 28
   public void setRadius(double r) {                     // Line 29
      this.r = r;                                        // Line 30
   }                                                     // Line 31
   public double circumference() {                       // Line 32
      double c;                                          // Line 33
      c = 2 * PI * r;                                    // Line 34
      return c;                                          // Line 35
   }                                                     // Line 36
   public double area() {                                // Line 37
      double a;                                          // Line 38
      a = PI * r * r;                                    // Line 39
      return a;                                          // Line 40
   }                                                     // Line 41
}                                                        // Line 42
```

Executing the first few lines of the program as done previously, the contour diagram in Fig. 5.11 shows the state of execution just prior to Line 9. Notice that each of the instances does not have a local constant PI. As mentioned previously in Sect. 2.7, just as the main program has a contour around it, as shown in Fig. 5.11, so does the class Circle. Using the word static creates the class constant PI that does not get allocated each time a new instance of the class Circle is created. When there is a reference to the constant PI, it is not found in the instance, but rather in the class. As can be seen, this saves memory, especially when many objects are created.

In contour diagrams, how can one distinguish the contour for the class itself from the contours associated with the instances of the class? One way is to note that variables of type `Circle` point to the instances of the `Circle` class. However, another way to help the reader is to allow the contour associated with the class itself to have the name of the class (in this case `Circle`) and then use a superscript for each instance of the class to indicate the order in which the objects were created as shown in Fig. 5.11. When necessary to help make this distinction clear, this text will use superscripts.

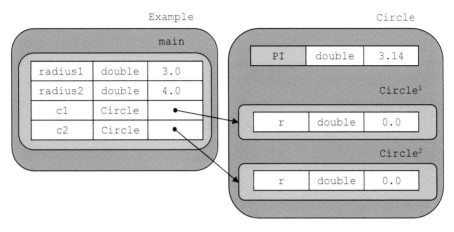

Fig. 5.11 State of execution prior to Line 9

Just as this text has previously not drawn the contour around the main program in the interest of saving space, it would also help to save space to not draw the contour around all the instances of each object. As can be seen in Fig. 5.11, it could get rather cumbersome to draw such large contours. However, on occasion it is still helpful to draw a contour to represent the class, so instead of drawing it around all the instances, it is sometimes convenient to draw it separately, with the understanding that all the instances are within that contour. This second alternative is shown in Fig. 5.12.

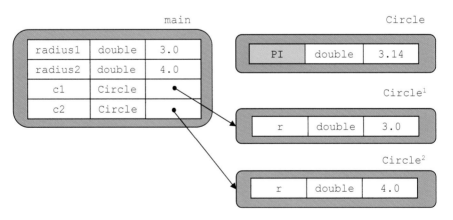

Fig. 5.12 Alternative contour diagram illustrating class constants

Figure 5.11 is the ideal drawing and it will be used as necessary. However, generally and if needed, the contour for the class using a class constant will be drawn as shown in Fig. 5.12, with the understanding that all instances will be within that contour.

5.5.2 Local, Instance, and Class Variables

Local and instance variables are similar to local and instance constants. In fact, the variables c and a representing the circumference and area in the previous section are local variables in the methods, and the variable r representing the radius in a Circle object is an instance variable. In trying to decide where a variable needs to be declared, it helps to ask which methods need access to the variable. For example, the variables c and a were used only by the circumference and area methods, so it made sense to declare them there. However, the variable r is used by both methods; hence, it makes sense to declare it once within the object instead of in both methods.

Although using the two local variables wasted a little memory, it made understanding the contours easier, and in this case it is not much of a problem. In fact, these variables are not even needed, because the expression to calculate each value could have been included in the return statement, as shown below:

```
public double circumference () {
    return 2 * PI * r;
}
public double area() {
    return PI * r * r;
}
```

It is sometimes benificial to write the initial version of the code using extra memory to help understand how it works and assist in debugging any logic errors, and then later the extra memory locations can be removed to make the code more efficient. This technique will become even more helpful when learning about recursion in Chap. 8.

As with the constants in the previous section, just as some variables are better placed in the object as instance variables instead of as local variables in the methods, there are cases where some variables should be declared as class variables instead of as instance variables. For example, what if one wanted to count each time a new object was created? Although this could be done in the main program, what if an object other than the main program was also creating the objects to be counted? In this case, the main program could not count them, nor could an instance variable be used, because each instance could not count how many other objects of its own type were created. As one might suspect, this would be a good candidate for a class variable.

A class variable is declared similarly to a class constant except the reserved word final is not used as shown in Line 15 of the following program which simulates a program that creates objects for charge cards that contain an account number:

```
class Example {                                             // Line 1
   public static void main(String[] args) {                // Line 2
      ChargeCard card1, card2, card3;                       // Line 3
      card1 = new ChargeCard();                             // Line 4
      card2 = new ChargeCard();                             // line 5
      card3 = new ChargeCard();                             // Line 6
      card1.setAccountNumber(12345678);                     // Line 7
      card2.setAccountNumber(23456789);                     // Line 8
      card3.setAccountNumber(34567890);                     // Line 9
      System.out.print("The number of charge cards is ");   // Line 10
      System.out.println(ChargeCard.cardCount);             // Line 11
   }                                                        // Line 12
}                                                           // Line 13

class ChargeCard {                                          // Line 14
   public static int cardCount = 0;                         // Line 15
   private int accNum;                                      // Line 16
   public ChargeCard() {                                    // Line 17
      accNum = 0;                                           // Line 18
      cardCount++;                                          // Line 19
   }                                                        // Line 20
   public void setAccountNumber(int accNum) {               // Line 21
      this.accNum = accNum;                                 // Line 22
   }                                                        // Line 23
   public int getAccountNumber() {                          // Line 24
      return accNum;                                        // Line 25
   }                                                        // Line 26
}                                                           // Line 27
```

Although it would be nice to create an indefinite number of objects, that would be difficult to illustrate using contours and would also be difficult to implement without the use of arrays which will be introduced in Chap. 7. Instead, this program creates only three ChargeCard objects to help illustrate the class variable cardCount. Notice that their class variable is initialized by the compiler to 0 in Line 15. Then each time a new instance of the class is created, the class variable cardCount is incremented in the constructor. The contour in Fig. 5.13 illustrates the state of execution just prior to Line 10 in the main program.

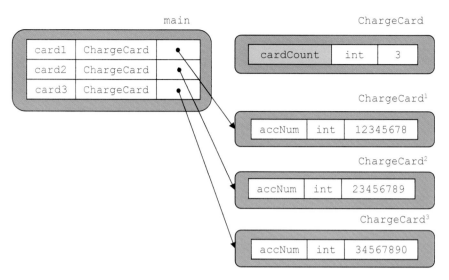

Fig. 5.13 State of execution prior to Line 10 in main

As can be seen, the class variable is shown in the ChargeCard contour which is accessible by all of the instances of that class, as discussed in the previous section. Also note that instead of using a variable such as card1 to gain access to a class variable, the name of the class ChargeCard in Line 11 is used instead. Further, the reader might have noticed that whereas the class constant in the previous section was declared as private, the class variable cardCount is declared as public. In one sense this might seem convenient, because the class variable is accessible in the main program in Line 11. However, as mentioned in Chap. 2 and as will be discussed in the next section, it is usually better to declare variables as private and access them using a public method.

5.5.3 Class Methods

Although declaring a class variable as public allowing it to be accessed from the main program works, it is not necessarily the best way to access class variables. Just as it is not a good idea to declare instance variables as public, the same applies to class variables. As before, it is better to declare class variables as private and then access them via a public class method. This is accomplished by declaring a method using the reserved word static as shown in the following modified program:

```
class Example {                                            // Line 1
   public static void main(String[] args) {                // Line 2
      ChargeCard card1, card2, card3;                       // Line 3
      card1 = new ChargeCard();                             // Line 4
      card2 = new ChargeCard();                             // line 5
      card3 = new ChargeCard();                             // Line 6
      card1.setAccountNumber(12345678);                     // Line 7
      card2.setAccountNumber(23456789);                     // Line 8
      card3.setAccountNumber(34567890);                     // Line 9
      System.out.print("The number of charge cards is ");   // Line 10
      System.out.println(ChargeCard.getCardCount());        // Line 11
   }                                                        // Line 12
}                                                           // Line 13

class ChargeCard {                                          // Line 14
   private static int cardCount = 0;                        // Line 15
   private int accNum;                                      // Line 16
   public ChargeCard() {                                    // Line 17
      accNum = 0;                                           // Line 18
      cardCount++;                                          // Line 19
   }                                                        // Line 20
   public void setAccountNumber(int accNum) {               // Line 21
      this.accNum=accNum;                                   // Line 22
   }                                                        // Line 23
   public int getAccountNumber() {                          // Line 24
      return accNum;                                        // Line 25
   }                                                        // Line 26
   public static int getCardCount() {                       // Line 27
      return cardCount;                                     // Line 28
   }                                                        // Line 29
}                                                           // Line 30
```

First, notice that the method getCardCount has been added at Line 27. The use of the reserved word static makes it a class method instead of an instance method. Also note that the method is declared as public and the class variable cardCount at Line 15 is now declared as private. Next, notice in Line 11 that instead of accessing the class variable, the class method getCardCount is invoked to return the value of cardCount. As before, the class method is invoked using the class name ChargeCard.

What is interesting to see is that when the main program invokes the class method getCardCount, the contour is not in one of the objects, but rather in the contour for the class ChargeCard as illustrated in Fig. 5.14 which shows the state of execution prior to Line 28 in the class method getCardCount. When Line 28 in the class method getCardCount is executed, it has access to the private class variable cardCount and will return the value 3 back to Line 11 in the main program.

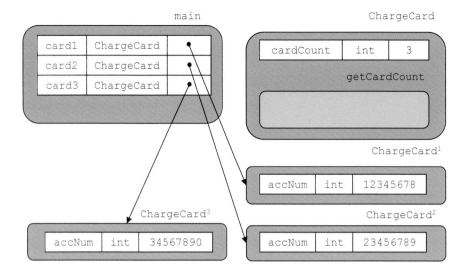

Fig. 5.14 State of execution prior to Line 28 in the `getCardCount` method

Given the above, one needs to plan carefully where various constants, variables, and methods are declared. As a general rule, it makes sense to declare constants as class constants since they cannot be modified, they are accessible to all methods in the objects within the class.. As another rule of thumb, it is generally a good idea to declare all variables as locally as possible. This helps organize a program and makes it easier to understand and maintain. However, if a method or object needs to communicate information with other methods or objects, then declaring the variables as instance or class variables makes sense. Although it might seem easy and be tempting to declare all variables as instance and class variables, this can make a program difficult to maintain and debug in the future. Likewise with methods, they should usually be declared as instance methods unless individual objects need to share a method, and then it should be declared as a class method. The key is to take the time when designing and creating a program to determine where each variable and method should be declared.

5.6 Complete Programs: Implementing Objects

The first complete program implements overloaded methods, and the second utilizes class data members and class methods.

5.6.1 Program Focusing on Overloaded Methods

After defining the `PointD` class earlier this chapter which represents a point, a class that represents a line will be developed in this section. Since a line consists of points, the `PointD` class can also be used. The main program will:

- Set points and lines
- Compare two lines
- Find the distance between a line and a point

A line can be defined in slope-intercept form $y = mx + b$, where m is the slope and b is the y-intercept, and the class will be named LineSI. The slope and y-intercept are kept in private instance variables, slope and intercept.

Because a user may like to define a line in several different ways and to reinforce the concept of overloaded constructors, six constructors will be provided. The default constructor without any parameters will set the value of the slope and the y-intercept to 0.0. The next constructor accepts the value for the slope as a parameter and sets the y-intercept to 0.0 creating a line going through the origin. The third constructor receives a LineSI object and copies the slope and y-intercept of the line to the new object, essentially creating an identical line. This constructor is sometimes referred as a copy constructor. The fourth constructor accepts two parameters and assigns these values to the instance variables, slope and intercept. A line can also be defined in two-point form as

$$y - y_0 = \frac{y_1 - y_0}{x_1 - x_0}(x - x_0)$$

where (x_0, y_0) and (x_1, y_1) are two different points on the line. So, the fifth constructor accepts two PointD objects, calculates the slope and the y-intercept, and assigns the results to appropriate data members. The last constructor receives the x and y coordinates of two points and calculates the slope and y-intercept. Initial implementations for the six overloaded constructors are shown below:

```
// First constructor of LineSI class:
public LineSI() {
    // using fourth constructor
    this(0.0, 0.0);
}

// Second constructor of LineSI class:
public LineSI(double slope) {
    // using fourth constructor
    this(slope, 0.0);
}

// Third constructor of LineSI class:
public LineSI(LineSI line) {
    // using fourth constructor
    this(line.slope, line.intercept);
}

// Fourth constructor of LineSI class:
public LineSI(double slope, double intercept) {
    this.slope = slope;
    this.intercept = intercept;
}

// Fifth constructor of LineSI class:
public LineSI(PointD pt1, PointD pt2) {
    // using fourth constructor
    this((pt2.getY()-pt1.getY()) / (pt2.getX()-pt1.getX()),
            ((pt2.getX()*pt1.getY()) -
            (pt1.getX()*pt2.getY()))/(pt2.getX()-pt1.getX()));
}

// Sixth constructor of LineSI class:
public LineSI(double x1, double y1, double x2, double y2) {
    // using fourth constructor
    this((y2-y1) / (x2-x1),
            ((x2*y1) - (x1*y2)) / (x2-x1));
}
```

All six overloaded constructors have the same name as the class and they are differentiated by their parameter lists. The first constructor has no parameters, the second and third constructors have one parameter, the fourth and fifth constructors have two parameters, and the sixth constructor has four parameters. Although both the second and third constructors have one parameter, the types are different; the second has one of type double and the third has one of type LineSI. The fourth and fifth constructors have two parameters; the fourth has two parameters of type double and the fifth has two parameters of type PointD.

The reserved word this in a constructor invokes the other constructor with the corresponding parameter list within the same class. So, calling the default constructor in the main method to create a LineSI object causes the fourth constructor to be called as well. The second, third, fifth, and sixth constructors also call the fourth constructor by using the reserved word this. As was discussed in Sect. 5.4, the advantage of using the word this is that if a change needs to be made to a common feature of all the constructors, only the fourth constructor needs to be modified. Also, notice that in the fourth constructor, the keyword this is used in order to distinguish between the data member and the parameter. This ensures that values in the parameters are correctly copied into the data members.

There will be two usual mutators to set each instance data member and two accessors to get the value of two data members as shown below:

```
// Mutator for slope:
public void setSlope(double slope) {
    this.slope = slope;
}

// Mutator for intercept:
public void setIntercept(double intercept) {
    this.intercept = intercept;
}

// Accessor for slope:
public double getSlope() {
    return slope;
}

// Accessor for intercept:
public double getIntercept() {
    return intercept;
}
```

In addition to the two mutators above, there will be three more mutators named setLine to set both instance data members at the same time. Like constructors, methods can also be overloaded. The setLine method is overloaded; one takes the values of the slope and the y-intercept, another takes the x and y coordinates of two points as parameters, and the last takes two PointD objects. Even though the first and the second setLine methods have the same number of parameters, the types are different; the first setLine method has two parameters of type double and the second has two parameters of type PointD. The detailed implementations of these three overloaded methods are shown below:

```
// First setLine method:
public void setLine(double slope, double intercept) {
    this.slope = slope;
    this.intercept = intercept;
}

// Second setLine method:
public void setLine(PointD pt1, PointD pt2) {
    // using first setLine method
    setLine((pt2.getY()-pt1.getY()) / (pt2.getX()-pt1.getX()),
            ((pt2.getX()*pt1.getY()) -
             (pt1.getX()*pt2.getY()))/(pt2.getX()-pt1.getX()));
}

// Third setLine method:
public void setLine(double x1,double y1,double x2,double y2) {
    // using first setLine method
    setLine((y2-y1) / (x2-x1),
            ((x2*y1) - (x1*y2)) / (x2-x1));
}
```

First, notice that the second and third setLine methods use the first setLine method. This is similar to the constructors, where all the other constructors invoked the fourth constructor.

If one looks carefully, it can be seen that the implementation of the fourth constructor and the first setLine method is the same. Also, notice that the code for the fifth constructor appears similar to the code for the second setLine method except that the constructor is invoking the fourth constructor and the setLine method is calling the first setLine method with the corresponding parameter list defined within the class. The calculations for the slope and y-intercept used as the formal parameters in the methods are exactly the same. The same thing can be said for the sixth constructor and the third setLine method. How can one avoid having duplicate code in the program? The answer is to invoke the setLine method in the constructor instead of repeating the same code twice. This would make sense when more complex computations need to be performed several times in the separate methods within the class as in the second and third setLine methods. The modification to the fourth, fifth, and sixth constructors is illustrated below:

```
// Fourth constructor of LineSI class, modified:
public LineSI(double slope, double intercept) {
    // using first setLine method
    setLine(slope, intercept);
}

// Fifth constructor of LineSI class, modified:
public LineSI(PointD pt1, PointD pt2) {
    // using second setLine method
    setLine(pt1, pt2);
}

// Sixth constructor of LineSI class, modified:
public LineSI(double x1, double y1, double x2, double y2) {
    // using third setLine method
    setLine(x1, y1, x2, y2);
}
```

The first setLine method can be further modified to avoid duplicate code. Notice that the two statements this.slope = slope; and this.intercept = intercept; are also in setSlope and setIntercept methods, respectively. Therefore, the original first setLine method can be rewritten as follows:

```
// First setLine method, modified:
public void setLine(double slope, double intercept) {
    // using setSlope and setIntercept methods
    setSlope(slope);
    setIntercept(intercept);
}
```

In order to understand the nesting of method calls in overloaded constructors and methods, consider what would happen when a LineSI object is created using a default constructor in the main method. Calling the default constructor would result in the fourth constructor being invoked. The fourth constructor will call the first setLine method which calls the setSlope and setIntercept methods to set the values of slope and intercept. Although at first this might seem more complicated, the purpose is to eliminate duplicate code making the program easier to maintain.

The last two methods are named compareLines and distance. The LineSI object, which calls the method compareLines, will be compared to the LineSI object passed to the method. It returns true when the two lines are the same and false when they are different. The LineSI object, which calls the method distance, calculates the distance from the object to the point passed as a parameter.

All the pieces are put together in the following class:

```
// definition of LineSI class

public class LineSI {
   // data members
   private static final double DEFAULT_VALUE = 0.0;
   private double slope;
   private double intercept;

   // constructors
   public LineSI() {
      // using fourth constructor
      this(DEFAULT_VALUE, DEFAULT_VALUE);
   }

   public LineSI(double slope) {
      // using fourth constructor
      this(slope, DEFAULT_VALUE);
   }

   public LineSI(LineSI line) {
      // using fourth constructor
      this(line.slope, line.intercept);
   }

   public LineSI(double slope, double intercept) {
      // using first setLine method
      setLine(slope, intercept);
   }

   public LineSI(PointD pt1, PointD pt2) {
      // using second setLine method
      setLine(pt1, pt2);
   }

   public LineSI(double x1, double y1, double x2, double y2) {
      // using third setLine method
      setLine(x1, y1, x2, y2);
   }

   // methods
   public void setSlope(double slope) {
      this.slope = slope;
   }

   public void setIntercept(double intercept) {
      this.intercept = intercept;
   }

   public void setLine(double slope, double intercept) {
      // using setSlope and setIntercept methods
      setSlope(slope);
      setIntercept(intercept);
   }
```

```
public void setLine(PointD pt1, PointD pt2) {
   // using first setLine method
   setLine(((pt2.getY()-pt1.getY())) / (pt2.getX()-pt1.getX()),
          ((pt2.getX()*pt1.getY()) -
          (pt1.getX()*pt2.getY())))/(pt2.getX()-pt1.getX())));
}

public void setLine(double x1,double y1,double x2,double y2) {
   // using first setLine method
   setLine(((y2-y1) / (x2-x1),
          ((x2*y1) - (x1*y2)) / (x2-x1));
}

public double getSlope() {
   return slope;
}

public double getIntercept() {
   return intercept;
}

public boolean compareLines(LineSI line) {
   boolean flag;
   flag = false;
   if (slope == line.slope && intercept == line.intercept)
      flag = true;
   return flag;
}

public double distance(PointD pt) {
   return Math.abs(slope*pt.getX() - pt.getY() +
          intercept) / Math.sqrt(Math.pow(slope, 2) + 1 );
}
}
```

Notice that along with the two private instance variables, the private class constant, DEFAULT_VALUE, was defined. It was declared as a class data member so that any method defined in the class can use it as a constant because the value does not need to be changed during execution. By declaring it as a class constant, it will avoid allocating memory for the same constant twice when used in the first and second constructors.

The Lines class in Fig. 5.15 will test the methods defined in LineSI. It will create two points and six lines using six different constructors. Then it will output the properties of the lines and the result from the compareLines and distance methods.

```
// a program to create lines and points, and output the
// information on them

public class Lines {
    public static void main(String[] args) {
        // declaration and initialization of variables
        PointD pt1, pt2;
        LineSI line1, line2, line3, line4, line5, line6;
        pt1 = new PointD(1.0, 4.0);
        pt2 = new PointD(-3.0, 2.0);
        line1 = new LineSI(pt1, pt2);                   // See Exercise 4
        line2 = new LineSI(line1);
        line3 = new LineSI(1.0, 2.0, 4.0, -1.0);
        line4 = new LineSI(0.5, 3.5);
        line5 = new LineSI();
        line6 = new LineSI(2.0);

        // output the information of lines
        System.out.println("line1: slope = " + line1.getSlope()
                        + ", intercept = " + line1.getIntercept());
        System.out.println("line2: slope = " + line2.getSlope()
                        + ", intercept = " + line2.getIntercept());
        System.out.println("line3: slope = " + line3.getSlope()
                        + ", intercept = " + line3.getIntercept());
        System.out.println("line4: slope = " + line4.getSlope()
                        + ", intercept = " + line4.getIntercept());
        System.out.println("line5: slope = " + line5.getSlope()
                        + ", intercept = " + line5.getIntercept());
        System.out.println("line6: slope = " + line6.getSlope()
                        + ", intercept = " + line6.getIntercept());

        // output the result from compareLines method
        if (line1.compareLines(line2))
            System.out.println("line1 and line2 are the same.");
        else
            System.out.println("line1 and line2 are not the same.");

        // output the result from compareLines method
        if (line4.compareLines(line5))
            System.out.println("line4 and line5 are the same.");
        else
            System.out.println("line4 and line5 are not the same.");

        // output the result from distance method
        System.out.printf("The distance between line3 and pt1 is "
                        + "%.2f.", line3.distance(pt1));
        System.out.println();

        // output the result from distance method
        System.out.printf("The distance between line6 and pt2 is "
                        + "%.2f.", line6.distance(pt2));
        System.out.println();
    }
}
```

Fig. 5.15 A client program for LineSI and PointD classes

The output from the program in Fig. 5.15 is given below:

```
line1: slope = 0.5, intercept = 3.5
line2: slope = 0.5, intercept = 3.5
line3: slope = -1.0, intercept = 3.0
line4: slope = 0.5, intercept = 3.5
line5: slope = 0.0, intercept = 0.0
line6: slope = 2.0, intercept = 0.0
line1 and line2 are the same.
line4 and line5 are not the same.
The distance between line3 and pt1 is 1.41.
The distance between line6 and pt2 is 3.58.
```

5.6.2 Program Focusing on Class Data Members and Class Methods

In this section, the ChargeCard class defined in Sect. 5.5.3 will be modified. Assume that a cardholder travels to Europe and uses the card for shopping. The amount charged in Euros should be converted into US dollars and added to the balance of the card. Using the application, a user should be able to:

• Open an account to receive a card
• Make purchases in either US dollars or Euros
• Print the current balance of the card

The program should perform the conversion from Euros to US dollars. The calculation used in conversion is the same for any purchase made in Euros; therefore, all the Card objects can share the code for the conversion. For this reason, the convertEurosToDollars method will be declared as a class method. The program also keeps track of the conversion rate named rate in the program. Since rate is used in the class method and a class method does not have an access to an instance data member, rate should be declared as a class data member. Because the conversion rate changes frequently, it should be declared as a variable, not a constant. The mutator and accessor for rate will also be class methods since they deal with a class data member. The following code segment implements the class data member and class methods discussed so far:

```
public class Card {
    // class data member
    private static double rate;

    // class methods
    public static double convertEurosToDollars(double euros) {
        return euros*rate;
    }

    public static void setRate(double aRate) {
        rate = aRate;
    }

    public static double getRate() {
        return rate;
    }
}
```

So far there is no instance data member or instance method implemented in the `Card` class; therefore, all the methods can be used without creating an object. The following `main` method will set the `rate` and output its value and the result of the conversion of 1.00 Euro to US dollars:

```
public class Purchases {
    public static void main(String[] args) {
        // output the information for Euros conversion
        Card.setRate(1.2128);
        System.out.println("rate = " + Card.getRate());
        System.out.printf("1.00 euro is equal to %.2f dollars.",
            Card.convertEurosToDollars(1.00));
        System.out.println();
    }
}
```

Notice that the three class methods are invoked using the class name `Card` in the dot notation. The following is the output from the above program:

```
rate = 1.2128
1.0  euro is equal to 1.21 dollars.
```

Now the data members, constructors, and instance methods can be added to the `Card` class. The additional data members include two class constants, DEFAULT_ACCOUNT_NUMBER and DEFAULT_BALANCE, and two instance variables, `accountNum` and `balance`. There will be two constructors: one default constructor and another constructor that has two formal parameters to store values in the instance variables. The `setAccountNum` method is a mutator to set the value of the variable `accountNum`. Both the `purchaseInDollars` and `purchaseInEuros` methods receive a formal parameter and increment the `balance` by the amount in the parameter. In the `purchaseInEuros` method, the amount of Euros passed to the method is converted to

US dollars by calling the `convertEurosToDollars` method. There will also be two accessors, `getAccountNum` and `getBalance`, to get the values of the two instance variables. The following program defines the `Card` class:

```
// definition of Card class

public class Card {
   // data members
   private static final int DEFAULT_ACCOUNT_NUMBER = 0;
   private static final double DEFAULT_BALANCE = 0.0;
   private static double rate;
   private int accountNum;
   private double balance;

   // class methods
   public static double convertEurosToDollars(double euros) {
      return euros*rate;
   }

   public static void setRate(double aRate) {
      rate = aRate;
   }

   public static double getRate() {
      return rate;
   }

   // constructors
   public Card() {
      // using second constructor
      this(DEFAULT_ACCOUNT_NUMBER, DEFAULT_BALANCE);
   }

   public Card(int accountNum, double amount) {
      // using setAccountNum and purchaseInDollars methods
      setAccountNum(accountNum);
      balance = amount;
   }

   // mutator methods
   public void setAccountNum(int accountNum) {
      this.accountNum = accountNum;
   }

   public void purchaseInDollars(double dollars) {
      balance += dollars;
   }
```

```
            public void purchaseInEuros(double euros) {
               balance += convertEurosToDollars(euros);
            }

            // accessor methods
            public int getAccountNum() {
               return accountNum;
            }

            public double getBalance() {
               return balance;
            }
         }
```

The complete `main` method in Fig. 5.16 includes the creation of a `Card` object, two purchases, one each in US dollars and Euros, and the output of the balance after each purchase.

```
// a program to create card, make purchases, and output balance

public class Purchases {
   public static void main(String[] args) {
      // output the information for Euros conversion
      Card.setRate(1.2128);
      System.out.println("rate = " + Card.getRate());
      System.out.println("1.00 euro is equal to "
        + Card.convertEurosToDollars(1.00) + " dollars.");

      // declaration and initialization of instance variables
      Card card;
      card = new Card(12345, 0.0);

      // purchase and output balance
      card.purchaseInDollars(100.00);
      System.out.println("after spending 100.00 dollars");
      System.out.print("card: Account Number = "
      + card.getAccountNum() + ", balance = ");
      System.out.printf("%.2f dollar",card.getBalance());
      System.out.println();

      // purchase and output balance
      card.purchaseInEuros(100.00);                    // See Exercise 5
      System.out.println("after spending 100.00 euros");
      System.out.print("card: Account Number = "
      + card.getAccountNum() + ", balance = ");
      System.out.printf("%.2f dollars",card.getBalance());
      System.out.println();
   }
}
```

Fig. 5.16 A client program for `Card` class

The following is the output from the program in Fig. 5.16:

```
rate = 1.2128
1.00 euro is equal to 1.2128 dollars.
```

```
after spending 100.00 dollars
card: Account Number = 12345, balance = 100.00 dollars
after spending 100.00 euros
card: Account Number = 12345, balance = 221.28 dollars
```

5.7 Summary

- In addition to primitive data types, objects can be sent to and returned from methods.
- Constructors and methods can be overloaded by having the same name but must have a different number of parameters, different types of parameters, or parameters of different types in a different order.
- The reserved word this is used to refer to instance variables when there are parameters of the same name and to constructors when one constructor is defined in terms of another.
- If a constant or variable is declared within a constructor or method, it is known as a local constant or variable.
- If a constant or variable is declared within an object, they are known as an instance constant or variable and can be accessed by any constructor or method within the object.
- The reserved word static causes a constant, variable, or method to be a class constant, variable, or method that can be accessed by an instance of the class.
- Take the time to determine where variables and methods should be declared to help balance readability, communication, debugging, maintainability, and memory allocation.

5.8 Exercises (Items Marked with an * Have Solutions in Appendix E)

1. Identify the valid and invalid overloaded constructors in the following code:

```
public class PointD {
    private double x;
    private double y;

  * // constructor 1
    public PointD() {
        ...
    }
    // constructor 2
    public PointD(double x) {
        ...
    }
  * // constructor 3
    public PointD(double y) {
        ...
    }
    // constructor 4
    public PointD(double x, double y) {
        ...
    }
    // constructor 5
    public PointD(double y, double x) {
        ...
    }
    // constructor 6
    public PointD(PointD pt) {
        ...
    }
}
```

2. Identify the valid and invalid overloaded methods in the following code:

```
public class PointD {
    private double x;
    private double y;

    // method 1
    public double distance(PointD pt) {
        ...
    }
  * // method 2
    public static double distance(PointD pt) {
        ...
    }
    // method 3
    public static double distance(PointD pt1, PointD pt2) {
        ...
    }
}
```

```
    // method 4
    public double distance(PointD pt1, PointD pt2) {
        ...
    }
    // method 5
    public PointD middle(PointD pt) {
        ...
    }
*   // method 6
    public PointD middle(PointD pt1, PointD pt2) {
        ...
    }
    // method 7
    public PointD middle(PointD pt1,PointD pt2,PointD pt3){
        ...
    }
    // method 8
    public PointD product(PointD pt) {
        ...
    }
    // method 9
    public double product(PointD pt) {
        ...
    }
*   // method 10
    public PointD product(double scalar) {
        ...
    }
    // method 11
    public PointD product(PointD pt, double scalar) {
        ...
    }
    // method 12
    public PointD product(double scalar, PointD pt) {
        ...
    }
}
```

3. A hexahedron is a three-dimensional shape with six faces. In this problem, a class which represents a hexahedron with squares at the top and the bottom as shown below will be implemented.

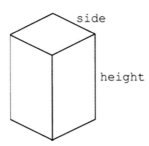

Assume that hexahedrons are made of different materials; therefore, the `weight` needs to be kept along with the `side` and the `height` in order to describe a particular hexahedron. The following code implements data members and a portion of the constructors of `Hexahedron` class. Complete the first six constructors to call the last one by using the reserved word `this`.

```java
public class Hexahedron {
    // data members
    private static final int DEFAULT_VALUE = 10;
    private static final double DEFAULT_WEIGHT = 10.0;
    private int side;
    private int height;
    private double weight;

    // constructors
    public Hexahedron() {
        // assign default values to all data members
    }

    public Hexahedron(int side) {
        // assign contents of parameter to side
        // assign default values to height and weight
    }
    public Hexahedron(double weight) {
        // assign contents of parameter to weight
        // assign default values to side and height
    }

    public Hexahedron(Hexahedron h) {
        // assign contents of data members of parameter
        // to side, height, and weight
    }

    public Hexahedron(int side, int height) {
        // assign contents of parameters to side and height
        // assign default value to weight
    }

    public Hexahedron(int height, double weight) {
        // assign contents of parameters to height and weight
        // assign default value to side
    }

    public Hexahedron(int side, int height, double weight) {
        this.side = side;
        this.height = height;
        this.weight = weight;
    }
    . . .
}
```

4. Draw contour diagrams to show the state of execution right after the execution of the statement `line1 = new LineSI(pt1, pt2);` in Fig. 5.15 in Sect. 5.6.1.
5. Draw contour diagrams to show the state of execution right after the execution of the statement `card.purchaseInEuros(100.00);` in Fig. 5.16 in Sect. 5.6.2.

6. Implement a class `Rectangle` which represents a rectangle shape as described below:

*A. The `Rectangle` class has one private class constant `DEFAULT_VALUE` that should be initialized to `0.0`.

*B. The `Rectangle` class has two private instance data members, `sideX` and `sideY`, of type `double`.

*C. The first constructor is a default constructor and calls the third constructor (described below) using the reserved word `this` to set instance data members to the default value.

D. The second constructor calls the third constructor (described below) using the reserved word `this`. It retrieves a `Rectangle` object as a formal parameter and copies `sideX` and `sideY` of the object to the new object.

E. The third constructor calls the `setSides` method (described below). Two formal parameters are used as the parameters for the `setSides` method.

*F. The mutator methods, `setSideX` and `setSideY`, each has one formal parameter and stores them in the instance data member.

G. Another mutator method, `setSides`, has two formal parameters and stores them in the instance data members by using the `setSideX` and `setSideY` methods (described above).

H. The accessor methods, `getSideX` and `getSideY`, return the value of the appropriate instance data member.

I. A method named `calcArea` computes the area of a rectangle and returns the computed area.

Next, write a client program to test the `Rectangle` class defined above. This class should be named `Rectangles` and should contain the `main` method which performs the following tasks:

a. Declare three `Rectangle` objects.
b. Create three `Rectangle` objects using the three different constructors.
c. Output the contents of `sideX` and `sideY` of the three objects.
d. Output the area of the third rectangle.

Here is some sample output:

```
rectangle1: sideX = 0.0, sideY = 0.0
rectangle2: sideX = 3.0, sideY = 4.0
rectangle3: sideX = 3.0, sideY = 4.0
rectangle3: area = 12.0
```

7. Expand the `PointD` class discussed in this chapter to include the quadrant information of a point. The *x*-axis and *y*-axis divide the plane into four regions called quadrants. The quadrants are labeled starting at the positive *x*-axis and going around counterclockwise as shown below:

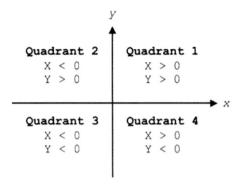

Write the new `PointD` class as described below. Points falling on the *x*-axis and *y*-axis are not considered to be in any quadrant, and therefore return the default value, 0:

A. The `PointD` class has two private class constants, `DEFAULT_VALUE` of type `double` and `DEFAULT_QUADRANT` of type `int`, that should be initialized to `0.0` and `0`, respectively.

B. The `PointD` class has two private instance data members, x and y, of type `double`.

C. The `PointD` class has one private instance data member `quadrant` of type `int`.

D. The first constructor is a default constructor and calls the third constructor (described below), by using the reserved word `this`, to set the instance data members to the default values.

E. The second constructor receives a `PointD` object as a formal parameter and stores the x, y, and `quadrant` of the object as the values of the instance data members.

F. Third constructor calls the `setPoint` method (described below). Its two formal parameters are used as the parameters for the `setPoint` method.

G. The mutator methods, `setX` and `setY`, have one formal parameter and call the `setPoint` method (described below). The `setX` method changes the value of data member x to the value of the parameter. The `setY` method changes the value of data member y to the value of the parameter.

H. Another mutator method, `setPoint`, has two formal parameters and stores these values in the instance data members, x and y. It also sets the correct value for the data member `quadrant` depending on the values of the two parameters.

I. The accessor methods, `getX`, `getY`, and `getQuadrant`, return the value of the appropriate instance data member.

Next, write a client program to test the `PointD` class defined above. Call this class `Points`. The `main` method should perform the following tasks:

    J.   Declare five `PointD` objects.

    K.   Create five `PointD` objects using the three different constructors. The points should be in three different quadrants and also the origin.

    L.   Output the contents of `x`, `y`, and `quadrant` for the five objects.

    M.   Change the value of `x` or `y` for one of the points using a mutator so that the point will move to a different quadrant.

Here is some sample output:

```
point1: (0.0, 0.0) in quadrant 0
point2: (2.0, -5.0) in quadrant 4
point3: (2.0, -5.0) in quadrant 4
point4: (2.0, 5.0) in quadrant 1
point5: (-2.0, 5.0) in quadrant 2
after calling set method
point3: (-2.0, -5.0) in quadrant 3
```

8. Describe how to differentiate methods with the same name defined in the same class.

9. Describe the use of the keyword `this`.

10. A part of the `LineSI` class from Section 5.6.1 is shown below. Identify necessary and unnecessary use of the keyword `this`.

```
public class LineSI {
    // data members
    private static final double DEFAULT_VALUE = 0.0;
    private double slope;
    private double intercept;

    // methods
    public void setSlope(double slope) {
        this.slope = slope;
    }

    public void setIntercept(double intercept) {
        this.intercept = intercept;
    }

    public void setLine(double slope, double intercept) {
        // using setSlope and setIntercept methods
        this.setSlope(this.slope);
        this.setIntercept(this.intercept);
    }

    public void setLine(PointD pt1, PointD pt2) {
        // using first setLine method
        this.setLine((pt2.getY()-pt1.getY()) /
                (pt2.getX()-pt1.getX()),
                ((pt2.getX()*pt1.getY()) -
                (pt1.getX()*pt2.getY()))/(pt2.getX()-pt1.getX()));
    }

}
```

11. Suppose the `Vehicle` class is defined to keep track of vehicles in a household. What kinds of instance data members, variables and constants, would be defined for such `Vehicle` objects? Do any useful class data members, variables and constants, for the `Vehicle` class? How about instance methods and class methods?

12. Write a complete program for the user to play a number guessing game. The computer generates a random number from 1-10, and the user gets one chance to guess that number. Output a message whether the guessed number was correct. After each game the player will be asked to play another game. When the user decides to stop, the winning percent of games will be displayed. The statement that will generate a random number from 1 to 10 inclusive is:

```
int computerNumber = (int) (Math.floor(Math.random() * 10) + 1);
```

First, define a class that represents one number guessing game which should include the `play` method that generates a random number, asks the user for input, checks if the user won, and displays the result. Make sure to keep track of the number of games played and the number of games the user won.

Next, implement a main program to play the number guessing game. Use a loop to play the game multiple times. At the conclusion display statistics of games.

Use an option dialog box like the blow for the user input. Option dialog boxes are discussed in Appendix A.7.

The user will be notified the result in the message dialog boxes that are similar to the ones shown below:

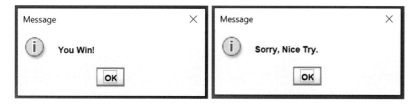

After each game, use a confirmation dialog box discussed in Appendix A.6 for the user to click on yes or no.

When the user clicks no, output the percent of winning games. Example is shown below:

6
Strings

James T. Streib[a]* and Takako Soma[a]

[a] Computer Science Program, Illinois College, Jacksonville, IL, USA

Abstract

This chapter discusses string variables and the `String` class. In addition to the concatenation of strings, various methods defined in the `String` class such as the `length`, `indexOf`, and `substring` methods are examined. The `toString` method which returns a string representation of the properties of an object is also shown along with a complete program implementing `String` objects.

Keywords

`String` Object; `String` Class; `ToString` Method; `String` Variables; Substring Method.

6.1 Introduction

Up till now, this text has focused on numerical values such as integers and real numbers. In this chapter the focus is text values. Characters are another fundamental type of data used on a computer, and a string in Java is a sequence of characters. Each programming language supports a particular character set which is a list of characters in a particular order. The ASCII (American Standard Code for Information Interchange) character set is the most common one. The basic ASCII set uses seven bits per character to support 128 different characters including letters, punctuation, digits, special symbols, and control characters. In order to support more characters and symbols from many different natural languages, Java uses the Unicode character set, which uses 16 bits per character, supporting 65,536 unique characters. ASCII is a subset of the Unicode character set.

Strings are not represented as a primitive data type such as `int`, `double`, or `char` but as an object of the `String` class. Text values can also be passed as an argument to methods such as `system.out.print` as described in Chap. 1. Similar to numbers, strings can be assigned to variables and manipulated using operators and methods defined in the `String` class.

6.2 String Class

The `String` class is a standard class, like the `Math` or `Scanner` classes, defined in the `java.lang` package. The following illustrates how a `String` variable is declared and a `String` object is created:

```
String fullName;
fullName = new String("Maya Plisetskaya");
```

After the variable `fullName` is declared as type `String`, the second statement creates an object with a value `"Maya Plisetskaya"` and then a reference to the new object is placed in the variable, fullName. The contour diagram in Fig. 6.1 illustrates the state of execution after the above two statements.

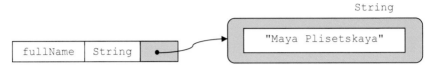

Fig. 6.1 An object of String class

Because the String class is a predefined class, a variable name is not in the contour diagram of the String object. Although the String class is not a primitive data type, a String object can be created by assigning a string within double quotes to a String variable, for example,

```
String fullName;
fullName = "Maya Plisetskaya";
```

Even though it looks like the text value is directly assigned to the variable, the variable fullName does not contain an actual value, like with a primitive data type, but rather an address of the object. The contour diagram after the above two statements will be exactly the same as the one shown in Fig. 6.1.

Further, notice that the following statements using the keyword new will assign a null value to the variable:

```
String fullName;
fullName = new String();
```

The same thing will also happen with a simple assignment statement:

```
String fullName;
fullName = null;
```

The differences between creating String objects using new statements and assignment statements will become more apparent in Sect. 6.4. Except for on a few occasions, the new statement will be used to create a String object in order to reinforce the ideas of object creation. In either case, once a String object is created, the string value inside of the object cannot be modified, which means that any of the characters in the string cannot be changed, nor can the string be shortened or lengthened. This property is called being *immutable*. If a string needs to be modified, an object of type StringBuffer which is a mutable sequence of characters can be used, but this is beyond the scope of this text.

6.3 String Concatenation

Although strings cannot be modified, there are a number of operators that can be used with strings. A useful String operation is concatenation accomplished by the use of a plus symbol, +, which was introduced briefly in Chap. 1 to support output. Two strings can be combined to create a new string. Consider the following example code segment:

```
String firstName, lastName, fullName;
firstName = new String("Maya");
lastName = new String("Plisetskaya");
fullName = firstName + " " + lastName;
```

A first name and a last name are assigned to separate variables, `firstName` and `lastName`, respectively, and then combined together using a string concatenation operator. A contour diagram for `fullName` is again exactly the same as the one in Fig. 6.1. Notice that a space is concatenated between `firstName` and `lastName`. Without it, `fullName` would have the first name and a last name combined together as in "MayaPlisetskaya".

A plus symbol was introduced as an arithmetic addition and as a concatenation in the output statements in _Chap. 1_ . When an operator represents more than one operation, it is called an *overloaded operator*. What happens if overloaded operators appear in the expression with mixed types? The Java compiler treats + as an arithmetic addition when both the left and right operands are numbers, otherwise it will treat it as a string concatenation. For example, what would the output be for the following code segment? Remember that the plus symbol is evaluated from left to right and the result of an expression with mixed types is `String` type.

```
int num1, num2;
String str1, str2;
num1 = 2;
num2 = 3;
str1 = new String("num1 + num2 = ");
str2 = new String(" = num1 + num2");
System.out.println(str1 + num1 + num2);
System.out.println(num1 + num2 + str2);
System.out.println(str1 + (num1 + num2));
```

The first print statement results in

```
num1 + num2 = 23
```

Since the left operand of the first plus symbol is `String` and the right operand is `int`, it will treat the contents of `num1` as `String`. Because the first plus sign was treated as concatenation, the left operand of the second plus sign is a `String` type. Further, the right operand of the second plus symbol is `int`; it will again treat the contents of `num2` as a `String`.

How about the second print statement? The first plus sign is treated as an arithmetic addition because the left and the right operands of the first plus sign are both `int` types. Then, the second plus symbol is treated as a string concatenation since the last operand is of type `String` and it is mixed-type operands. The output will be

```
5 = num1 + num2
```

In the third print statement, parentheses will force (num1 + num2) to be evaluated first. Therefore, the second + is treated as an arithmetic addition. The result will be

```
num1 + num2 = 5
```

Another operator that can be used on String objects is a shortcut operator, +=. It has the same effect as the shortcut of arithmetic addition discussed in Chap. 1 and is left as an exercise at the end of the chapter.

6.4 Methods in String Class

There are over 50 methods defined in the String class that can be found in the Java API specification document on the Oracle website at

   http://docs.oracle.com/javase/7/docs/api/java/lang/String.html

In this section, six of the most commonly used ones will be discussed: length, indexOf, substring, equals, equalsIgnoreCase, and charAt.

6.4.1 The length Method

In order to find the number of characters in a String object, the length method is used. For example, if the variable fullName refers to the string "Maya Plisetskaya", then

```
fullName.length()
```

will return the value 16 because there are 16 characters in the string. Notice that a space between the first name and the last name is counted as a character. If the string is empty, applying the length method results in 0.

6.4.2 The indexOf Method

A character in a string can be referred to by its position, or in other words its index, in the string. The index of the first character is 0, the second character is 1, and so on as illustrated in Fig. 6.2.

0	1	2	3	4	5	6	7	8	9	10	11	12	13	14	15
M	a	y	a		P	l	i	s	e	t	s	K	a	y	a

Fig. 6.2 Index of characters in the string

To find the position of a substring of a string, the indexOf method can be used. The method will return the position of the first character of the substring in the string. Here are some examples using fullName:

Statement	return value
fullName.indexOf("Maya")	0
fullName.indexOf("set")	8
fullName.indexOf("Set")	-1
fullName.indexOf("ya")	2
fullName.indexOf(" ")	4

The first statement returns 0 because "Maya" occurs at the beginning of the string. The word "set" starts at the position 8. The return value −1 from the third statement indicates that the substring does not exist in the string. Since it performs a case-sensitive search, it did not find "Set" starting with an uppercase letter. There are two occurrences of "ya" at the position 2 and 14. Since if there is more than one occurrence of the substring in the string, the position of the first character of the first matching substring is returned, the fourth statement returns 2. As it was mentioned before, a space is considered to be a character; therefore, the last statement returns 4 which is the position of the space in the string.

6.4.3 The substring Method

On some occasions, one's name needs to be printed in a format of a last name, a comma, a space, and a first name. How can it be formatted if the full name is given in a first name, a space, and a last name? The answer is that the first name and the last name can be extracted from the full name and rearranged. In order to extract a substring from a string, a substring method can be used. A substring method takes two integers as arguments: the position of the first letter of the substring and the position of the last letter of the substring + 1. Using the string in Fig. 6.2, this means that the statement fullName.substring(8, 11); will return "set". Here are some more examples:

statement	return value
fullName.substring(0, 4)	Maya
fullName.substring(2, 2)	an empty string
fullName.substring(10, 6)	runtime error
fullName.substring(18, 20)	runtime error

The second statement will create a String object with empty string. The third example gives a runtime error because the first argument should be the same as or smaller than the second. In the fourth example, the arguments should be in the range of 0–16, otherwise they are out of bounds and cause a runtime error.

Obtaining a first name, "Maya" from fullName is not very difficult. A statement fullName.substring(0, 4) would work. However, consider when the fullName contains a different name, for example, "George Balanchine". fullName.substring(0, 4); would return Geor, which is not the first name. How can this be changed so that the statement will extract the first name from any full name? Notice that the first name and the last name are separated by a space. So, using a position of the space spacePos = fullName.indexOf(" "), a first name can be easily extracted from any full name as in fullName.substring(0, spacePos). Once the first name is obtained, how can the last name be extracted? Remember the last name starts right after the space, so the position of the first letter of the last name is spacePos + 1. When does it end? It ends at the end of the string. Since fullName.length() returns 16 for "Maya Plisetskaya", which is the position of the last letter of the last name + 1, this is perfect for the second parameter of substring method for extracting a last name. All the pieces are put together in the following program:

```java
import java.util.*;

class FormatName {
    public static void main(String[] args) {
        // declaration and initialization of variables
        String fullName, firstName, lastName;
        int spacePos, len;
        Scanner scanner;
        scanner = new Scanner(System.in);

        // input name
        System.out.print("Enter full name, first name " +
                              "followed by last name: ");
        fullName = scanner.nextLine();

        // extract firstName and lastName
        spacePos = fullName.indexOf(" ");
        len = fullName.length();
        firstName = fullName.substring(0, spacePos);
        lastName = fullName.substring(spacePos+1, len);

        // output name
        System.out.println(lastName + ", " + firstName);
    }
}
```

Alternatively, without declaring variables, spacePos and len, one could use return values from indexOf and length methods as arguments for the substring method.

```java
firstName = fullName.substring(0, fullName.indexOf(" "));
lastName = fullName.substring(fullName.indexOf(" ")+1,
    fullName.length());
```

Which way is better? The first option allocates memory for two more variables, spacePos and len; however, it does not call indexOf method twice as in the second option. For a small example like this, it does not matter which option one uses. For large programs, try to remember not to waste too much memory by declaring unnecessary variables and also try not to invoke complex methods multiple times. One should always be aware of a trade-off between space and time, and create a very good balance between the two when developing a large application.

An example of the input and output from the above program is shown below:

```
Enter full name, first name followed by last name: Maya Plisetskaya
Plisetskaya, Maya
```

6.4.4 Comparison of Two `String` Objects

While a double equal sign, ==, was used to compare primitive data types, comparing two `String` objects takes extra care. Examine the following code segment:

```
String str1, str2;
str1 = new String("saddles");
str2 = new String("saddles");
System.out.println(str1 == str2);
```

Is the output `true` or `false`? As a matter of fact, it prints `false`. Why does the comparison of `str1` and `str2` return `false`? Both `String` variables seem to contain the same value, `"saddles"`, but remember that a `String` variable contains a reference to the `String` object, not the string itself. Since `str1` and `str2` are two completely different objects, two variables refer to different addresses shown below:

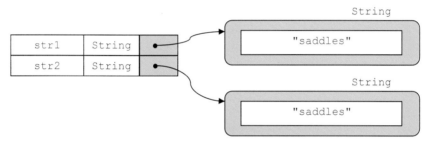

The correct way to compare the contents of `String` object is to use a `String` method, `equals`.

```
System.out.println(str1.equals(str2));
```

The above statement will output `true` since both `str1` and `str2` have the same value. The `equals` method does not compare the references, but rather the contents of the strings being referenced. What about when a `String` object is created by assigning a string literal?

```
String str3, str4;
str3 = "halters";
str4 = "halters";
System.out.println(str3 == str4);
System.out.println(str3.equals(str4));
```

Interestingly, both print statements return `true`. This is because when the value is assigned to `str4`, the Java compiler will search the existing `String` objects for an exact match. If it finds one, which is the case here, a new `String` object is not created. Instead, the variable is assigned a reference to the existing `String` object show below:

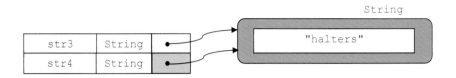

Of course, if the contents of one `String` variable is copied to another `String` variable, both variables would point to the same object as shown below because what is copied is the address of the object:

```
String str5, str6;
str5 = new String("bridles");
str6 = str5;
System.out.println(str5 == str6);
System.out.println(str5.equals(str6));
```

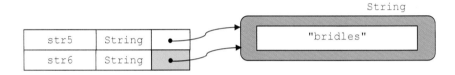

As can be seen in the above contour diagram, both print statements return `true`. Recall that this is exactly the same situation discussed in Sect. 2.9 , where variables of `Number` objects, num1 and num2, are referencing the same object containing the integer 5 after the assignment statement num1 = num2 shown in Fig. 2.24 repeated below:

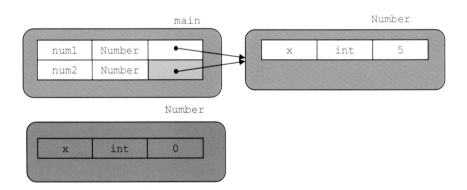

The contour diagram showed that the intended task of copying the integer 5 from num1 to num2 was not accomplished. In general it is not a good idea to have two variables pointing to the same object, unless it is a `String` object. If the contents of the object num1

is referring to were modified by using a mutator method, the contents of the object `num2` is referring to would be automatically changed because they are pointing to the same object. Is it the same way with `String` objects? If one were to execute the following statement to modify the contents of `str5`,

```
str5 = "reins";
```

the Java compiler would search the existing `String` objects for one containing `"reins"`. So far, two objects with `"saddles"`, one object with `"halters"`, and one object with `"bridles"` have been created. Since it does not find an object with `"reins"`, a new `String` object will be created. Therefore, `str5` and `str6` will be referencing different `String` objects as shown below:

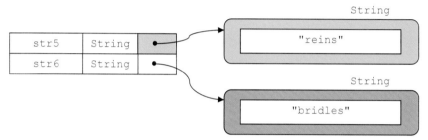

Now, the following statements will both return `false`:

```
System.out.println(str5 == str6);
System.out.println(str5.equals(str6));
```

Unlike with `num1` and `num2`, because of the immutable characteristic of `String` type, there is no danger of modifying the content of one object when two `String` variables are referencing the same object.

6.4.5 The equalsIgnoreCase Method

Assume that a program to play a Tic Tac Toe game has been written. At the end of each game, a user will be asked if he or she would like to play another game. For example, consider the code segment in Fig. 6.3:

```
boolean selection;
Scanner scanner;
String response;
selection = true;

scanner = new Scanner(System.in);
while(selection) {
    // play one Tic Tac Toe game
    System.out.print("Would you like to play another
                                Tic Tac Toe game? ");
    response = scanner.next();
    if(!response.equals("yes"))
        selection = false;
}
```

Fig. 6.3 Use of a method from String class to compare strings

Because of the !, the condition of the if statement is true when a user does not enter yes. Then, the variable selection will be changed to false, and eventually the program stops. What happens if a user wanted to play another game and entered Yes instead of yes? Because the equals method checks for an exact match, the if condition again is true. In case the user types yes in different ways, the if condition can be modified to

```
if(!(response.equals("yes") || response.equals("Yes") ||
response.equals("YES")))
    selection = false;
```

Then, the user can enter "yes", "Yes", "YES" to continue. Actually, there is a way to include all the combinations of upper- or lowercase characters in the word "yes" such as "yEs", "yeS", and "yES". One can compare the content of String objects ignoring the case of characters in the string. An equalsIgnoreCase method compares the content of a String object to that of another String object ignoring case considerations. Two strings are considered to be equal if they are of the same length and corresponding characters in the two strings are equal ignoring the case of the characters. In other words, the search can be done in a case-insensitive way. One can rewrite the if condition as

```
if(!response.equalsIgnoreCase("yes"))
    selection = false;
```

Given the equalsIgnoreCase method, the user can enter "yes", "Yes", "YES" or any other combination of uppercase or lowercase characters in the word "yes" to continue.

6.4.6 The charAt Method

The charAt method returns the character stored at the specified position in the string. For example, if the variable fullName refers to the string "George Balanchine", then fullname.charAt(0) will return the value "G" because the character "G" is the first character. The statement fullname.charAt(2) will return the value "o" because the index of the character "o" is 2. Suppose one likes to know the number of occurrences of certain character in a string, for instance, the character "G" in `fullname`. Each character in the `fullname` can be checked using the `charAt` method inside the loop and a counter can be incremented. The following code segment counts the number of "G" characters in "George Balanchine":

```
String fullname;
int i, count;
fullname = "George Balanchine";
count = 0;
char letter;

for(i=0; i<fullname.length(); i++) {
    letter = fullname.charAt(i);
    if(letter == 'G')
        count++;
}
System.out.println("The name George Balanchine contains "
              + count + " of character 'G's.");
```

An output from the above code segment would be

```
The name George Balanchine contains 1 character 'G's.
```

Notice that it only counts the capital letter "G" and ignores lowercase letter "g". If both uppercase and lowercase letters need to be counted, the `if` condition would look like

```
if(letter == "G" || letter == "g")
```

and the code will return 2 because one uppercase "G" and one lowercase "g" exist in "George Balanchine". A summary of some of the methods in the `String` class can be found in Table 6.1.

Table 6.1 Various methods in the `String` class

Method	Function preformed	Arguments	Value returned
charAt(pos)	Returns character at given index	int	Char
equals(str)	Compares strings	String	Boolean
equalsIgnoreCase(str)	Compares strings ignoring case	String	Boolean
indexOf(str)	Returns index of first occurrence of substring	String	Int
length()	Returns length of string	None	Int
substring(pos,pos)	Returns substring of string	int, int	String

6.5 The `toString` Method

The overriding method, `toString`, receives no parameters and returns a `String` type. Although overriding methods will be discussed further in Chap. 9, it is introduced here because it is a useful method that helps output data stored in objects. Prior to demonstrating how `toString` works, the `PointD` class from Fig. 5.4 in Chap. 5 is relisted in Fig. 6.4.

```
class Example {
    public static void main(String[] args) {
        PointD middle;
        PointD p1, p2;
        p1 = new PointD();
        p2 = new PointD();
        p1.setX(4.0);
        p1.setY(4.0);
        p2.setX(8.0);
        p2.setY(7.0);
        middle = p1.midPoint(p2);
        System.out.print("The mid-point between (");
        System.out.print(p1.getX() + "," + p1.getY());
        System.out.print(") and (" + p2.getX() + ",");
        System.out.print(p2.getY()+") is (" + middle.getX());
        System.out.println("," + middle.getY() +")");
    }
}

class PointD {
    private double x, y;
    public PointD() {
        x = 0.0;
        y = 0.0;
    }
    public void setX(double xp) {
        x = xp;
    }
    public void setY(double yp) {
        y = yp;
    }
    public double getX() {
        return x;
    }
    public double getY() {
        return y;
    }
    public PointD midPoint(PointD p) {
        PointD mid;
        mid = new PointD();
        mid.setX( (x+p.getX()) / 2 );
        mid.setY( (y+p.getY()) / 2 );
        return mid;
    }
}
```

Fig. 6.4 A client program and PointD class

The main method in Fig. 6.4 creates objects of the PointD class and finds the midpoint of the two points. After executing the program, the output is

```
The mid-point between (4.0,4.0) and (8.0,7.0) is (6.0,5.5)
```

What would happen if the last five print statements of the main method were replaced by the following statement?

```
System.out.println(middle);
```

This statement is trying to output `middle` which is a `PointD` object. Does it output the contents of x and y of `middle`? The answer is no. Instead, the output would look like the following:

```
PointD@ae3364
```

What is this? Is it garbage? The answer to the second question is no, it is not garbage. However, it is not very useful information at this level of programming. The `System.out.println` outputs the name of the class `PointD`, an @ symbol, and the memory address of the object in hexadecimal (base 16) representation. Since each time the program is run the object might be in a different location in memory, the output may be different every time the program is executed. In order to output the contents of x and y, one needs to use accessor methods, such as `getX` and `getY` as done in Fig. 6.4. However, wouldn't it be nice if there was a method to return the contents of an object? A `toString` method could be written in the `PointD` class to return a string representation of the contents of the data members of an object. The method could return x and y as the location of a point in the format (x, y) and would be written as follows:

```
public String toString() {
    return "(" + x + "," + y + ")";
}
```

Since the values in x and y are concatenated with strings, they are converted to type `String` and would be returned as a `String`. Then, in the following statement, the object `middle` can call the `toString` method

```
System.out.println(middle.toString());
```

and the above statement will produce an output of

```
(6.0,5.5)
```

Now, if the last five print statements in the `main` method in Fig. 6.4 were replaced by the following code,

```
System.out.println("The mid-point between "
 + p1.toString() + " and " + p2.toString() + " is "
 + middle.toString());
```

it would produce the same output as the original code as follows:

```
The mid-point between (4.0,4.0) and (8.0,7.0) is (6.0,5.5)
```

The usefulness of a `toString` method will be appreciated more when objects are discussed further in <u>Chap. 9</u>.

6.6 Complete Program: Implementing `String` Objects

In this section, an application which outputs course information will be developed. The program will:

- Ask the user for a name of a class. The input consists of a department code, a course number, and a course title, such as "CS 360 Theory of Computation".
- Process the input.
- Output the title of the class, level of the class, and the department that offers the class.

An example of the input and output for the Theory of Computation course would be

```
Enter the course: CS 360 Theory of Computation
The class, "Theory of Computation", is a
junior level class offered by the
Computer Science department.
```

and the input and output for a Calculus course could be

```
Enter the course: MA 213 Calculus I
The class, "Calculus I", is a
sophomore level class offered by the
Mathematics department.
```

When the user provides input, the program will create an object and store pieces of information inside of the object. The name of the department will be determined by the department code which is the first piece of the input. The course number is the second piece of the input, and the course title is the rest of the input. The level of the course will be obtained by checking the course number. Figure 6.5 contains the code defining the class for a Course object.

```
// definition of Course class
class Course {
    // data member
    private String department;
    private String number;
    private String name;
    private String level;

    // constructor
    public Course() {
        this("", "", "");
    }

    // constructor
    public Course(String dept, String number, String name) {
        setDepartment(dept);
        setNumber(number);
        setName(name);
        setLevel();
    }

    // mutator methods
    public void setDepartment(String dept) {
        if(dept.equals("CS"))
```

```
                department = "Computer Science";
        else
            if(dept.equals("MA"))
                department = "Mathematics";
            else
                department = "undetermined";
    }

    public void setNumber(String number) {
        this.number = number;
    }

    public void setName(String name) {
        this.name = name;
    }

    public void setLevel() {
        String str;
        char num;
        str = number.substring(0, 1);
        num = str.charAt(0);
        switch(num) {
            case '1': level = "first-year";
                      break;
            case '2': level = "sophomore";
                      break;
            case '3': level = "junior";
                      break;
            case '4': level = "senior";
                      break;
            default:  level = "undetermined";
        }
    }

    // accessor methods
    public String getDepartment() {
        return department;
    }

    public String getNumber() {
        return number;
    }

    public String getName() {
        return name;
    }

    public String getLevel() {
        return level;
    }
}
```
Fig. 6.5 Course class

The Course class consists of four data members that are all instance variables, two constructors, and mutators and accessors for each data member. The setDepartment method accepts a department code as a parameter, then the if-then-else structure determines the department, and the value is assigned to the data member. The setLevel method uses the value of data member, number, to figure out the level of the class. In order to use a case structure, the first character of number is extracted as a String and converted to a character since only char, byte, short, or int types can be used in the case statement. The charAt method is used to convert a string to a character. It takes a position of a character in a string and returns a character. The main program which uses Course class is shown in Fig. 6.6.

```java
// a program to output course information

import java.util.*;

class Courses {
    public static void main(String[] args) {
        // declaration and initialization of variables
        Course course;
        String str, dept, number, name;
        Scanner scanner;
        scanner = new Scanner(System.in);

        // input course
        System.out.print("Enter the course: ");
        str = scanner.nextLine();
        dept = str.substring(0, str.indexOf(" "));
        str = str.substring(str.indexOf(" ")+1, str.length());
        number = str.substring(0, str.indexOf(" "));
        name = str.substring(str.indexOf(" ")+1, str.length());
        course = new Course(dept, number, name);

        // output course information
        System.out.println();
        System.out.println("The class, \"" + course.getName() +
                                            "\", is a ");
        System.out.println(course.getLevel() +
                            " level class offered by the ");
        System.out.println(course.getDepartment() +
                                    " department.");
    }
}
```

Fig. 6.6 A client program for Course class

After the user enters an input, pieces of information are extracted and used to create a Course object. Notice that in order to include a double quote in a string literal, a backslash is used as in \", which was discussed in the output section of Chap. 1 . This application can be extended to accommodate more departments and graduate level classes. Course objects can also be stored in an array for further manipulation which will be discussed in Chap. 7 .

6.7. Summary

- A String object can be created by using new, =, or += operators.
- String objects are immutable, which means their contents cannot be changed.
- When a String object is created by assigning a string literal, the Java compiler will search the existing String objects for an exact match. If it finds one, the variable is assigned a reference to the existing String object.
- When a String object is created using the keyword new, a new object will be created even if there already exists an object with the same string value.
- Individual characters of a string are numbered starting from 0.
- When an equals method is applied to String objects, it compares the contents of the objects being referenced.
- To compare the contents of String objects, a == operator cannot be used since it compares the references to objects.
- Some String methods include indexOf, length, substring, equals, equalsIgnoreCase, and charAt.

6.8 Exercises (Items Marked with an * Have Solutions in Appendix E)

1. Identify the errors in the following code segments:

    A. ```
    String text1;
    text1 = new String(girth);
    ```

    *B. ```
    String text2;
    text2 = new Text("shedding blade");
    ```

    C. ```
    String text3;
    text3 = new Sting("grazing muzzle");
    text3.indexOf("muzz");
    text3.length(5);
    ```

    D. ```
    String text4 = String("Feeders");
    System.out.println(text4);
    ```

    E. ```
    String text5 = "Stall Fork";
    String text6 = "Stall ";
    String test7 = text5 - text6;
    System.out.println(text7);
    ```

    F. ```
    String text8 = 'Hey Bags';
    System.out.println("text8 is " + text8);
    ```

2. Determine the return value for each of these expressions, assuming the following declaration:

```
String org;
org = new String ("American Quarter Horse Association");
```

   A.   `org.substring(5, 8)`
*B.   `org.length()`
   C.   `org.substring(9, 22)`
*D.   `org.substring(17, 19) + org.substring(20, 22)`
   E.   `org.substring(15, 16) + org.substring(18, 19)`
         `+ org.substring(13, 14)`
         `+ org.substring(org.length()-5, org.length())`
   F.   `org += org`

3. Draw contour diagrams to show the state of execution after the execution of the following code segment:

```
String s1, s2, s3, s4;
s1 = new String("stirrup irons");
s2 = "stirrup irons";
s3 = new String("stirrup irons");
s4 = s2;
```

4. Determine the output from the following code segment:

```
String star;
star = "*";
int i;
for (i=0; i<5; i++) {
   System.out.println(star);
   star += star;
}
```

5. Write a program that asks the user for a positive integer, receives input as a `String`, and outputs a string with commas in the appropriate places. For example, if the input is

```
1000000
```

then the output is

```
1,000,000
```

6. Repeat the previous exercise using dialog boxes for input and output. An input dialog box is used to input a positive integer. Then, a message dialog box displays a string with commas in the appropriated places.

7. Write a program for a given word and string that will

   a.   Check if the word is in the string.
   b.   Count all occurrences of the word in the string.
   c.   Remove all occurrences of the word from the string.

*8. With a given `String` object called `org` containing a value `"American Quarter Horse Association"`, write a program to output an abbreviation of the string, `AQHA`.

9. Modify the previous program to ask a user for a name of his or her organization and print an abbreviation of the name. Realize that the name of the organization consists of any number of words.

10. Repeat the previous exercise using dialog boxes for input and output. An input dialog box is used to input a name of the organization. Then, a message dialog box displays the abbreviation of the name.

7

Arrays

James T. Streib[a*] and Takako Soma[a]

[a] Computer Science Program, Illinois College, Jacksonville, IL, USA

Abstract

Arrays and array processing are illustrated in the chapter starting with declaration, access, input and output. In addition to simple processing, the passing of an array to and from a method is demonstrated. Other processing includes reversing, searching (sequential and binary), and sorting an array using the bubble sort. Also, two-dimensional arrays and arrays of objects are introduced, along with a complete program.

Keywords

One and Two dimensional Arrays; Sequential Search, Binary Search; Bubble Sort.

7.1 Introduction

Similar to a string which can store a group of characters, an array can be used to store numbers of type `int` or `double`. Not only can arrays store numbers, but they can also be used to store strings, objects, and even other arrays. Arrays are extremely useful to store data that needs to be processed more than once, such as data that needs to be searched or sorted.

Related to an array are the predefined `Array` and `Vector` classes which are beyond the scope of this text, because before learning how to use these classes, it is good to understand how to input, process, and output data using arrays. This chapter will first introduce the reader to declaring an array, and as in the past the best way to learn is to get started with an example.

7.2 Array Declaration

When declaring an array, the type of data that will be stored in the elements of the array must be specified. For example, to declare a memory location to store a reference to an array of type `int` called `number`, one would write the following:

```
int number[];
```

Alternatively, and used more often, the above could be declared as

```
int[] number;
```

This reserves a memory location called `number`, the square brackets indicate that it will be an array, and the word `int` indicates that each element of the array can contain an integer. Initially, the memory location `number` will contain a `null` reference, which means it does not initially reference anything, as shown below.

number

In order to create an array of three elements, the following instruction is needed:

```
number = new int[3];
```

Although the word new has also been used to create a new object, here it is used to create a new array. The number in the square brackets indicates the length of the array, in this case three elements. In this example, the first element is number[0] and the last one is number[2]. As with simple variables, the contents of the array are initialized to 0, but as in Chap. 1 this text will assume that the contents are indeterminate. Lastly, a reference to the array is placed into the memory location number via the assignment symbol and is represented as an arrow in the following diagram:

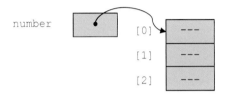

Alternatively the previous two lines could be combined as follows:

```
int[] number = new int[3];
```

Although this takes up less space, the other two statements will be used more frequently to reinforce the concepts of declaration and allocation. As another alternative, a constant can be declared and used in the new statement. The advantage to this technique is that when iterating in a loop to process or output an array, the same constant can be used both to declare the array and as the end value of a for loop as will be seen in the next section:

```
final int ARRAYSIZE = 3;
int[] number;
number = new int[ARRAYSIZE];
```

As another alternative, an array can be declared and initialized using the following technique:

```
int[] number = {0,0,0};
```

While this is somewhat useful for small arrays, it would be impractical to initialize hundreds of elements. Though often smaller arrays will be initialized this way in order to save space, an alternative is presented in the next section.

7.3 Array Access

Assuming that an array has been created at the beginning of the program using the statements in the preceding section, the array can now be accessed. In order to access an individual element of an array, the name of the array is followed by the index of the element to be accessed. For example,

```
number[0] = 5;
```

indicates that the 0th element of the array, the first element, takes on the value of 5. This is illustrated in the following diagram:

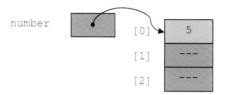

Be sure not to confuse the index, 0, with the contents of the array, 5. Notice that the 0th element of the array now contains the number 5. Should the contents of the first element need to be copied into the third element, it could be accomplished as follows:

```
number[2] = number[0];
```

and would be represented as shown below:

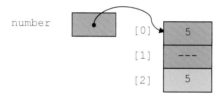

When accessing various elements of an array, be careful not to try to access or alter any elements outside the range of the array. In the example above, do not try to access `number[-1]` or below, or try to access `number[3]` or above, because an execution error will occur.

Although the accessing of individual elements can be useful in particular instances, it is often more practical to be able to access all of the array elements. As an example, what if the elements of the array need to be initialized to zero? If only three elements need to be initialized, the technique illustrated at the end of the previous section could be used, but what if instead of three elements, one hundred elements needed to be initialized? Clearly, listing out one hundred individual zeros would be impractical. Instead, as mentioned previously in Chap. 4 , this can be accomplished by using an iteration structure. Though any of the loop structures can be used, under different circumstances some iteration structures are better choices than others.

For example, if each element of the above array needs to be initialized to zero, which loop would be the best choice? Since there is a fixed number of elements to be initialized, then a fixed iteration loop structure could be used, specifically the `for` loop as shown below:

```
for(int i=0; i<3; i++)
    number[i] = 0;
```

Notice that the loop control variable is of type `int` and iterates from 0 to 2 corresponding to the three elements of the array. For each iteration of the loop, the number 0 is placed into the `i`th element of the array. As when accessing individual elements of an array, be careful not to have the loop try to access elements that are outside the range of the array, such as `number[-1]` or `number[3]` because again an execution error will occur.

Assuming the declaration of the constant `ARRAYSIZE` in the previous section, the above code segment could be rewritten as follows:

```
for(int i=0; i<ARRAYSIZE; i++)
   number[i] = 0;
```

Another alternative to the programmer-defined constant `ARRAYSIZE` is to use the public constant `length` associated with the array as shown in the following code segment:

```
for(int i=0; i<number.length; i++)
   number[i] = 0;
```

Although this would not be helpful in creating the array, this is otherwise helpful because one would not have to remember the name of the programmer-defined constant. Also notice that a set of parentheses does not appear after the word `length` as it does with strings, as in `.length()` as discussed in Chap. 6 . The reason is that `.length()` is a method with an empty argument list for use with strings, whereas `.length` is a public constant associated with an array. At first it can be a little hard to distinguish between the two, but with time and practice, it becomes easier to remember.

In both cases, whether using either the programmer-defined constant or the public constant, they can be convenient when inputting, processing, or outputting the contents of an entire array. However, there are many times when an array is not entirely filled, so using either type of constant is not as useful as one might think as shown in the next section.

7.4. Input, Output, Simple Processing, and Methods

Although initializing an array is useful in some circumstances, more often data will need to be input by the user. The data input into the array is often processed and the array might subsequently be output. The first subsection examines the input, the second shows how to output an array, the third demonstrates some simple processing, and the fourth subsection illustrates passing an array to and from a method.

7.4.1 Input

As in the preceding section, assume that the following declarations are made at the beginning of the program and prior to the following input code segments:

```
int[] number;
number = new int[3];
```

If there are exactly three items that need to be input into the three element array above, then the `for` loop is again the logical choice. As with input of data into simple variables, a prompt should be used:

```
for(int i=0; i<3; i++) {
   System.out.print("Enter integer number " + (i+1) + ": ");
   number[i] = scanner.nextInt();
}
```

Note that the loop control variable is part of the prompt to help the user know what number is being entered. Although the array elements are numbered 0 to 2, the i+1 in the prompt allows the user entering the data to think in the more familiar terms of 1 to 3. Further note that the i+1 is in parentheses so the plus sign will be treated as addition instead of concatenation. Lastly, since the value of i+1 in the prompt is not assigned back into i, the value of the loop control variable and the index for the array is not altered. The format of the prompts with sample input is as follows:

```
Enter integer number 1: 5
Enter integer number 2: 7
Enter integer number 3: 10
```

Of course as discussed in Chap. 4 and assuming the declaration of the integer variable n, a user could be prompted for the number of integers to be entered as in the following:

```
System.out.print("Enter the # of integers to be entered 1 - 3: ");
n = scanner.nextInt();
for(i=0; i<n; i++) {
   System.out.print("Enter integer number " + (i+1) + ": ");
   number[i] = scanner.nextInt();
}
```

However, what if the user needs to enter fewer items into the array than were initially allocated? In the above example, if the user only needs to enter two items, then only the last element would go unused. Further, what if an array were declared to hold 1,000 elements, but the user only needed to enter 20 items? The result would be that there would be 980 empty elements in the array, which would be a waste of memory. More problematic is what if the user of the above code segment needed an array of size 100 rather than an array of size 3 elements? Although the program could be modified and recompiled, this is not a viable option for a user who does not know how to program. Fortunately, there is a solution to this problem. The following declaration of the variable to hold the reference to the array would still occur at the beginning of the program as follows:

```
int[] number;
```

Then, instead of having the allocation of memory using the `new` statement and a constant prior to the input code segment, it could appear after the prompt for the number of items to be entered into the array as follows:

```
System.out.print("Enter the # of integers to be entered: ");
n = scanner.nextInt();
```

```
number = new int[n];
for(i=0; i<n; i++) {
   System.out.print("Enter integer number " + (i+1) + ": ");
   number[i] = scanner.nextInt();
}
```

Notice that the reference to the array is created after the prompt and input for the number of integers to be entered into the variable n. The advantage to this technique is that no wasted memory locations are declared. More importantly there are enough elements in the array for the user to enter the data and the user is not limited to a fixed number of data items.

However, as discussed in Chap. 4 , a problem with the above code is what if the user miscounts the number of data items to be entered and enters the wrong number of items to be input? Although the array will be declared to the size entered, the user might end up having more data to enter than was allowed for in the array or the user might have less data than expected and the for loop might iterate more times than needed.

As before, a better solution might be to use a sentinel control loop. If one uses the code from Chap. 4 and alters it to substitute an array element instead of a simple variable, one might write something similar to the following code segment. However, there is still a problem with this code segment:

```
// *** Caution: Incorrectly implemented code ***
i = 0;
System.out.print("Enter a non-negative integer ");
System.out.print("or a negative integer to stop: ");
number[i] = scanner.nextInt();
while(number[i] >= 0) {
   i++;
   System.out.print("Enter a non-negative integer ");
   System.out.print("or a negative integer to stop: ");
   number[i] = scanner.nextInt();
}
```

As indicated by the comment prior to the code, the above code segment is implemented incorrectly. Although it appears to input all the valid data into the array, what is the problem? The problem is that the sentinel value is also input into the array. While this is not a major issue, the array would have to be declared to be one element larger to accommodate the sentinel value. Further, one would need to write all subsequent code to not process or output the sentinel value, which could be a potential source of logic errors.

The best solution is not to put the sentinel value in the array in the first place. How could this be done? The problem is that both input statements put the values directly into the array. As an alternative, the value could be input to a temporary variable and checked to see whether it is a sentinel value before putting it into the array. However, instead of adding a couple of extra if statements, note that the while loop already checks for the sentinel value. If the value in the temporary variable is not a sentinel value, the body of the loop is entered and the value in the temporary variable can be copied into the array. On the other hand, if the value in the temporary variable is a sentinel value, the loop is not executed and the sentinel value is not placed in the array. A good name for the temporary variable is `temp` as in the following segment:

```
i = 0;
System.out.print("Enter a non-negative integer ");
System.out.print("or a negative integer to stop: ");
temp = scanner.nextInt();
while(temp >= 0) {
   number[i] = temp;
   i++;
   System.out.print("Enter a non-negative integer ");
   System.out.print("or a negative integer to stop: ");
   temp = scanner.nextInt();
}
```

However, what is preventing the user from entering more data than there is space for in the array? Assume that the array is fixed at a particular size as in the following declaration and allocation:

```
final int ARRAYSIZE = 10;
int[] number;
number = new int[ARRAYSIZE];
```

Note that a constant is being used for the allocation of the array. The `while` statement in the above code segment can now be altered using the constant to ensure that the user does not enter more data than was allocated for the array as shown below:

```
while(temp >= 0 && i < ARRAYSIZE) {
```

or alternatively

```
while(temp >= 0 && i < number.length) {
```

Whereas the previous example using the `for` loop had the advantage that the array was the exact size the user wanted, the disadvantage was that the user might miscount the number of data items to be entered. However, the advantage of the sentinel controlled loop above is that it does the counting for the user, but the disadvantage is that it is still using a fixed-size array. Can't the user enter the size of the array? It is possible that they could, but then same problem could occur as before and the user might miscount the number of items to be input. Further, the code in the sentinel controlled loop is doing the counting of the number of items, and the array has to be declared before the data is input.

In the field of computer science, there are always trade-offs, and it is up to the designers of the algorithms to determine the best possible solution to the problem at hand. As will be seen in subsequent courses in computer science, the concept of a linked list is helpful in solving the above problem, but it should be noted that that solution is not without its own set of limitations. Another possible solution to the current problem, when there are more data items to be entered into an array than has been allocated, is to have the program allocate an array of a larger size, say twice as large, then copy the contents of the old array into the new one and allow the user to continue to enter data into the new array. Although this solution might slow down the processing, it does avoid the consequences of an array that is not large enough and this is left as an exercise at the end of the chapter. However, in this text when using the sentinel controlled loop, the emphasis will be on selecting the right size array in the first place.

7.4.2 Output

The output of an array could be done as the data is input, but then the output would be intermixed with the input. A better solution is to output the contents of the array after all the data has been input. But how does one know how many data items have been input when using a sentinel controlled loop? The answer is with the variable i used in the previous code segment. Since a fixed number of values have been input, a for loop is the best choice for output. The for loop could be written to iterate i times, but since i is typically used as a loop control variable, it might be better to copy the value in i to another variable such as n and then have the for loop reuse the variable i as a loop control variable and iterate n times. It is also helpful to add a column heading prior to the output of the contents of the array as shown in the following code segment:

```
n = i;
System.out.println();
System.out.println("Integers");
System.out.println();
for(i=0; i<n; i++)
   System.out.println("   " + number[i]);
```

Note that a blank line is output both before and after the column heading, Integers. Assuming some values have already been input to the array, the output would look as shown below:

```
Output

Integers

   5
   7
   9
```

Also note that the underlined word Output is not part of the output from the code segment but rather helps one see where the output begins and the blank line both before and after the column heading.

7.4.3 Simple Processing

What if the data needs to be modified prior to output? As a simple example, what if the output was to be the original numbers doubled? There are two ways that this can be accomplished. The first is to just output the number doubled but not alter the contents of the array as follows:

```
for(i=0; i<n; i++)
   System.out.println(" " + (number[i] * 2) );
```

However, what if the specifications actually indicate that the contents of the array should be altered and then output? This can be accomplished by the following code segment:

```
for(i=0; i<n; i++)
   number[i] = number[i] * 2;
for(i=0; i<n; i++)
   System.out.println(" " + number[i] );
```

Notice that in this instance the contents of the array are actually altered in the first loop and then output in the second loop. However, as an aside, can this be done in only one loop? The answer is yes as can be seen below:

```
for(i=0; i<n; i++) {
   number[i] = number[i] * 2;
   System.out.println(" " + number[i]);
}
```

Clearly, the second solution is the better of the two. Although there will be times when there is no choice but to have a separate loop for processing the data in an array, as will be seen in the next section, it is usually better to combine the two tasks into one loop, if at all possible.

Returning to the previous example of not altering the array and only modifying the output or writing code to actually alter the array prior to output, which one is the correct solution to the problem? It depends upon the specifications for the program and how the program might be modified in the future. If the specifications require only the output of the new numbers and the array needs to retain the original values for subsequent processing, then the first version is the preferred method. However, if the specifications indicate that the numbers are to be altered and subsequent processing depends upon the altered numbers, then the second way is better. If it is unclear, it is usually better to ask to determine which of the two is the best way to solve the problem, and in this text if it is not specified, it should be assumed that the contents of the array ought to be altered.

7.4.4 Passing an Array to and from a Method

An array can be passed to and from a method fairly easily. For simplicity, assume there is a 3-element array to be input and output. From the main program, one method could be called to input data into the array and another method to output the array as follows:

```
int[] number;
number = inputNumber();
outputNumber(number);
```

The call to inputNumber will prompt for and input integers into a local 3-element array as shown below:

```
public int[] inputNumber() {
   int[] num = new int[3];
   for(int i=0; i<num.length; i++) {
      System.out.print("Enter an integer: ");
      num[i] = scanner.nextInt();
   }
   return num;
}
```

Since the array is allocated locally, there is no reason to allocate an array in the main program. At the end of the method, a reference to the array is returned to the calling program. Note that a copy of the entire array is not returned, but only the reference. The variable num in the method points to the array, a copy of the reference is passed back to the main program, and the copy is assigned to the variable number as shown in the following diagram:

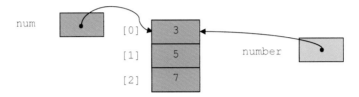

Just as a reference to an array can be sent back from a method, it can be sent to a method too. Again, a copy of the entire array is not passed to the method outputNumber, but only the reference is sent to the method via a parameter:

```
public void outputNumber(int[] num) {
   for(int i=0; i<num.length; i++)
      System.out.println(num[i]);
}
```

Since arrays can become quite large, sending and returning only the reference makes it very practical.

7.5 Reversing an Array

As an example of a type of processing that can be done with an array, what if one wanted to output the integers that were input in reverse order? Although one does not need to reverse the contents of an array very often, it does introduce a number of interesting ideas that pertain to processing data in an array and will help in subsequent sections. There are two ways that this reversing can be accomplished. The first is to input the values using a loop such as the sentinel controlled loop in the previous section and then output the contents of the array in reverse order. How can this be accomplished? Instead of starting at zero, the loop would need to start at the opposite end of the array. But where should this be? If the array is called number as in the last section and instead its length is 8, should it start at position 8, ARRAYSIZE, or number.length? No, because recall that an 8-element array would be numbered from 0 to 7, not 1 to 8. So should it start from position 7, ARRAYSIZE-1, or number.length-1? That depends on how many integers are in the array. If there are only six integers in the array, then it should not start from position 7, but rather from position 5. Why not 6? For the same reason just mentioned, if there are six integers in an array, they would typically occupy elements 0 to 5. So if there are n integers in an array, the output should start from position n-1 as shown in the following code segment:

```
for(i=n-1; i>=0, i--)
    System.out.println(number[i]);
```

Notice that the loop control variable starts at n-1, the loop continues while i is greater than or equal to 0, and that i is decremented each time through the loop. Although this would output the array in reverse order to the user, have the values in the array changed? The answer is no. So what if instead of outputting the array in reverse order, one actually wanted to reverse the contents of the array? One way to accomplish this task is to declare another array and then copy the contents of the first array into the second array in reverse order. However, what is a possible drawback with this solution? The problem is that it takes two arrays or twice as much memory. In this example, it would require two 10-element arrays for a total of 20 elements. For a small array this is not much of a problem, but for a very large array, this would entail a substantial amount of memory. Instead, the solution is to reverse the array in place, thus using only one array.

The algorithm takes the first data item and the last data item and swaps them. Then, the second data item and the second to the last data item are swapped, and so on as shown in Fig. 7.1.

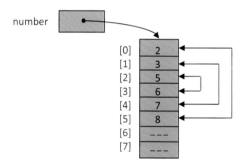

Fig. 7.1 Reversing an array

Again, one needs to be careful not to swap elements that do not contain values. When n equals 6, element 0 is swapped with the n-1 element, then element 1 is swapped with the n-2 element, and so on. The loop control variable can be used for elements 0, 1, and 2, but how does one access elements n-1, n-2, and n-3? One solution is to use a second variable such as j so that when the loop control variable, say i, is incremented, the variable j is decremented. But are two variables really needed? If one thinks about it, one should be able to see a pattern in accessing both ends of the data. When i is zero, the contents of location 0 needs to be swapped with location n-1. Although a little difficult to see here, in the first instance i is equal to 0, so n-1 could be thought of as n-i-1. However, sometimes a pattern is difficult to see in the first instance, but can be seen a little better in subsequent instances. Consider the next case when i is 1, it needs to be swapped with n-

2. Since i would be equal to 1, n-2 could again be thought of as n-i-1. So instead of using two indexes, only one index is needed, which is a little more elegant.

Lastly, the matter of the swap needs to be considered. If the contents of two simple variables need to be swapped, how can this be accomplished? When the value of one variable is transferred to another variable, the previous contents of the variable being swapped into are destroyed, so the previous contents need to be stored in a temporary memory location, often called temp. First the contents of the variable x need to be put aside in the temporary memory location temp using a temp = x; instruction.

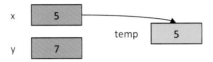

Once the contents of variable x have been moved into temp, the contents of variable y can be copied into the variable x using an x = y; instruction.

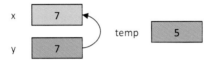

Now that the contents of y have been copied into x, the contents of temp can be copied into the variable y using a y = temp; instruction.

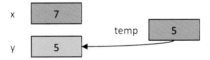

The whole sequence of instructions is as follows:

```
temp = x;
x = y;
y = temp;
```

So how can this be used with an array? Instead of using simple variables, the corresponding location of the array can be substituted using the variables i and n-i-1 as discussed above and shown below:

```
temp = number[i];
number[i] = number[n-i-1];
number[n-i-1] = temp;
```

Assuming i is equal to 0 and n is equal to 6, then going from left to right in Fig. 7.2 the execution of the three instructions is shown in the dashed boxes above each array.

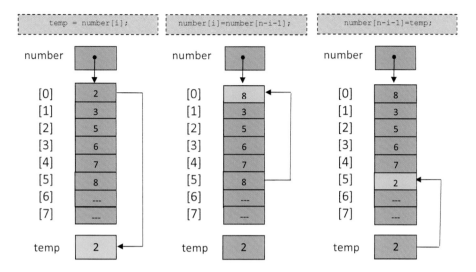

Fig. 7.2 Swapping items in an array

Putting it all together with the loop results in the following code segment. However, one needs to be careful when writing the code to solve this problem. For example, can the error in the following code segment be spotted?

```
// *** Caution: Incorrectly implemented code ***
for(i=0; i<n; i++) {
    temp = number[i];
    number[i] = number[n-i-1];
    number[n-i-1] = temp;
}
```

The swapping is okay, but what about the number of times the `for` loop iterates? At first one might think that the `for` loop is iterating one more or one less time than it should, but look at the code again. The problem is that after i gets halfway through the loop and has swapped the first half with the second half of the array, the loop continues and swaps the second half back with the first half of the array. This can be a tough problem for a beginning programmer to detect, because after supposedly reversing the array, and subsequently outputting the array, there appears to be no change in the order! Rather, the loop should only go halfway through the array and then stop. This makes sense when there is an even number of values in the array, but what if there is an odd number of items in the array as in Fig. 7.3?

number

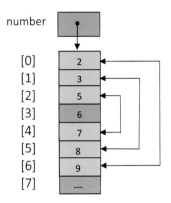

[0] 2
[1] 3
[2] 5
[3] 6
[4] 7
[5] 8
[6] 9
[7] ---

Fig. 7.3 Reversing an odd number of items in an array

Certainly, one does not need to swap the center item with itself. If there are 7 items in the array and n equals 7, then 7 divided by 2 is 3. Isn't it 3.5? No, recall that when an integer is divided by an integer, the answer is an integer. The result is that the loop will iterate 3 times and swap the first three data items with the last three in the array. The correct code can be found below:

```
// *** Correctly implemented code ***
for(i=0; i<n/2; i++) {
    temp = number[i];
    number[i] = number[n-i-1];
    number[n-i-1] = temp;
}
```

After reversing the array, it can be output. Since the output looks the same as when just outputting the array in reverse order without actually reversing the contents of the array, the difference between the two ways of approaching the problem might seem subtle to a beginning programmer. However, that is exactly the point that is trying to be made in the previous section. Just because the output might look the same does not mean the code has been written correctly. It is important to understand the specifications before attempting to write a program. Does the user or instructor just expect a listing in reverse order, or is there a plan to have subsequent code process the data in reverse order? Of the two, the second example is probably the better choice because if any subsequent code expects the array to be modified, it is important to actually reverse the array. A code segment illustrating the input, reversing, and output is given in Fig. 7.4.

```
int i,n;
final int ARRAYSIZE = 8;
int[] number;
number = new int[ARRAYSIZE];
System.out.print("Enter a non-negative integer ");
System.out.print("or a negative integer to stop: ");
temp = scanner.nextInt();
while(temp >= 0 && i < ARRAYSIZE) {
    number[i] = temp;
    System.out.print("Enter a non-negative integer ");
    System.out.print("or a negative integer to stop: ");
    temp = scanner.nextInt();
    i++;
}
n = i;
for(i=0; i<n/2; i++) {
    temp = number[i];
    number[i] = number[n-i-1];
    number[n-i-1] = temp;
}
System.out.println();
System.out.println("Reversed");
System.out.println();
for(i=0; i<n; i++)
    System.out.println("    " + number[i]);
```

Fig. 7.4 Code segment to input, reverse, and output

As can be seen, the segment uses a sentinel controlled loop to count and input the integers into the array and then copies the number of integers into n. It then reverses the integers in the array and lastly outputs the contents of the array.

7.6 Searching an Array

One of the benefits of storing data on a computer is that it can easily be retrieved. For example, once data has been placed into an array, it can subsequently be searched to see if a particular item is in the array. There are two common ways to search for data in an array, the sequential search and binary search.

7.6.1 Sequential Search

A sequential search is just as it sounds; the data in the array is searched in sequence from the beginning of the array to the end. It is similar to an instructor hunting for a particular exam in a stack of random exams on a desk, where he or she would start at the top of the pile of exams and proceed to the end. If he or she were lucky, in the best-case scenario, it might be the first one on the pile of exams. In the worst-case scenario, it would be the last one in the pile of exams. If there are n exams in the stack, it could take 1 to n times of picking up and looking at the exam to determine whether it is the correct one. However, usually it will be somewhere in between the first and last exams, and one could say that on average it will take $n/2$ times to find the exam. Of course, once the exam is found, there is no need to continue looking through the pile of exams and the searching can stop. Further, if the instructor is searching for more than one of the student's exams in the stack, then searching would continue until the end of the stack. Lastly, it is possible that the exam is not in the pile of exams, so in that case it is not found.

This is essentially the algorithm that can be used when performing a sequential search on an array. Searching through the pile of exams is equivalent to searching through an array which can be accomplished using a loop. If the number of items in the array is known, such as n, a for loop could be used. Then, each element in the array can be compared to the item being searched. However, once it is found, there is no reason to continue searching through the array, so the loop should stop before reaching the end. Since there are two reasons why the loop might stop, the for loop might not be the best choice. Although a for loop could be used, the code for it is rather unstructured and the while loop is probably the better choice. Once the item being searched for is found, a boolean flag can be set and checked in the while loop to indicate that further iteration is no longer necessary. What if there are duplicates in the array? The iteration would need to continue and the possibility of searching for duplicates is left as an exercise at the end of the chapter.

The name of the flag variable could be anything, but since it is indicating whether or not the item was found, the variable name found is a good one. Before entering the loop, the item has not been found, so the found flag can be initially set to false. The loop can then search until either the item is found or all the values in the array have been searched. Then, for each iteration of the loop, an if statement can compare whether the current item in the array is equal to the item being searched, and if so, the found flag is set to true. Otherwise, the found flag remains false. Assuming the array already contains various values, the code in Fig. 7.5 prompts for and inputs the value to be searched.

```
System.out.print("Enter the item to be searched for in the array: ");
item = scanner.nextInt();
found = false;
i=0;
while(i<n && !found)
    if(item == number[i])
        found = true;
    else
        i++;
if(found)
    System.out.prinln(item + " was found at location " + i);
else
    System.out.println(item + " was not found");
```

Fig. 7.5 Sequential search

When the execution of the code segment is complete, if item was found, then the found flag will be true and i will indicate the location it was found. If the item was not found in the array, the found flag will remain false. Note that an && is used in the while statement, because only while both i is less than n and found is false should the loop continue to iterate. Also notice that !found is used in the while loop instead of found != true or found == false. Since the found flag is a boolean variable, it will contain either true or false, so it is not necessary to compare it to true or false. Likewise, in the if statement after the while loop found == true is not used because if the found flag is true, it is unnecessary to compare it to true.

7.6.2 Binary Search

A sequential search is useful when items are in random order, but what if the data to be searched are not in random order? Returning to the pile of exams, what if they were in alphabetical order? Wouldn't it be easier and faster to find the particular exam in question? For example, if a person's last name began with the letter A, then it would appear toward the top of the stack of exams, and if a person's last name began with the letter Z, then it would appear toward the bottom. If someone's last name began with the letter T, it would not make sense to start at the top and work their way down. Although unlikely, it is possible that the stack of exams contains only people whose last names begin with the letters S through Z, so starting at the other end might not be a good idea either.

The safe route is to just split the stack of exams into two halves and determine whether the Ts are in the top half or the bottom half. In the case where the names on the exams begin with A through Z and in the middle is a name starting with the letter M, an exam with a name beginning with the letter T would be in the bottom half. In the case where the stack contains names that start with the letters S though Z, and if the name on the exam in the middle starts with the letter X, then the exam with the letter T would be in the top half. In either case, with just one comparison, the task of searching has been cut in half.

The beauty of this technique is that after the stack of exams has been cut in two, the process can be repeated. Using the first example with the second half of exams from M through Z, it could then be cut in half again, where maybe the middle exam has a name that starts with the letter S and again the letter T would be in the second half. When the half with names starting with S through Z is cut in half again, and assuming the middle exam has a name that starts with the letter V, then the letter T would be in the first half. If at any time when the stack is cut in half and the exam being searched for happens to be in the middle, the processing would stop. This process would continue until there is only one exam left, and if it is not the exam being searched for, then the exam is not found.

Consider the code segment in Fig. 7.6 which searches any array of integers. Notice that i is the lower index, j is the upper index, and mid is the middle position of the array to be searched.

```
System.out.print("Enter the item to be searched for in the array: ");
item = scanner.nextInt();
i = 0;
j = n - 1;
mid = (i + j) / 2;
while(i <= j && item != number[mid]) {
    if(item < number[mid])
        j = mid - 1;
    else
        i = mid + 1;
    mid = (i + j) / 2;
}
if(item == number[mid])
    System.out.println(item + " was found at location " + mid);
else
    System.out.println(item + " was not found");
```

Fig. 7.6 Binary search

Should item be the middle integer, then it is found. Otherwise, depending on if the item is less than or greater than the middle integer, j or i takes on the value of mid − 1 or mid + 1, respectively. The search continues until item is found in the middle or i is greater than j indicating that item is not in the array.

Note that whereas the sequential search can work with either unsorted or sorted data, the binary search can only work with sorted data. Further, if the data is unsorted, then only the sequential search can be used.

7.6.3 Elementary Analysis

Although at first the binary search might seem a little slow, it really is quite fast. For example, to make it simple, assume that there are 64 items (which is a power of 2) to be searched and the item is not in the list. When the array of 64 is cut in half, there would be 32 items to be searched. When 32 is cut in half, there are 16 to be searched, and 16 cut in half is 8. Half of 8 is 4, half of 4 is 2, and half of 2 is 1. The original stack of 64 is cut in half 6 times. That means with just 6 comparisons, the item would be found or not found in the worst-case scenario. With a sequential search, the worst-case scenario would take 64 times, where 6 is clearly better than 64.

When one is first learning about logarithms, they are usually in base 10. Recall that 10^3 is equal to 1,000 and $\log_{10} 1,000 = 3$. However, since the above example is a binary search and if one thinks about it, 2^6 is equal to 64 and $\log_2 64$ equals 6. One will find in computer science that many algorithms will be binary in nature so when one sees a logarithm, it will usually be $\log_2$. Further, should the subscript be missing, then in the field of computer science, it can usually be assumed that the default is $\log_2$.

Returning back to the binary search, it was seen that a group of 64 could be searched in 6 comparisons. If 1,024 integers were in an array, it would take just 10 comparisons in the worst case to find the item being searched, since 2^{10} equals 1,024 and $\log_2 1,024$ equals 10. This is much better than the sequential search which would take 1,024 comparisons to find an integer in an array in the worst case, and on average it would take 1,024/2 times which equals 512. What if the number of items being searched is not a power of two? For example, what if there were 1,000 items to be searched? The answer is that it would be no worse than the next highest power of two, which in this case would be 1,024.

So far, only concrete numbers have been used, but can this idea be generalized to an unknown number of items in an array? Yes, assume that there are n items in an array. If a sequential search were used, then the average case would be n / 2 and the worst case would be n, whereas with the binary search the worst case would be $\log_2$ n. This concept of comparing algorithms is a very important one in the field of computer science, where the relative speed of algorithms can be compared with each other. A common notation is to use the capital letter O to compare the relative order of magnitude of various algorithms, and the use of the capital letter O is called Big O notation (pronounced Big Oh). So in the worst case the sequential search is said to be of order n or O (n) and in the worst case the binary search is said to be of order log n, or O (log n). Although introduced here and used on occasion elsewhere in this text, this concept becomes much more frequent in subsequent courses such as a second course in computer science that examines data structures or a course on advanced data structures and/or algorithm analysis.

7.7 Sorting an Array

As has been seen, the binary search is much faster than the sequential search. Its disadvantage is that the data must be in order. But how does the data get in the proper order? One way is to have the data entered in the proper order to begin with. However, that would require a lot of effort on behalf of the person entering the data. Instead, wouldn't it be more convenient to just enter the data in any order and let the power of the computer do the work of sorting the data? The answer is yes as will be seen shortly.

There are many algorithms that have been developed to sort data. Some are sufficiently fast with small sets of data, but as the number of items to be sorted becomes larger, they are not very efficient. There are other algorithms that excel at large amounts of data but are not as efficient on smaller sets. There are still other algorithms that work well on data that has already been partially sorted, and others that are more efficient when the data is totally random. The more efficient an algorithm, the more complicated it is, and these are usually learned in subsequent computer science courses or texts. For now, this text will examine one of the simpler algorithms known as the bubble sort. As a way to help understand the bubble sort, this text breaks it into two separate sorting algorithms, where the basics are presented as the simplified bubble sort and then modified to help its efficiency, where the modified version is the true bubble sort.

7.7.1 Simplified Bubble Sort

Assuming one wants to sort data in ascending order (from the smallest to the largest), the bubble sort gets its name from the way the smaller values slowly move up toward the top of an array, as bubbles might slowly move up in a glass of soda. The bubble sort works by comparing pairs of adjacent integers and if the pair is out of order, swapping the two integers as shown in Fig. 7.7 which should be read from left to right, top to bottom.

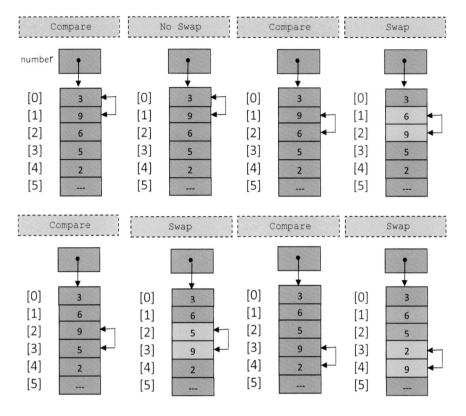

Fig. 7.7 First pass of the bubble sort

As can be seen, the first and second integers are compared, and if they are in the correct order, they remain as they are, but if the integers are out of order, they are swapped. This process is repeated for each pair of adjacent integers. Given an array of 5 data items, four pairs of integers are compared.

After the first pass through the array, note that the smallest integer has moved up one position. Also, note that the bottom integer in the array is now the largest one. After one pass, there is no need to subsequently compare the bottom integer. So when going through a second pass comparing the pairs of integers, the loop can iterate one less time.

But how many of these passes need to be made? If the first time through there are four pairs of integers to be compared and the second time there is one less integer to be sorted, then the second time through there would be only three pairs of numbers to be compared. It would follow that the third time through there would be two pairs and the fourth time there would be only one pair of integers to be compared. The result is that for 5 integers, there would be four passes through the array, each comparing one less pair of integers. If there were n integers in an array, then it would follow that n-1 passes would need to occur. To make this happen in a program, it should be apparent that a loop is needed. Further, the loop would need to iterate n-1 times. Since it is a number based on n, then a for loop would be a good choice.

If the number of passes needs a loop, it should seem clear that the comparison of the pairs of integers within each pass also needs a loop. However, the number of pairs of integers to be compared is different each time. How can this problem be resolved? Notice that the number of pairs of integers that need to be compared decreases by one each time. Is there a variable that could be used for this? If there are n-1 comparisons the first time, n-2 the second time, and so on, and further if the outer loop control variable, say i, is going from 0 to 3, then that variable could be used to determine the number of comparisons. So when i is 0 the first time, n-i-1 would be equal to 4; then when i is equal to 1 the second time, then n-i-1 would be equal to 3; and so on. The expression n-i-1 should look familiar from the code for reversing an array, and this expression comes in handy on many occasions.

Lastly, which two elements would need to be compared each time? Since i is used for the outer loop, then j could be used for the inner loop. So for the first time through when j is equal to 0, the 0th and 1st elements would be compared, which would be the j and j+1 elements, and when j is equal to 1, it would compare the 1st and 2nd elements and so on. The swap would be similar to the one developed in the previous section, except it would be between the two compared elements, j and j+1, as shown in the following code segment:

```
for(i=0; i<n-1; i++)
   for(j=0; j<n-i-1; j++)
       if(number[j]>number[j+1]) {
          temp = number[j];
          number[j]= number[j+1];
          number[j+1] = temp;
       }
```

The reader is encouraged to walk through the code segment to see how the algorithm works. Again, notice how the smallest number slowly moves or bubbles its way to the top of the array during each pass, thus giving the name to the bubble sort. To analyze the speed of this algorithm, it should be noticed that the outer loop iterates n-1 times. However, when doing analysis like this, the one less time than n that it loops is not very significant for a very large number n, so it is said to be of order n. The inner loop iterates one less time on each pass going from n-1 to 1 times, where it could be said that it loops on average n/2 times. But again, for a very large n, the division by two would still be a large number, so it is also said to be of order n. Recall from Chap. 4 that two nested loops each iterating n times the total number of iterations would be n*n, or n^2. Since in the current example, one loop is nested inside the other and also each loop is iterating approximately n times, this algorithm is of order n^2, or $O(n^2)$.

7.7.2 Modified Bubble Sort

In the previous simplified sorting algorithm, does it make any difference whether the data in the array is in reverse order, random order, or already sorted? The answer is no, because the outer loop will still iterate $n-1$ times and the inner loop will still iterate $n/2$ times. Although this does not make a difference if the array is in reverse order, nor does it make a lot of difference if the array is totally random, what if the array is already sorted? Granted this might not happen very often, but if it was already sorted, it would still take $O(n^2)$ to sort an already sorted array. Is there some way that this can be improved? During the first pass through the array, if there are no swaps between any of the pairs of elements, then it would be known that the array is already in order. Can the program be modified to take advantage of this scenario? Yes, a boolean flag can be used to indicate whether a swap has or has not occurred, and a good name for this flag is swap.

The first for loop could be replaced with a while loop that not only checks to see how many passes have occurred but also checks to see if a swap has occurred. If a swap has not occurred, then another pass is not necessary. Initially the swap flag could be set to true prior to any code to indicate that a swap has occurred. This would force the execution of the first time through the outer loop. The first thing to be done inside to the loop is to reset the swap flag to false, so in case there are no swaps during the inner loop, then no subsequent passes through the outer loop need to occur. Lastly, should a swap occur in the if statement, the swap flag is sent to true, thus forcing another pass through the outer loop:

```
swap = true;
i = 0;
while(i < n-1 && swap) {
    swap = false;
    for(j=0; j<n-i-1; j++)
        if(number[j] > number[j+1]) {
            swap = true;
            temp = number[j];
            number[j] = number[j+1];
            number[j+1] = temp;
        }
    i++;
}
```

As before, notice that swap is used in the while loop instead of swap == true or swap != false. Also notice the addition of the extra set of braces for the while loop, because now syntactically there are three statements in the body of the loop: the setting of swap to false, the for statement, and the increment of i. Lastly, notice that if there is more than one swap in the inner for loop, the swap is set repetitively to true. Although this seems a little redundant, it is quicker and easier to just keep setting swap back to true than adding code to check to see if it is already set to true.

The result is that if the data in the array is in reverse order, there is no increase in the speed of the algorithm. However, if the data is already in order, then there is only one pass through the outer loop, and the inner loop iterates $n-1$ times. So, this algorithm with data already sorted is O(n), and the bubble sort is one of the fastest sorting algorithms for data that is already in order. Although this might seem a little confusing to use a sorting algorithm with data that is already sorted, the algorithm also works fairly well for data that is close to being in order. If only a few items need to be swapped, then the outer loop will only iterate a few times, until there is a pass without any swaps, in which case the outer loop stops iterating. So in cases where data is possibly in order, or close to being in order, the bubble is a very good sort. However, for large amounts of data that is in reverse order, close to being in reverse order, or totally random, the bubble sort is not the best choice. As will be seen in later courses, there are a number of other sorting algorithms that can handle these situations much faster. Nonetheless for this text, the bubble sort provides a good starting point for understanding how sorting algorithms work and can be used to sort small sets of data.

7.8 Two-Dimensional Arrays

The preceding sections introduced how to declare variables for one-dimensional arrays, how to create them, and how to access elements in them. One-dimensional arrays work well when dealing with a set of data such as a collection of grades for one student. However, what if there are multiple sets of data, such as grades for several students? Then, the data could be stored in a two-dimensional array, which are sometimes called a 2D array.

7.8.1 Declaration, Creation, and Initialization

Suppose that there are four students in a class and they each took three exams. Instead of creating four separate one-dimensional arrays in order to record the exam scores for each student, one two-dimensional array can be used to store all the scores. Three exam scores for each student are kept in a row; therefore, there will be four rows and three columns in the table. Assume that the scores are of type `int` and the name of the array is `scores`. To declare a two-dimensional array, two sets of brackets are required. The first one is for the rows and the second one is for the columns as shown below:

```
int scores[][];
```

which is equivalent to

```
int[][] scores;
```

The two sets of brackets could be after or prior to the name of the array and the second example above is used more often. A diagram after the declaration is shown below:

The following creates a two-dimensional array of four by three integer values:

```
scores = new int[4][3];
```

The number 4 in the first set of brackets specifies the number of rows and the number 3 in the second set of the brackets specifies the number of columns. The diagram in Fig. 7.8 illustrates the array after its creation. Notice that a two-dimensional array is actually an array of one-dimensional arrays, meaning that it consists of an array in which each element is a one-dimensional array.

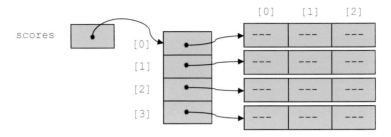

Fig. 7.8 After creation of 2D array

An array can be declared and created at the same time using the following statement:

```
int[][] scores = new int[4][3];
```

The diagram for the above statement is the same as that in Fig. 7.8. Again, in order to reinforce the concepts of declaration and allocation, two separate instructions are used in this text.

To access the data in a two-dimensional array, two subscripts or indices are used, one for the row number and the other for the column number. As in a one-dimensional array, each index is of type `int` and starts from 0 in the array. The first exam score of the first student is stored in `scores[0][0]`, the second exam score is stored in `scores[0][1]`, and the third exam score is stored in `scores[0][2]`. The scores for the second student are kept in `scores[1][0]`, `scores[1][1]`, and `scores[1][2]`. The scores for the third and fourth students are stored in a similar fashion. Suppose that the first student made a 72 on the first exam, an 85 on the second exam, and a 91 on the third exam. Then, the following statements store the scores for the first student in the appropriate positions in the array:

```
scores[0][0] = 72;
scores[0][1] = 85;
scores[0][2] = 91;
```

If the second student made 95, 89, and 90 on the three exams, the statements below will initialize the scores for the second student:

```
scores[1][0] = 95;
scores[1][1] = 89;
scores[1][2] = 90;
```

Scores for the third and fourth students can be entered in a similar manner. The diagram in Fig. 7.9 shows the two-dimensional array after the initialization.

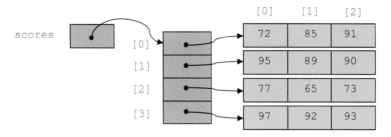

Fig. 7.9 After initialization of 2D array

Alternatively the following statement will declare, create, and initialize a two-dimensional array:

```
int[][] scores = {{72, 85, 91},
                  {95, 89, 90},
                  {77, 65, 73},
                  {97, 92, 93}};
```

The size of the array is determined by the number of values provided in the set of braces without explicitly specifying it inside the brackets. The diagram after the above statement is equivalent to the one in Fig. 7.9.

7.8.2 Input and Output

Although the techniques of assigning data used in the previous section are adequate for testing programs, how can the data be entered by the user? It is similar to a one-dimensional array, but instead of using a simple `for` loop, a nested `for` loop is used as shown below:

```
int[][] scores;
scores = new int[4][3];
for(int i=0; i<4; i++) {
   for(int j=0; j<3; j++) {
      System.out.print("Student " + (i+1) + ", exam "
      + (j+1) + ": ");
      scores[i][j] = scanner.nextInt();
   }
   System.out.println();
}
```

Notice that each position in the array can be accessed using two index variables, `i` and `j`, for the row number and the column number, respectively, inside the loop. A portion of the output with sample input is as follows:

```
Student 1, exam 1: 72
Student 1, exam 2: 85
Student 1, exam 3: 91

Student 2, exam 1: 95
Student 2, exam 2: 89
Student 2, exam 3: 90
```

. . .

Alternatively, the number of rows and columns could be entered by the user, and a two-dimensional array could then be created dynamically as discussed in Sect. 7.4. Once scores are in the array, one can output them using a nested `for` loop. Suppose three exam scores for each student are to be output in a row. The code segment below outputs the column labels first followed by the row labels and scores:

```
System.out.println("                    exam 1 exam 2 exam 3");
for(int i=0; i<4; i++) {
   System.out.print("Student " + (i+1));
   for(int j=0; j<3; j++)
      System.out.print("      " + scores[i][j]);
   System.out.println();
}
```

Notice that the print statement for the column headings is outside the nested `for` loop, since they are only output once. The print statement for the row label is located prior to the inner `for` loop, which means it is output every time the control variable `i` of the outer `for` loop changes. Also notice that three scores for each student are output on the same line using the `print` in the inner `for` loop. The `println` after the inner `for` loop moves the cursor to the next line for the next student. The output from the above code segment is as follows:

```
          exam 1 exam 2 exam 3
Student   1     72     85     91
Student   2     95     89     90
Student   3     77     65     73
Student   4     97     92     93
```

What if all the scores of thee exams need to be output line by line as shown below?

```
          Student 1  Student 2  Student 3  Student 4
exam   1     72         95         77         97
exam   2     85         89         65         92
exam   3     91         90         73         93
```

Again, a nested `for` loop can be used. In order to access all the scores in one column of the array before going to the next column, the column number has to remain the same in an outer `for` loop, while the row number is changing in the inner for loop. This is left as an exercise at the end of the chapter.

7.8.3 Processing Data

Using the array `scores`, how can the average of the three exam scores for the first student be calculated? All the scores for the first student are stored in the first row of the two-dimensional array. In order to find the average, the values in the first row have to be added together and divided by the number of exams. The following formula will find the average for the first student:

```
(scores[0][0] + scores[0][1] + scores[0][2])/3;
```

The average exam scores of other students can be found in the similar way. However, if the instructor would like to find the averages for a large class, it would not be efficient to list the formula for each student.

To process arrays, the `length` field is useful as discussed earlier in this chapter. When an array is created, a reference to the array is stored in the variable. At the same time, the length of the array is stored in an instance constant named `length`. For a one-dimensional array, the `length` holds the number of elements in the array. Since a two-dimensional array is an array of one-dimensional arrays, there are several `length` fields associated with it. They keep track of the number of rows and the number of columns for each row. With the array shown in Fig. 7.9, the length of the array `scores` can be obtained by `scores.length` which is the size of the one-dimensional array that the variable `scores` is referring to. In this case, the value would be 4 indicating the number of rows. As shown in Fig. 7.9, the elements of the array, `scores[0]`, `scores[1]`, `scores[2]`, and `scores[3]`, are references to one-dimensional arrays. Therefore, their length can be obtained by `scores[0].length`, `scores[1].length`, `scores[2].length`, and `scores[3].length`. Since it is a four by three array, all of them have a value of 3 indicating that the number of columns of the array `scores` is 3.

Returning back to finding the average of all the exam scores for the first student, a `for` loop can be used as shown below:

```
double total, average;
total = 0.0;
for(int j=0; j<3; j++)
    total = total + scores[0][j];
average = total/3;
```

The variable `total` contains the total of the three exam scores and the variable `average` holds the average. The variable `total` is initialized to `0.0` at the beginning, and inside the `for` loop, the three test scores, `scores[0][0]`, `scores[0][1]`, and `scores[0][2]`, are added together. The row number is fixed at 0 and the value of the index variable j changes from 0 to 2 accessing the scores of the first student. Since there are three exams, the `total` was divided by 3. Although the elements of the array `scores` are of type `int`, the value for `average` most likely requires more precision. Therefore, both the `total` and `average` were declared as type `double` in order to avoid integer division. Using the `length` field, the above code can be rewritten as

```
double total, average;
total = 0.0;
for(int j=0; j<scores[0].length; j++)
   total = total + scores[0][j];
average = total/scores[0].length;
```

Notice that `scores[0].length` gives the number of the columns of the two-dimensional array, which is 3 in this example, indicating the number of exams. How can the above code be changed to find the average exam scores of all four students? Since the formula to find the average is the same for all the students, a outer `for` loop can be used as shown below:

```
double total, average;
for(int i=0; i<4; i++) {
   total = 0.0;
   for(int j=0; j<scores[i].length; j++)
      total = total + scores[i][j];
   average = total/scores[i].length;
   System.out.printf("average for student " + (i+1) + ": %5.2f",
   average);
   System.out.println();
}
```

Notice that the outer `for` loop is used to specify the particular student. All the 0's in the brackets in the previous code indicating the first student are replaced by the index variable `i` which changes from 0 to 3 for the 4 students in the class. Of course, the value 4 can be replaced by the `length` field as shown below:

```
double total, average;
for(int i=0; i<scores.length; i++) {
   total = 0.0;
   for(int j=0; j<scores[i].length; j++)
      total = total + scores[i][j];
   average = total/scores[i].length;
   System.out.printf("average for student " + (i+1) + ": %5.2f",
   average);
   System.out.println();
}
```

The `scores.length` gives the number of rows of the two-dimensional array. In this example it is 4, which is the number of students. Assuming that the size of the array is the same as the number of student and exams, the advantage of using the `length` field is that no matter how many students or exams, the same code can be used to find the average.

The next question is can the average of the first, second, and third exams be found using a loop? The answer is yes. However, careful consideration should be taken concerning the order of the elements accessed in a two-dimensional array. In the previous example, the elements of the array were accessed in row-wise fashion. In order to find the average score for each exam, they have to be accessed in column-wise fashion. The key is the index variables `i` and `j`. In order to access all the data in one column, the column number has to remain the same while the row number is changing. The following code illustrates how the averages of the three exams are calculated:

```
double total, average;
for(int j=0; j<scores[0].length; j++) {
   total = 0.0;
   for(int i=0; i<scores.length; i++)
      total = total + scores[i][j];
   average = total/scores.length;
   System.out.printf("average for Exam " + (j+1) + ": %5.2f",
   average);
   System.out.println();
}
```

In the above code, the outer and inner `for` loops are swapped from the previous code segment, so that while the value of j remains the same, the value of i changes inside the inner `for` loop. Notice that the value of j changed from 0 to 2 indicating there are three exams. Even though the `scores[0].length` is used in the condition of the outer `for` loop, any of the values from `scores[1].length` through `scores[3].length` could be used since they all have the same value for the number of columns.

7.8.4 Passing a Two-Dimensional Array to and from a Method

A two-dimensional array can be passed to a method just as a one-dimensional array can be passed to a method. The following program implements a method that calculates and outputs the average of the exam scores for each student in the class. The `studentsAvg` method is called from the `main` method:

```
public class ExamScores {
   public static void main(String[] args){
      int[][] scores = {{72, 85, 91},
                        {95, 89, 90},
                        {77, 65, 73},
                        {97, 92, 93}};

      // method invocation
      studentsAvg(scores);
   }

   public static void studentsAvg(int[][] inArray) {
      double total, average;
      for(int i=0; i<inArray.length; i++) {
         total = 0.0;
         for(int j=0; j<inArray[i].length; j++)
            total = total + inArray[i][j];
         average = total/inArray[i].length;
         System.out.printf("average for student " + (i+1)
                           + ": %5.2f", average);
         System.out.println();
      }
   }
}
```

The output from the above code is shown below:

```
average for student 1: 82.67
average for student 2: 91.33
average for student 3: 71.67
average for student 4: 94.00
```

Alternatively, since a two-dimensional array is an array of one-dimensional arrays, each row can be passed to the method separately. The method `studentAvg` implemented below takes a one-dimensional array of exam scores for one student as a parameter, calculates the average, and returns it:

```
public static double studentAvg(int[] inRow) {
   double total, average;
   total = 0.0;
   for(int i=0; i<inRow.length; i++)
      total = total + inRow[i];
   average = total/inRow.length;
   return average;
}
```

How is the method above invoked? Since the method accepts an array of three scores for one student, as in `studentAvg(scores[0])`, it will return the average score for the first student. The average score for each student can be found by calling the method inside the loop as shown below:

```
double average;
for(int i=0; i<scores.length; i++) {
    average = studentAvg(scores[i]);
    System.out.printf("average for student " + (i+1) + ": %5.2f",
    average);
    System.out.println();
}
```

Notice that when the method `studentAvg` was called, `score[i]` was sent to the method as an argument. Further, it is an element of a one-dimensional array which has a reference to another one-dimensional array that has the scores for one student.

Just like a two-dimensional array can be sent to a method, it can be returned from a method. The following example shows how a two-dimensional array is created inside the method `getScores` and returned to the `main` method. There is no need to create an array in the `main` method after the declaration because the reference to the newly created array in the method `getScores` will be assigned to the variable `scores` when the flow of control returns from the method:

```
public class ExamScores {
    public static void main(String[] args){
        int[][] scores;
        scores = getScores();
    }

    public static int[][] getScores() {
        int[][] array = {{72, 85, 91},
                         {95, 89, 90},
                         {77, 65, 73},
                         {97, 92, 93}};
        return array;
    }
}
```

Notice that the return type of the method `getScores` is `int[][]`, which means it will return the reference to a two-dimensional array of `int` type.

7.8.5 Asymmetrical Two-Dimensional Arrays

Suppose that nonstop flights from several cities need to be recorded. A two-dimensional array can be used to keep this information. Each row can contain the list of destinations from a particular city. For example, there may be direct flights to Chicago, St. Louis, and Dallas/Fort Worth from City1, while Dallas/Fort Worth may be only the city reached from City2, and so on. It is possible that each city has a different number of nonstop flights to the destinations, which means that each row could have a different number of columns. Can a two-dimensional array have rows of unequal lengths? The answer is yes, because a two-dimensional array is an array of one-dimensional arrays and each one-dimensional array can be created separately using a different size. Before creating an asymmetrical two-dimensional array, consider the example from the previous section. Instead of creating an array `scores` using the following statements,

```
int[][] scores;
scores = new int[4][3];
```

a one-dimensional array of size 4 can be created first and then for each row a one-dimensional array of the size 3 can be created next as shown below:

```
int[][] scores;
scores = new int[4][];
scores[0] = new int[3];
scores[1] = new int[3];
scores[2] = new int[3];
scores[3] = new int[3];
```

The same thing can be accomplished using a loop.

```
int[][] scores;
scores = new int[4][];
for(int i=0; i<4; i++)
   scores[i] = new int[3];
```

Returning back to the flights example, the second alternative above can be used to create a two-dimensional array with rows of unequal lengths. Suppose there are three cities and the first city has three nonstop flights, the second city has one, and the third city has two. The following will declare and create an array `city`:

```
String[][] city;
city = new String[3][];
city[0] = new String[3];
city[1] = new String[1];
city[2] = new String[2];
```

The code below will assign values (ORD for Chicago, STL for St. Louis, and DFW for Dallas/Fort Worth) in the one-dimensional array for the first city:

```
city[0][0] = "ORD";
city[0][1] = "STL";
city[0][2] = "DFW";
```

Alternatively the following statement will accomplish declaration, creation, and initialization in one statement:

```
String[][] city = {{"ORD", "STL", "DFW"},
                    {"DFW"},
                    {"ORD", "DFW"}};
```

The following diagram shows the array `city`:

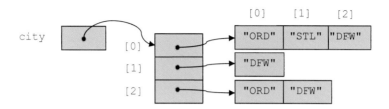

Two-dimensional arrays are examples of multidimensional arrays. The same principle can be applied to *n*-dimensional arrays, where *n* can be any integer value. A three-dimensional array is left as an exercise at the end of the chapter.

7.9 Arrays of Objects

Looking at the scores example from Sect. 7.8, the two-dimensional array `scores` keeps only students' exam scores. It would be nice if the names of the students were associated with their scores. So far arrays with only primitive data types, strings, and arrays have been discussed. As seen in the preceding sections, an array is a collection of data of the same type regardless of the number of dimensions. Therefore, the scores of type `int` and the student names of type `String` cannot be stored together in a simple array, because a two-dimensional array whose columns contain values of different data types is not allowed.

To get around this problem, a one-dimensional array of `String` type can be used for the name along with a two-dimensional array `scores`. The array could be declared as `studentName` which would be of size 4 containing the names of four students. The three scores in the one-dimensional array `scores[0]` would correspond to the student at `studentName[0]`, the scores in `scores[1]` would be made by the student at `studentName[1]`, and so on. This technique of using two separate arrays, called parallel arrays, is useful when a programming language does not support objects or other structures.

In Java, instead of using parallel arrays, associated data can be encapsulated into an object, and a one-dimensional array of these objects can be created. Objects that represent the name of the student and the test scores can be described by the class `Student`. The name of the student and their test scores will be declared as instance variables, and a constructor and four accessors for each data member are defined in the class `Student` as shown below:

```
public class Student {
   private String name;
   private int exam1, exam2, exam3;

   public Student(String name, int score1, int score2, int score3) {
      this.name = name;
      exam1 = score1;
      exam2 = score2;
      exam3 = score3;
   }

   public String getName() {
      return name;
   }

   public int getExam1() {
      return exam1;
   }

   public int getExam2() {
      return exam1;
   }

   public int getExam3() {
      return exam1;
   }
}
```

In the `main` method, a one-dimensional array of type `Student` is declared, and an array of size four is created using the following statements:

```
Student[] scores;
scores = new Student[4];
```

The execution of the above code will result in the diagram shown below:

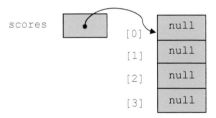

Notice that only the array is created and the elements of the array `scores` are initially `null`. Therefore, each individual object has to be created and the reference to it has to be placed in the array. Each object of type `Student` will contain the last name of the student and three test scores. The following statement will create an object and assign the reference to the object to the first position of the array, `scores[0]`:

```
scores[0] = new Student("Fonteyn", 72, 85, 91);
```

Similar statements will be used to place the other students in the array. Figure 7.10 illustrates the array of objects.

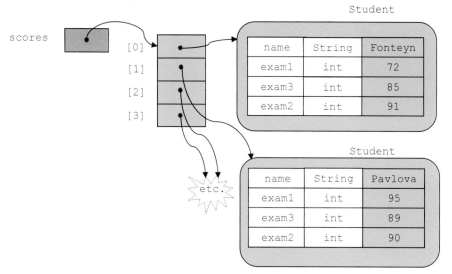

Fig. 7.10 Array `scores` with four objects of the type `Student`

The following program will output the contents of the array `scores`, using a loop and accessors:

```
public class ExamScores {
    public static void main(String[] args){
        Student[] scores;
        scores = new Student[4];
        scores[0] = new Student("Fonteyn", 72, 85, 91);
        scores[1] = new Student("Pavlova", 95, 89, 90);
        scores[2] = new Student("Baryshnikov", 77, 65, 73);
        scores[3] = new Student("Nureyev", 97, 92, 93);

        System.out.printf("%12s%11s%11s%11s",
                        "Name", "Exam 1", "Exam 2", "Exam 3");
        System.out.println();
        for(int i=0; i<scores.length; i++) {
            System.out.printf("%12s%11d%11d%11d", scores[i].getName(),
                        scores[i].getExam1(),
                        scores[i].getExam2(),
                        scores[i].getExam3());
            System.out.println();
        }
    }
}
```

Notice that `scores[i]` refers to an object of type `Student` in the array `scores`. Here an indexed expression is used to refer to an object instead of a simple variable. Therefore, the same syntax can be used to call the object's method such as in `scores[i].getName()`. The output from the above code is shown below:

Name	Exam 1	Exam 2	Exam 3
Fonteyn	72	85	91
Pavlova	95	89	90
Baryshnikov	77	65	73
Nureyev	97	92	93

The average test scores of each student or each exam can be calculated using the accessors defined in the class `Student`.

7.10 Complete Program: Implementing an Array

Using an array, a program which calculates the standard deviation of a set of data will be developed in this section. The program will:

* Allow the user to enter the number of items and the actual data
* Compute the standard deviation of the data
* Display the standard deviation

The standard deviation, represented by the symbol sigma, σ, is a measure of the spread of the data. If the distribution is roughly bell shaped and symmetric, then most of the data, approximately 68 %, lie within one standard deviation of the mean between (*mean* – σ) and (*mean* + σ), and almost all the data, approximately 95 %, lie within two standard deviations of the mean between (*mean* – 2σ) and (*mean* + 2σ). The definition of the standard deviation is

$$\sigma = \sqrt{\frac{1}{n}\sum_{i=1}^{n}\left(x_i - \bar{x}\right)^2}$$

First, the mean $\bar{x}$ is determined, which is the sum of the data divided by the number of data values. Then, the mean is subtracted from every number $\left(x_i - \bar{x}\right)$ to get the list of deviations. Next, the resulting deviations are squared giving $\left(x_i - \bar{x}\right)^2$. Then, the squares are added to get their sum $\sum_{i=1}^{n}\left(x_i - \bar{x}\right)^2$. The result is divided by the number of items in the list to get the variance. Lastly, to obtain the standard deviation, the square root of the variance is calculated.

If only the mean of the numbers was to be calculated, there is no reason to store the data in an array. Inside a loop the numbers the user enters can be summed and then the average can be computed outside the loop. However, to find the standard deviation, the data must be stored in some way because the deviations need to be calculated by the formula $\left(x_i - \bar{x}\right)$ using the mean and the original data.

Declaring variables to store all the numbers is one way, but using an array is a better solution when the size of the data is large. Assuming that the numbers are all stored in an array named `array`, the following code will find the mean of the numbers in the array:

```
total = 0;
for(int i=0; i<array.length; i++)
    total = total + array[i];
mean = total/array.length;
```

The next step is to square each of the differences and add them together as shown below:

```
total = 0;
for(int i=0; i<array.length; i++)
    total = total + Math.pow(array[i] - mean, 2);
```

Note that the method `pow` from the `Math` class is useful here. The following code calculates the variance by dividing the total by the number of items in the array:

```
variance = total/array.length;
```

Finally, the standard deviation can be computed by taking the square root of the variance as illustrated below:

```
sigma = Math.sqrt(variance);
```

Notice another method `sqrt` in the `Math` class is used here. In the complete program, three methods are defined to get data from the user, calculate the standard deviation, and output the result. These three methods, `getData`, `computeStdDev`, and `outputStdDev`, will be called from the `main` method. The complete program is shown below:

```java
import java.util.*;

public class StandardDeviation {
    public static void main(String[] args){
        //declaration of variables
        int[] data;
        double sigma;

        // input data
        data = getData();

        // compute standard deviation
        sigma = computeStdDev(data);

        // output standard deviation
        outputStdDev(sigma);
    }

    // input data
    public static int[] getData() {
        Scanner scanner = new Scanner(System.in);
        int size;
        int[] array;

        // input number of data
        System.out.print("Enter the number of data: ");
        size = scanner.nextInt();

        // create array
        array = new int[size];

        // initialize array
        for(int i=0; i<size; i++) {
            System.out.print("Enter the data " + (i+1) + ": ");
            array[i] = scanner.nextInt();
        }

        return array;
    }
```

6. Write the following code segments concerning a three-dimensional array.

    A. Write a statement to declare a 3 by 2 by 5 three-dimensional array of type `int`.

    B. Write a statement to create the array declared in the previous question.

    C. Using `i`, `j`, and `k` as index variables, write a code segment to store the value `i*j*k` in every position of the three-dimensional array created previously.

*7. Using the array `scores` discussed in Sect. 7.8.2, write a code segment to output all the exam scores stored in the array. Each row should contain scores for all four students as shown below:

```
           Student 1   Student 2   Student 3   Student 4
exam 1        72          95          77          97
exam 2        85          89          65          92
exam 3        91          90          73          93
```

8. Using the array `scores` discussed in Sect. 7.8, write a method to find the average for a particular exam. The method should take a reference to a two-dimensional array and a column number as arguments. Then, implement a `main` method to find the average for each exam by calling a method inside a loop and output them.

9. Using the array `scores` discussed in Sect. 7.9, write a code segment to find the lowest score in the entire array and output it.

10. Using the array `scores` discussed in Sect. 7.9, write a code segment to find the highest score for each exam and output the score along with the student's name.

11. Write a code segment to perform a sequential search on a one-dimensional array. Assume that the set of data could contain duplicates. If the item being searched for is found in the array, record the number of the occurrences also.

12. Develop a program to store names in a one-dimensional array. The program should initially create a one-dimensional array which holds ten `String` values. As the user enters names one by one, each name will be stored in the array. Whenever the array becomes full, create a new array that is twice the size of the previous array, copy the data over to the new array, and continue input.

13. Write a complete program to create an array of `Card` object discussed in Sect. 5.6.2. The program should ask a user for the number of cards and using a loop to initialize each card. Perform a couple of transactions on each card and then output the current balance of each card.

8
Recursion

James T. Streib[a]* and Takako Soma[a]

[a] Computer Science Program, Illinois College, Jacksonville, IL, USA

Abstract

This chapter examines recursion using contour diagrams. The power function and Fibonacci numbers are used as examples. In addition to contour diagrams, stack frames and a tree of calls are shown as alternative ways of visualizing the recursive process. As with other chapters, a complete program is provided.

Keywords

Recursive Call; Power Function; Fibonacci Numbers; Stack Frames, Tree of Calls, Greatest Common Divisor.

8.1 Introduction

In Chap. 4 , the topic of iteration was discussed as a way to solve various problems using loop structures. In this chapter, an alternative method to solve similar problems using *recursion* is presented. Whereas iteration tends to use less memory and is faster, recursion tends to use more memory and is slower. If recursion is not as efficient in terms of speed and memory, why would one want to use it? The reason is that some problems lend themselves better to a recursive solution than to an iterative solution. Many mathematical solutions are expressed more clearly using a recursive definition, and many data structures and algorithms can be written easier using recursion resulting in a less complicated program.

Since many programmers learn iteration first, sometimes the subsequent change to recursion can be a little difficult, although the reverse can be true as well. However, by using simple examples and contours, this transition can be made easier. With time and practice, one learns that recursion is a powerful tool for solving complex problems.

8.2 The Power Function

Recall from Sect. 4.4 the assumption that Java did not contain the `pow` method in the `Math` class, so a `for` loop was used to calculate the power function, x^n. As a brief review, the iterative solution to the problem began by initializing the variable `answer` to `1`, used a `for` loop that iterated `n` times, and each time through the loop the variable `answer` was multiplied by `x`.

Just as there was a pattern to finding an iterative solution, there is a pattern to solving a problem recursively. As with iteration, recursion also needs three parts: initialization, test, and change. However, instead of typically starting the first case with the number `1` and working forward as with iteration, in a sense recursion tends to look at the last case and

© The Author(s), under exclusive license to Springer Nature Switzerland AG 2023
J. T. Streib and T. Soma, *Guide to Java*, Undergraduate Topics in Computer Science,
https://doi.org/10.1007/978-3-031-22842-1_8

work backward. So instead of starting at 1, recursion starts with the largest number as its initialization. As with iteration, it helps first to see if a pattern can be found using specific values. For example, assume x is equal to 2 for the power function x^n with the pattern presented in Sect. 4.4 repeated below:

$2^0 = 1$
$2^1 = 1 * 2 = 2$
$2^2 = 1 * 2 * 2 = 4$
$2^3 = 1 * 2 * 2 * 2 = 8$
.

.

$2^n = 1 * 2 * 2 * 2 * \ldots * 2$ (n times)

First, note that 2^3 is equal to $1*2*2*2$ and that 2^2 is equal to $1*2*2$. Given this, couldn't the definition of 2^3 be thought of in terms of 2^2? In other words, couldn't $1*2*2*2$ be defined as $2^2 *2$? The answer is yes, where 2^2 can substitute for the $1*2*2$ portion of $1*2*2*2$ and 2^3 can be defined recursively in terms of 2^2. This process can continue, where 2^2 can be defined as $2^1 *2$ and 2^1 can be defined as $2^0 *2$. Just as something needs to change in the body of a loop, this is the change portion of recursion.

Given there can be an infinite loop in iteration, there can also be "infinite" recursion. However, instead of looping forever, the program would recurse trying to solve the power function in terms of 2^{-1}, 2^{-2}, and so on until there is no more memory. Just as there needs to be a test to ensure that iteration does not continue indefinitely, there needs to be a test so that recursion does not continue indefinitely. Since 2^0 equals 1, this is where recursion should stop and this is often known as the base case or terminal case. Rewriting part of the pattern from above, it would look as follows:

$2^0 = 1$
$2^1 = 2^0 * 2 = 2$
$2^2 = 2^1 * 2 = 4$
$2^3 = 2^2 * 2 = 8$

This is good for 2^3, but what about 2^n? Looking at the above pattern, notice that each time the value for n is decreased by 1. Again, note that $2^3 = 2^2 *2$, $2^2 = 2^1 *2$, and so on. In terms of n, this can be rewritten as $2^n = 2^{n-1} *2$, so the last line of the original definition could be

$2^n = 2^{n-1} * 2$

Further, instead of using 2 for x, the entire definition could be rewritten in terms of x as follows:

$x^0 = 1$
$x^1 = x^0 * x$
$x^2 = x^1 * x$
$x^3 = x^2 * x$
.

.

$x^n = x^{n-1} * x$

However, the above still looks like an iterative definition, and there is a much more concise way of writing a recursive definition. For the sake of convenience, it helps to assume that neither x nor n is negative and that x and n are not both 0, since 0^0 is undefined. Then for all cases where n is greater than 0, the last line could be used. In the case where n is 0, the first line could be used as the base or terminal case. The resulting recursive definition is as follows:

$$x^n = \{\text{if } n > 0, \text{ then } x^{n-1} * x, \text{ otherwise } 1\}$$

This forms the basis of the method which could be written as follows:

```
public static int power(int x, int n) {
   int answer;
   if (n > 0)
      answer = power(x,n-1)*x;
   else
      answer = 1;
   return answer;
}
```

Notice the method is declared as `static`, so that a class does not need to be defined nor does an object need to be created as discussed in _Chap. 5_. Further, note that a local variable `answer` has been declared. As will be discussed later, this will waste memory in recursion, but for now using a memory location will be very helpful in tracing through the program using contour diagrams. After the code is understood using contours, the method can be rewritten to save memory as will be shown later. More importantly, notice that the `power` method is calling itself. Is that legal? Yes it is, but as discussed above, there needs to be a way to stop the recursion, and that is the purpose of the else section and the terminal case of `answer=1`. Of course a main program will need to be written to drive the method as shown in Fig. 8.1 with line numbers to help facilitate seeing the code execute via contours.

```
import java.util.*;                                    // Line 1
class Ch8Sample1 {                                     // Line 2
   public static void main(String[] args){             // Line 3

      Scanner scanner;                                 // Line 4
      scanner = new Scanner(System.in);                // Line 5

      int x,n,answer;                                  // Line 6

      System.out.println();                            // Line 7
      System.out.print("Enter an integer for x: ");    // Line 8
      x = scanner.nextInt();                           // Line 9
      System.out.print("Enter an integer for n: ");    // Line 10
      n = scanner.nextInt();                           // Line 11

      System.out.println();                            // Line 12

      if(x>=0 && n>=0 && !(x==0 && n==0)) {            // Line 13
         answer = power(x,n);                           // Line 14
         System.out.println("The answer is " + answer);// Line 15
      }                                                // Line 16
      else                                             // Line 17
         System.out.println("Power not calculated");    // Line 18
   }                                                   // Line 19

   public static int power(int x, int n) {             // Line 20
      int answer;                                      // Line 21
      if(n > 0)                                         // Line 22
         answer = power(x,n-1)*x;                        // Line 23
      else                                             // Line 24
         answer = 1;                                    // Line 25
      return answer;                                    // Line 26
   }                                                   // Line 27

}                                                      // Line 28
```

Fig. 8.1 main program and power method

Before calling the power method, notice that the main program checks whether x is greater than or equal to 0, that n is greater than or equal to 0, and that x and n are not both 0. It is often best to first test the base case to ensure that it is working properly. So to start, assume that the user has entered a value of 2 for x and 0 for n. Since n is not greater than 0, there should be no recursion, and answer is assigned a value of 1 which is returned to the main program and output. Because this is a simple instance, a contour will not be written for this case.

However, what if x is equal to 3 and n is equal to 2? This is when things start to get interesting and contours are very helpful. Figure 8.2 shows the state of execution just prior to Line 22 in power.

Ch8Sample1

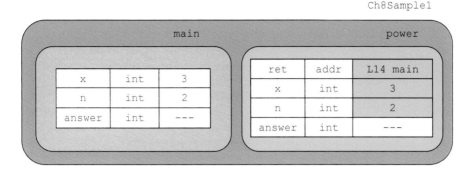

Fig. 8.2 Contour prior to the execution of Line 22 in the first call to power

As discussed in Chap. 1 , although typically the contour for Ch8Sample1 would not be drawn, it is helpful to see it in this case. Since the power method is static, notice that an object is not created nor is there a reference to an object. Instead, the contour for power is drawn in the class Ch8Sample1, just as the main method which is also declared as static. As can be seen in the contour for power, there is a new cell called ret. This is not the value returned from a method, but rather indicates where the method will return upon completion. Whereas previously it was fairly clear where a method was returning, with recursion and its multiple calls, it might not be so obvious. The ret cell also has listed a type of addr which is an abbreviation for address. Although there is not a type associated with this cell as there is with other variables and parameters, the address is the place where the flow of control will be transferred when the method is finished. Lastly, note that the line number is abbreviated as L14 and the name of the method main is included in the cell. Although in this case it should be apparent that Line 14 is in main, indicating the name of the method will be important as will be seen shortly.

Since n is greater than 0, once Line 23 has begun to execute, the first thing that needs to be done is recursively call the power function. Figure 8.3 shows the state of execution just prior to Line 22 in the second call to the power method.

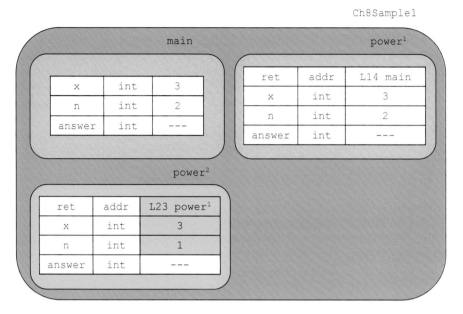

Fig. 8.3 Contour prior to the execution of Line 22 in the second call to `power`

As can be seen, there are now two contours depicting the `power` method. Similar to when there was more than one object of the same type in Chap. 5, notice that superscripts have again been employed to distinguish between the two contours. Also note that when calling `power` a second time, the value of n has been decremented by 1. Lastly, notice that the `ret` field points back to Line 23 in the first call to `power`. Of course, when Line 22 in the second call to `power` is executed, n is still greater than 0, and there is another call to `power` as shown in Fig. 8.4 illustrating the state of execution prior to Line 22.

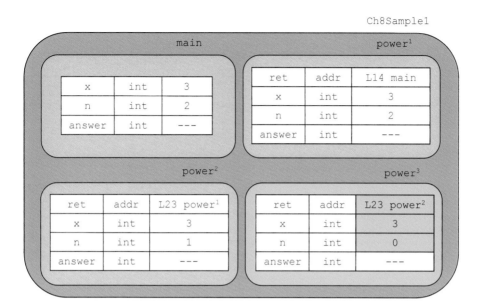

Ch8Sample1

Fig. 8.4 Contour prior to the execution of Line 22 in the third call to `power`

The third contour has now been added, where the return is to Line 23 in the second call to `power` and n is equal to 0. This time when Line 22 is executed, n is no longer greater than 0, but rather equal to 0, so instead of making the recursive call in the then section of the `if` statement, the else section is executed. This is the terminal case and no more recursive calls will occur. Instead 1 is assigned to `answer`, and Fig. 8.5 shows the state of execution prior to Line 26 in the third call to `power`.

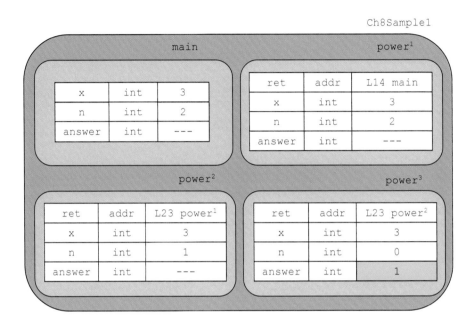

Fig. 8.5 Contour prior to the execution of Line 26 in the third call to `power`

After the execution of Line 26, the value in `answer` is returned to Line 23 in the second call to `power`. Then the value 1 is multiplied by the value 3 in `x`. The result is then placed into the variable `answer`, and Fig. 8.6 shows the state of execution prior to Line 26 in the second call to `power`.

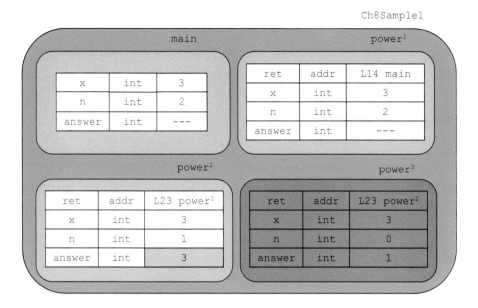

Ch8Sample1

Fig. 8.6 Contour prior to the execution of Line 26 in the second call to `power`

Of course, the first thing one notices is that the contour for the third call to `power` is now shaded light red to indicate that it is deallocated. Also, the value 3 is in `answer` ready to be returned to the first call to `power`. As before, contours can simply be erased as done in Fig. 8.7 which shows the state of execution prior to Line 26 in the first call to `power`.

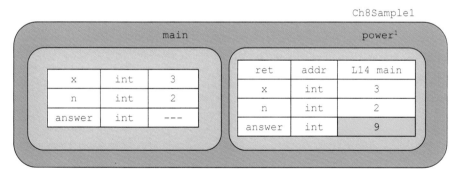

Ch8Sample1

Fig. 8.7 Contour prior to the execution of Line 26 in the first call to `power`

Notice that the value 3 returned from the second call to `power` has been multiplied by the value 3 in `x` and the result 9 is placed in `answer`. The flow of control continues to Line 26, and the value 9 is returned back to the calling program. The 9 is then placed into answer as illustrated in Fig. 8.8 which shows the state of execution just prior to Line 15 in main.

Ch8Sample1

main		
x	int	3
n	int	2
answer	int	9

Fig. 8.8 Contour prior to the execution of Line 15 in the first call to main

Looking back at the base case in Fig. 8.5, notice that there were a lot of memory locations used to find answer in Fig. 8.8. If recursion takes up so much memory, why use it? Again, some problems are more naturally expressed using recursion than iteration. Further, with memory being much less expensive than it was in the past, the use of recursion is much less costly. Still, some larger problems can use quite a bit of memory, and there are some techniques to cut down on its usage. For example, the previous method used a variable answer each time a contour was created. Instead of assigning the result of the calculation to a variable, it can simply be returned to the calling method as shown in the following segment:

```
public static int power(int x, int n) {
   if (n > 0)
      return power(x,n-1)*x;
   else
      return 1;
}
```

Of course, the method uses two return statements, which is considered unstructured programming. Again, if memory is a concern, this might be a justifiable trade-off. It is often helpful to initially write an algorithm with some built-in inefficiencies to ensure that it is working properly and then optimize the code, rather than initially try to optimize the code and risk, creating a code that does not work correctly in the first place.

8.3 Stack Frames

Notice that each time a recursive call occurs, another contour is drawn, and each time a new contour is created, more memory is used. Contours are helpful in understanding of the process of recursion. But how is this actually accomplished in the computer? It is done using a *stack*. A stack is known as a LIFO structure, which stands for Last In First Out. That means that the last item put on the stack is the first one taken off the stack, not unlike a stack of papers on a desk. The process of putting an item on a stack is known as a push operation, and the task of removing an item is known as a pop operation.

When a method is called the first time, the values are stored in the variables, like when the first contour is drawn. However, in the program there is only one set of variables. What would happen when there is a recursive call to a method? What happens to the values in the variables? Instead of drawing a new contour, the variables in the contour need to be reused. The result is that all the variables in the method, along with some other possible information associated with the method, form what is known as a stack frame and it is pushed onto the stack. Once the values from the variables are stored on the stack, new values can now be stored in the variables. Each time there is another recursive call, the process is repeated. When there is a terminal case, the process reverses itself. As a simple example, assume there is only one recursive call. The values are pushed onto the stack and the variables reused. Then after the terminal case, the values can be popped off the stack and be placed back into the variables, and the processing can complete.

Using the same example from the previous section calculating 3^2 and using only a partial contour diagram, Fig. 8.9 is the state of execution just prior to Line 26 in the program in Fig. 8.1 in the third call to `power`.

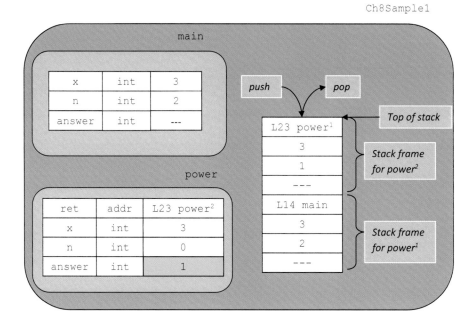

Fig. 8.9 Contour and stack prior to the execution of Line 26 in the third call to power

Figure 8.9 corresponds to Fig. 8.5 in Sect. 8.1. Note first that there is only one contour for power. Even though it represents power[3], it is just labeled power since the contour is used for all calls to power. As each call is made, the contents of the power contour are pushed onto the stack. When power[1] called power[2], the variables in power[1] were pushed onto the stack so that power[2] could use the variables in the contour. Then when power[3] was called, the contents for power[2] were pushed onto the stack so that power[3] could use the contour. Once power[3] is ready to return to power[2], the stack frame for power[2] is popped off the stack and put back into the contour, and so on. Simply stated, each new contour created after the first one means another stack frame needs to be pushed onto the stack, and each time a contour is deallocated, that means that a stack frame is popped off the stack.

Note that the names of the cells and their types are not pushed onto the stack, but only the contents are pushed onto the stack. However, also notice that the order in which they are pushed is the same as they occur in the contour so one can determine which cell is which. Although one could draw the stack with the other information, it gets a little cumbersome, and this is one of the reasons why contours are sometimes a little more convenient.

But wasn't it said that each recursive call wastes memory? The answer is yes, because the stack is implemented in the computer's memory and each time a stack frame is pushed onto the stack, more memory is used. If infinite recursion occurs, oftentimes a message will be output saying something to the effect that there is a stack overflow, meaning that the stack is full and no memory is available to push more items onto the stack.

Notice that using contours and stack frames are just two ways of looking at the same process. Although the stack frame model is more accurate, it is a little more cumbersome to draw, whereas the contour model is easier to draw and makes it easier to keep track of previous values. The importance of keeping track of previous values will become even more apparent in the next section with a more involved use of recursion.

8.4 Fibonacci Numbers

Another example of the use of recursion is the calculation of Fibonacci numbers that one may have encountered in a mathematics course. The Fibonacci numbers can be defined as follows:

Fibonacci(0) = 0
Fibonacci(1) = 1
Fibonacci(2) = 0 + 1 = 1
Fibonacci(3) = 1 + 1 = 2
Fibonacci(4) = 1 + 2 = 3
Fibonacci(5) = 2 + 3 = 5
Fibonacci(6) = 3 + 5 = 8

Although this is an iterative definition, it can help in the finding of a recursive definition. First, notice the base or terminal cases for 0 and 1. Then notice that any other given line is the addition of the two previous lines. For example, Fibonacci(6) is the sum of the numbers 3 and 5, which are the answers for the fourth and fifth Fibonacci numbers. In other words, couldn't Fibonacci(6) be defined in terms of adding Fibonacci(5) and Fibonacci(4)? The answer is yes, but what would the nth Fibonacci number look like? It would be as follows:

Fibonacci(n) = Fibonacci(n − 1) + Fibonacci(n − 2)

Putting the base case and the nth case together, the definition of the Fibonacci numbers for nonnegative integers would be as follows:

Fibonacci(n) = { if n = 0 or n = 1, then n,
otherwise Fibonacci(n−1) + Fibonacci(n−2) }

Given this definition, the code can then be written. As in the previous sections, it helps to use local variables to make the reading of contour diagrams easier.

```
public static int fib(int n) {
    int answer1,answer2,answer;
    if (n > 1) {
        answer1 = fib(n-1);
        answer2 = fib(n-2);
        answer = answer1 + answer2;
    }
    else
        answer = n;
    return answer;
}
```

Again notice that the method is static and the name of the method is fib to save space in subsequent contour diagrams. Putting the above method together with a main program and adding Line numbers results in the program in Fig. 8.10.

```
import java.util.*;                                           // Line 1
class Ch8Sample2 {                                            // Line 2
   public static void main(String[] args){                    // Line 3

      Scanner scanner;                                         // Line 4
      scanner = new Scanner(System.in);                        // Line 5

      int n,answer;                                            // Line 6

      System.out.println();                                    // Line 7
      System.out.print("Enter an integer for n: ");            // Line 8
      n = scanner.nextInt();                                   // Line 9
      System.out.println();                                    // Line 10

      if (n >= 0){                                             // Line 11
         answer = fib(n);                                      // Line 12
         System.out.println("The answer is " + answer);        // Line 13
      }                                                        // Line 14
      else                                                     // Line 15
         System.out.println("Fibonacci not calculated");       // Line 16

      System.out.println();                                    // Line 17
   }                                                           // Line 18

   public static int fib(int n) {                              // Line 19
      int answer1,answer2,answer;                              // Line 20
      if (n > 1) {                                             // Line 21
         answer1 = fib(n-1);                                   // Line 22
         answer2 = fib(n-2);                                   // Line 23
         answer = answer1 + answer2;                           // Line 24
      }                                                        // Line 25
      else                                                     // Line 26
         answer = n;                                           // Line 27
      return answer;                                           // Line 28
   }                                                           // Line 29

}                                                              // Line 30
```

Fig. 8.10 Fibonacci program

The main program checks for a negative number before calling the fib method. In the case where the input of n is either a 0 or 1, the result is just a simple call to the terminal case, and a corresponding value of 0 or 1 is returned to the main program and output. However, more interesting is a nonterminal case, such as when n is equal to 3. Figure 8.11 shows the state of execution just prior to Line 21 in the first call to fib.

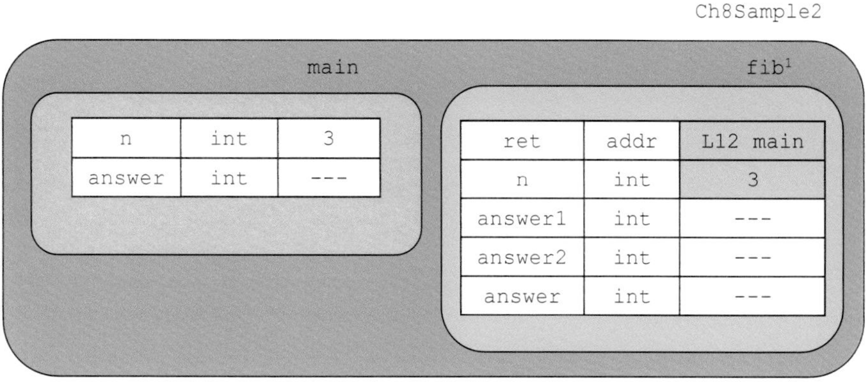

Fig. 8.11 Contour prior to the execution of Line 21 in the first call to `fib`

As before, notice `L12 main` in the `ret` cell and the superscript for `fib` indicating the first call. Since 3 is greater than 1, the then portion of the `if` is taken. Then a recursive call is made as shown in Fig. 8.12 just prior to the execution of Line 21 in the second call to `fib`.

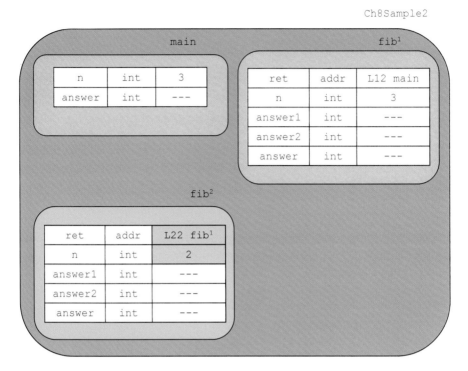

Fig. 8.12 Contour prior to the execution of Line 21 in the second call to `fib`

In the second call to `fib`, the parameter n has been decremented by 1. Since 2 is greater than 1, another call is made, and Fig. 8.13 shows the state of execution prior to Line 21 in the third call to `fib`.

Ch8Sample2

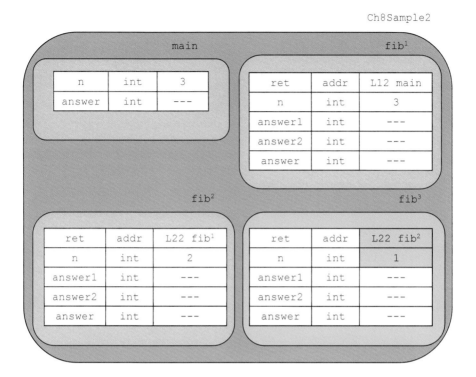

Fig. 8.13 Contour prior to the execution of Line 21 in third call to `fib`

At Line 21, since `n` is no longer greater than `1` and the condition for the `if` statement is `false`, the else portion is executed and `answer` is set to `1`. This value is then returned to Line 22 in the second call to `fib`, and the value `1` is stored in the variable `answer1` as shown in Fig. 8.14 just prior to the execution of Line 23.

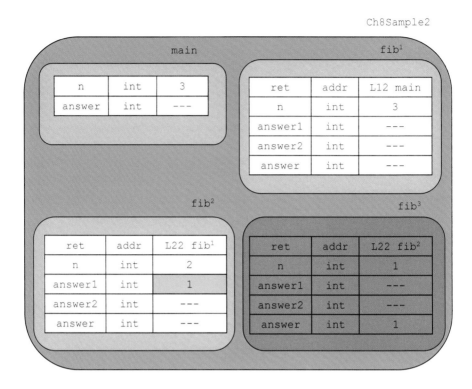

Fig. 8.14 Contour prior to the execution of Line 23 in the second call to `fib`

Notice that the variable `answer` in the third call to `fib` is 1 and that the contour is shaded light red. Further, note that there are no values in `answer1` and `answer2` in the third call to `fib`, because it was a terminal case and no recursive calls were made. Again, notice the value 1 has been returned to the second call to `fib` and stored in `answer1`. However, instead of the flow of control returning back to the first call to `fib` as it did in the `power` example, there is another call to `fib` to calculate `answer2`. So Fig. 8.15 shows the state of execution prior to Line 21 in the fourth call to `fib`.

Ch8Sample2

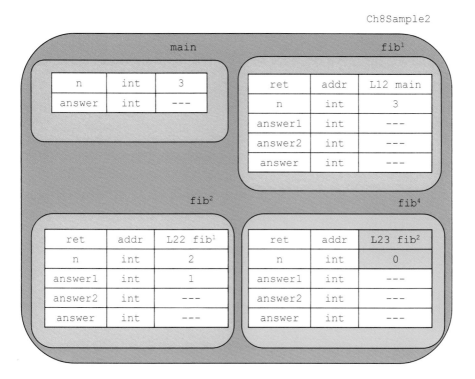

Fig. 8.15 Contour prior to the execution of Line 21 in the fourth call to fib

At first glance, it might appear that the contour for the third call to fib is no longer shaded gray. However, look carefully and notice that it is not the third call but rather it is labeled the fourth call to the method fib, the value for n is 0, and ret references Line 23 in the second call to fib. This is the calculation for the second part of the second Fibonacci number. As before, n is not greater than 1, so the else section of the if statement is executed and answer is assigned a value of 0 that is returned to the second call. Figure 8.16 illustrates the state of execution prior to Line 24 in the second call to fib.

Ch8Sample2

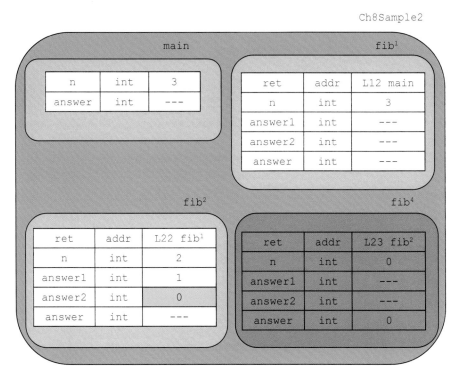

Fig. 8.16 Contour prior to the execution of Line 24 in the second call to fib

As before, the contour for the fourth call to fib has been shaded light red to indicate deallocation, and the value 0 is returned to answer2 in the second call to fib. When Line 24 is executed, the values in answer1 and answer2 are added together and stored in answer. Then answer in the second call to fib is returned to answer1 in the first call to fib as shown in Fig. 8.17 illustrating the state of execution just prior to Line 23.

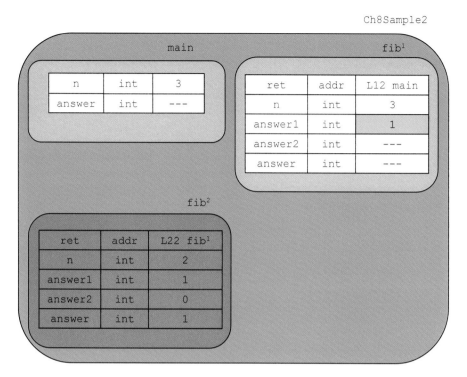

Fig. 8.17 Contour prior to the execution of Line 23 in the first call to `fib`

Note now that the fourth call to `fib` has been erased so as not to cause confusion with the second call to `fib` which is now shaded light red to indicate it has been deallocated. Also, `answer` in the second call to `fib` now contains the sum of `answer1` and `answer2`. Further, the value 1 in `answer` in the second call to `fib` has been returned to `answer1` in the first call to `fib`. Even though there have been a number of calls, the second half of the calculation still needs to be determined. Figure 8.18 shows the state of execution prior to Line 21 in the fifth call to `fib`.

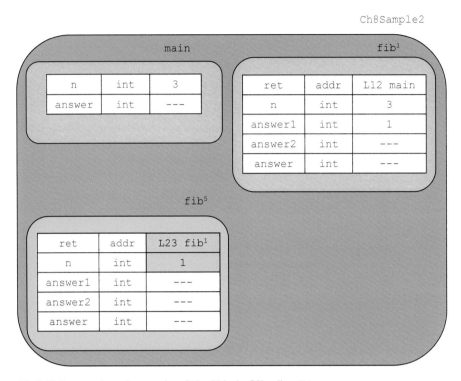

Fig. 8.18 Contour prior to the execution of Line 21 in the fifth call to `fib`

As before, notice this is not the second call to `fib`, but rather it is the fifth call to `fib` to calculate `answer2` in the first call to `fib`. Since `n` is not greater than `1`, the else portion of the `if` statement in the fifth call to `fib` is executed, and a `1` is placed in `answer` and returned back to the first call to `fib`. Figure 8.19 shows the state of execution prior to Line 24 in the first call to `fib`.

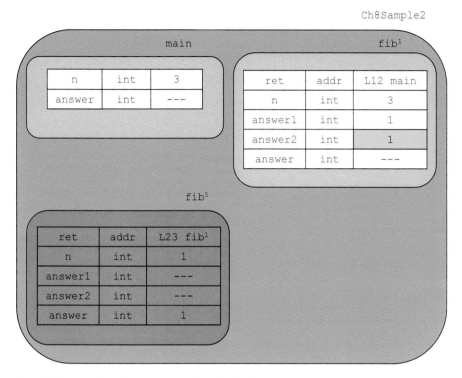

Fig. 8.19 Contour prior to the execution of Line 24 in the first call to `fib`

The fifth call to `fib` is now shaded light red indicating deallocation, and the value in `answer` is returned to `answer2` in the first call to `fib`. The values in `answer1` and `answer2` in the first call to `fib` are then added together and stored in `answer`, which is returned and assigned to `answer` in `main`. Figure 8.20 shows the state of execution prior to `answer` being output in Line 13 in `main`.

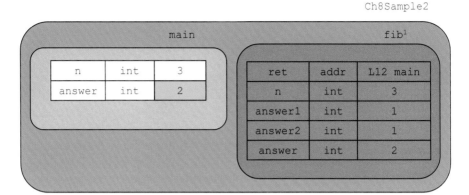

Fig. 8.20 Contour prior to the execution of Line 13 in main

As can be seen, the first call to fib is shaded light red to indicate deallocation, and answer in main contains the value 2 that was returned. Granted, this seems like a lot of work to calculate a Fibonacci number, but it shows the amount of memory that would be involved. Although there were a total of five calls to fib, only three contours were activated at any given time. As with the power method previously, the number of memory cells can be decreased by eliminating the temporary variables answer1, answer2, and answer as shown in the following code segment:

```
public static int fib(int n) {
   if (n > 1) {
      return fib(n-1) + fib(n-2);
   else
      return n;
}
```

As before, this introduces the unstructured practice of two return statements, but if memory is an issue, then this is a possible alternative. An even more efficient solution is to use iteration, which was an exercise in Chap. 4 .

As with the power function, a stack could also be used to represent recursion, but with more complex algorithms, it can be a little confusing. Yet another way to represent recursion is to use a tree of calls. The tree is drawn from the top down with the first call at the top which is called the root. Then each call after that represents a branch and terminal calls are referred to as leaves. The tree of calls for the Fibonacci number problem is shown in Fig. 8.21.

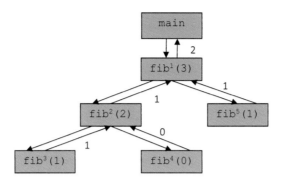

Fig. 8.21 Tree of calls for `fib(3)`

Notice that `main` makes a call to `fib¹ (3)`, which then calls `fib² (2)`, which then calls `fib³ (1)`. Once it is calculated, `fib³` returns the value 1 back to `fib²`, which calls `fib⁴` to calculate `fib(0)`. Then the sum of those two can be returned to `fib¹` which calls `fib⁵` to calculate `fib(1)`. When that is completed, a 1 is returned to `fib¹`, which then adds the two numbers and returns a 2 to `main`.

Which is a better method to walk through recursion: stack frames, a tree of calls, or contours? It depends on the situation. As stated previously, stack frames are the most realistic but it is harder to use to keep track of each call. A tree of calls is short and convenient but lacks much of the detail. Given the drawbacks of these two extremes, this is why contours are used in this text. As one gets more proficient with recursion, one might gravitate to using a tree of calls for a simple problem, but still using contours when a problem gets more complicated or using stack frames when an accurate picture is needed.

8.5 Complete Program: Implementing Recursion

A program which computes the greatest common divisor of two integers using recursion will be developed in this section. The program will

- Ask the user to enter two integers
- Compute the greatest common divisor
- Display the result

Of all the integers that divide the two numbers given, the largest is known as the greatest common divisor. For example, the positive divisors of 36 are 1, 2, 3, 4, 6, 9, 12, 18, and 36, and the positive divisors of 8 are 1, 2, 4, and 8. Thus, the common divisors of 36 and 8 are 1, 2, and 4. It follows that the greatest common divisor of 36 and 8 is 4. The Euclidean algorithm which computes the greatest common divisor of two integers starts with a pair of positive integers. It forms a new pair that consists of the smaller number of the two and the remainder which is obtained by dividing the larger number by the smaller number. This process repeats until one number is zero, and then the other number is the greatest common divisor of the original pair. The following illustrates how the greatest common divisor of 36 and 8 is found. First, 36 divided by 8 is 4 with a remainder of 4 ($4 = 36 - 4 \times 8$). Then,

8 divided by 4 is 2 with a remainder of 0 ($0 = 8 - 2 \times 4$). Since the last remainder is zero, the algorithm ends with 4 as the greatest common divisor of 36 and 8.

A recursive method to find the greatest common divisor of two positive integers can be defined by the following:

$$\gcd(num1, num2) = \{ \text{if } num2 \geq 1, \quad \text{then } \gcd(num2, \quad \text{mod}(num1, num2))$$

$$\text{otherwise, } num1 \}$$

Recall from _Sect. 1.7_ that % is the mod operator and if num1 and num2 are integers, num1%num2 returns the remainder. For example, 36%8 is 4. The implementation of the method gcd is shown below:

```
public static int gcd(int num1, int num2) {
   if(num2 >= 1)
      return gcd(num2, num1%num2);
   else
      return num1;
}
```

The above method can be invoked for the pair 36 and 8 by

```
int result;
result = gcd(36, 8);
```

After the execution of the method, the variable result will contain 4. In order to compute the greatest common divisor of 36 and 8, how many method calls were made? The first method call was gcd(36, 8), the next call was gcd(8, 4), and then gcd(4, 0) which was the last method call, resulting in a total of three method calls. The complete program with a main method is shown below:

```
import java.util.*;

class Gcd {
   // method to compute greatest common divisor
   private static int gcd(int num1, int num2) {
      if(num2 >= 1)
         return gcd(num2, num1%num2);
      else
         return num1;
   }

   public static void main(String[] args) {
      // declaration and initialization of variables
      int n, k, result;
      Scanner scanner = new Scanner(System.in);

      // input two integers
      System.out.print("Enter first number: ");
      n = scanner.nextInt();
```

```
        System.out.print ("Enter second number: ");
        k = scanner.nextInt ();

        // compute greatest common divisor
        result = gcd (n, k);

        // output greatest common divisor
        System.out.println ();
        System.out.println ("The greatest common divisor of " + n
                        + " and " + k + " is " + result + ".");
    }
}
```

When the above code is compiled and executed using the sample input of 36 and 8, the output of the program is as follows:

```
Enter first number: 36
Enter second number: 8
The greatest common divisor of 36 and 8 is 4.
```

8.6 Summary

- It helps to hunt for patterns when trying to create a recursive definition.
- Be sure to identify the base or terminal case.
- Without a base case, "infinite" recursion will occur.
- When using contours, it is helpful to use local variables to store information.
- To optimize recursion, eliminate local variables.
- Drawing a stack frame and creating a tree of calls are alternatives to contour diagrams.

8.7 Exercises (Items Marked with an * Have Solutions in Appendix E)

1. Draw series of contour diagrams to show the state of execution of the program in Fig. 8.1 for $x = 2$ and $n = 3$.
2. Draw series of contour diagrams to show the state of execution of the program in Fig. 8.10 for $n = 2$.
3. Given the complete program in Sect. 8.4, what would happen if the numbers 36 and 8 were input in reverse order? How many contours for gcd would need to be drawn?
4. Consider the program in Fig. 8.10 where Lines 22 and 23 are swapped. Draw a series of contour diagrams to show the state of execution for $n = 3$.
5. Trace the program in Fig. 8.1 for $x = 2$ and $n = 5$ and draw the tree similar to the one in Fig. 8.21.
6. Trace the program in Fig. 8.10 for $n = 5$ and draw the tree similar to the one in Fig. 8.21.
*7. Write a recursive method to reverse a given string. The method accepts a string as a parameter and returns the reverse of the string. For example, if the argument is Java, then the method returns avaJ.
8. Write a recursive method to multiply two positive integers using repeated addition.
*9. Write a recursive method to compute the factorial of a nonnegative integer using

the definition shown below:

$$\text{factorial}(n) = \left\{ \text{if } n \geq 1, \text{ then } n * \text{factorial}(n-1), \text{ otherwise}, 1 \right\}$$

10. Write a recursive method to compute the binomial coefficient using the definition shown below:

$$\text{binomial}(n,k) = \left\{ \text{if } k = 0 \text{ or } n = k, \text{ then} 1, \right.$$

$$\left. \text{otherwise}, \text{binomial}(n-1, k-1) + \text{binomial}(n-1, k) \right\}$$

11. Find a reference on how to convert a decimal number to a binary number [10] and then write a recursive method to perform the conversion.

12. Write a recursive method to output a string a certain number of times. A user will input a string and how many time the string will be printed. An example output to print "Book" 5 times along with the number is given below:

```
Enter a string: Book
Number of times to repeat: 5

Book #1
Book #2
Book #3
Book #4
Book #5
```

13. Write a recursive method to take 5 numbers as inputs and outputs the maximum number of these numbers.

9

Objects: Inheritance and Polymorphism

James T. Streib[a*] and Takako Soma[a]

[a] Computer Science Program, Illinois College, Jacksonville, IL, USA

Abstract

This chapter returns to objects and explores the concept of inheritance. Contours are used to explain how a subclass is extended and inherits data members and methods from a superclass. Further, protected variables and methods along with abstract classes are discussed. Another object-oriented programming concept, polymorphism, which is a useful tool for developing software, is introduced. A complete program implementing inheritance and polymorphism is included.

Keywords

Inheritance; Subclass; Superclass; Protected Variables; Abstract Classes; Polymorphism.

Objects were introduced in Chap. 2 , and topics such as passing objects, method overloading, and class methods were discussed in Chap. 5 . In this chapter the concepts of inheritance, overriding methods, abstract classes, and polymorphism will be illustrated. At first these concepts might sound a little bit intimidating, but introducing them with simple programs and contour diagrams makes the concepts easier to understand.

9.1 Inheritance

An important concept in object-oriented programming is software reuse. Writing a program when the same code needs to be written and rewritten with minor variations can be time-consuming and can also waste memory. Further, if the code has already been written for one situation, rewriting it not only wastes time and memory, but the chance of making a logic error in subsequent versions also increases. Instead, it makes sense to reuse software that has already been written and tested. A further advantage of software reuse is with the maintaining of code. When a segment needs to be changed, it only needs to be changed in one place, and again the chance of introducing logic errors decreases. An important way of maximizing software reuse is through *inheritance*.

When a new class is created using inheritance, the new class can inherit data members and methods from an already existing class. The existing class is known the parent class and the new class is called the child class. Also, the parent class is sometimes called the base class and the child class is called the derived class. An even more common name for the base class is the superclass, and the derived class is then called the subclass.

As an example, a regular polygon has equal length sides. Further, a three-sided regular polygon is an equilateral triangle, a four-sided regular polygon is a square, a six-sided regular polygon is a hexagon, and an eight-sided regular polygon is an octagon. Although

J. T. Streib and T. Soma, *Guide to Java*, Undergraduate Topics in Computer Science,
https://doi.org/10.1007/978-3-031-22842-1_9

there exists a generic formula for the area for an n-sided regular polygon, this text will use the specific algebraic formulas for each of the regular polygons to help illustrate the concepts of inheritance, overriding methods, abstract classes, and polymorphism.

The specific equations for the area of each of these polygons share a common part: the length of one of its sides squared or s^2. One might recognize this is also the equation for a square, and because a square is such a simple example, it is not included in subsequent examples. Since this equation is shared by all the other equations, it can be made local to the class for a regular polygon. As a result, a regular polygon can be thought of as the superclass, and the triangle, hexagon, and octagon can be thought of as subclasses.

Using a simple example, consider the RegPoygon class as shown in Fig. 9.1. Given the previous chapters on classes, the RegPoygon class should look fairly familiar. Notice the local private variable lenSide which is for the length of a side. The constructor initializes the variable with the value sent via the parameter. Further, there is one method that squares the length of the side using the pow method from the Math class. Lastly, as before, there is a local variable in the method that helps when using contour diagrams, but if memory were an issue, it could be eliminated and the expression could be used in the return statement.

```
class RegPolygon {
    private int lenSide;

    public RegPolygon(int lenSide) {
        this.lenSide = lenSide;
    }

    public double calcRegPolyArea() {
        double a;
        a = Math.pow(lenSide, 2);
        return a;
    }
}
```

Fig. 9.1 RegPolygon class

A main program segment that tests this class is shown in Fig. 9.2. Again, the statements in this program should be fairly familiar. A value is input from the user and a new instance of the RegPolygon class is created using the value that was input. Then the method is invoked and the value returned is output.

```
RegPolygon polygon;
int lenSide;
double area;

System.out.print("Enter the length of a side: ");
lenSide = scanner.nextInt();

polygon = new RegPolygon(lenSide);
area = polygon.calcRegPolyArea();

System.out.println();
System.out.printf("The area is: %5.2f", area);
```

Fig. 9.2 Main program segment using the `RegPolygon` class

However, what if one wanted to write a new class for a triangle with a method to calculate the area of a triangle? One could just write the necessary expression and be done with it.

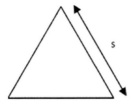

However, as mentioned previously, isn't a triangle a regular polygon? The equation for the area of an equilateral triangle is $\sqrt{3}/4s^2$ which includes s^2. If the `RegPolygon` class already exists, then couldn't methods of that class be used? The answer as one might suspect is yes. The `RegPolygon` class would then be the superclass and the `Triangle` class would be a subclass, and the `Triangle` class could inherit methods from the `RegPolygon` class. Another way of saying this is that the `Triangle` class is an extension of the `RegPolygon` class.

How is this accomplished in a program? The first line in the `Triangle` class would indicate that it `extends` the `RegPolygon` class as follows:

```
class Triangle extends RegPolygon {
```

By doing so, the `Triangle` class now has access to the data member, method, and constructor in the `RegPolygon` class. So instead of having to rewrite code segments, it can now reuse these code segments. How is this accomplished?

First, it helps to look at the constructor for the `Triangle` class. Since the `RegPolygon` class already contains the variable `lenSide` and a `Triangle` is an extension of a `RegPolygon`, instead of declaring a local private variable, the variable in the `RegPolygon` class could be reused. And instead of initializing it in the `Triangle` class, the constructor in the `RegPolygon` class can also be reused. The constructor in the superclass `RegPolygon` is invoked by using `super(lenSide)` as shown in the following constructor:

```
public Triangle(int lenSide) {
   super(lenSide);
}
```

Note that in order to invoke the constructor of the superclass, `super(lenSide)` must be the first line in the constructor as shown above. To calculate the area of a triangle, one would need to multiply $\sqrt{3}/4$ by the results returned from the method `calcRegPolyArea` in the `RegPolygon` class as shown below:

```
public double calcArea() {
   double area;
   area = Math.sqrt(3.0) / 4.0 * calcRegPolyArea();
   return area;
}
```

Unlike the constructor, the invoking of other methods can occur anywhere in a method. As before, there is a local variable `area` declared in the method which will help later when creating contour diagrams. Would the word `super` need to be used as it was in the constructor? The answer in this case is no, but it is optional as in `super.calcRegPolyArea()`. Are there cases where `super` is needed? Yes, it is required in the constructor and in some other special cases as will be shown shortly. However, as a general rule, if it is not needed, do not include it. Before proceeding, it is helpful to see the complete `Triangle` class as shown in Fig. 9.3.

```
class Triangle extends RegPolygon {

    public Triangle(int lenSide) {
        super(lenSide);
    }

    public double calcArea() {
        double area;
        area = Math.sqrt(3.0) / 4.0 * calcRegPolyArea();
        return area;
    }
}
```

Fig. 9.3 `Triangle` class

As always, it helps to see the main program segment that invokes the method in the `Triangle` class as shown in Fig. 9.4. The main program inputs `lenSide` for the triangle. It then creates a new instance of the `Triangle` class by invoking the constructor, which as seen in Fig. 9.3 invokes the constructor of the `RegPolygon` class. It then invokes the `calcArea` method of the `Triangle` class which subsequently invokes the `calcRegPolyArea` method of the `RegPolygon` class. Lastly, the `area` is output. But how does this look using contour diagrams? To do so requires putting Figs. 9.1, 9.3, and 9.4 together in a complete program with line numbers as shown in Fig. 9.5.

```
Triangle triangle
int lenSide;
double area;

System.out.print("Enter the length of a side: ");
lenSide = scanner.nextInt();

triangle = new Triangle(lenSide);

area = triangle.calcArea();
System.out.println();
System.out.printf("The area is: %5.2f", area);
```

Fig. 9.4 Main program segment using the `Triangle` class

```
import java.util.*;                                          // L 1
public class Ch9Sample1 {                                    // L 2
    public static void main(String [] args){                 // L 3
        Scanner scanner;                                     // L 4
        scanner = new Scanner(System.in);                    // L 5

        Triangle triangle;                                   // L 6
        int lenSide;                                         // L 7
        double area;                                         // L 8

        System.out.print("Enter the length of a side: ");    // L 9
        lenSide = scanner.nextInt();                         // L 10

        triangle = new Triangle(lenSide);                    // L 11
        area = triangle.calcArea();                          // L 12

        System.out.println();                                // L 13
        System.out.printf("The area is: %5.2f", area);       // L 14
        System.out.println();                                // L 15
    }                                                        // L 16
}                                                            // L 17

class Triangle extends RegPolygon {                          // L 18
    public Triangle(int lenSide) {                           // L 19
        super(lenSide);                                      // L 20
    }                                                        // L 21

    public double calcArea() {                               // L 22
        double area;                                         // L 23
        area = Math.sqrt(3.0) / 4.0 * calcRegPolyArea();     // L 24
        return area;                                         // L 25
    }                                                        // L 26
}                                                            // L 27

class RegPolygon {                                           // L 28
    private int lenSide;                                     // L 29

    public RegPolygon(int lenSide) {                         // L 30
        this.lenSide = lenSide;                              // L 31
    }                                                        // L 32

    public double calcRegPolyArea() {                        // L 33
        double a;                                            // L 34
        a = Math.pow(lenSide, 2);                            // L 35
        return a;                                            // L 36
    }                                                        // L 37

}                                                            // L 38
```

Fig. 9.5 Complete main program with the RegPolygon and Triangle classes

As in previous chapters, not every step will be shown using contour diagrams, but steps will be shown only at critical points to illustrate how the code executes. Assuming that the user inputs 2 for the lenSide, a good first stopping point in the execution of the program is just prior to Line 20 (abbreviated L 20 in Fig. 9.5) in the Triangle class as shown in Fig. 9.6.

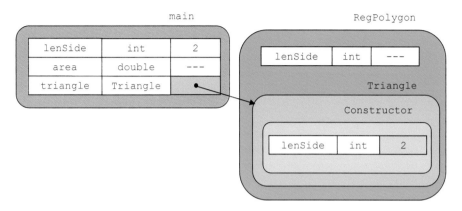

Fig. 9.6 Contour just prior to the execution of Line 20

Although the contour for a constructor is often not shown, it is shown here to help with understanding the flow of control of the program. First note that the parameter `lenSide` contains the value 2 passed from the main program, but it has not yet been assigned to the variable `lenSide` in the `RegPolygon` object. Further notice that the contour for `Triangle` is nested inside the contour for the `RegPolygon` class. As might be suspected, the reason for this is because `RegPolygon` is the superclass and `Triangle` is the subclass. As in the past, since `Triangle` is nested inside `RegPolygon`, it now has access to the non-private variable in `RegPolygon`. In other words, it can inherit the non-private variable in `RegPolygon`. As the execution of `super(lenSide)` occurs, the flow of control is transferred to the constructor in `RegPolygon`, and Fig. 9.7 shows the state of execution just prior to Line 32.

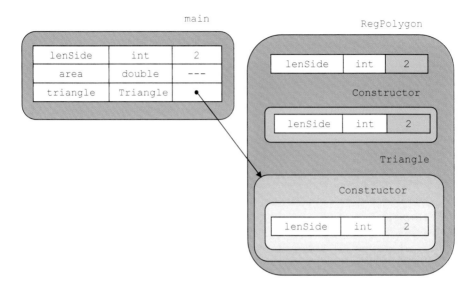

Fig. 9.7 Contour just prior to the execution of the end of the constructor at Line 32

The value in the argument lenSide in the Triangle constructor is transferred to the parameter lenSide in the RegPolygon constructor, and from there it is assigned to the data member lenSide in RegPolygon. Notice in Fig. 9.7 that both the parameter lenSide in RegPolygon constructor and the variable lenSide in RegPolygon now contain the value 2 from lenSide in Triangle. After the constructor in RegPolygon is done, it returns to the constructor for Triangle and control is returned to the main program. Figure 9.8 shows the state of execution just prior to Line 12.

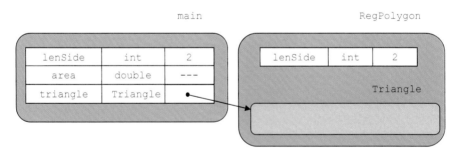

Fig. 9.8 Contour just prior to the execution of Line 12 in main

Notice that the two contours for the constructors are gone and again the variable lenSide in RegPolygon now contains a 2. The method calcArea is then invoked, and the state of execution just prior to Line 24 is shown in Fig. 9.9.

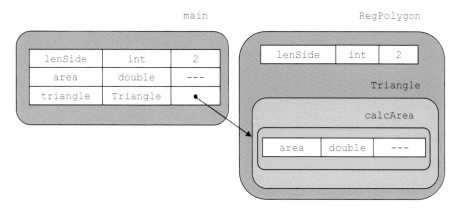

Fig. 9.9 Contour prior to the execution of Line 24 in calcArea

Since Triangle is a subclass of RegPolygon, the contour for the method calcArea is created in Triangle as the constructor was previously. Then as Line 24 is executed, the method calcRegPolyArea is invoked, and the value for the variable a is calculated as shown just prior to Line 36 in Fig. 9.10.

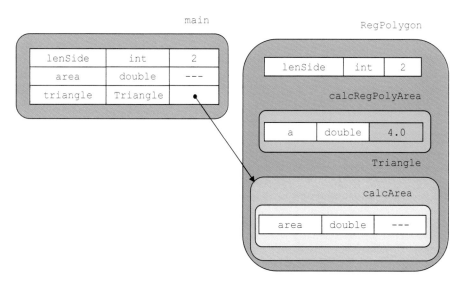

Fig. 9.10 Contour just prior to the execution of Line 36 in calcRegPolyArea

Upon return from the method calcRegPolyArea, the state of execution just prior to Line 25 is shown in Fig. 9.11. Lastly, control is returned to the main program as shown just prior to output of the area on Line 14 in Fig. 9.12.

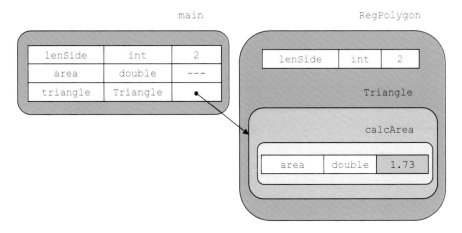

Fig. 9.11 Contour prior to the execution of Line 25 in calcArea

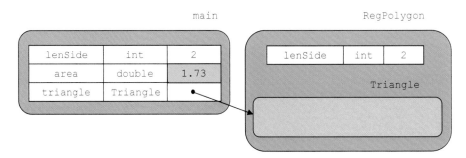

Fig. 9.12 Contour prior to the execution of Line 14 in the main program

However, what if the name of the calcArea method in the Triangle class was changed to calcRegPolyArea? Would this cause a problem with the method calcRegPolyArea in the RegPolygon class? The answer is yes, because calcRegPolyArea in the Triangle class would have the same number and type of parameters as the calcRegPolyArea method in the RegPolygon class. A method in a subclass that has the same name, the same number of parameters, and the same type of parameters as another method in the superclass is known as an *overriding method*. Does this mean that there cannot be two methods of the same name, the same number of parameters, and same type of parameters, one in the superclass and one in the subclass? The answer is no, but if there is an overriding method, how does one access the method in the superclass? If `calcRegPolyArea` is invoked in the subclass, the method in the subclass would be used, and in this case it would recursively call itself which is not what is intended. As mentioned earlier, there are instances where the word `super` must be used and this is one of those instances. So, should one want to access the `calcRegPolyArea` method in the superclass, then the word `super` is no longer optional and must be used as shown in the segment in Fig. 9.13.

```
public double calcRegPolyArea() {
    double area;
    area = Math.sqrt(3.0) / 4.0 * super.calcRegPolyArea();
    return area;
}
```

Fig. 9.13 Overriding the `calcRegPolyArea()` method

First, note that the name of the method has been changed from `calcArea` to `calcRegPolyArea`. Further, by including the word `super` prior to the call to `calcRegPolyArea`, the method in the superclass `RegPolygon` is invoked instead of recursively calling the `calcRegPolyArea` method in the subclass. Again, in this case the word `super` is not optional. Using the word `super` only when it is needed helps alert other programmers reading the code that there are two methods of the same name. For now, instead of changing the method name to `calcRegPolyArea`, the program in Fig. 9.5 will retain the method name `calcArea`.

9.2 Protected Variables and Methods

In the program in Fig. 9.5, what would happen if a method in the `Triangle` class tried to access the variable in the `RegPolygon` class? Specifically, what if the constructor in the `Triangle` class tried to access the variable `lenSide` in the `RegPolygon` class? The answer is the same as if trying to access the variable from the main program. If a variable is `private`, then it can only be accessed by methods in the `RegPolygon` class; thus the variable `lenSide` is initialized using the constructor.

However, if a variable were made `public`, then the methods of the subclass could access it. Unfortunately, the variable would also be accessible from the main program as well. Is there a way that would allow only methods in the subclass to access a variable in the superclass, but still not allow the variable to be accessed from the main program? The answer is yes. Instead of `private` or `public` access, `protected` access can be used as shown in the following:

```
protected int lenSide;
```

Now instead of initializing the variables via the `RegPolygon` constructor, the variables can be accessed directly as in the following modified `Triangle` constructor:

```
public Triangle(int lenSide) {
    super.lenSide = lenSide;
}
```

To access the variable `lenSide` in the `RegPolygon` class, notice the use of the word `super`. Also note that `this` could have been used instead of `super`, but the use of the word `super` is preferred because it alerts programmers who might subsequently read the code that the variable is not located in the current class but rather in the superclass.

Since the `RegPolygon` constructor would no longer be invoked, it could be deleted. However, if it was retained, but not invoked, a default constructor would need to be added to the `RegPolygon` class as follows:

```
public RegPolygon() {
}
```

Although accessing a variable in this manner works and is better than declaring a variable as `public`, it can still suffer from some of the same problems as being declared `public` when there are a large number of subclasses. As a result, given a choice between accessing a `protected` variable or accessing a `private` variable via a method, this text will generally choose the latter as shown previously in Fig. 9.5.

However, notice in Fig. 9.5 that although the variables in the `RegPolygon` class are `private`, the methods are `public`. While this is acceptable when access to the method is needed by both the main program and a subclass, what if access is only needed via the subclass and not from the main program? Is there a way that this can be accomplished? Again, as might be suspected, just as variables can be made accessible only by a subclass, this can also be true for methods. This is accomplished again using `protected` instead of `public` as shown in the following headings:

```
protected RegPolygon(int lenSide) {

protected double calcRegPolyArea() {
```

This corresponds to the previous suggestion that variables should remain `private` and only accessed through methods. Further, these methods can only be accessed from other methods within the class or any subclasses, and not from the main program.

9.3 Abstract Classes

Given the program in Fig. 9.5, there is nothing preventing the main program from creating an instance of the `RegPolygon` class. Although not very useful, even if the variable `lenSide` is `private` and the methods are `protected`, an instance could be created. Is there a way to make it so that an instance of the class cannot be created? Yes, and it is known as an `abstract` class. The result is that subclasses can still be defined, yet an instance of the superclass cannot be created. The following first line of the `RegPolygon` class shows how this is accomplished:

```
abstract class RegPolygon {
```

If it is possible to create an abstract class, is it also possible to create an abstract method? The answer again is yes. When creating an abstract method, the heading is declared in the superclass, but the body of the method is not defined as in the following:

```
public abstract double calcArea();
```

Again, note that there is no body to the method and the first line of the method ends in a semicolon. If the heading is in the superclass and there is no body to the method, where is the body defined? The complete method is defined in the subclass as it was before and as shown below:

```
public double calcArea() {
    double area;
    area = Math.sqrt(3.0) * calcRegPolyArea() / 4.0;
    return area;
}
```

If the above method is the same as before, what is the advantage of doing this? The advantage is that it allows different subclasses to have different methods using the same heading to meet the needs of each subclass. For example, instead of a triangle, consider an octagon:

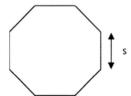

The name for this new class could be Octagon. Further, since the equation for an octagon is $2(1+\sqrt{2})s^2$, it could also be a subclass of the RegPolygon class. Since the formula s^2 is the same, the calcRegPolyArea method of the RegPolygon class could be invoked, but unlike the calculation for the area of the triangle, it would not need to be multiplied by $\sqrt{3}/4$ but rather multiplied by $2(1+\sqrt{2})$. There is no change to the Triangle class and the new Octogon class is as follows:

```
class Octagon extends RegPolygon {
    public Octagon(int lenSide) {
        super(lenSide);
    }
    public double calcArea()
        double area;
        area = 2.0 * (1.0 + Math.sqrt(2.0)) * calcRegPolyArea();
        return area;
    }
}
```

Note in the first line that the Octagon class extends the RegPolygon class. Next, notice in the calcArea method that calcRegPolyArea() is not multiplied by $\sqrt{3}/4$ but rather by $2(1+\sqrt{2})$ as mentioned above.

Note that an abstract class does not have to have any abstract methods, but if a class has abstract methods, the class needs to be declared as an abstract class. Using an abstract method in the superclass forces both subclasses to define different `calcArea` methods, and if the methods were not declared, a syntax error would occur. This is a handy feature to have when there are some differences in various subclasses, yet it is desired to retain some commonality among the subclasses.

9.4 Polymorphism

Another important feature of object-oriented programming is *polymorphism*, where the type of an object that is referenced by a superclass variable is determined at runtime instead of at compile time. This concept will be illustrated with the help of examples below.

In Java, a variable of a superclass type can reference an object of any of its subclasses. In other words, both an object of the superclass and an object of a subclass can be referenced by a variable of the superclass type. Consider the definition of the class `RegPolygon` shown in Fig. 9.1 which is repeated below for convenience:

```
class RegPolygon {
   private int lenSide;
   public RegPolygon(int lenSide) {
      this.lenSide = lenSide;
   }
   public double calcRegPolyArea() {
      double a;
      a = Math.pow(lenSide, 2);
      return a;
   }
}
```

Further, the class `Triangle` from Fig. 9.3, with the modification described in Fig. 9.13 with the method `calcArea` renamed to `calcRegPolyArea`, is shown below:

```
class Triangle extends RegPolygon {
   public Triangle(int lenSide) {
      super(lenSide);
   }
   public double calcRegPolyArea() {
      double area;
      area = Math.sqrt(3.0) / 4.0 * super.calcRegPolyArea();
      return area;
   }
}
```

The class `Triangle` is a subclass of the class `RegPolygon`, and the method `calcRegPolyArea` in the `Triangle` class is overriding the method `calcRegPolyArea` in the `RegPolygon` class. Suppose two variables of type `RegPolygon` are declared in the `main` method as follows:

```
RegPolygon shape1, shape2;
```

Naturally, a reference to an object of the class `RegPolygon` can be assigned to these variables. For example, the following statement assigns an object of the `RegPolygon` class to the variable `shape1`.

```
shape1 = new RegPolygon(5);
```

In addition, a reference to an object of the class `Triangle` can also be assigned to these variables. The following statement assigns an object of the `Triangle` class to the variable `shape2`.

```
shape2 = new Triangle(2);
```

Next, using the method `calcRegPolyArea` defined in both the class `RegPolygon` and the class `Triangle`, the square of the side and the area of the triangle will be calculated. For the object `shape1`, the code segment can be found in Fig. 9.14. This code segment will output the area with a side of 5 as

```
area of shape1: 25.00
```

```
double area1;
shape1 = new RegPolygon(5);
area1 = shape1.calcRegPolyArea();
System.out.printf("area of shape1: %.2f", area1);
```
Fig. 9.14 Code segment finding the square of the side of `shape1`

Now, what would happen when the code segment in Fig. 9.15 is executed for the object `shape2`? Recall that the variable `shape2` is declared as of type `RegPolygon`, and a reference to the `Triangle` object is assigned to it. Will the method `calcArea` defined in the class `RegPolygon` be invoked and return `25.00`? The answer is no. Instead it will output the following:

```
area of shape2: 1.73
```

```
double area2;
shape2 = new Triangle(2);
area2 = shape2.calcRegPolyArea();
System.out.printf("area of shape2: %.2f", area2);
```
Fig. 9.15 Code segment finding the area of `shape2`

This is the area of a triangle with a side of length 2. The reason is that the type of the object invoking the method `calcRegPolyArea` determines which `calcRegPolyArea` method is called, either the one in the class `RegPolygon` or the one in the class `Triangle`. Even though the variable `shape2` is of type `RegPolyton`, it references a `Triangle` object because that is the type assigned to it during runtime by the `shape2=new Triangle(2);` statement. This means that the `Triangle` object is invoking the method `calcRegPolyArea` defined in the class `Triangle` when it is executed.

This is an example of polymorphism. Variables shape1 and shape2 could reference either a RegPolygon object or a Triangle object. At compile time, it cannot be determined what type of the object they will reference. However, at runtime when the object invokes the method calcRegPolyArea, the type of the object is determined and the appropriate calcRegPolyArea method is called.

If a variable of a superclass type can reference an object of a subclass type, can a variable of a subclass type reference an object of a superclass type? The answer is no. Consider the following code segment:

```
Triangle shape3;
shape3 = new RegPolygon(6);
```

The second statement causes a compile-time error, because a reference variable of a subclass type is not allowed to reference an object of its superclass. As one might suspect, the following statement is also incorrect,

```
shape3 = shape1;
```

because the variable shape1 is referencing an object of type RegPolygon. What about the following statement?

```
shape3 = shape2;
```

At first it looks okay since the variable shape3 is of type Triangle and the variable shape2 references an object of the Triangle class. But, the answer is again no. It causes a compile-time error because even though shape2 references a Triangle object, the variable shape2 is of type RegPolygon. However, the following statement is legal:

```
shape3 = (Triangle) shape2;
```

The above statement uses a typecast operator, discussed in Chap. 1 , which allows shape3 of type Triangle to reference the Triangle object that shape2 of type RegPolygon references.

Suppose another subclass of the class RegPolygon named Hexagon is defined. The equation for a hexagon is $3\sqrt{3}/2s^2$ as shown below:

```
class Hexagon extends RegPolygon {
    public Hexagon(int lenSide) {
        super(lenSide);
    }
    public double calcRegPolyArea() {
        double area;
        area = 3.0 * Math.sqrt(3.0) / 2.0 * super.calcRegPolyArea();
        return area;
    }
}
```

As discussed above, a variable of the class RegPolygon can reference an object of the class Hexagon, but a variable of the Hexagon class cannot reference an object of the RegPolygon class. Also, a variable of the Hexagon class cannot reference an object of

the Triangle class, and vice versa, since the Hexagon class and the Triangle classes
are both subclasses of the RegPolygon class, also known as *sibling* classes.

Returning to the output of the code segments in Figs. 9.14 and 9.15, instead of
displaying the words "shape1" and "shape2" as shown below, would it be better if
the type of the polygon is output?

```
area of shape1: 25.00
area of shape2: 1.73
```

Is there a way to determine the type of an object during the runtime and output it? The
answer is yes. To determine the type of an object, Java provides the operator
instanceof. This operator is especially useful because the variable of a superclass can
reference an object of either its own class or a subclass type. Consider the following
expression:

```
shape1 instanceof Triangle
```

This expression evaluates to true if the variable shape1 refers to an object of the
class Triangle; otherwise it evaluates to false. Using the operator instanceof, the
printf statements in Figs. 9.14 and 9.15 can be rewritten as follows:

```
if(shape1 instanceof Triangle)
   System.out.printf("area of triangle: %.2f", area1);
else
   System.out.printf("square of side: %.2f", area1);
System.out.println();
if(shape2 instanceof Triangle)
   System.out.printf("area of triangle: %.2f", area2);
else
   System.out.printf("square of side: %.2f", area2);
System.out.println();
```

The output of the above code segment is

```
square of side: 25.00
area of triangle: 1.73
```

Since the variable shape1 references a RegPolygon object, the first if condition
returns false. Therefore the printf statement in the else block was executed stating
that the square of the side is calculated. For shape2, the then portion of the second if
statement was executed. However, what would happen if there are a large number of shapes
whose areas need to be calculated? Instead of having each object calling the
calcRegPolyArea method separately and having if statements for the output, an array
of objects can be used to simplify the program.

Consider the creation of an array with different types of regular polygons. If the array
is declared as a type RegPolygon, each element of the array could be an object of its
subclasses. The following code segment declares and creates an array named shapes of
type RegPolygon with five elements, which can be the Triangle class or the

Hexagon class:

```
RegPolygon[] shapes;
shapes = new RegPolygon[5];
```

The following statements create either a Triangle object or a Hexagon object and place them in the array:

```
shapes[0] = new Hexagon(3);
shapes[1] = new Triangle(2);
shapes[2] = new Triangle(5);
shapes[3] = new Hexagon(4);
shapes[4] = new Triangle(4);
```

Once all the objects are stored in the array, a for loop can be used to calculate the areas and output them along with the type of the shape.

```
for(int i=0; i<shapes.length; i++) {
   area = shapes[i].calcRegPolyArea();
   if(shapes[i] instanceof Triangle)
      System.out.printf("area of triangle: %.2f", area);
   else
      System.out.printf("area of hexagon: %.2f", area);
   System.out.println();
}
```

The output of the above code segment is of the same form as before:

```
area of hexagon: 23.38
area of triangle: 1.73
area of triangle: 10.83
area of hexagon: 41.57
area of triangle: 6.93
```

Again, the advantage of using an array is that the program does not need to have a series of calculations for the area and if statements, but rather only one calculation and if statement placed inside a loop.

9.5 Complete Program: Implementing Inheritance and Polymorphism

Combining all the material from this chapter, one can now develop a program that illustrates the concepts of inheritance and polymorphism. In this section, a program which keeps track of an employee's information for a company will be developed. The program will

- Allow a user to enter the employee information
- Compute the compensation for each employee
- Display the results

Suppose each employee has a unique ID number and is either a full-time or a part-time employee. Full-time employees are salaried and part-time employees are paid hourly.

Therefore, the company keeps track of the salary for each full-time employee and the hourly rate and the number of hours worked for each part-time employee. Since every employee has an ID number as a common field and other field(s) depending on the type of employment, the concept of inheritance can be used to organize the data. The `Employee` class could be the superclass and there could be two subclasses, a `FullTime` class and a `PartTime` class. The `Employee` class could have a data member named `id` of type integer and two methods, one constructor and a method `toString`, as discussed in Sect. 6.5 . The `toString` method returns a descriptive text and the contents of the variable `id` as a `String` type for the purpose of displaying information about the object. The definition of the `Employee` class is shown below:

```
class Employee {
   private int id;
   public Employee(int id) {
      this.id = id;
   }
   public String toString() {
      return "An employee with ID " + id;
   }
}
```

The `FullTime` class inherits the `id` field from the parent class `Employee` and has one additional data member of its own, `salary` of type `double`. The `id` is also inherited by the `PartTime` class. Two more data members, `hourlyRate` and `hoursWorked` of type `double`, are declared in the `PartTime` class to determine the compensation. Both subclasses have a method `toString` which is an overriding method of the one in the `Employee` class. They also have a method named `compensation` to calculate the pay for the particular month. Both the `FullTime` class and the `PartTime` class are shown below:

```
class FullTime extends Employee {
   private double salary;

   public FullTime(int id, double salary) {
      super(id);
      this.salary = salary;
   }

   public String toString() {
      String str;
      str = String.format(super.toString()
            + " is a full-time employee \n"
            + "with salary $%.2f.\n", compensation());
      return str;
   }

   public double compensation() {
      return salary;
   }
}

class PartTime extends Employee {
   private double hourlyRate;
   private double hoursWorked;

   public PartTime(int id, double hourlyRate, double hoursWorked) {
      super(id);
      this.hourlyRate = hourlyRate;
      this.hoursWorked = hoursWorked;
   }

   public String toString() {
      String str;
      str = String.format(super.toString()
            + " is a part-time employee \n"
            + "with wages $%.2f.\n", compensation());
      return str;
   }

   public double compensation() {
      return hourlyRate * hoursWorked;
   }
}
```

Notice that the method toString defined in the Employee class is invoked from the toString method of both subclasses using the method call super.toString(). The next two lines append the type of employment and the result from the compensation method as defined and calculated in its own class. The compensation method in the FullTime class simply returns the content of the variable salary, and the compensation method in the PartTime class calculates the wage multiplying the hourly rate by the number of hours the employee worked. The format method in the toString method, which is similar to printf, is a class method defined in the String class and is used to format the `double` number.

As discussed in <u>Sect. 2.10</u>, Unified Modeling Language (UML) diagrams help one to see the relationships among the various classes. Figure 9.16 shows how the `Employee`, `FullTime`, and `PartTime` classes can be displayed using UML class diagram notation.

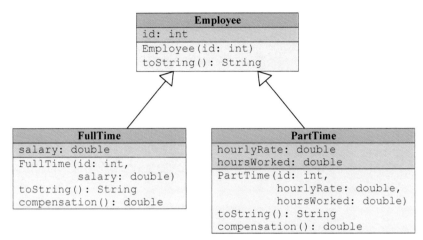

Fig. 9.16 UML class diagram of the `Employee`, `FullTime`, and `PartTime` classes

As can be seen, each box represents a particular class. The name of the class is in the top section of the box. A list of the data members is located in the middle section, and the list of the methods is in the bottom section. Two arrows show the relationship between the parent class and the two child classes. In the `FullTime` class, the middle section contains the data member `salary` and its type `double` following the colon. The list of methods includes the constructor `FullTime` along with the two methods, `toString` and `compensation`. The parameter list (`id: int, salary: double`) for the constructor indicates that `id` and `salary` are of type `int` and `double`, respectively, and are used to assign the values to the data members. By having an empty parameter list in the parentheses, both `toString` and `compensation` methods do not receive any information and return a value of type `String` and `double`, respectively.

In the `main` method, an array of `Employee` type is created with the number of employees that the user inputs, and the information about each employee is collected from the user inside the `for` loop. After all the information is entered, the compensation for each employee is calculated and displayed using polymorphism. The complete main program is shown below:

```java
import java.util.*;

public class Company {
    public static void main(String[] args) {
        Employee[] employee;
        int numEmp, id;
        double salary, hourlyRate, hoursWorked;
        String type;
        Scanner scanner;
        scanner = new Scanner(System.in);

        System.out.print("Enter number of employees: ");
        numEmp = scanner.nextInt();
        employee = new Employee[numEmp];
        System.out.println();

        for(int i=0; i<employee.length; i++) {
            System.out.print("Enter id of employee " + (i+1) + ": ");
            id = scanner.nextInt();
            System.out.print("Enter either 'f' for full-time or ");
            System.out.print("'p' for part-time: ");
            type = scanner.next();
            if(type.equals("f")) {
                System.out.print("Enter salary of employee "
                                + (i+1) + ": ");
                salary = scanner.nextDouble();
                employee[i] = new FullTime(id, salary);
            }
            else {
                System.out.print("Enter hourly rate of employee "
                                + (i+1) + ": ");
                hourlyRate = scanner.nextDouble();
                System.out.print("Enter number of hours worked: ");
                hoursWorked = scanner.nextDouble();
                employee[i] = new PartTime(id, hourlyRate, hoursWorked);
            }
            System.out.println();
        }

        for(int i=0; i<employee.length; i++)
            System.out.println(employee[i].toString());
    }
}
```

In the first for loop, notice that after an ID number is entered, the program asks the user if the employee is full-time or part-time. Depending on the type of the employment, only the necessary information is prompted for in the then or else section of the if statement. A for loop is also used for output. Because of the use of polymorphism, the type of the object at a particular position in the array is determined dynamically and the appropriate toString method is executed. When the above program is compiled and executed using the sample input of three employees, the output appears as given below:

```
Enter number of employees: 3

Enter id of employee 1: 12345
Enter either 'f' for full-time or 'p' for part-time: f
Enter salary of employee 1: 55000.00

Enter id of employee 2: 67890
Enter either 'f' for full-time or 'p' for part-time: p
Enter hourly rate of employee 2: 14.50
Enter number of hours worked: 42

Enter id of employee 3: 34567
Enter either 'f' for full-time or 'p' for part-time: p
Enter hourly rate of employee 3: 9.5
Enter number of hours worked: 15

An employee with ID 12345 is a full-time employee
with salary $55000.00.

An employee with ID 67890 is a part-time employee
with wages $609.00.

An employee with ID 34567 is a part-time employee
with wages $142.50.
```

As can be seen from the above output, the user entered information for one full-time and two part-time employees.

9.6 Summary

- The word extends is used to create a subclass.
- When accessing a constructor in a superclass, super must be used. It must also be the first line of the constructor of the subclass.
- An overriding method is one in a subclass that has the same name, the same number of parameters, and the same type of parameters as the one in the superclass.
- When there is not an overriding data member or method in a subclass, super is optional and generally not used. However, if there is an overriding data member or method in the subclass and the one in the superclass needs to be accessed, super is required.
- Use protected when variables or methods in a superclass are to be accessed only in the superclass and its subclasses.
- If the superclass is an abstract class, it can be extended by subclasses, but a new instance of the superclass cannot be created.
- The heading of an abstract method is placed in the superclass followed by a semicolon, and in the subclasses, the method must eventually be implemented.
- An abstract class does not need to include abstract methods, but if a class has abstract methods, the class must be declared as an abstract class.

- Polymorphism means the type of an object that is referenced by a superclass variable is determined at runtime.
- A variable of a superclass type can reference an object of its subclass type.
- A variable of a subclass type cannot reference an object of its superclass type.
- A variable of a subclass type cannot reference an object of another subclass type that shares the same parent. The two subclasses are known as sibling classes.
- The operator `instanceof` determines the type of an object.

9.7 Exercises (Items Marked with an * Have Solutions in Appendix E)

1. Suppose that `Staff`, `Faculty`, and `StudentWorker` are the subclasses of the `Employee` class. Indicate whether the following statements are syntactically correct or incorrect. If incorrect, indicate what is wrong with the statement:

   A. `Employee employee = new Faculty();`
   *B. `Staff staff = new Employee();`
   *C. `StudentWorker student = new StudentWorker();`
   D. `Faculty faculty = new Staff();`

2. The `Triangle` class is derived from the `RegPolygon` class. Using the UML diagrams shown below, complete the following:

```
                        RegPolygon
 lenSide: int
 RegPolygon()
 RegPolygon(lenSide: int)
 setLenSide(lenSide: int)
 getLenSide(): int
 calcRegPolyArea(): double
 toString(): String
 equals(regPolygon: RegPolygon): boolean
 makeCopy(regPolygon: RegPolygon)
```

```
                         Triangle
 Triangle()
 Triangle(lenSide: int)
 calcRegPolyArea(): double
 toString(): String
 equals(triangle: Triangle): boolean
 makeCopy(triangle: Triangle)
```

   A. List any overloaded methods in the RegPolygon and Triangle classes.

*B. List any overriding methods in the RegPolygon and Triangle classes.

   C. If the variable lenSide is a private data member of the RegPolygon class, is lenSide accessible from the Triangle class?

*D. If the variable lenSide is a protected data member of the RegPolygon class, is lenSide accessible from the Triangle class?

   E. If the variable lenSide is a protected data member of the RegPolygon class, is lenSide accessible from the main method?

*3. Implement a class Engineer which extends from the FullTime class discussed in Sect. 9.5. Include a data member which describes the type of engineering and a method toString.

4. Write a class Vehicle which keeps a vehicle identification number, license plate number, and a number of axles. Derive two classes from the Vehicle class named Car and Truck. Include a data member for the number of passengers in the Car class and a data member for the towing capacity for the Truck class. All three classes should have a toString method to be able to output information about a particular vehicle.

5. Suppose that two different types of sources are used in a term paper: books and journal articles. The following UML diagram illustrates how the sources are organized.

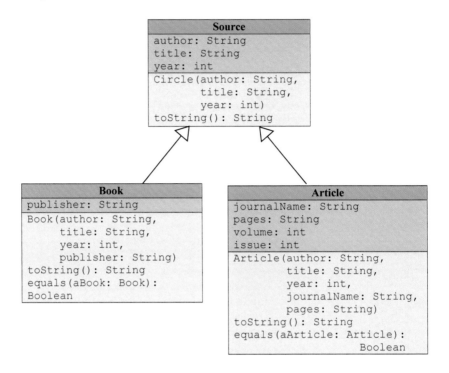

First, implement the three classes, Source, Book, and Article, and then write a main method to use them. In the main method, ask the user to enter the number of references, create an array of type Source using the size the user entered, use a loop to ask the user to enter the information for each reference (book or journal article), and then output the contents of each object.

6. In Problem 4, the Vehicle, Car, and Truck classes were implemented. Vehicles could include more such as motorcycles, buses, trains, ships, and airplanes. Using UML diagrams, organize these vehicles. Add appropriate data members and methods in the diagram for each type of vehicle.

7. In this chapter, the Triangle and Octagon classes were extended from RegPolygon class. Define the Square class which is a subclass of the RegPolygon

and have the `calcArea` method in the `Square` class call `calcRegPolyArea` method to calculate the are of square.

8. Define the `Heptagon` class as a subclass of `RegPolygon` class.

10

Elementary File Input and Output

James T. Streib[a*] and Takako Soma[a]

[a] Computer Science Program, Illinois College, Jacksonville, IL, USA

Abstract

This chapter discusses elementary files, including how to obtain data from a file and how to save output to a file. It also discusses how the file location is specified. Two complete programs, one performing matrix multiplication using a data stored in a file, and another sorting string data from a file, are included.

Keywords

Text File; Input File; Output File; Token; File Object.

10.1 Introduction

Simple input using a standard input device such as a keyboard and simple output using a standard output device such as a monitor were introduced in Chap. 1 . With a small amount of data, entering data using the keyboard works fine; however, with a large set of data, it can become troublesome. Recall the example discussed in Chap. 4 , where the list of exam scores was entered from a keyboard and the average was calculated using a loop structure. Since the example used only three exam scores, it was not much trouble. However, if there were 100 or more students in the class and the exam scores are used several times for analysis, it would be inefficient to type scores at the keyboard each time the program is executed. In addition to the inconvenience of typing a large amount of data, typing can generate errors and cause erroneous results. Just like using a keyboard for input, sending output to the monitor also works well if the amount of information displayed is small; however, if a large number of statistics must be output or the results need to be distributed, the use of a monitor is not particularly a good option.

What can be done about the limitations associated with getting input from the keyboard and sending output to the monitor? A solution is to use files, where they can be used to store all the input and output data. Another advantage of using files is that they can be created before running a program. Further, if the results are output to a file, a program does not have to be executed over and over to see the same result, and the file can be distributed easily. A file can be created for input to a program or the output examined using a utility program. This chapter will discuss how to obtain data from and save output to the file.

10.2 File Input

When the `Scanner` class was introduced in Java 5.0, also known as Java[TM] 2 Platform Standard Edition 5.0 Development Kit (JDK 5.0), it significantly simplified the process of input both by reading data from the keyboard and a file. This is because the `Scanner` object processes a data line as a sequence of tokens. A *token* is an individual item that is a string of characters separated by delimiters. Any character can be designated as a delimiter, but white space such as a blank, a tab, a newline, or a return is the most commonly used. For the file input, instead of associating an object of type `Scanner` to the standard input device, `System.in`, it is associated to an object of type `File`. The `File` class represents files and directory pathnames. Some of the purposes of this class are to create files and directories, and to search files. The following statement

```
Scanner inFile = new Scanner(new File("grades1.txt"));
```

will associate an object `inFile` of type `Scanner` to a data file `grades1.txt`. For now, assume that the file resides in the same directory as the Java program. The way to specify the input file in a different directory will be discussed in Sect. 10.5. The name of the file is `grades1.txt`, and it is passed as an argument to the constructor of the `File` class. Since the `Scanner` class is in the `java.util` package and the `File` class is in the `java.io` package, both packages have to be imported at the beginning of the program as shown below:

```
import java.util.*;
import java.io.*;
```

Once import statements are included, the methods such as `nextInt` and `next` discussed in <u>Chap. 1</u> can be used to input data from the file, just the same way an object of the `Scanner` class has been used to input the data from the standard input device.

The program in Fig. 10.1 will read numbers from the `grades1.txt` file and output the average.

```
import java.util.*;
import java.io.*;

public class GradesVersion1 {
    public static void main(String[] args) throws IOException {
        int score;
        double totalExam1, average1;

        Scanner inFile = new Scanner(new File("grades1.txt"));

        totalExam1 = 0;
        for(int i=0; i<3; i++) {
            score = inFile.nextInt();
            System.out.println("score " + (i+1) + ": " + score);
            totalExam1 = totalExam1 + score;
        }
        average1 = totalExam1/3;
        System.out.println();
        System.out.printf("average: %.2f",average1);

        inFile.close();
    }
}
```

Fig. 10.1 A simple program that inputs data from a text file

Notice that `throws IOException` is added in the `main` method header. An exception represents an error condition or an unexpected event that occurs during the normal course of program execution. Since exceptions are discussed in Appendix B, this section briefly mentions just enough about them to enable the program to use file input and output. When the program performs file processing operations, there is a chance that a system error will occur. For example, the system may not be able to locate the file or an error could occur during a file read operation. For this reason, Java requires an application to deal with exceptions in some form. A simple solution is to add a `throws` clause in the method header, and then the system will handle the exception by simply halting execution. Finally, notice that the last statement in the program is `inFile.close();` which closes the input file `grades1.txt` with which `inFile` was associated.

Assuming the file `grades1.txt` contains the following three values as shown below, a `for` loop is used to read the scores.

```
71
60
75
```

The output from the code in Fig. 10.1 is

```
score 1: 71
score 2: 60
score 3: 75
average: 68.67
```

Similar to the `File` class, an object of the `FileReader` class could be associated to the file and used to create an object of the `Scanner` class. The following three statements

```
Scanner inFile
   = new Scanner(new FileReader("grades1.txt"));
```

and

```
Scanner inFile
   = new Scanner(new FileReader(new File("grades1.txt")));
```

along with the following discussed earlier

```
Scanner inFile = new Scanner(new File("grades1.txt"));
```

are all equivalent when creating a `Scanner` object for the purpose of the input. Besides using `File` and `FileReader` for file input, the `File` class is used to handle files in general, such as creation and deletion of files, and the `FileReader` class is used for reading character files. For more information, the definition of `File` and `FileReader` classes can be found in the Java API specification document on the Oracle website.

Next, how can the code in Fig. 10.1 be modified if the number of scores in the input file is not known in advance? A sentinel value -1 could be added to an input file as shown below:

```
71
60
75
-1
```

and the following code segment illustrates how a variation of the sentinel-controlled loop introduced in Sect. 4.2 could be used.

```
numStudents = 0;
totalExam1 = 0;
score = inFile.nextInt();
while(score >= 0) {
   numStudents++;
   System.out.println("score " + numStudents + ": " + score);
   totalExam1 = totalExam1 + score;
   score = inFile.nextInt();
}
average1 = totalExam1/numStudents;
System.out.println();
System.out.printf("average: %.2f", average1);
```

The variable numStudents is used to store the number of scores and calculate the average after the loop. However, what if one did not want to include a sentinel value in the data file? It would seem that the program should be able to keep reading the integers using a loop until there are no more scores in the file. Fortunately, the hasNextInt method can be used to check if another integer value exists in the file. If it does not find an integer, the method returns false. Using a while loop, the execution could continue to the statement that follows the loop. The revised loop is shown below:

```
numStudents = 0;
totalExam1 = 0;
while(inFile.hasNextInt()) {
   score = inFile.nextInt();
   numStudents++;
   System.out.println("score " + numStudents + ": " + score);
   totalExam1 = totalExam1 + score;
}
average1 = totalExam1/numStudents;
System.out.println();
System.out.printf("average: %.2f", average1);
```

The advantage to this technique is that the file does not need to contain a sentinel value, nor does the loop need a priming read. In addition to the method hasNextInt, there are a number of similar methods in the Scanner class that can be used with different types of data as listed in Table 10.1.

Table 10.1 Selected methods of the `Scanner` class

Method	Return Type	Description
hasNext()	Boolean	Returns `true` if there is another token available for input.
hasNextDouble()	Boolean	Returns `true` if the next token is a `double` value.
hasNextInt()	Boolean	Returns `true` if the next token is an `int` value.
hasNextLine()	Boolean	Returns `true` if there is another line available for input.
next()	String	Return the next token.
nextDouble()	Double	Return the next token as a `double` value.
nextInt()	Int	Return the next token as an `int` value.
nextLine()	String	Return the next line of input as a string. It may contain several tokens and spaces. The newline character \n could be there, but it is not included in the string.

Next, consider the case where the input file `grades2.txt` contains two sets of exam scores per line and the column headings as shown below:

```
Exam1  Exam2
71     95
60     80
75     76
```

The task is to find the average score of both sets of exam scores. Since the first two items in the file are not scores, they have to be extracted using the `next` method instead of the `nextInt` and assigned to the `String` variables to be output later. Notice in the following code that both sets of scores are read and added to the appropriate variables during each iteration of the `while` loop before moving on to the next line. Further, since the number of students is not known in advance, it is necessary for the program to count the number of input lines using the variable `numStudents` as shown in Fig. 10.2.

```
public class GradesVersion2 {
    public static void main(String[] args) throws IOException {
        String str1, str2;
        int score, numStudents;
        double totalExam1, totalExam2, average1, average2;

        Scanner inFile = new Scanner(new File("grades2.txt"));

        numStudents = 0;
        totalExam1 = 0;
        totalExam2 = 0;
        str1 = inFile.next();
        str2 = inFile.next();
        System.out.println("             " + str1 + " " + str2);
        while(inFile.hasNextInt()) {
            numStudents++;
            score = inFile.nextInt();
            System.out.print("Student " + numStudents + ":  "
                                        + score + "    ");
            totalExam1 = totalExam1 + score;
            score = inFile.nextInt();
            System.out.println(score);
            totalExam2 = totalExam2 + score;
        }
        average1 = totalExam1/numStudetns;
        System.out.println();
        System.out.printf(str1 + " average: %.2f", average1);
        Average2 = totalExam2/numStudetns;
        System.out.println();
        System.out.printf(str2 + " average: %.2f", average2);

        inFile.close();
    }
}
```

Fig. 10.2 A program that inputs data from a text file

The output from the program would look like the following:

```
            Exam1 Exam2
Student 1:   71     95
Student 2:   60     80
Student 3:   75     76
Exam1 average: 68.67
Exam2 average: 83.67
```

Each individual score was output as they were read from the file inside the loop, and the last two lines were output after the calculation of the average outside the loop.

10.3 File Output

To send output to a file, the classes PrintWriter and FileWriter are used. The PrintWriter class prints formatted text using methods like print, println, and printf. The FileWriter class is a counterpart of FileReader class and is meant for writing streams of characters. As with the FileReader class, the PrintWriter and `FileWriter` classes are contained in the package `java.io` which needs to be imported at the beginning of the program. For file output, a variable of type `PrintWriter` is declared and associated with the destination, the file where the output will be stored. Suppose the output is to be stored in the file `outs.txt` in the same directory as the source code. Again, the way to specify the output file in a different directory will be discussed in Sect. 10.5. Consider the following statement:

```
PrintWriter outFile
   = new PrintWriter(new FileWriter("outs.txt"));
```

This statement creates an object of type `PrintWriter` named `outFile` and associates it with the file `outs.txt`. An output file does not have to exist before it is opened for output. If it does not exist, the system creates an empty file in the current directory. If the designated output file already exists, a new empty file with the same name will be created, replacing the previous file of the same name. Sometimes, however, there is a time when new data should be appended to the end of the data that already exists in the file. The `FileWriter` class has an overloaded constructor that takes two arguments as in

```
PrintWriter outFile
   = new PrintWriter(new FileWriter("outs.txt", true));
```

The first argument is a name of the file and the second argument is a Boolean value. If it is `true` and the file already exists, the contents of the file will not be erased and the new data will be appended to the end of the file. If the argument is `false` and the file already exists, it will be replaced by the new one. If the `boolean` value is not included in the argument list, the value `false` is assumed and an existing file will be replaced. Finally, in any case, if the file does not exist, a new file is created.

Similar to the `Scanner` class, an object of the `File` class could be associated to the file. Using an overloaded constructor of the `PrintWriter` class and a `File` object as an argument to create a `PrintWriter` object is shown below:

```
PrintWriter outFile
   = new PrintWriter(new File("outs.txt"));
```

Another overloaded constructor of the `PrintWriter` class simply takes a filename as an argument just like the `Scanner` class as shown below:

```
PrintWriter outFile = new PrintWriter("outs.txt");
```

The advantage of using an object of the class `FileWriter` over the `File` class or a simple filename is the ability of appending text, if it is desired.

Once the object of type `PrintWriter` is created, the methods such as `print`, `println`, and `printf` can be applied to the object `outFile` just the same way they have been used with the `System.out`. When the output is completed, the output file should be closed by using the method `close` shown in the following statement:

```
outFile.close();
```

Data to be written to a file is stored in an output buffer in memory before it is written to the file. Closing a file ensures that any data remaining in the buffer will be emptied. If the file is not closed, it is not considered an error, but it could be possible that not all the information generated by the program will be sent to the output file. Therefore, it is good practice to always close the output file. The program in Fig. 10.2 is modified to output the result to the file `outs.txt` as shown in Fig. 10.3.

```
import java.util.*;
import java.io.*;
public class GradesVersion3 {
    public static void main(String[] args) throws IOException {
        String str1, str2;
        int score, numStudents;
        double totalExam1, totalExam2, average1, average2;

        Scanner inFile = new Scanner(new FileReader("grades2.txt"));
        PrintWriter outFile = new PrintWriter(new File("outs.txt"));

        numStudents = 0;
        totalExam1 = 0;
        totalExam2 = 0;
        str1 = inFile.next();
        str2 = inFile.next();
        outFile.println("              " + str1 + " " + str2);
        while(inFile.hasNextInt()) {
            numStudents++;
            score = inFile.nextInt();
            outFile.print("Student " + numStudents + ":   "
                            + score + "    ");
            totalExam1 = totalExam1 + score;
            score = inFile.nextInt();
            outFile.println(score);
            totalExam2 = totalExam2 + score;
        }
        average1 = totalExam1/numStudents;
        outFile.println();
        outFile.printf(str1 + " average: %.2f", average1);
        average2 = totalExam2/numStudents;
        outFile.println();
        outFile.printf(str2 + " average: %.2f", average2);

        inFile.close();
        outFile.close();
    }
}
```

Fig. 10.3 A program that outputs data to a text file

The program in Fig. 10.3 will have the same output as the program in Fig. 10.2, but this time, it will be output to the file `outs.txt`. To see the output, simply open the file using a utility program and examine the results.

10.4 File Input and Output Using an Array

Assuming the scores from different exams are kept in separate files, how can the scores in each file be processed using the same program? It would not be a good idea to have the input filename hardcoded into the program. Instead, the program should allow the user to enter the filename. Also, after the scores are processed, the results can also be stored in a user-specified file. If variables are used for the name of both input and output files, it is not necessary to change and to compile the code every time the program is executed for a different set of data.

If every course has a different number of students, the number of scores in the input file is not known in advance. Suppose that an array of the same size as the number of scores were to be created, then the scores would need to be counted and the count stored in a variable would be used to allocate the array. In order to count scores, every score is read without being stored or used for calculations. The code segment in Fig. 10.4 will count scores in the file.

```
// get name of input file from user
System.out.print("Enter input filename: ");
inFileName = scanner.next();

// open input file
inFile = new Scanner(new File(inFileName));

// count number of scores in input file
numStudents = 0;
while(inFile.hasNextInt()) {
    numStudents++;
    inFile.nextInt();
}
```

Fig. 10.4 A code segment that counts the data in an input file

Note that the user is prompted for and inputs the name of the file. Further, notice that inside the while loop, although the exam scores were read from the file using the statement inFile.nextInt(); because the return values were not used for any calculations at this point, they were not stored in memory. The instruction inFile.nextInt(); was simply used to count the number of exam scores. At the end of the while loop, the variable numStudents will have the number of scores in the file. The next step is to create an array of the size numStudents, read the scores from the file again, and this time store them in the array. Consider the following code segment that could be added to the code in Fig. 10.4 to do these tasks:

```
// ** Caution - Possible incorrectly implemented code ** //
// create array of size numStudents
scores = new int[numStudents];
// read scores from input file and save them in array
for(i=0; i<numStudents; i++)
    scores[i] = inFile.nextInt();
```

The above code is syntactically correct. However, when it is executed, a runtime error will be encountered and the program will halt unexpectedly. What is wrong with it? The problem is that after all the scores are read once, the end of the data file is reached and there is nothing left to read. In order to start back at the beginning of the input file, a solution is to close and reopen the file. Once the numbers are stored in the array, the average of the scores will be found. If the average is less than 70, then points are added to every student's score in order to make the average equal to 70. The following is the entire program:

```java
import java.util.*;
import java.io.*;

public class GradesVersion4 {
    public static void main(String[] args) throws IOException {

        // declaration and initialization of variables
        int[] scores;
        int numStudents;
        double total, average;
        String inFileName, outFileName;
        Scanner scanner, inFile;
        PrintWriter outFile;
        scanner = new Scanner(System.in);

        // get name of input file from user
        System.out.print("Enter input filename: ");
        inFileName = scanner.next();

        // open input file
        inFile = new Scanner(new File(inFileName));

        // count number of scores in input file
        numStudents = 0;
        while(inFile.hasNextInt()) {
            numStudents++;
            inFile.nextInt();
        }

        // close input file
        inFile.close();

        // open input file
        inFile = new Scanner(new File(inFileName));

        // create array of size numStudents
        scores = new int[numStudents];

        // read scores from input file and save them in array
        for(int i=0; i<numStudents; i++)
            scores[i] = inFile.nextInt();

        // close input file
        inFile.close();

        // find average
        total = 0.0;
        for(int i=0; i<scores.length; i++)
            total = total + scores[i];
        average = total/numStudents;
```

```
// check if average is less than 70
if(average > 70)
    System.out.println("no score adjustment needed");
else {
    // add points to each score
    for(int i=0; i<numStudents; i++)
        scores[i] += Math.ceil(70-average);

    // get name of output file from user
    System.out.print("Enter output filename: ");
    outFileName = scanner.next();

    // open output file
    outFile = new PrintWriter(new FileWriter(outFileName));

    // output result to output file
    for(int i=0; i<numStudents; i++)
        outFile.println(scores[i]);

    // close output file
    outFile.close();
    }
  }
}
```

If the grades1.txt file shown below is used again as an input file,

```
71
60
75
```

and the user entered grades1adj.txt for the output file as shown below,

```
Enter input filename: grades1.txt
Enter output filename: grades1adj.txt
```

after the execution, the grades1adj.txt file would contain the following:

```
73
62
77
```

which consists of the scores after being adjusted.

10.5 Specifying the File Location

Before reading the contents of the file or writing data to a file, a File object could be created and associated to the file. Consider a file structure in Windows® operating system as shown below:

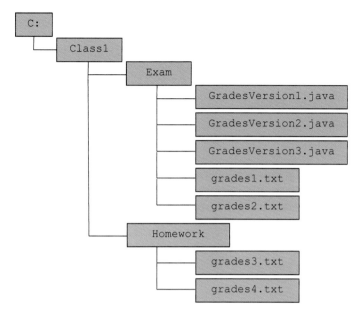

Assuming the current directory is `Exam` and the program is in the `GradesVersion3.java` file, the following statement will create an object of type `File` named `file` by invoking a constructor:

```
File file = new File("grades2.txt");
```

The argument to the constructor designates the name of the file to access. The system assumes the file is located in the current directory of the program. It is also possible to open a file that is stored in a different directory by providing an absolute pathname and a filename. An absolute pathname is the full pathname beginning with the disk drive name. Therefore, the absolute pathname for a file `grades3.txt` in the `Homework` directory in the `Class1` directory is

```
C:\Class1\Homework\grades3.txt
```

A statement in `GradesVersion3.java` program that associates the input file `grades3.txt` to an object of type `File` would be

```
File file = new File("C:\\Class1\\Homework\\grades3.txt");
```

Notice that there are two backslashes to separate directories, `Class1` and `Homework`, and a directory and a file, `Homework` and `grades3.txt`. Recall from Chap. 1 that in order to insert special characters such as a double quotation mark and backslash into a string, Java requires a \ in front of the character like \" and \\, respectively.

Since other operating systems use a forward slash character / to separate directories and a file in the pathname, the forward slash is also allowed in a program run on the Windows® operating system to describe the pathname in order to maintain the consistency across the different computer platforms as in

```
File file = new File("C:/Class1/Homework/grades3.txt");
```

An absolute pathname can also be used with constructors of the `FileReader` and `FileWriter` classes. A pathname a user enters through the keyboard can be stored in the variable of type `String` and used as a parameter, just like the simple filename discussed in the previous section.

10.6 Complete Programs: Implementing File Input and Output

Two complete programs will be discussed here. The first one deals with storing data into a two-dimensional array while reading the data from the file and appending the results into the existing file. The second program deals with strings. The list of strings will be read from the file and placed in the array. After they are sorted, the results will also be stored in the file.

10.6.1 Matrix Multiplication

This section designs a program that performs matrix multiplication. Given two matrices A and B, where both A and B contain 2 rows and 2 columns, the matrix product of A and B is matrix C that contains 2 rows and 2 columns. The entry in matrix C for row i column j, $C_{i,j}$ is the sum of the products of the elements for row i in matrix A and column j in matrix B. That is,

$$\begin{bmatrix} a_{00} & a_{01} \\ a_{10} & a_{11} \end{bmatrix} \times \begin{bmatrix} b_{00} & b_{01} \\ b_{10} & b_{11} \end{bmatrix} = \begin{bmatrix} a_{00} \times b_{00} + a_{01} \times b_{10} & a_{00} \times b_{01} + a_{01} \times b_{11} \\ a_{10} \times b_{00} + a_{11} \times b_{10} & a_{10} \times b_{01} + a_{11} \times b_{11} \end{bmatrix}$$

The program asks a user to enter the name of the file which contains the matrices A and B. Consider the file `matrix.txt` which is used as an input file as shown below.

```
1 2
3 4
5 6
7 8
```

In this example, the matrix A is $\begin{bmatrix} 1 & 2 \\ 3 & 4 \end{bmatrix}$ and the matrix B is $\begin{bmatrix} 5 & 6 \\ 7 & 8 \end{bmatrix}$, and the program will read these values and place them in the two-dimensional arrays named `matrix1` and `matrix2`. The result of the matrix multiplication is saved in the two-dimensional array named `matrix3` and will be appended to the input file `matrix.txt`. The entire program is show below:

```
import java.util.*;
import java.io.*;

public class MatrixMult {
    public static void main(String[] args) throws IOException {

        // declaration and initialization of variables
        int[][] matrix1, matrix2, matrix3;
        int i, j;
        String fileName;
        Scanner scanner, inFile;
        PrintWriter outFile;

        matrix1 = new int[2][2];
        matrix2 = new int[2][2];
        matrix3 = new int[2][2];

        scanner = new Scanner(System.in);
        System.out.print("Enter filename: ");
        fileName = scanner.next();

        // open input file
        inFile = new Scanner(new File(fileName));

        // read two matrices from file
        for(i=0; i<2; i++)
            for(j=0; j<2; j++)
                matrix1[i][j] = inFile.nextInt();
        for(i=0; i<2; i++)
            for(j=0; j<2; j++)
                matrix2[i][j] = inFile.nextInt();

        // close input file
        inFile.close();

        // matrix multiplication
        for(i=0; i<2; i++)
            for(j=0; j<2; j++)
                matrix3[i][j] = matrix1[i][0]*matrix2[0][j]
                             + matrix1[i][1]*matrix2[1][j];

        // open output file
        outFile = new PrintWriter(new FileWriter(fileName, true));

        // append result to output file
        outFile.println();
        for(i=0; i<2; i++) {
            for(j=0; j<2; j++)
                outFile.print(matrix3[i][j] + " ");
            outFile.println();
        }

        // close output file
        outFile.close();
    }
}
```

Notice there are two nested `for` loops to obtain two matrices from the file and place them in the two-dimensional arrays. Since the same file is used for both input and output, the `inFile` is closed after the reading of the matrices. When the same file is opened for output, the second argument of the `FileWriter` constructor is set to be `true` for appending. After the output of a blank line, the result of the matrix multiplication $\begin{bmatrix} 19 & 22 \\ 43 & 50 \end{bmatrix}$ is added to the end of the file `matrix.txt` as shown below:

```
1 2
3 4
5 6
7 8
19 22
43 50
```

10.6.2 Sorting Data in a File

Another program that deals with file input and output is one that sorts string values stored in the file and outputs the results to another file. The input file `terms.txt` consists of one integer and a list of strings as shown below:

```
15
variables
input
output
arithmetic
class
object
contour
selection
iteration
array
recursion
inheritance
polymorphism
exception
file
```

The number 15 indicates the number of words stored in the file. After this number is input, an array of 15 elements is created, and the strings are read and saved in the array. Then the words in the array are sorted using the `sort` method which is a class method of the `Arrays` class. This predefined `sort` method uses a merge sort that is usually discussed in subsequent courses and texts on data structures or algorithm analysis. Here, since the focus is file input and output, a preexisting method is used instead of writing a sort method, although the bubble sort discussed in Chap. 7 could be used instead and is left as an exercise at the end of the chapter. Finally, the sorted list is output to the file `sortedTerms.txt`. The following is the entire program:

```java
import java.util.*;
import java.io.*;

public class SortTerms {
    public static void main(String[] args) throws IOException {

        // declaration and initialization of variables
        String[] term;
        int i, numTerms;
        String fileName;
        Scanner scanner, inFile;
        PrintWriter outFile;

        // open input file
        inFile = new Scanner(new File("terms.txt"));

        // open output file
        outFile = new PrintWriter(new FileWriter("sortedTerms.txt"));

        // input number of strings
        numTerms = inFile.nextInt();
        term = new String[numTerms];

        // read words from file
        for(i=0; i<numTerms; i++)
            term[i] = inFile.next();

        // sort terms
        Arrays.sort(term);

        // output result to file
        for(i=0; i<numTerms; i++) {
            outFile.println(term[i]);
        }

        // close input file
        inFile.close();

        // close output file
        outFile.close();
    }
}
```

After the above code is executed, the output file `sortedTerms.txt` would contain a list of sorted words as shown below:

```
arithmetic
array
class
contour
exception
file
inheritance
input
```

```
iteration
object
output
polymorphism
recursion
selection
variables
```

10.7 Summary

- The `Scanner` class is used to read a text file.
- The `File` class and the `FileReader` class can be used to create an object of the `Scanner` class that opens a text file for input.
- After creating an object of the `Scanner` class to access a text file as input, the methods such as `nextInt` and `next` from the `Scanner` class can be used to read the file.
- The `PrintWriter` class is used for file output.
- When the class `PrintWriter` is used to open a text file for output, a new file is created regardless of whether the file with the same name exists.
- The `File` class or the `FileWriter` class can also be used to create an object of `PrintWriter` class that opens a text file for output.
- In order to append data to the end of a text file, set the second argument of the constructor of the class `FileWriter` to `true`. If the second argument is not present, the value `false` is assumed and an existing file will be replaced.
- After creating an object of the `PrintWriter` class for output, the methods such as `print`, `println`, and `printf` from the `PrintWriter` class can be used to write data to the text file.
- Once all of the operations intended to carry out on a given file have been completed, both the input file and output file should be closed by using the method `close`.

10.8 Exercises (Items Marked with an * Have Solutions in Appendix E)

1. Indicate whether the following statements are syntactically correct or incorrect. If incorrect, indicate what is wrong with the statement:

   A. `Scanner inputFile = new Scanner(new file(Sample.dat));`
 *B. `File in = new File(new FileReader("in.txt"));`
   C. `FileWriter out = new FileWriter(new`
      `PrintWriter("o.txt"));`
 *D. `PrintWriter out = new PrintWriter("out.txt");`
   E. `FileWriter out = new File(new FileWriter("result.out"));`

2. Consider a program that reads data from an input file named `in.dat`, performs calculations, and outputs the results to a file named `result.out`.

   A.   What would happen if the file `in.dat` did not exist before the program is executed?

   B.   What are the contents of the file `in.dat` after the execution of the program?

   C.   What would happen if the file `result.out` did not exist before the program is executed?

   D.   What could happen if the output file was not closed at the end of the execution?

*3. Write a program that asks a user to enter a file name and three numbers, and then store the three numbers in the user-specified file. After the execution of the program, open the file with a utility program to make sure the three numbers are there.

4. Write a program that reads the three numbers from the file created in the previous exercise. After the data are read, display the smallest and the largest of the three numbers.

5. Write a program that asks a user to enter the name of a file, and count and display the number of words that appear in the user-specified file. Use a utility program to create a simple text file that can be used to test the program.

6. Write a program that prompts a user to enter the name of a file and a word. The program should then count all occurrences of the word in the file and display the number of occurrences. Use a utility program to create a simple text file that has many words in it and that can be used to test the program.

7. Rewrite the program that sorts string values stored in the file described in Sect. 10.6.2 so that it uses the bubble sort discussed in Sect. 7.7.2.

8. Write a program that prompts a user to enter the name of a file and a word. The input file should be a simple text file that contains a list of words. Use a binary search to look for he word the user entered and display if the word was found in the list or not.

9. Perform matrix multiplications discussed in Sect. 10.6.1 using non-square matrices.

11
Bit Manipulation

James T. Streib[a*] and Takako Soma[a]

[a] Computer Science Program, Illinois College, Jacksonville, IL, USA

Abstract

This chapter explores bit manipulation including bit-wise logic, shifting, and rotation.

Keywords

Bit-wise Logic, Shifting, Rotation.

11.1 Introduction

Although assembly languages are exceptionally adept for manipulating bits (binary digits), the language C and the subsequent C-based languages such as C++ and Java also have bit manipulation capabilities as well. Instead of having to learn the assembly language of a particular processor, one can just use a C-like language without having to learn a new assembly language, provided there is a translator available for that processor.

So why would one want to manipulate bits in a programming language? The reason is that when interfacing with various devices at a lower-level, various bits within a word of memory might need to be checked and altered in order to communicate with a particular device. This could be especially true for those who are in the engineering disciplines. This chapter can also serve as a precursor to a course on computer organization and assembly language. Although the actual manipulation of a device is beyond the scope of this text, the prerequisite fundamentals of bit manipulation are presented here. It is highly recommended that one has read Section 3.5 of this text prior to reading this chapter and for more information beyond the scope of this chapter, see a text such as *Guide to Assembly Language: A Concise Introduction* [10].

11.2 Simple Conversions

When manipulating bits, binary or base-2 is used instead of decimal or base-10. However, on occasion it is helpful to be able to convert between these two numbering systems. Since this chapter will not be performing any arithmetic, only a cursory overview of the binary or base-2 numbering system will be presented here.

As is already known, the base-10 or decimal numbering system contains ten digits, 0 through 9; however, the base-2 numbering consists of only two digits, 0 and 1. Whereas each position in base-10 is arithmetic a power of 10, each position in binary is a power of 2. For example, the number 124 in base 10 is as follows:

$1 * 10^2 + 2 * 10^1 + 4 * 10^0$

Then converting the powers of ten and since 10^0 equals 1, the equivalent is

$1 * 100 + 2 * 10 + 4 * 1$

which equals 124. Although this seems rather redundant, it forms the basis for all other numbering systems. So, for example, the number 1101 in base-2 is represented as follows:

$1 * 2^3 + 1 * 2^2 + 0 * 2^1 + 1 * 2^0$

Again converting the powers of 2 and since 2^0 is 1, the equivalent would be

$1 * 8 + 1 * 4 + 0 * 2 + 1 * 1$

which equals 13 in base-10. In fact, this is an easy way to convert base-2 numbers to base 10. Another example is what would 11010 be in base 10? Since the digits are only 1 or 0, only the converted powers of 2 that are preceded by 1 need to listed as follows:

$16 + 8 + 2$

which equals 26 in base-10. The reverse of converting base-10 to base-2 is just a little more complicated, but for small numbers the subtraction method works well. One just needs to identify the largest power of 2 that might fit into the base-10 number and then put that number into the corresponding position of the powers of two for a base-2 number. Since really large numbers can be difficult to work with, these examples will be limited to 8-bit numbers where typically 8 bits make up a *byte*. The following place holders show the powers of two for each bit position in a byte:

```
|___|___|___|___|___|___|___|___|
128 64  32  16  8   4   2   1
```

For example, using the number 108, 128 cannot be subtracted from 108 (without having a negative number), so a 0 is put into the 128 position. A 64 could be subtracted from 108, so a 1 is put into the 64 position and subtracting 64 from 108 leaves 44. Then the largest power of 2 that can be subtracted from 44 is 32, so a 1 is put into that position and 32 is subtracted from 44 leaving 12. Since 16 cannot be subtracted from 12, a 0 is placed into the 16 position. So far, the number looks as follows:

```
|_0_|_1_|_1_|_0_|___|___|___|___|
128 64  32  16  8   4   2   1
```

Continuing, an 8 can be subtracted, so a 1 is put into that position, and the 8 is subtracted from 12 leaving 4. Lastly, 4 can be subtracted from 4, so a 1 is put into that position. Since 4 subtracted from 4 leaves 0, the remaining positions are filled with zeros and the process is complete.

|_0_|_1_|_1_|_0_|_1_|_1_|_0_|_0_|
128 64 32 16 8 4 2 1

In another example, what would the number 68 be in base 2? Since a 64 can be subtracted from 68, a 1 is placed in the 64 position and a 4 is leftover. Of course, all that is left to do is put a 1 in the 4 position and the rest of the positions are filled with zeros.

|_0_|_1_|_0_|_0_|_0_|_1_|_0_|_0_|
128 64 32 16 8 4 2 1

In converting in either direction, the other method converting back can be used to check one's work. Although this does not guarantee that the answer is correct (since one might have made a mistake in both directions), it does help to catch a number of errors.

11.3 Declarations and Assignments

Although entire 64-bit words of memory can be manipulated in Java, it can get rather cumbersome trying to illustrate their operations. Again, only 8-bits will be used. Further, since the memory locations will often not be used in arithmetic operations, only unsigned binary numbers will be considered.

Looking back at Table 1.1, notice that the type `byte` might fulfill these two qualifications. Unfortunately, the string methods needed to display binary numbers cause bytes to be converted to integers prior to converting them to strings. As a result, and as will be seen in the complete program in Section 11.7, it is easier to just use integers and display only the lower eight bits of the integer. The result is that to declare a variable the following can be used:

```
int num;
```

To initialize the memory location to 0, either it can be done in the declaration statement above or by the assignment statement below:

```
num = 0;
```

So far, this hardly looks any different than using decimal declaration and assignment statements. This is due in part to the fact the first two numbers, 0 and 1, in both the base-2 and base-10 numbering systems are the same.

But since this chapter is dealing with only 0s and 1s and only 8-bits, it is helpful to other readers of the code to both show all eight bits and indicate that the number is indeed a binary number as follows:

```
num = 0b00000000;
```

The Ob indicates that the number is a binary number and the eight zeros further illustrates that 8 bits are being used. Although not necessary in the example above, the use of the Ob in the following example is very necessary:

```
num = 0b00000100;
```

If the Ob was left off the example above, the number would be interpreted as 100 in base 10 instead of the number 4 in base-2. Again, although there technically wouldn't be any harm in leaving off the leading zeros, it does help reinforce to others that 8 bits are being used.

11.4 Bit-wise Logic Operations

As should be recalled from Section 3.5, the logic operators *and*, *or*, and *not* (&&, | |, and !), are extremely useful in creating more complex conditional statements in if, case, and while statements. However, as cautioned in Section 3.5 leaving off the second & or | can cause potential serious errors. By leaving off the second symbol, one has created what is known as bit-wise logic symbols. Instead of dealing with the truth or falsity of an expression, one is testing the individual bits within a memory location which is the subject of this section.

To avoid confusion when talking about bit positions, typically the right-most bit is position 0 and the left-most bit is the nth-1 bit position. If an 8-bit memory location is being used, n would be equal to 8, so the left-most position would be the 7th position.

```
|__|__|__|__|__|__|__|__|
  7  6  5  4  3  2  1  0
```

There are four bit-wise logic operations that can be used in Java, *and*, *or*, *xor*, and *not* represented by &, |, ^, and ~, respectively. The *and* and *or* instructions work similarly to the previous logic instructions, except instead of dealing with true and false, these new instructions deal with 1's and 0's, where a 1 is the equivalent to true and 0 is the equivalent to false. The result is 1 & 1 is 1 and all other combinations are 0. With the | inclusive-or instruction, if one or the other bit position, or both are 1, the result is 1, otherwise the result is 0. With the ^ exclusive-or, if one or the other position is 1, the result is 1. However, if both positions are 1 or both 0, the result is 0. An easy way to remember the distinction between these two instructions is recall that | includes the case where both operands are 1, whereas the ^ excludes this case and the result is 0. Of course, the not operation ~ changes 1 to 0 and vice versa. All of the above are represented in table 11.1.

Bit-wise Operation	Java Symbol
and	&
inclusive – or	|
exclusive - or	^
not	!

Table 11.1 Bit-wise logical operators

For example, assuming that `num1 = 0b11001100` and `num2 = 0b11110000`, what would be the result of

```
ans = num1 & num2;
```

To help determine the result, the following can be helpful where the only positions that contain two ones in the same bit position are the first two on the left so that the result in `ans` is shown below:

```
num1 = 11001100
num2 = 11110000
     & ──────────
 ans = 11000000
```

Given the same two values in `num1` and `num2`, what would be the result of the | inclusive-or operation? If either of the bit positions contains a 1 or both are 1 the result is a 1, so that `ans` is as follows:

```
num1 = 11001100
num2 = 11110000
     | ──────────
 ans = 11111100
```

Continuing, given the same initial values, what would be the result of the ^ exclusive-or operation? Only when there is a 1 in a bit-position and the other is a 0 is the result 1, otherwise the result is 0 as shown below:

```
num1 = 11001100
num2 = 11110000
     ^ ──────────
 ans = 00111100
```

Of course, the ~ not operations just reverse the bits so that

```
ans = ~ num1;
```

would result in:

```
num1 = 11001100
    ~  ‾‾‾‾‾‾‾‾
 ans = 00110011
```

11.5 Testing, Clearing, Setting, and Toggling

Given the above, what are some possible uses for these bit operations? They can be used for testing, clearing, setting, and toggling various bit positions. For example, assume that num contains the following bit pattern:

```
int num = 0b00100110;
```

and that the 2nd bit position (3rd from the right) needs to be checked to see if it is set to 1. How could this be accomplished? What needs to be done is to mask out all the other bit positions to 0 and not alter bit position 2. Which operation could be used for clearing out all of the other bits? Recall that when using an & only bit positions that are both 1's will still be 1 so that 0 & 1, 1 & 0, or 0 & 0 would be 0. The result is that a mask of 0b00000100 could be used. If bit position 2 is a 1 it will remain a 1 and if it is a 0 it will remain a 0 as shown for both cases below:

```
 num = 00100110              num = 00100010
mask = 00000100             mask = 00000100
   &  ‾‾‾‾‾‾‾‾                 &  ‾‾‾‾‾‾‾‾
 ans = 00000100              ans = 00000000
```

The result in ans could be used in a subsequent if statement to output a message or the expression itself could be used in an if statement, both as shown below. If the expression only needs to be checked once, then the one on the right could be used or if the expression might be needed to be checked again later in the program, the one on the left is preferred to avoid the possibility of subsequent keying errors.

```
ans = num & mask;
if(ans == 0b00000100)              if(num & mask == 0b00000100)
   System.out.println("Bit 2 set");      System.out.println("Bit 2 set");
```

Alternatively, after the operation with the mask one could check to see whether the result is not equal to 0, since only bit 2 could be set and otherwise the result would be all zeros. In another example, what if bit position 2 in num needed to be cleared to 0 without altering the other bit positions? The operation above should give a clue, where the & operation can be used to clear some bit positions and not alter others. Instead of a mask with a 1 in bit-position 2, there would be a 0 in bit-position 2 with all other positions being a 1 as follows:

```
  num  = 00100110              num  = 00100010
 mask  = 11111011             mask  = 11111011
      & ————————                   & ————————
  num  = 00100010              num  = 00100010
```

If bit position 2 contained a 1, it now contains a 0 and if the position contained a 0 it remains a 0. Note that all the other bit positions remain unchanged using the above mask in the following instruction:

```
num = num & mask;
```

Instead of clearing out bit position 2 in num, what if it needed to be set to 1 without altering any of the other bit positions? In this case the | operation would work best where bit-2 in the mask would be set to 1 since 1 | 0 is 1 and 1 | 1 is also 1. All the other bits would be set to 0 so that the rest of the bits would remain unchanged as shown below:

```
  num  = 00100110              num  = 00100010
 mask  = 00000100             mask  = 00000100
      | ————————                   | ————————
  num  = 00100110              num  = 00100110
```

Note that when bit position 2 is already a 1 it remains a 1 but when the position is a 0 it is set to a 1 while all the other positions remain the same using the mask above and the following instruction:

```
num = num | mask;
```

Lastly, what if bit position 2 needed to be toggled from a 1 to 0 or from a 0 to a 1. At first it might seem that the ~ operation might be the best choice, but it would toggle all the bits which in this case is not what is intended. Instead, the ^ exclusive-or would work and bit-2 in the mask would be set to a 1, where 1 ^ 1 is 0 and 0 ^ 1 is 1. All the other bits would be set to 0 so that the rest of the bits would remain unaltered.

```
  num  = 00100110              num  = 00100010
 mask  = 00000100             mask  = 00000100
      ^ ————————                   ^ ————————
  ans  = 00100010              ans  = 00100110
```

In both cases above, bit-2 is toggled and the rest of the bits remain unchanged using the following code.

```
num = num ^ mask;
```

If more than one bit needed to be toggled such as both bits 2 and 3 above, all that needs to be done is change the mask to 0b00001100. The same is true for all of the other examples where different masks can be used to manipulate various bits and these are left as exercises.

Since the above operations are extremely useful in modifying individual bits or groups of individual bits and have been summarized in Table 11.2.

Operation	Logic
Set	Or
Test	And
Clear	And
Toggle	Xor

Table 11.2 Set, test, clear, and toggle

11.6 Shifting

In addition to manipulating individual bits or groups of bits all at once, sometimes it is necessary to manipulate individual bits one at a time. Instead of having to have eight groups of instructions to check eight bits one at a time, the individual bits could be manipulated one at a time in a loop. In order to check the individual bits, the left-shift << and right-shift >>> instructions can be used. Assume that num is declared as follows:

```
int num = 0b11000111;
```

Again, technically an int variable is 32-bits long and would look as follows:

```
00000000000000000000000011000111
```

As before, this would be cumbersome to deal with each time. So, for convenience only 8 bits will be shown to illustrate many of the concepts. The result is that this text will pretend that a word of memory is only 8-bits long and the above will only be displayed as the following:

```
11000111
```

To illustrate how the left-shift works, assume the following instruction:

```
num = num << 1;
```

The above would cause each bit to be shifted to the left one bit and the right-most bit would then contain a 0. Further, the left-most bit would fall off the left and the results would be as follows:

```
10001110
```

Starting again with the original declaration for num,

```
int num = 0b11000111;
```

the contents for num could be shifted to the right. However, in Java there are two different shifts to the right: the arithmetic right-shift >> and the logical right-shift >>>. When dealing with signed numbers, the left-most bit is considered to be the sign-bit. Briefly, when dealing with an arithmetic right-shift instead of zero filling in on the left, the sign-bit is copied in order to maintain the proper sign of the number. However, since the discussion of how signed numbers are stored in memory is beyond the scope of this text and as mentioned at the beginning of this chapter, a computer organization text or an assembly language text should be consulted for further information [10]. Would there be a distinction between an arithmetic left-shift and a logical left-shift? The answer is no, thus the need for only one symbol, <<.

Since the process of performing logical bit manipulation is usually performed only on unsigned numbers, the logical right-shift >>> can be used. So given the following instruction:

```
num = num >>> 1;
```

the result is as follows:

```
01100011
```

Note that the 1 in the right-most position has moved off the right end and a 0 has moved in on the left-end. Although a number other than 1 can be used to indicate the number of positions to move, each bit cannot be tested. However, this deficiency can be rectified by using a loop as shown below.

For example, what if the number of bits that are set to 1 in bit positions 0 through 3 need to be counted? Since only 4 bits are to be checked, a for loop would be a good choice. Further, the count of the number of 1s should be initialized to 0. Also, instead of being input (which will be discussed in the next section), assume num is declared as given below. Note that the contents of num will be destroyed by the process of shifting so it is advisable to save the contents in a variable such as saveNum prior to the manipulation and restore num afterwords. Given all of the above, the following initial code segment is provided:

```
int num = 0b00001101, mask = 0b00000001;
int saveNum, count;
saveNum = num;
count = 0;
for (i=1; i<=4; i++) {

}
num = saveNum
```

Recalling the bit manipulation techniques in the previous section and using Table 11.2, the & operation is the best choice. Then the right-most bit of num can be tested to see if it is equal to 1 as shown below:

```
if (num & mask == 0b00000001)
   count ++;
```

Then the contents of num could be shifted to the right for subsequent counting as follows:

```
num = num >>> 1;
```

Putting it all together and outputting count, the segment would look as follows:

```
int num = 0b00001101, mask = 0b00000001;
int saveNum, count;
saveNum = num;
count = 0;
for (int i=1; i<=4; i++) {
   if (num & mask == 0b00000001)
       count ++;
   num = num >>> 1;
}
num = saveNum
System.out.println("The count is: " + count);
```

11.7 Precedence

Just as there is a precedence for arithimetic operators as discussed in Section 1.8 and a precedence for logical operators as discussed in Section 3.5, there is a precedence for bit-wise operators as well as shown in Table 11.3.

Operator	Precedence
innermost nested ( )	Highest
~	
<< , >>>	
&	
^	
|	
Tie - left to right	Lowest

Table 11.3 Bit-wise precedence

Notice that the shift operators are all at the same level of precedence and hold a place lower than *parentheses* and the *not* operator, yet above the *and*, *exclusive-or* and *inclusive-or*. Note that due to the possibility of logic errors and to help others understand the logic, it is typically not recommended to include the shift operators in the same expression as the other bit-wise opeators.

Looking only at the bit-wise logic operators, they have a similar precedence to the logical operators of Section 3.5. For example, looking only at the bit-wise operators what would be the result of the following:

```
w = 0b10110111;
x = 0b11011110;

z = ~w | x;
```

The highest prioity would be the ~ operator so `~0b10110111` would be `0b01001000` and then performing the or operation with ~w would be as shown below:

```
~w =  01001000
 x =  11011110
  |  ─────────
 z =  11011110
```

Assuming the existence of another variable y as given below, what would the result of the following be?

```
y = 0b00111011;

z = w | x & y;
```

Recalling that & has a higher precedence than |, the following would be the intermediate result represented by i:

```
 x =  11011110
 y =  00111011
  &  ─────────
 i =  00011010
```

Then the | can be performed as follows:

```
 w =  10110111
 i =  00011010
  |  ─────────
 z =  10111111
```

Given the sometimes complicated nature of bit-wise logic it is helpful to perform calculations by hand before coding them in a program to avoid time consuming debugging later. Note that the DeMorgan's rules as presented in Section 3.5 also apply to bit-wise operations and this is left as an exercise in Section 11.10.

11.8 Complete Program: Implementing Bit-wise Operators

To test all of the logic and shift instructions it is helpful to have a program to see how they work. Although some calculators have bit manipulation functions it is further helpful to have a program to also see how the code is implemented.

The program in Fig. 11.1 uses three methods to help clean up the `main` method. The first method called is `input8` which inputs a manipulation binary number consisting of only 1s and 0s. This is accomplished by using:

```
bNum = scanner.nextInt(2);
```

The number 2 above indicates that base-2 will be used for input. Further, so that only the lower eight binary digits will be used, recall that the `&` operation is useful for this task as follows:

```
bNum = bNum & 0b11111111;
```

Even though the upper 0s in the mask are not shown, all the bits to the left of bit 7 will be cleared to zeros and the lower 8 bits will remain intact.

Note that here and elsewhere in the program, whenever a binary number is entered, it is echoed using the method `output8`. Although this can be removed, it is helpful to confirm what one has entered. Speaking of the output method `output8`, it uses the `toBinaryString` method to convert the number in `bNum` to a string as shown below:

```
bString = Integer.toBinaryString(bNum);
```

If one has wondered why the variables used in this program are not declared as a byte instead of an integer, the problem is with the `toBinaryString`. As mentioned previously, in the conversion from a number to a string, it does not matter if `bNum` is declared as `byte`, it will convert the number to an integer before converting it to a string. Thus, instead of fighting this process, it is simply easier to declare the variables as an integer initially. Continuing, once converted to a string the code below will output the right-most 8 bits.

```
zString = String.format("%8s", bString).replace(' ','0');
```

The result is that even when trying to format the string as `%8s` in the `String.format` method, all the leading 0s in the string will unfortunately be output which can be distracting. So using the `replace` method, all the leading 0s will be replaced with spaces and they will not be output with the `%8s` in the `format` method which makes for much nicer looking output. Although all of this might be a little confusing, this code can be used in subsequent programs and thus the reason for supplying it in this section as a complete program.

Returning back to the main program, to make the input easier, only a single character is used to represent the various operations to performed, where `L` and `R` are used to represent the operations `<<` and `>>>`, respectively. Further, the use of single characters is helpful in the subsequent `switch` statement as will be discussed shortly. Of course, this can be improved upon and is left as an exercise.

Next, since some of the operators are unary operators such as ~, they only require one operand. However, others such as & require two, so an `if` statement is used to input the second operand as needed.

The `switch` statement is convenient for performing the various operations based on the character entered previously. Again, the results of some of these operations can move bits into the upper bit positions of an `int` variable, such as the left-shift operator, so they should be cleared out. Likewise, the ~ not operator can change the 0s in the upper bits to 1s and they would need to be cleared also, thus the reason for the following statement after the `switch` statement:

```
answer = answer & 0b11111111;
```

Again, the purpose of this complete program is not only to illustrate the results of various operations, but also to help one implement some of the pesky details needed to input, output, and use only the lower 8 bits of a 32-bit integer. Further, it can serve as an example for other programs and as a source of modifications, all as suggested in the exercises.

```
import java.util.*;

class Bitp1 {
   static Scanner scanner;
   public static void main (String [] args){

      int x,y=0,answer=0;
      char op;

      // input binary x
      x =  input8();
      // output to verify input
      output8(x);

      // input operation code
      scanner = new Scanner(System.in);
      System.out.println();
      System.out.print("Enter an operation ( |, ^ , & , ~ ,"
      + " L , R ): ");
      op = scanner.next().charAt(0);

      // check binary operators
      if (op=='|' || op == '^' || op == '&') {
         // input binary y
         y = input8();
         //ouptut to verify input
         output8(y);
      }

      // check and perform operation
      switch (op) {
          case '|': answer = x | y;
                  break;
          case '^': answer = x ^ y;
                  break;
```

```
                case '&': answer = x & y;
                        break;
                case 'L':
                case 'l': answer = x << 1;
                        break;
                case 'R':
                case 'r': answer = x >>> 1;
                        break;
                case '~': answer = ~x;
                        break;
                default:
                    System.out.println("Invalid entry");
        }
        // Clear upper bits
        answer = answer & 0b11111111;
        // ouput results
        System.out.println();
        output8(answer);
        System.out.println();
    }

    // input 8 binary bits
    public static int input8 () {
        int bNum;
        scanner = new Scanner(System.in);
        System.out.println();
        System.out.print("Enter a binary number: ");
        // input base 2
        bNum = scanner.nextInt(2);
        // clear upper bits
        bNum = bNum & 0b11111111;
        return bNum;
    }

    // output 8 binary characters
    public static void output8 (int bNum) {
        String bString,zString;
        // convert to string
        bString = Integer.toBinaryString(bNum);
        // insert leading zeros and output
        zString = String.format("%8s", bString).replace(' ','0');
        System.out.println(" The binary number is: " + zString);
    }
}
```

Fig. 11.1 Complete program for testing bit-wise operators

As a sample of the input and output of the program in Fig. 11.1, consider the following two examples. Of course the reader is encouraged to try other data and operations and possibly make some changes as suggested in the exercises or by one's instructor.

```
Enter a binary number: 11001100
 The binary number is: 11001100

Enter an operation ( |, ^ , & , ~ , L , R ): &

Enter a binary number: 11110000
 The binary number is: 11110000

 The binary number is: 11000000


Enter a binary number: 11000111
 The binary number is: 11000111

Enter an operation ( |, ^ , & , ~ , L , R ): R

 The binary number is: 0110001
```

11.9 Summary

- The inclusive-or includes the case when both operands are 1s and the result is 1, whereas the the exclusive-or excludes this case.
- To set, toggle, clear, and test bits, use the |, ^, and in the last two cases & instructions, respectively.
- If data is needed later, be sure to save it when using any of the bit-wise logic instructions or the << and >>> instructions.
- The precedence rules for bit-wise operators are similar to the ones for logical operators in Section 3.5 and are summarized in Table 11.3.

11.10 Exercises (Items Marked with an * Have Solutions in Appendix E)

Some of these problems can be solved using a calculator or the complete program in Section 11.8 but it is advisable not to use them in order to gain practice and further because these tools might not be available during a quiz or exam.

1. Convert the following binary numbers to their decimal equivalent:

    *A. 00101111
    B. 01010010
    *C. 01110110
    D. 00111001

2. Convert the following decimal numbers to their binary equivalent:

    *A. `33`
    B. `72`
    *C. `120`
    D. `145`

3. Given the following variables, give the result of each of the following operations (show all 8 bits):

```
int num1 = 0b00110101, num2 = 0b11001010, ans;
```

    *A.   `ans = num1 & num2;`
    B.   `ans = num1 | num2;`
    *C.   `ans = ~num2;`
    D.   `ans = num1 ^ num2;`

4. In addition to the variables in problem 3 above, assume the existence of the following variable and answer the following questions:

```
int num3 = 0b10101100;
```

    *A.   `ans = -num1 & (num2 | num3);`
    B.   `ans = num1 | num2 ^ num3;`
    *C.   `ans = ~ (num1 | num3);`
    D.   `ans = num1 ^ num2 & num3;`

5. Converrt the following expressions using DeMorgan's rules:

    A. `z = ~x | ~y;`
    B. `z = ~(x | y);`

6. Given a variable `num1`, perform each of the following operations. Show all 8 bits positions in the masks.

    A. Clear bits 5 and 6.
    B. Set bits 0 and 1.
    C. Toggle bits 2, 5, and 7.
    D. Shift to the left 2 bits
    E. Shift logically to the right 3 bits.

7. What would happen to an 8-bit word if it was shifted 8 bits to the left? What would happen if shifted logically 8 bits to the right?

8. Modify the complete program in Section 11.8 to input << instead of L and >>> instead of R. Further, modify to program to allow the user to enter the number of bits to shift to the left or right.

9. Read another source on arithmetic right shifts such as *Guide to Assembly Language* [10] and then modify the complete program in Section 11.8 to include the arithmetic right shift >>.

10. Assume that an int variable status indicates the current state of an automobile according to the following table. Write a complete program to input the 8-bits of status and for each bit, output the appropriate message starting with bit 0. Note that a loop does not need to be used.

Bit Message

0   Low oil pressure
1   Low fuel
2   Low tire pressure
3   Low battery voltage
4   Low washer fluid
5   Dirty air filter
6   Dirty cabin filter

12

Introduction to Parallel Processing Programming

Abstract

This chapter discuses parallel processing and parallel programming. After the brief introduction of common microprocessor systems, programming in multi-core shared memory multiprocessor systems is introduced using Pyjama. A parallel program and a serial program are compared by taking the running time of both program executions.

Keywords

Parallel program, Shared memory multiprocessor, Pyjama

Suppose a group of building blocks are counted by color before creating a miniature city. If there are about 1000 blocks and 4 different colors: red, blue, yellow, and orange; how long does it take to count them by color? Unsurprisingly, it could take a long 40 minutes. If someone could help, would it take less time? Of course. How long would it be? At half the time, 20 minutes. What if two more people, total of 4 people, count the 1000 blocks by color? Would it take 10 minutes? If several people perform the task simultaneously, it will take less time to complete it.

This idea can be applied when running computer programs. Instead of using one processor, a task can be divided into several processors and each processor performs a part of the task at the same time in parallel. In this chapter a concept of parallel computation and parallel programming will be introduced.

12.1 Multiprocessor Systems

Most modern micro computers have multi-core processors that consist of a number of independent processing units called *physical cores* or cores. A *core* is a well-partitioned piece that is capable of independently performing all functions of a processor. It is the same as the Central Processing Unit (CPU) in a general-purpose microprocessor.

A shared memory multiprocessor is a computer system in which two or more processors share a common main memory. Each processor can directly access any data location in the main memory and at any time a different processor can execute different instructions on different data.

A single physical CPU core with *hyperthreading* capability appears as two logical CPUs, also called *logical cores* or logical processors, to an operating system. Although the operating system sees two processors, the actual CPU hardware has only a single set of execution resources for two logical cores. The CPU pretends it has more physical cores than it does, and it uses its own logic to speed up program execution. When subcomponents of the core are not being used for certain types of instructions, another instruction can be executed, so the core could work on 2 things concurrently.

A dual-core processor with hyper-threading consists of 2 physical cores and appears as 4 cores (logical cores) to the operating system. If a system has four dual-core processors with hyper-threading, the operating systems sees 16 logical cores. Similarly, a quad-core processor with hyper-threading provides 8 logical cores as shown in Fig. 12.1. The LC in the figure stands for a logical core. Hyperthreading can help speed up the system, however logical cores are not true CPUs as the physical cores are and parallelism in its real sense is not attainable on a single-core processor.

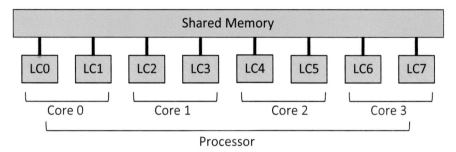

Fig. 12.1 A quad-core processors with hyper-threading shared-memory multiprocessor system

12.2 Programming Multi-core and Shared Memory Multiprocessor Using Pyjama

Among many different parallel and distributed systems, multi-core and shared memory multiprocessors are commonly used. In this section, programming such systems is introduced using Pyjama [11]. Pyjama is a Java version of OpenMP [6] which is a widely used application programming interface that is suited for the implementation of multithreaded programs.

12.2.1 Using Pyjama to Write Multithreaded Programs

A parallel program running on a shared memory multiprocessor usually consists of multiple threads. A *thread* of execution is the smallest sequence of programmed instructions that can be managed independently by an operating system's scheduler. The implementation of threads and processes differs from one operating system to another, but in most cases a thread is contained inside a process. The multiple threads in a given process run in a shared memory space, whereas processes do not share resources. Therefore, threads in different process do not share resources. The number of threads may vary during program execution but at any time each thread is being executed on one logical core. If there are less threads than logical cores, some logical cores are kept idle. If there are more threads than logical cores, the operating system applies *multiprogramming* among threads running on the same logical cores. Multiprogramming is where multiple application programs reside in the main memory on a processor system and the operating system executes part of one application program in a thread, then part of another application program in a thread, and so on. To the user, it appears that all programs are executing at the same time. However, since there is only one processor, there is no true simultaneous execution of different programs.

A multithreaded program can be written in different programming languages using many different libraries and frameworks. Using the programming language Java, the Runnable class can be used. Another approach is to use Pyjama which is a parallel programming environment best suited for writing parallel programs that are to be run on shared memory systems. The combination of compiler directives and library functions can provide a programming environment where the programmer can focus mostly on the program and algorithms, and less on the details of the underlining computer system.

12.2.2 "Hello World"

Consider the Output program back in Fig. 1.8 which prints "Hello World" once on the monitor. In order to run the program using the command prompt instead of using an IDE; first go to the folder where the program resides and then use the command "javac" to compile the program as shown below:

```
>javac Output.java
```

If the javac command was not recognized, search for the javac executable file in the system and set a path. For example, if the file is located in the C:\Program Files\Java\jdk-16.0.1\bin directory, the following command can be used in order to set the PATH environment variable.

```
>set path=C:\Program Files\Java\jdk-16.0.1\bin
```

The executable file javac can be referred to once the path is set. Then the next command tells the Java compiler and interpreter where to find the source files. The period indicates the current directory.

```
>set classpath=.
```

To execute the program, the "java" command is used as follows:

```
>java Output
```

In the Command Prompt window, the following output will be seen:

```
Hello World
```

Next, assuming the system has 4 processors, the program can be modified to run using 4 processors and output "Hello World" once from each processor. Four processors will run the same code independently and simultaneously. To illustrate Pyjama API elements, the program in Fig. 1.8 is used and modified as shown in Fig. 12.2. Pyjama provides directives that tell the compiler about the parallelism in the source code and creates instructions for generating the parallel code which is the multithreaded translation of the source code. A line beginning with `//#omp` is treated as a compiler directive by the Pyjama compiler but ignored as comments by the other compilers.

```
public class OutputParallel {
   public static void main(String[] args) {
       int numThreads;
       numThreads = 4;
       System.out.println("Hello World Program");
       //#omp parallel num_threads(numThreads)
       {
           int myID;
           myID = Pyjama.omp_get_thread_num();
           System.out.println("Hello World from thread " + myID);
       }
       System.out.println("End");
   }
}
```

Fig. 12.2 Hello World! using 4 processors

This program starts as a single thread, which is the first thread, that prints out "`Hello World Program`". Once the flow of control reaches the `parallel` directive, 3 additional threads are created. Clauses can be used along with directives to further specify the behavior. The `num_threads` clause tells how many threads are used in the parallel section. All 4 threads, the initial thread and newly created threads, execute the statement immediately following the directive: in this example each thread prints out "`Hello World from thread `" and its unique thread number obtained by calling the method, `omp_get_thread_num`. When all threads finish printing, 3 threads created by the `parallel` directive are terminated, the program continues as a single thread that prints out "`End`", and terminates the program.

After downloading Pyjama [2], to compile the program shown in Fig. 12.2 use the command as follows:

```
>java -jar Pyjama-3.1.0.jar OutputParallel.java
```

A jar file is a collection of class files that are compiled java programs. The `-jar` option is used to specify the jar file to run the main program contained in the jar file in order to compile the `OutputParallel` program. To run it, use the command:

```
>java -cp Pyjama-3.1.0.jar;. OutputParallel
```

Notice that to run the `outputParallel` program, the `-CP` option is used to specify the jar file that contains the necessary class files. The jar file along with the main program in this case `outputParallel` are executed together. Since the number of threads is specified to 4, the program might print out a line from the 4 threads in the following order:

```
Hello World Program
Hello World from thread 3
Hello World from thread 1
Hello World from thread 2
Hello World from thread 0
End
```

If the program is run again, it may print:

```
Hello World Program
Hello World from thread 1
Hello World from thread 0
Hello World from thread 2
Hello World from thread 3
End
```

Notice that during the first run, the thread 3 printed "Hello World" first, then the threads 1, 2, and 0. The second time, the thread 1 printed first, then the threads 0, 2, and 3 followed.

Once the threads are started, it is up to the underlying operating system to carry out scheduling and to resolve competition for the single standard output. Therefore, if the program is run several times, "Hello World" will most likely be printed from the 4 processors in a different order each time.

12.2.3 Sorting Building Blocks

Returning back to the idea of building block pieces, counting blocks is faster if several people work together. This will be demonstrated by writing both serial code and parallel code where Fig. 12.3 contains the serial code. There are 1000 blocks stored in a one-dimensional array, called blocks. By calling the getBlocks method one of the 4 colors; red, blue, yellow, and orange will be assigned in each element of the array. The color is randomly chosen. Then, the program will check each element in the array and if the contents is "Red" the counter for the red pieces called numRed will be incremented by one. If it is "Blue" then the numBlue variable is incremented, and so on. After that, the number of blocks will be printed by color.

```
public class CountBlocksSerial {
    public static void main(String[] args) {
        int numRed, numBlue, numYellow, numOrange;
        String[] blocks;
        blocks = new String[1000];
        numRed = numBlue = numYellow = numOrange = 0;
        getBlocks(blocks);
```

```
        for(int i=0; i<blocks.length; i++) {
            if(blocks[i].equals("Red"))
                numRed++;
            if(blocks[i].equals("Blue"))
                numBlue++;
            if(blocks[i].equals("Yellow"))
                numYellow++;
            if(blocks[i].equals("Orange"))
                numOrange++;
        }

        System.out.println("Number of red blocks is " + numRed);
        System.out.println("Number of blue blocks is "
                            + numBlue);
        System.out.println("Number of yellow blocks is "
                            + numYellow);
        System.out.println("Number of orange blocks is "
                            + numOrange);
    }

    public static void getBlocks(String[] blocks) {
        int color;
        for(int i=0; i<blocks.length; i++) {
            color = (int) (Math.floor(Math.random() * 4));
            switch(color) {
                case 0: blocks[i] = new String("Red");
                        break;
                case 1: blocks[i] = new String("Blue");
                        break;
                case 2: blocks[i] = new String("Yellow");
                        break;
                case 3: blocks[i] = new String("Orange");
                        break;
            }
        }
    }
}
```

Fig. 12.3 Serial building blocks counting program

The sample output is shown below:

```
Number of red blocks is 232
Number of blue blocks is 247
Number of yellow blocks is 251
Number of orange blocks is 270
```

As can be seen, since the color of the building blocks was chosen randomly, each color has about the same number of blocks. The serial code imitates one person counting blocks. Now to simulate the counting of building blocks by several people, the task of counting blocks is distributed among several processors to run in parallel.

The parallel program shown in Fig. 12.4 starts as a single thread. Once the flow of control reaches the `parallel` directive, several additional threads are created. There are two clauses for the `parallel` directive, the `num_threads` and the `shared` in order to specify the further behavior. The number of threads that perform the parallel section is determined by the `num_threads` clause. In Pyjama, variables declared before a parallel block can be accessed by all the threads by listing in the `shared` clause. They include `blocks`, `numThreads`, `numBlocks`, `numRed`, `numBlue`, `numYellow`, and `numOrange`. Variables declared in the parallel block such as `myPart`, `myID`, `myFirstPos`, `myLastPos`, `myNumRed`, `myNumBlue`, `myNumYellow`, and `myNumOrange` can only be accessed by a single thread. All threads including the initial thread and the newly created threads execute statements immediately following the `parallel` directive. When all threads finish the parallel section, threads created by the `parallel` directive are terminated and the program continues as a single thread that outputs the results and terminates the program.

The number of processors and the number of building blocks to run the program will be specified by the user during the command line execution. Any information typed after the main class name on the command line when invoking the interpreter using the `java` command is called a command-line argument and can be referenced in the program. The arguments are always treated as a list of strings and in this program the array that stores command-line arguments is called `args`. The program uses two command-line arguments. The number of threads read from the command line is stored as the first argument in `args[0]` and the number of blocks is the second argument stored in `args[1]`. Then the following two assignment statements assign the number of processors in the `numThreads` variable and the number of blocks in `numBlocks` after converting `String` values to `int` using the `parseIntg` method defined in the `Integer` class.

```
numThreads = Integer.parseInt(args[0]);
numBlocks = Integer.parseInt(args[1]);
```

Note that without recompiling the program, it can be executed again, giving it different command-line arguments, and producing different results.

If there are 1000 building blocks and 4 helpers, each will count 250 blocks by color. How can the blocks stored in a one-dimensional array be divided among 4 processors in the program? The first processor will have blocks located position from 0 to 249 in the array, the second processor from 250 to 499, the third processor from 500 to 749, and the fourth processor from 750-999. The number of blocks that each processor deals with can be found by total number of blocks divided by the number of processors. In this example 250 (= `1000 / 4`) is stored in the `myPart` variable. The position of the first block each processor handles can be found using a formula, `myPart * myID`. The `myID` variable contains the ID number of processor that is found by calling the method `Pyjama.omp_get_thread_num()`. If 4 processors are used, each processor would have ID number 0, 1, 2, or 3. Therefore, the processor 0 will check the element staring from 0 (=`myPart` `*` `myID` `=` `250` `*` `0`) and the last position plus one which will be used in the `for` loop is 250 (= `myFirstPos` + `myPart` = `0` + `250`). For the second processor, `myFirstPos` is 250 (= `myPart` `*` `myID` `=` `250` `*` `1`) and `myLastPos` has 500 (= `myFirstPos` + `myPart` = `250` + `250`), and so on. The `if(myID == numThread-1)` statement takes care when the `numBlocks` does not divide exactly by `numThreads`.

After all processors finish counting the number of blocks in 4 different colors and storing the value in local variables such as `myNumRed` that is only visible by an individual processor, values would be summed up and placed into the global variables such as `numRed` that are accessible by all the processors. As individual processors can access any memory location in the main memory and execute instructions independently, it may result in a *race condition* which is a situation where the result depends on a random precise timing of read/load and write/store accesses to the same location in the main memory. Using 4 processors, P0, P1, P2, and P3, suppose P0 counted 42 red blocks and stored 42 in its own `myNumRed`, P1 had 62 and stored 62 in its own `myNumRed`, P2 had 50, and P3 had 76. The total is 230 and `numRed` should be 230 at the end.
The `numRed` is initially 0 and suppose P1 reads the content of `numRed` as 0, adds 62 to 0, and stores 62 in `numRed`. Next, P3 read the value 62 in `numRed`, adds 76 to 62, and updates `numRed` to 138. If P0 does the same followed by P2, there will be no problem. The `numRed` would have the value 230 in conclusion. However, since each processor could access memory anytime in any order, if P3 reads the value of `numRed` after P1 reads the value 0 but before performing addition and updating the variable, P3 would read 0 in the `numRed`. While P1 adds 62 to 0 and updates the variable `numRed` to 62, P3 adds 76 to 0 and updates `numRed` to 76 after P1's update, erasing the value 62 that P1 puts in earlier, which means 62 was not included in the total number of red blocks after all.

To avoid race conditions described above, the assignment to update variables `numRed`, `numBlue`, `numYellow`, and `numOrange` can be put inside a *critical section* – a part of a program that is performed by at most one thread at a time. This is achieved by the `critical` directive which is applied to the statement or a block immediately flowing it shown in Fig 12.4. The program works correctly because the `critical` directive performs locking around the code it contains, i.e., the code that access variables `numRed`, `numBlue`, `numYellow`, and `numOrange` and thus prevents race conditions.

```
public class CountBlocksParallel {
   public static void main(String[] args) {
       int numThreads;
       int numBlocks;
       int numRed, numBlue, numYellow, numOrange;
       String[] blocks;
       numRed = numBlue = numYellow = numOrange = 0;
       numThreads = Integer.parseInt(args[0]);
       numBlocks = Integer.parseInt(args[1]);
       blocks = new String[numBlocks];
```

```
      getBlocks(blocks);

      //#omp parallel num_threads(numThreads) shared(blocks,
            numThreads,numBlocks,numRed,numBlue,
            numYellow,numOrange)
      {
         int myPart, myID, myFirstPos, myLastPos;
         int myNumRed, myNumBlue, myNumYellow, myNumOrange;
         myNumRed = myNumBlue = myNumYellow = myNumOrange = 0;
         myPart = numBlocks / numThreads;
         myID = Pyjama.omp_get_thread_num();
         myFirstPos = myPart * myID;
         if(myID == numThreads-1)
            myLastPos = numBlocks;
         else
            myLastPos = myFirstPos + myPart;

         for(int i=myFirstPos; i<myLastPos; i++) {
            if(blocks[i].equals("Red"))
               myNumRed++;
            if(blocks[i].equals("Blue"))
               myNumBlue++;
            if(blocks[i].equals("Yellow"))
               myNumYellow++;
            if(blocks[i].equals("Orange"))
               myNumOrange++;
         }
         //#omp critical
         {
            numRed += myNumRed;
            numBlue += myNumBlue;
            numYellow += myNumYellow;
            numOrange += myNumOrange;
         } // end of critical section
      } // end of parallel section

      System.out.println("Number of red blocks is " + numRed);
      System.out.println("Number of blue blocks is "
                           + numBlue);
      System.out.println("Number of yellow blocks is "
                           + numYellow);
      System.out.println("Number of orange blocks is "
                           + numOrange);
   }

   public static void getBlocks(String[] blocks) {
      int color;
      for(int i=0; i<blocks.length; i++) {
         color = (int) (Math.floor(Math.random() * 4));
         switch(color) {
            case 0: blocks[i] = new String("Red");
                    break;
```

```
                case 1: blocks[i] = new String("Blue");
                        break;
                case 2: blocks[i] = new String("Yellow");
                        break;
                case 3: blocks[i] = new String("Orange");
                        break;
            }
        }
    }
}
```

Fig. 12.4 Parallel building blocks counting program

To compile and run the program shown in Fig. 12.4 use the following commands. Note that it will use 4 threads to count 1000 building block by colors.

```
>java -jar Pyjama-3.1.0.jar CountBlocksParallel.java
>java -cp Pyjama-3.1.0.jar;. CountBlocksParallel 4 1000
```

The sample output is shown below:

```
Number of red blocks is 251
Number of blue blocks is 249
Number of yellow blocks is 254
Number of orange blocks is 246
```

12.3 Analysis

How can one compare a parallel program and a serial program? The running time or execution time of both program executions could be measured and compared. Also, the program in Fig. 12.4 can be executed using a different number of threads.

The execution time is measured using the Date class in the java.util package. A Date object can call the getTime method of the Date class to record the start time. After the section that is being measured is completed, the end time is recorded. By subtracting the start time from the end time, the elapsed time in milliseconds can be obtained. In order to use the Date class, the following import statement that was introduced in Sect. 1.2.2 needs to be added to the program:

```
import java.util.*;
```

Then, the two lines shown below are included in the declaration section at the beginning of the program.

```
    Date startTime, endTime;
    Double elapsedTimeInSec;
```

Further, the following statements should be added before and after the parallel section in Fig. 12.4 which includes the critical sections since the critical section is performed by an individual processor.

```
startTime = new Date();   // current time at start
// parallel section
   ...
// end of parallel section
endTime = new Date();   // current time at end
elapsedTimeInSec = (endTime.getTime() - startTime.getTime())
                   / 1000.0;
System.out.println(numBlocks + " blocks are counted by "
                   + numThreads + " processors and took "
                   + elapsedTimeInSec + " secs.");
```

The running times of the program with 1, 2, 3, 4, 5, 6, 7 and 8 threads using 1,000,000 blocks are shown in the Fig. 12.5. The timing was taken 10 times for each case and the average was used to plot the results. The x-axis is the number of threads and y-axis is the timing in seconds. As can be seen and as expected, the timing decreases as the number of threads increases. Then, why does the graph become flat for using more than 4 threads? This is because the program was run using the computer that has a dual-core processor with hyper-threading which consists of 2 physical cores and appears as 4 logical cores to the operating system. When the tasks are divided into more than 4 parts, the operating system scheduled them among 4 logical cores. Also notice that the huge drops in execution times from number of threads from 1 to 2. This is because tasks are performed truly in parallel using 2 physical cores in the system.

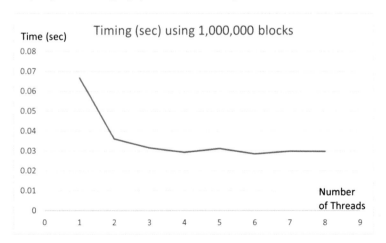

Fig. 12.5 Running times of the program in Fig. 12.4

It is also good to know how many times the parallel execution is faster than the sequential exertion. *Speedup* is measured in the time it took to complete in sequential code divided by the time it took to complete in parallel code. It is a measure that demonstrates the relative benefit of solving a problem in parallel. Speedup can be defined as follows:

$$S = \frac{T_{sequential}}{T_{parallel}}$$

When the program in Fig. 12.4 was executed using 1 thread it took 0.0667 seconds on average and took 0.0361 seconds on average with 2 threads running on two cores. Therefore, the speedup is 1.848 (= 0.0667 / 0.0361). Using 3 threads, the speedup was 2.111 (= 0.0667 / 0.0316) and using 4 threads 2.269 (= 0.0667 / 0.0294). Assuming the system has 4 physical processors, theoretically the speedup using 2 processors would be 2, 3 with 3 processors, and 4 with 4 processors, and it can never exceed the number of processors. Notice that the best speedup was achieved when using 2 threads due to the simultaneous execution on 2 physical cores. Although the speedup was observed in general in this example, it was not optimal. This may be because there are only two physical cores even though the operating system sees 4 logical cores. Also, it may be due to how the parallel program was implemented using critical section. The use of critical sections slows down the program because at any moment at most one thread can perform the addition and assignment while all other threads are kept waiting.

12.4 Complete Program: Implementing Parallel Inner Product

Combining all the material from this chapter, one can now write a simple parallel program. In this section, a program to compute an inner product of two vectors will be developed. An inner product is used in geometry and physics and defined for a vector $a = [a_0, a_1, a_2]$ and a vector $b = [b_0, b_1, b_2]$ as:

$$a \cdot b = a_0 \times b_0 + a_1 \times b_1 + a_2 \times b_2$$

The number of processors and the size of vectors will be specified by the user during the command line execution. The number of processors the user selected is stored in the numThreads variable and the size of vectors stored in vecSize. The two vectors are initialized to random numbers. Each processor will determine the part of vectors that it is responsible for calculating before performing the computation. Since updating innerProduct by all processors may cause race conditions, it is placed inside the critical section. The complete program is given in Fig. 12.6.

```
public class InnerProductParallel {
    public static void main(String[] args) {
        int numThreads, vecSize;
        int innerProduct;
        innerProduct = 0;
        numThreads = Integer.parseInt(args[0]);
        vecSize = Integer.parseInt(args[1]);
        int[] a, b;
        a = new int[vecSize];
        b = new int[vecSize];
```

```
      getVec(a);
      getVec(b);

      // parallel section
      //#omp parallel num_threads(numThreads)
            shared(numThreads, innerProduct, vecSize, a, b)
      {
         int myPart, myID, myFirstPos, myLastPos;
         int myInnerProduct;
         myInnerProduct = 0;
         myPart = vecSize / numThreads;
         myID = Pyjama.omp_get_thread_num();
         myFirstPos = myPart * myID;
         if(myID == numThreads-1)
            myLastPos = vecSize;
         else
            myLastPos = myFirstPos + myPart;

         // multiplication and addition
         for(int i=myFirstPos; i<myLastPos; i++)
            myInnerProduct = myInnerProduct + (a[i] * b[i]);

         // critical section: update innerProduct
         //#omp critical
         {
            innerProduct += myInnerProduct;
         } // end of critical section
      } // end of parallel section

      // print the contents of vectors if the size is small
      if(vecSize <= 10) {
         System.out.print("a = [");
         for(int i=0; i<vecSize; i++)
            System.out.print(a[i] + " ");
         System.out.println("]");
         System.out.print("b = [");
         for(int i=0; i<vecSize; i++)
            System.out.print(b[i] + " ");
         System.out.println("]");
      }
      System.out.println("Inner Product is " + innerProduct);
   }

   public static void getVec(int[] array) {
      for(int i=0; i<array.length; i++)
         array[i] = (int)(Math.floor(Math.random() * 1000));
   }
}
```

Fig. 12.6 Parallel inner product program

The sample output using arrays of size 5 running on one processor is found below to show the correctness of the program. Note that in order to see the benefit of running the program in parallel, the size of the data has to be large.

```
a = [305 652 524 445 503 ]
b = [270 129 796 227 903 ]
Inner Product is 1138786.
```

12.5 Summary

- A parallel program divides a task and executes each task at the same time using multiple processors.
- A thread is a sequence of programmed instructions that can be managed independently by an operating system's scheduler.
- A shared memory multiprocessor is a computer system in which two or more processors share a common main memory.
- A race condition is a situation where the result depends on random precise timing of read/load and write/store accesses to the same location in the main memory.
- A critical section is a part of a program that is performed by at most one thread at a time to avoid a race condition.
- A speedup is measured in the time it took to complete a sequential code divided by the time it took to complete a parallel code.
- Better speedup can be observed using number of physical cores compared to using logical cores since logical cores are not true CPUs and parallelism in its real sense is not attainable.

12.6 Exercises (Items Marked with an * Have Solutions in Appendix E)

1. Review the Section 12.2.3 and find the myFirstPos and myLastPos for each processor for the following cases.

   *A. when numThreads = 4 and numBlocks = 1500
    B. when numThreads = 6 and numBlocks = 1500
    C. when numThreads = 6 and numBlocks = 1500

2. Would it help to place the section where each processor prints "Hello World" in Fig. 12.2 in the critical section? If so why and if not, why not?

3. Plot execution times of several runs of the complete program shown in Fig. 12.6 with a different number of threads and see the speed up.

4. Write both serial code and parallel code to find a maximum number stored in 2-dimensional array. Plot execution times of several runs with a different number of threads and to see the speed up.

*5. Write both serial code and parallel code to perform vector addition. Plot execution times of several runs with a different number of threads and to see the speed up. (Note: only the answer to the serial and parallel programs will be given in the Appendix E)

6. Write both serial code and parallel code to perform matrix-matrix multiplication. Plot execution times of several runs with a different number of threads and to see the speed up.

Appendix A: Explanation and Elaboration of Concepts in Chapter 1

This appendix includes a detailed explanation and an elaboration of the code used in Chapter 1. Note that in addition to the new material, some of the items from Chapter 1 might be explained once more for the sake of continuity. For experienced programmers with knowledge of OOP in another language, the various sections can be read as needed. However, for a reader that is new to OOP, it is advisable that Chapters 2 and 5 be read prior to Section A.1 and Chapter 9 prior to Section A.4.

A.1 Skeleton Program and "Hello World"

As introduced in Section 1.1 and 1.2, the skeleton and "Hello World" programs introduced the basic structure of a Java program and simple output. The "Hello World" program from Figure 1.2 is shown again here in Figure A.1.

```
class Output {
    public static void main(String[] args) {
        System.out.println("Hello World!");
    }
}
```

Fig. A.1 Hello World program revisisted

The first line in the program begins with the reserved word `class`. A class is a definition of a group of objects that includes data members (places to store data) and methods (places to put the program logic). The word `Output` is an identifier and the class name usually beginning with a capital letter is provided by the programmer. The definition of the class consisting of the data and methods is placed between the first opening brace and the last closing brace, { }.

This class has one method definition starting on the second line. The first three words in the second line are reserved words. The word `public` is the access or visibility modifier and the `main` method is always defined using `public` visibility, so that the program can be executed by the interpreter. The word `static` means this is a class method, and the `main` method is always declared `static` so that it can be executed without creating an instance of the class. The word `void` means that `main` is a non-value-returning method. Next, `main` is the name of the method and the instructions in the `main` method will be executed first. Inside of the parentheses after the name of the method, parameters are listed along with their types to allow the method to receive values. The parameter called `args` is of type `String` and the square brackets, `[]`, indicate `args` is an array, where strings

J. T. Streib and T. Soma, *Guide to Java*, Undergraduate Topics in Computer Science, https://doi.org/10.1007/978-3-031-22842-1

and arrays were discussed in Chaps. 6 and 7 , respectively. The definition of the `main` method also starts with an opening brace and ends with a closing brace.

Inside the braces, a sequence of instructions would be placed. For now, it contains a `System.out.println("Hello World!");` statement as discussed in Chapter 1 and elaborated on in the next section. Note that GUI-Based output is discussed in Section A.4.

A.2 Text-based Output: `print` and `println`

Recall the following statement from the previous section which outputs "Hello World" and moves the cursor to the next line:

```
System.out.println("Hello World!");
```

However, what would happen should one leave off the `ln` portion of the `println`, as shown below?

```
System.out.print("Hello World!");
```

Given the previous description concerning the `println`, the output would be as follows:

```
Hello World!_
```

At first glance, this does not appear to be much different than the original sample output. However, if one looks carefully, note the location of the cursor. It is not on the second line but rather at the end of the string. The statement outputs the string to the screen, but with the absence of the `ln`, the cursor does not move down to the next line. In fact, if the cursor does not show up on the screen, one would not notice the difference. Even though it might not be detected on the screen, it is important to know where the cursor is located, so that subsequent input and output is correct.

Again recall the following statements from Section 1.3 which outputs the words `"Hello"` and `"World!"` on two separate lines with the cursor on the third line.

```
System.out.println("Hello");
System.out.println("World!");
```

However, what if one accidently used two separate `System.out.print` statements instead?

```
System.out.print("Hello");
System.out.print("World!");
```

The output would appear as given below:

```
HelloWorld!_
```

Note that this output appears similar to using a single `System.out.print` statement as shown previously. Why are they similar? After the first `System.out.print` output the word `Hello`, the cursor stayed on the same line and did not move to the second line. So, when the second `System.out.print` was executed, the word `World!` was output on the same line, and since there was no `ln` in the second statement, the cursor stayed on the same line. One might also notice there is no space between the two words. Why did this happen? Since there is no space at the end of the first string within the double quotes, nor a space at the beginning of the second string, a space did not appear in the output.

Although this is similar to the example using the `System.out.print`, could it be changed to mimic the first example in this section? The answer is yes, as in the following example:

```
System.out.print("Hello ");
System.out.print("World!");
System.out.println();
```

In this case, the word `Hello` followed by a space would be output, and then the word `World!` would be output. The last line would output nothing, because there is no string in the parentheses, but the `ln` would cause the cursor to move down to the next line as shown below:

```
Hello World!
```
—

Although the above three-line code segment produces the same output as the original single-line statement, why would one want to use this latter example? Usually, one would not and a single statement is usually preferable to using multiple statements.

As a last example of formatting output, recall the following code segment from Section 1.6.1 which outptuts "Hello" and "World!" separated by a blank line. With the cursor following on the fourth line?

```
System.out.println("Hello");
System.out.println();
System.out.println("World!");
```

However, what if one wanted to output two blank lines, would the following code segment work?

```
System.out.print("Hello");
System.out.println();
System.out.println();
System.out.println("World!");
```

At first glance, it might appear to work, but look carefully. Notice that the first statement does not contain a `println` but rather only a `print`. The result would be exactly the same as the previous code segment since the first statement outputs the word `Hello`, but does not move the cursor down to the next line on the screen. The second statement is a `System.out.println`, and it moves the cursor down from the first line to the second line of output. The second `System.out.println` creates a single blank line.

Unfortunately, this is a mistake that is sometimes made by beginning Java programmers, where they assume that anytime there is a `System.out.println();` a blank line is produced. The only time a blank line is produced is when there is not a preceding `System.out.print` statement.

The correct code segment to produce two blank lines is given below. Note that the first statement is a `System.out.println`.

```
System.out.println("Hello");
System.out.println();
System.out.println();
System.out.println("World!");
```

This is yet another reason why one should tend to avoid using the `System.out.print` statement unless under special circumstances such as with prompts for input as discussed in Section 1.7.1. and when one needs to break up an output line using multiple statements as dicussed in Chap. 3 on selection statements.

A.3 Text-based Input

Figure A.2 is the program from Figure 1.11. The `import` statement on the first line allows the use of the predefined `Scanner` method for input. All the predefined classes and methods in the Java API are organized into packages where a package is like a folder in which classes can be stored. The `import` statement identifies those packages that will be used in a program. For example, the following statement imports the `Scanner` class of the `java.util` package:

```
import java.util.Scanner;
```

A second option uses an asterisk to indicate that any class inside the package might be used in the program. Thus, the statement

```
import java.util.*;
```

allows any of the classes in the `java.util` package to be referenced. The second option is used in the program shown in Fig. A.2.

```
import java.util.*;
class InputOutput {
    public static void main(String[] args) {
        int num;

        Scanner scanner;
        scanner = new Scanner(System.in);

        num = scanner.nextInt();

        System.out.println("The integer is " + num);
    }
}
```

Fig. A.2 Program to input an integer revisisted

Note that the `System.out.println`, `System.out.print`, and `System.out.printf` statements were used in Chapter 1 for output and the `java.lang` package which includes the `System` class was not imported at the beginning of the program. This is because the `java.lang` package, which includes the `System` and `Math` classes, is used extensively, and it is automatically imported into all Java programs.

Returning back to Fig. A.2, in order for input to work properly, one needs a place to store the data entered. As should be known, the first statement in the body of the main method declares the variable `num` as type `int`. The next statement is the declaration of the variable `scanner` of type `Scanner` as shown below:

```
Scanner scanner;
```

`Scanner` is not a primitive data type like `int` or `double`, but rather a class. Then the following statement,

```
scanner = new Scanner(System.in);
```

creates a new instance of the `Scanner` class, or in other words a `Scanner` object. Unlike output, input is not directly supported in Java; however, the `Scanner` class can be used to create an object to get input from the keyboard. Java uses `System.in` to refer to the standard input device, which is the keyboard. The above statement then assigns a reference to the new object to the variable `scanner`.

The next statement below shows how the `Scanner` object is used to scan the input for the next integer. The method `nextInt` will make the system wait until an integer is entered from the keyboard, and then the integer input is assigned to the variable `num`:

```
num = scanner.nextInt();
```

The value in `num` can then be output as done in Figure A.2. Of course, it is usually best to provide a *prompt* to let the user know what should be input as originally shown in Fig 1.12.

A.4 Overview of Java Packages

In Chap. 9, the concept of inheritance was introduced. Using inheritance, a more specified class called a subclass can be defined from an existing class called a superclass and the subclass inherits, or extends, the superclass. Most of the standard classes are subclasses of other standard classes, which are themselves subclasses of other classes, forming an inheritance hierarchy. The inheritance hierarchy of standard classes can be found in the Oracle Java API documentation at http://docs.oracle.com/javase/7/docs/api/index.html.

The class `Object` is the root of the class hierarchy in Java, meaning the `Object` class is directly or indirectly a superclass of all the predefined and user-defined classes. The commonly used classes such as `Math.String` and `System` are subclasses of the `Object` class. The list below shows the inheritance hierarchy of some classes and where they are discussed in the text:

- `java.lang.Object`
  - `java.io.File` (Chap. 10)
  - `java.awt.Component` (Appendix A, Section A.5)
  - `java.lang.Math` (Chap. 1)
  - `java.lang.Number` (Chap. 1)
  - `java.lang.String` (Chap. 6)
  - `java.lang.System` (Chap. 1)
  - `java.lang.Throwable` (Appx. B)
  - `java.util.Scanner` (Chap. 1)
  - `javax.swing.ImageIcon` (Appendix A, Section A.5)

For example, the `Number` class is a subclass of the `Object` class and subclasses of the `Number` class includes `Byte`, `Double`, `Float`, `Integer`, `Long`, and `Short` classes that are also introduced in Chap. 1.

In Java, classes are grouped into packages according to functionality. Many of the commonly used classes reside in the `java.lang` package and any class in the package is automatically available to all Java programs. To use a class that is not in the `java.lang` package, the compiler needs to know where to find the class. To do this, an `import` statement is inserted at the top of the program before the `class` statement that begins the program as described in Chapter 1.

As mentioned in Chap. 2, one of the advantages of an object-oriented programming language like Java is that a well-written class can be reused. Java provides thousands of predefined classes that can be used to add functionality to programs. Collections of related classes are organized in a package and can be imported into programs.

A.5 More on GUI-based Output and Input

Output and input using message dialog boxes and input dialog boxes were introduced in Chap. 1. In this section packages, where the GUI classes are contained, are discussed in addition to the overloaded methods of `showMessageDialog` and `showInputDialog`. The inheritance hierarchy of the `JOptionPane` class is shown below:

- `java.lang.Object`
- `java.awt.Component`
  - `java.awt.Container`
    - `javax.swing.JComponent`
      - `javax.swing.JOptionPane`

Each successive subclass inherits everything from its superclass and either adds new features or replaces the inherited ones. The `javax.swing.JOptionPane` is a subclass of `java.swing.JComponent` class, which is a subclass of `java.awt.Container`, class and so forth. As discussed in Chap.1 a dialog box created using the statement `JOptionPane.showMessageDialog(null, "Hello, World!");` will display in the center of the screen. If the dialog box is to appear in the specific location on the screen, a `JFrame` object can be passed to the `showMessageDialog` method. As can been seen in the class hierarchy of the `Frame` class below and the `JOptionPane` classes above, they share the same grandparent, `java.awt.Container`.

```
- java.lang.Object
    - java.awt.Component
        - java.awt.Container
            - java.awt.Window
                - java.awt.Frame
```

As shown below, after creating an instance of the `JFrame` class, calling the `setVisible` method with `true` makes the frame visible on the screen. The `setLocation(100, 100)` makes the frame appear 100 pixels down and 100 pixels to the right from the top-left corner of the screen. The message dialog box will appear on the top of the frame.

```
JFrame frame = new JFrame();
frame.setVisible(true);
frame.setLocation(100, 100);
JOptionPane.showMessageDialog(frame, "Hello World!");
```

There are two overloaded `showMessageDialog` methods. Using them, there is an option of selecting an icon to be displayed in the message box: an error message icon, an information message icon, a warning message icon, a question message icon, or no icon. A customized icon can also be placed in the dialog box. An icon helps the user identify the kind of message that is being displayed. The following example outputs a text "Cinders and ashes!" in the dialog box and "Warning" in the title bar. A warning message icon is also displayed by sending an argument, `JOptionPane.WARNING_MESSAGE`, to the `showMessageDialog` method.

```
JOptionPane.showMessageDialog(null,
                             "Cinders and ashes!",
                             "Warning",
                             JOptionPane.WARNING_MESSAGE);
```

The dialog box looks like the following when the statement above is executed.

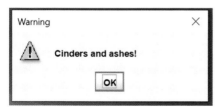

The argument ERROR_MESSAGE can be used to display an error message icon including INFORMATION_MESSAGE for an information message icon, WARNING_MESSAGE for a warning message icon, QUESTION_MESSAGE for a question message icon, and PLAIN_MESSAGE for no icon. The INFORMATION_MESSAGE is the default value if the type of the message was not specified.

To display a customized icon, suppose a picture of the sun is created using drawing software and saved as sun.jpg. The image file should be placed in the directory where the Java main program resides. In the program an ImageIcon object is created and associated with the sun.jpg image as shown below. The JOptionPane.PLAIN_MESSAGE is sent to the showMessageDialog method as the third argument, so that no predefined icon will be displayed. Instead, the picture of the sun will appear sending the sunIcon object to the method.

```
ImageIcon sunIcon = new ImageIcon("sun.jpg");
JOptionPane.showMessageDialog(null,
                              "It is a sunny day!",
                              "Today",
                              JOptionPane.PLAIN_MESSAGE,
                              sunIcon);
```

The above statements display the following message dialog box with a smiley sun drawing.

There are 4 overloaded showInputDialog methods besides the one mentioned in Chap. 1. As with message dialog boxes, an icon showing the type of the message and a customized icon can be passed to the methods. The showInputDialog methods also accepts initial (default) values placed in the input field. A dropdown menu can also be added to the text box.

An example using the showInputDialog method with 7 arguments is shown below. The first argument, null, displays the dialog box in the center of the screen. The second argument is a string to display in the dialog box. The third argument is a string to display in the title bar. The fourth argument displays a question mark icon in the dialog box. The fifth argument is null since no customized icon is used. The sixth argument is an array containing the possible selections: First-year, Sophomore, Junior, or Senior. The seventh argument is the value used to initialize the input field, which in this case is the first string First-year in the possibleValues array. The `showInputDialog` method returns the value the user selected which is a reference to the object of type `Object` meaning an object of any type. The object is typecast into the `String` type so that the value of type `String` can be stored in `selectedValue`.

```
String[] possibleValues = {"First-year", "Sophomore",
                           "Junior", "Senior"};
String selectedValue =
               (String)JOptionPane.showInputDialog(null,
               "What is your classification?",
               "Input",
               JOptionPane.QUESTION_MESSAGE, null,
               possibleValues, possibleValues[0]);
```

When the statement above is executed, the dialog box shown below appears on the screen with a default value, "First-year" in the text box.

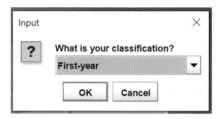

The user can select, for example, "Junior" from the drop-down menu as shown below and click OK button.

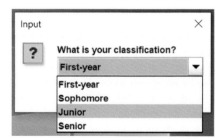

A.6 Confirmation Dialog Boxes

In addition to the message dialog boxes and input dialog boxes introduced previously, two additional dialog boxes are discussed in this section and the next section: confirmation dialog boxes and option dialog boxes.

A confirmation dialog box gives buttons to select, and when a user clicks one of the buttons, it returns an integer value. Recall the code segment from Fig. 6.3 in Chap. 6 that checks the string value the user enters after playing one Tic Tac Toe game to determine if the user wants to play another game. Again, assuming the program to play a Tic Tac Toe game has been written, the code segment in Fig. 6.3 can be rewritten using a confirmation dialog box as shown below instead of having the user enter "yes" or "no" :

```
int selection;
do {
    // play one Tic Tac Toe game
    selection = JOptionPane.showConfirmDialog(null,        //#1
    "Would you like to play another Tic Tac Toe game?", //#2
    "Confirmation",                                       //#3
    JOptionPane.YES_NO_OPTION);                           //#4
} while(selection == JOptionPane.YES_OPTION);
```

The showConfirmDialog method passes four arguments labeled in the comment to the right as #1 through #4 . The first argument, null , places the dialog box in the center of the screen. The second argument is a descriptive message to be output above the buttons in the dialog box to inform the user what should be done. The third argument is the title of the dialog box that appears in the window's title bar. The fourth argument defines the set of option buttons that appear at the bottom of the dialog box. The JOptionPane.YES_NO_OPTION option displays a **Yes** button and a **No** button. The integer returned from the method indicates which option was selected by the user. When the user clicks the **Yes** button in the dialog box shown below, an integer value 0, which is the value of the constant JOptionPane.YES_OPTION, is returned. When the user clicks the **No** button, an integer value 1, which is the value of the constant JOptionPane.NO_OPTION, is returned. Therefore, the return value from the confirmation dialog box could be 0 or 1, and the programmer does not have to remember the actual value returned for the specific case. Whatever the value is, if the user clicks the **Yes** button, the return value should match with the value of the constant JOptionPane.YES_OPTION . Thus, all the programmer has to write is selection == JOptionPane.YES_OPTION instead of comparing the return value with the actual integer.

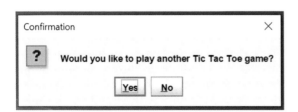

With the above code, if the user clicks the **Yes** button after playing one Tic Tac Toe game, a new game will start. The user keeps playing as long as the **Yes** button is selected. When the code segment above is actually executed, since it does not contain the code which implements the Tic Tac Toe game, it simply keeps showing the confirmation dialog box inside the loop until the user clicks the **No** button.

A.7 Option Dialog Boxes

In addition to the `JOptionPane.YES_NO_OPTION` option that was discussed in the previous section, the `JOptionPane` class defines another set of option buttons that appear in the dialog box including `JOptionPane.YES_NO_CANCEL_OPTION` which displays **Yes, No,** and **Cancel** buttons and `JOptionPane.OK_CANCEL_OPTION` which displays **OK** and **Cancel** buttons. Is there any way the buttons other than **Yes**, **No**, **Cancel**, or **OK** could be displayed in the dialog box? The answer is yes. An option dialog box allows a programmer to create custom buttons using an array structure introduced in Chap. 7 .

As an example, assume that every conference attendee will fill out a survey at the conclusion of the conference. Each question will appear in the dialog box and an attendee will select one of the buttons. An example question is shown below:

As can be seen, there are six option buttons with custom labels and a conference attendee can click any of them. Besides displaying a question and buttons, the program needs to know which button the user pressed and stores the information. The code to display the above dialog box is shown below:

```
int selection;
String[] options;
options = new String[6];
options[0] = "N/A";
options[1] = "awful";
options[2] = "poor";
options[3] = "average";
options[4] = "good";
options[5] = "excellent";
selection = JOptionPane.showOptionDialog(null,      //#1
    "Overall, What did you think of the conference?", //#2
    "Conference Survey",                              //#3
    JOptionPane.DEFAULT_OPTION,                       //#4
    JOptionPane.QUESTION_MESSAGE,                     //#5
    null,                                             //#6
    options,                                          //#7
    "average");                                       //#8
```

As before, the first argument of the `showOptionDialog` method indicates the placement of the dialog box. The `null` value centers the dialog box on the screen. The second argument is the question displayed above the option buttons. The third argument is the title of the dialog box which appears in the window's title bar. The fourth argument indicates the set of option buttons. The `DEFAULT_OPTION` is used since the programmer will define buttons in the seventh argument. If the predefined option such as `JOptionPane.YES_NO_OPTION` is used, then the seventh argument would be set to `null`. The fifth argument defines the style of the message. Here one of the default icons, `QUESTION_MESSAGE`, is used to display a question mark. The sixth argument can place additional icons in the dialog box. In this example, since the question mark icon is already added by the previous parameter, the `null` value is used to not display any more icons. The seventh argument specifies the buttons. The labels of the buttons are stored in the `String` array named `options`. The last argument allows a programmer to specify an initial choice. Since the argument is `"average"`, the **average** button is outlined, and if the user simply presses the **enter** key without choosing any of the buttons, the **average** button will be selected as a default. The `showOptionDialog` method returns an `int` value indicating the button that was activated. It basically returns the index value of the array `options`. For example, when the **N/A** button is selected, it returns the value `0` because the `String` value `"N/A"` is stored in the first location of the array, and when the **awful** button is clicked, the value `1` is returned. The integer value from each question can be used to create the result of the survey.

For more information about dialog boxes, please refer to the Java API specification document at the Oracle website at http://docs.oracle.com/javase/7/docs/api/index.html .

Appendix B: Exceptions

Building robust programs is essential to the practice of programming. Robust programs are able to handle error conditions gracefully. If a program crashes when an invalid input is entered, the program is not very robust. This appendix describes a process called exception handling which can be used to improve the robustness of the program to prevent it from crashing and allow it to terminate in a controlled manner.

B.1 Exception Class and Error Class

An *exception* represents an execution error, an error condition, or an unexpected event that occurs during the normal course of program execution. It is an instance of a class in the Java Application Programming Interface (API) which is a predefined set of classes that can be used in any Java program. The Java API contains an extensive hierarchy of exception classes. A portion of the hierarchy is shown in Fig. B.1.

- Throwable
    - Error
        - OutOfMemoryError
        - StackOverflowError
        - AssertionError
    - Exception
        - IOException
            - CharConversionException
            - EOFException
            - FileNotFoundException
        - RuntimeException
            - ArithmeticException
            - IllegalArgumentException
                - NumberFormatException
            - IndexOutOfBoundsException
                - ArrayIndexOutOfBoundsException
                - StringIndexOutOfBoundsException
            - NullPointerException
            - NoSuchElementException
                - InputMismatchException

Fig. B.1 Hierarchy of exception classes

As one can see, all of the classes in the hierarchy are subclasses of the `Throwable` class. Just below the `Throwable` class are the classes `Error` and `Exception`. Subclasses of the `Error` class are for exceptions when a critical error occurs, such as an internal error in the Java interpreter which indicates it has run out of resources and cannot continue operating. Subclasses of the `Exception` class include `IOException` and `RuntimeException` which also serve as superclasses to other classes. `IOException`

J. T. Streib and T. Soma, *Guide to Java*, Undergraduate Topics in Computer Science, https://doi.org/10.1007/978-3-031-22842-1

is the superclass for exceptions related to input and output operations. `RuntimeException` serves as the superclass for exceptions that result from programming errors, such as an out of bounds array index.

When an exception occurs, it is said to have been *thrown*. Unless an exception is detected by the program and dealt with, it causes the program to halt. To detect whether an exception has been thrown and prevent it from halting the program, Java allows programmers to create an exception handler which is a section of code that is executed when an exception is thrown. *Exception handling* is the process of catching an exception and then handling it. If the program does not provide an exception handler, the system uses the default exception handler, which outputs an error message and stops the program. The next section will show how exceptions can be caught and processed.

B.2 Handling an Exception

Consider the following program which asks a user for a test score and then outputs it. When the program in Fig. B.2 is executed using a sample input of 80, the output is as follows:

```
Enter the score: 80
Your score is 80.
```

```java
import java.util.*;

class ScoreVersion1 {
    public static void main(String[] args) {
        int score;
        Scanner scanner;
        scanner = new Scanner(System.in);
        System.out.print("Enter the score: ");
        score = scanner.nextInt();
        System.out.println("Your score is " + score + ".");
    }
}
```

Fig. B.2 A program without exception handling

When a valid input is entered, the program terminates successfully. What happens if the real number 80.0 is entered instead of an integer? The program will halt in the middle of the execution and gives the error message shown below:

```
Enter the score: 80.0
java.util.InputMismatchException
    at java.util.Scanner.throwFor(Scanner.java:840)
    at java.util.Scanner.next(Scanner.java:1461)
    at java.util.Scanner.nextInt(Scanner.java:2091)
    at java.util.Scanner.nextInt(Scanner.java:2050)
    at ScoreVersion1.main(ScoreVersion1.java:9)
```

This error message indicates the system has caught an exception called the `InputMismatchException`, because the value entered was of type `double` which cannot be read using the `nextInt` method. If the input was 8o, the digit 8 and a lower-case letter o, the system will catch the same exception because the combination of a number

8 and a lower case letter o is not an integer. In the absence of an exception handler by a programmer, a single thrown exception will most likely result in program termination. Instead of depending on the system for exception handling, one can write code that catches and handles exceptions to increase the program's robustness.

To handle an exception, a try-catch control statement is coded. In order to catch an InputMismatchException exception, the following code can be used:

```
try {
    // try block
}
catch (InputMismatchException exception) {
    // catch block
}
```

After the keyword try, a block of code follows inside braces. This block of code is known as a try block. A try block has one or more statements that can potentially throw an exception, such as input statements. After the try clause comes a catch clause. A catch clause begins with the keyword catch, followed by a parameter declaration which includes the name of an exception class and a parameter. If the code in the try block throws an exception of the InputMismatchException class, an object of the InputMismatchException class is created. It will be caught by the catch clause and referenced by the variable exception. Then, the code in the catch block is executed. Note that both the try block and the catch block require braces.

From the code shown in Fig. B.2 , the statement score = scanner.nextInt(); should be placed inside the try block because it can potentially throw an exception when a user enters a non-integer value. The statements that are executed in response to the thrown exception are placed in the matching catch block. To simply display an error message and continue when the exception is thrown, a try-catch statement can be added to the code in Fig. B.2 as shown below:

```
import java.util.*;

class ScoreVersion2 {
    public static void main(String[] args) {
        int score;
        Scanner scanner;
        scanner = new Scanner(System.in);
        System.out.print("Enter the score: ");
        try {
            score = scanner.nextInt();
            System.out.println("Your score is " + score + ".");

        }
        catch (InputMismatchException exception) {
            System.out.println("Error: Score must be integer.");
        }
    }
}
```

If there are several statements in the `try` block, they are executed in sequence. When one of the statements throws an exception, control is passed to the matching `catch` block and the statements inside the `catch` block are executed. The execution then continues to the statement that follows the `try-catch` statement, ignoring any remaining statements in the `try` block. For example, if the user enters 8o, a number 8 and a lower case letter o , an exception is thrown, the program will skip the second statement, `System.out.println("Your score is " + score + ".");` in the `try` block, and the error message in the `catch` block will be output. Since there are no more statements in the program, it will terminate. The output would then look like the following:

```
Enter the score: 8o
Error: Score must be integer.
```

If no statements in the `try` block throw an exception, then the `catch` block is ignored and execution continues with the statement following the `try-catch` statement. For example, the input 80 will result in the following:

```
Enter the score: 80
Your score is 80.
```

By adding the `try-catch` statement, the program will not crash when a non-integer value is entered. However, it would be nice if the user is asked to re-enter the input in order to continue. To accomplish this, the entire `try-catch` statement can be placed inside a loop as shown in Fig. B.3 .

```java
import java.util.*;

class ScoreVersion3 {
    public static void main(String[] args) {
        boolean flag;
        int score;
        Scanner scanner;
        scanner = new Scanner(System.in);
        flag = true;
        while(flag) {
            System.out.print("Enter the score: ");
            try {
                score = scanner.nextInt();
                flag = false;
            }
            catch (InputMismatchException exception) {
                scanner.next();
                System.out.println("Error: Score must be integer.");
            }
        }
        System.out.println("Your score is " + score + ".");
    }
}
```

Fig. B.3 Program with exception handling

Notice that the variable `flag` is initialized to `true` at the beginning so the program will ask the user to enter the score at least once inside the `while` loop. In order to break out of the `while` loop, the contents of `flag` must be changed to `false`. The use of the `boolean` variable `flag` was discussed in Chaps. _3_ and _4_ , where it was used with selection and iteration structures, respectively. In this example, the only time that control should break out of the `while` loop is when the user enters an integer value. Therefore, the value of the `flag` is changed right after the `nextInt` method. If an integer is entered, the execution continues to the statement that follows the `while` loop, instead of jumping to the `catch` clause. Also, notice the first statement `scanner.next();` inside the `catch` block. This removes the non-integer input value that caused an exception from the input buffer. Otherwise, the `nextInt` method processes the same invalid input from the first attempt over and over resulting in an infinite loop because the value would never be removed from the buffer and be assigned to the variable. The following output shows that the program will keep asking the user for input until valid value is entered:

```
Enter the score: 80.0
Error: Score must be integer.
Enter the score: 8o
Error: Score must be integer.
Enter the score: eighty
Error: Score must be integer.
Enter the score: 80
Your score is 80.
```

As can been seen in the fourth attempt, the user finally entered an integer value which caused the program to break out of the while loop and output the score.

B.3 Throwing Exceptions and Multiple `catch` Blocks

Compared to the original code in Fig. B.2 , the code with a `try-catch` statement in Fig. B.3 is more robust because the program does not crash when a non-integer value is entered. However, what happens if a negative integer is entered? Because a negative integer is still an integer, the program proceeds producing an erroneous result and does not throw an exception. Since the score should not be a negative number or greater than 100, the program should only accept a value in the range of 0 and 100. Before writing the program using the exception handling feature, one without `try-catch` blocks will be first developed to show the difference between the two techniques.

Because the user could enter non-integer values, it is not wise to use the `nextInt` method to read the input because it may cause abnormal termination when the input cannot be read as integer. Therefore, the input will be read as a `String` and checked to ensure that it consists of only digits. If it contains characters and decimal points, it cannot be an integer. If it is actually a number without a decimal point, it will be converted to the `int` type. Then, if it is between 0 and 100, the input is valid. The program below does these tasks:

```
import java.util.*;

class Score {
    public static void main(String[] args) {
        boolean flag, isInt;
        int i, score = 0;
        char c;
        String str;
        Scanner scanner = new Scanner(System.in);
        flag = true;
        while(flag) {
            System.out.print("Enter the score: ");
            str = scanner.next();

            isInt = true;
            i = 0;
            if(str.charAt(i) == '-' && str.length() > 1)
                i++;
            else
                if(str.length() == 0)
                    isInt = false;

            while(isInt && i < str.length()) {
                c = str.charAt(i);
                if(c < '0' || c > '9')
                    isInt = false;
                i++;
            }

            if(!isInt)
                System.out.println("Error: Score must be integer.");
            else {
                score = Integer.parseInt(str);
                if(score < 0 || score > 100)
                    System.out.println("Error: Score must be in 0-100.");
                else
                    flag = false;
            }
        }
        System.out.println("Your score is " + score + ".");
    }
}
```

As before, the while loop will repeat until the user enters an integer value between 0 and 100 inclusive. Notice that the input is read using the method next instead of nextInt . This will allow both digits and characters to be read as String. After checking for a leading minus sign, the inner loop goes through each character in the input string to see if it lies between "0" and "9" in the Unicode character set. The if statement following checks the boolean variable isInt , and if the input consists only of digits and an optional minus sign, it will contain the value true . If this is the case, then the input is converted into an integer using the parseInt method defined in Integer class, which takes a String and returns a value of int type. If the number is in the correct range, another boolean variable flag is set to false to break out of the while loop.

The following output shows that the program recovers not only from non-integer input but also an out of range integer value:

```
Enter the score: 8o
Error: Score must be integer.
Enter the score: 180
Error: Score must be in 0-100.
Enter the score: 80
Your score is 80.
```

A program which does the same task as above can be written using a try-catch block as shown in Fig. B.4 . In this program, notice that the input is checked in the `try` block to see if it is in the correct range. If it is not, an exception is thrown by using the `throw new RuntimeException();` statement. It creates an object of the `RuntimeException` class using a `new` statement. In the corresponding `catch` block, the thrown exception is caught, the reference to the object is assigned to the parameter `exception`, and the error message is displayed. Theoretically in the `throw` statement, any instance of the `Throwable` class or its subclasses including the `Error` class can be created. However, programs should not try to handle objects of the `Error` class or its subclasses. In general, only an instance of `Exception` class or its subclasses should be handled by programs, and this is why an object of the `RuntimeException` class that is a subclass of the `Exception` class was thrown in Fig. B.4 .

```
import java.util.*;

class ScoreVersion4 {
    public static void main(String[] args) {
        boolean flag;
        int score;
        Scanner scanner;
        scanner = new Scanner(System.in);
        flag = true;
        while(flag) {
            System.out.print("Enter the score: ");
            try {
                score = scanner.nextInt();
                if(score < 0 || score > 100)
                    throw new RuntimeException();
                flag = false;
            }
            catch (InputMismatchException exception) {
                scanner.next();
                System.out.println("Error: Score must be integer.");
            }
            catch (RuntimeException exception) {
                System.out.println("Error: Score must be in 0-100.");
            }
        }
        System.out.println("Your score is " + score + ".");
    }
}
```

Fig. B.4 A program with multiple `catch` blocks

Also notice that there are multiple `catch` blocks in the code shown in Fig. B.4 . When there are multiple `catch` blocks in a `try-catch` statement, they are checked in the order they are listed. Once a matching `catch` block is found, none of the subsequent ones are checked. Using the same input as before, when the input 80 is entered during the first iteration of the while loop, an InputMismatchException will be thrown and control looks for a matching catch block. In this case, the first catch block is executed, and then control will go back to the beginning of the while loop ignoring the second catch block. When the input 180 is entered, which is a valid integer value, the if condition is checked. Because the condition is false , a RuntimeException is thrown and control searches a matching catch block. Since this exception is not an object of the InputMismatchException class, the first catch block is skipped and the second catch block is executed. If the exception is thrown and there is not a matching catch block, then the system will handle the thrown exception by halting execution.

Because the execution classes form an inheritance hierarchy, it is important to place the catch block for specialized exception classes before those for the more general exception classes. For example, consider the reversed order of the catch blocks from Fig. B.4 as shown below:

```
// ** Caution - Incorrectly implemented code ** //
try {
    score = scanner.nextInt();
    if(score < 0 || score > 100)
        throw new RuntimeException();
    flag = false;
}
catch(RuntimeException exception) {
    System.out.println("Error: Score must be in 0-100.");
}
catch(InputMismatchException exception) {
    scanner.next();
    System.out.println("Error: Score must be an integer.");
}
```

This results in a compiler error with the message:

```
exception java.util.InputMismatchException has already been caught
```

Why? Recall that the InputMismatchException class is a subclass of the RuntimeException class as shown in Fig. B.1 and partially repeated below:

- Exception
    - IOException
        - ...
    - RuntimeException
        - ...
        - NoSuchElementException
            - InputMismatchException

When the object of the InputMismatchException class is thrown, the first catch block is executed and all other catch blocks are ignored. This means that the second `catch` block will never be executed because any exception object that is an instance of the `RuntimeException` class or its subclasses will match the first `catch` block.

When there are multiple `catch` blocks, each `catch` clause has to correspond to a specific type of exception. With the example above, since the `InputMismatchException` class is a subclass of the `RuntimeException` class, both exceptions could be caught by the `catch` clause with `RuntimeExeption`. Further, having two `catch` clauses for the same type of exception in the `try-catch` statement, as shown below, will cause the compiler to issue an error message "exception `java.lang.RuntimeException has already been caught`" in the second `catch` clause.

```
try {
   score = scanner.nextInt();
   if(score < 0 || score > 100)
      throw new RuntimeException();
   flag = false;
}
catch(RuntimeException exception) {
   scanner.next();
   System.out.println("Error: Score must be an integer.");
}
catch(RuntimeException exception) {
   System.out.println("Error: Score must be in 0-100.");
}
```

If there is a block of code that needs to be executed regardless of whether an exception is thrown, then the `try-catch` statement can include a `finally` block which must appear after all of the `catch` blocks. Consider the following `while` loop modified from Fig. B.4 with a `finally` block added at the end of the `try-catch` statement:

```
while(flag) {
    System.out.print("Enter the score: ");
    try {
        score = scanner.nextInt();
        if(score < 0 || score > 100)
            throw new RuntimeException();
        flag = false;
    }
    catch (InputMismatchException exception) {
        scanner.next();
        System.out.println("Error: Score must be integer.");
    }
    catch (RuntimeException exception) {
        System.out.println("Error: Score must be in 0-100.");
    }
    finally {
        System.out.println("End of try-catch statement.");
    }
}
```

The output using the same input values, 8o, 180, and 80, is shown below:

```
Enter the score: 8o
Error: Score must be integer.
End of try-catch statement.
Enter the score: 180
Error: Score must be in 0-100.
End of try-catch statement.
Enter the score: 80
End of try-catch statement.
Your score is 80.
```

Since the first two inputs were invalid, both an error message from the `catch` block and a message from the `finally` block were output. The last input did not throw an exception, so all the `catch` blocks were skipped, but the message from the `finally` block was still displayed.

B.4 Checked and Unchecked Exceptions

Among the exceptions, including the ones listed in Fig. B.1 , there are two categories: checked and unchecked. *Unchecked exceptions* are those that inherit from the `Error` class or the `RuntimeException` class. They are also called *runtime exceptions* because they are detected during runtime. As mentioned before, the exceptions that inherit from the `Error` class are thrown when a critical error occurs, and therefore they should not be handled by the program. Exceptions that were handled in the previous sections are all instances of the `RuntimeException` class or its subclasses. However, in general not all the possible exceptions from the `RuntimeException` class are handled in the program because handling each one of them in the program is not practical. As a result, exception handling should only be used when the problem can be corrected, and simply catching and ignoring any exception is a bad practice.

A `RuntimeException` indicates programming errors, so it could possibly be avoided altogether by writing better code. However, large applications might never be entirely bug-free, and exception handling can be used to display an appropriate message instead of surprising the user by an abnormal termination of the program. If the application is running critical tasks and must not crash, exception handling can be used to log the problem and the execution can continue.

All exceptions that are not inherited from the `Error` class or the `RuntimeException` class are called *checked exceptions* because they are checked during compile time. Consider a program which opens a file, reads numbers from the file, and outputs the total. Suppose the `scores.txt` file contains the following data and exists in the same directory as the `.java` file:

```
70
80
90
```

The code in Fig. B.5 opens the `scores.txt` file, reads three numbers from the file, and outputs the total. What happens during the compilation of the program? The compiler will issue an error message `"Unreported exception java.io.FileNotFoundException; must be caught or declared to be thrown"` for the line `inFile = new Scanner(new File("scores.txt"));` because this statement can potentially throw a checked exception. If the file `scores.txt` does not exist as discussed in Chap. 10 , the checked exception of a `FileNotFoundException` has to be thrown. A simple solution to eliminate this error is to add a `throws` clause, `throws IOException` , in the method header. The `throws` clause informs the compiler of the exceptions that could be thrown from a program. If the exception actually occurs during runtime, because the system could not find the file `scores.txt` , the system will deal with the exception by halting execution. Consider the following modified version of the code from Fig. B.5 :

```java
import java.util.*;
import java.io.*;

public class TotalVersion2 {
    public static void main(String[] args) throws IOException {
        int total;
        Scanner inFile;
        total = 0;

        inFile = new Scanner(new File("scores.txt"));
        for(int i=0; i<3; i++)
            total = total + inFile.nextInt();
        System.out.println("Total = " + total);
    }
}
```

```
import java.util.*;
import java.io.*;

public class TotalVersion1 {
    public static void main(String[] args) {
        int total;
        Scanner inFile;
        total = 0;

        inFile = new Scanner(new File("scores.txt"));
        for(int i=0; i<3; i++)
            total = total + inFile.nextInt();
        System.out.println("Total = " + total);
    }
}
```

Fig. B.5 A program with a checked exception

Notice that `throws IOException` is added in the `main` method header. The `FileNotFoundException` could be used in the header instead of `IOException` since it is the class that the exception object is actually created from. However, because the `IOException` class is a superclass of the `FileNotFoundException` class as shown below from Fig. B.1 , the `throws` clause with `IOException` can catch the instance of the `FileNotFoundException` class. Including the more general exception class in the header is useful since it can catch exceptions of all the subclasses.

```
−   Exception
     −   IOException
              −   CharConversionException
              −   EOFException
              −   FileNotFoundException
     −   RuntimeException
              −   ...
```

The other way to handle a checked exception is to include the `try-catch` statement in the body of the program. Because the statement `inFile = new Scanner(new File("scores.txt"));` could possibly throw a checked exception, it should be included inside the `try` block. The statements that should be executed in response to the thrown exception are placed in the matching `catch` block. To simply display an error message and continue when the exception is thrown, a `try-catch` statement is added to the code in Fig. B.5 as shown below:

```
import java.util.*;
import java.io.*;

public class TotalVersion3 {
   public static void main(String[] args) {
      int total;
      Scanner inFile;
      total = 0;

      try {
         inFile = new Scanner(new File("scores.txt"));
         for(int i=0; i<3; i++)
            total = total + inFile.nextInt();
      }
      catch(FileNotFoundException exception) {
         System.out.println("Error: File not found.");
      }
      System.out.println("Total = " + total);
   }
}
```

If the designated file does not exist in the system, the program will stop whether a `try-catch` block exists or not. However, without a `try-catch` block, the execution stops abnormally, and with a `try-catch` block, the program terminates normally. If it was a part of a larger application program, it would be convenient if the program did not crash just because it did not find one file, but continued the execution of the next part of the program.

Appendix C: Javadoc Comments

In Chap. 1 , different ways of documenting a Java program were discussed. As was mentioned, comments are intended for programmers and are ignored during execution. However, documentation is an important aspect of developing applications. In the real world, once an application is released, programming bugs that were not detected during development need to be fixed and new features may be added. Often those who modify a program are not the ones who developed it. The documentation then becomes very helpful for a programmer attempting to understand somebody else's program. This appendix explains more about specialized comments called *Javadoc* .

C.1 Javadoc

Java provides a standard form for writing comments and documenting classes. Javadoc comments in a program interact with the documentation tool also named Javadoc, which comes with the Java Development Kit (JDK). The Javadoc tool reads the Javadoc comments from the source file and produces a collection of HyperText Markup Language (*HTML*) pages, which can be read and displayed by web browsers. These pages look just like the Java API specification document at the Oracle website at http://docs.oracle.com/javase/7/docs/api/index.html . The HTML pages created by the Javadoc tool contain only documentation and no actual Java code. The documentation allows programmers to understand and use the classes someone else has written without seeing how they are actually implemented.

Javadoc comments begin with a slash followed by two asterisks /** and end with an asterisk followed by a slash */ . Many programmers also place a single asterisk * at the start of each line in the comment as shown in the program in Fig. C.1 . Although they have no significance and the Javadoc tool ignores them, they make it easy to see the entire extent of the comments in the program.

J. T. Streib and T. Soma, *Guide to Java*, Undergraduate Topics in Computer Science, https://doi.org/10.1007/978-3-031-22842-1

```java
import java.util.*;

/**
 * A program to calculate two roots of a quadratic equation.
 * Assume that a <> 0 and the relationship b^2 >= 4ac holds,
 * so there will be real number solutions for x.
 *
 * @author James T. Streib and Takako Soma
 */
public class QuadEq {
    /**
     * This method inputs three numbers then calculates and
     * outputs two roots.
     */
    public static void main(String[] args) {
        // declaration and initialization of variables
        double a, b, c, root1, root2, sqrtDiscr;
        Scanner scanner;
        scanner = new Scanner(System.in);

        // input a, b, and c
        System.out.print("Enter a: ");
        a = scanner.nextDouble();
        System.out.print("Enter b: ");
        b = scanner.nextDouble();
        System.out.print("Enter c: ");
        c = scanner.nextDouble();

        // compute the two roots
        sqrtDiscr = Math.sqrt(Math.pow(b,2) - 4*a*c);
        root1 = (-b + sqrtDiscr) / (2*a);
        root2 = (-b - sqrtDiscr) / (2*a);

        // output two roots
        System.out.println();
        System.out.println("Two roots of the equation, " + a
                        + "*x*x + " + b + "*x + " + c + " = 0, are");
        System.out.printf("%.2f and %.2f.", root1, root2);
    }
}
```

Fig. C.1 A program with Javadoc comments

The Javadoc comments for the class are placed between the `import` statements and the class header. After the description of the class, the rest of the comment consists of a series of *Javadoc tags*, which are special markers that begin with the @ symbol. Each tag tells the Javadoc tool certain information. The documentation for a class will usually contain an author tag. The Javadoc tag `@author` indicates the name of the programmer(s) who created the class. The Javadoc comments for the description of a method are placed above the method header. As an example, two Javadoc comments are added to the `QuadEq` class discussed in Chap. 1 and shown in Fig. C.1 .

The use of Javadoc comments does not preclude the use of other types of comments in the program. In addition to the Javadoc comments in Fig. C.1 , the regular comments with two slashes `//` are used to describe the sections of the code. Since Javadoc comments included in the HTML page are the only ones describing the class, its data members, and its methods, the comments describing the sections will not appear in the HTML page even if they are written as Javadoc comments. However, the comments in the middle of the code are still important when a programmer is reading to understand the code. Therefore, Javadoc comments are useful for a programmer who simply uses the classes without looking at the implementation, and other comments in the code are helpful for a programmer who is actually modifying the code.

Once all the Javadoc comments are added to the class, the next step is to generate the corresponding HTML documentation file. Many Java editors and Integrated Development Environments (IDEs) include a menu option that can be used to generate a Javadoc documentation file quickly and easily. Part of the resulting HTML page for the QuadEq class is shown below:

In the nicely formatted HTML page, the description of the class which has been added to the program as a Javadoc comment is shown. The author tag appears in boldface and the names of the authors are shown as well. Since there is no constructor defined in the class, a system-generated default constructor is listed in the Constructor Summary section. The

Method Summary section contains only the `main` method along with the Javadoc comments added in the program because only one method exists in the class.

C.2 More Javadoc Tags

The format of the Javadoc comments for a method is similar to the one for a class. In addition to a general description, a number of Javadoc tags can be included. The main purpose of the comments for a method is to record its purpose, a list of any parameters passed to the method, and any value returned from the method. If the method receives a parameter, the `@param` tag is used, and if the method returns a value, the `@return` tag is added. The Javadoc comments for the method `convertEurosToDollars` as defined in the `Card` class from Sect. 5.6.2 are shown below:

```
/**
 * Convert the passed value to Dollars.
 *
 * @param euros the amount in Euros
 * @return the amount in Dollars
 */
public static double convertEurosToDollars(double euros) {
    return euros*rate;
}
```

Notice that the Javadoc comments for the method need to be placed just above the method header. Each parameter of the method is documented by using a tag `@param`, followed by the name and the description of the parameter. A description of a return value is listed after the Javadoc tag `@return`. Notice the effect of the `@param` and `@return` tags in the following HTML document for the above method:

Method Detail

---

convertEurosToDollars

`public static double convertEurosToDollars(double euros)`

Convert the passed value to Dollars.

Parameters:
euros - the amount in Euros
Returns:
the amount in Dollars

The Javadoc comments for a constructor can be defined in a manner similar to the one for a method, except it does not have a `@return` tag. In addition to the above tags, if the method could throw exceptions, they can be listed using the `@throws` tag, just like the `@param` and the `@return` tags in the Javadoc comments. The topic of exceptions is discussed in Appendix B.

More complex methods may need complete precondition and postcondition lists. Also an example of how the method is used may be useful information for other programmers. The tags such as @precondition , @postcondition , and @example that are not predefined in the Javadoc tool can be created by programmers. Since the convertEurosToDollars is a simple method, only the @example tag will be added to the Javadoc comments as shown below:

```
/**
 * Convert the passed value to Dollars.
 *
 * @param euros the amount in Euros
 * @return the amount in Dollars
 * @example conversion of 1.00 Euros to US dollars -
 * Card.convertEurosToDollars(1.00);
 */
public static double convertEurosToDollars(double euros) {
   return euros*rate;
}
```

Note that in order to include the user-defined tags in the documentation, the HTML page may need to be generated from a command line if the Java editor does not have a capability of including the options, as will be discussed in the next section. The HTML document for the above method also appears in the next section.

Similar to the standard classes, programmer-defined classes and HTML documentation can be shared with other programmers. First, .java files are written in the usual way but include the Javadoc comments described in this appendix. After they are compiled, the .class files can be moved to a location where other programmers can have access to them. Then the Javadoc tool can be run on each .java file to create an HTML page, and all Javadoc HTML files can be moved to a public place where a web browser could be used to read them. This way, by importing the classes at the beginning of the Java program, the programmer-defined classes are available to other programmers without compiling them just like the standard classes.

C.3 Generating Javadoc Documentation from a Command Line

An HTML page can also be generated from a command line. In the command prompt window, the commands javac and java are used to compile and run Java programs, respectively. Similarly, the javadoc command is used for generating Javadoc documentation files. For example, to generate a Javadoc documentation file for the QuadEq class, the following command is used:

```
javadoc QuadEq.java
```

After the command is executed, a collection of HTML files will be created. The documentation can be viewed by opening the file index.html and clicking the QuadEq link.

When a programmer-defined tag such as @example is included in the source code, options need to be included in the command line to generate the HTML. The following command can be used to create Javadoc documentation for the `Card` class which implements the method.

```
convertEurosToDollars:
javadoc -private -author -tag param -tag return
-tag example:a:"Example:" Card.java
```

The `-private` option generates the documentation for the class, variables, and methods including the `public`, `protected`, and `private` members of the class. The `-author` option puts the author tag in boldface followed by the author's name in the documentation. The other options starting with `-tag` indicate the order in which the tags appear in the HTML file: the parameter(s) first, then the return specification, and finally the example. Two of these options, `param` and `return`, are predefined in the Javadoc system, so only `-tag param` and `-tag return` are listed. However, because an `example` tag is not predefined in Javadoc, the extra information at the end such as `:a:"Example:"` is needed and indicates how the tag is to appear in the documentation. The `a:` means that all occurrences of the `@example` tag should be put in the documentation along with a heading, which in this case is **Example:** as it appears in the quotation marks. Headings will always appear in boldface in the documentation created by the `javadoc` command. The following is the HTML document for the method `convertEurosToDollars` that is generated after the `@example` tag is added to the source code.

Method Detail

---

convertEurosToDollars

```
public static double convertEurosToDollars(double euros)
```

Convert the passed value to Dollars.

Parameters:
euros - the amount in Euros

Returns:
the amount in Dollars

Example:
conversion of 1.00 Euros to US dollars Card.convertEurosToDollars(1.00);

For more information about Javadoc, refer to the Java API specification document at the Oracle website at
http://docs.oracle.com/javase/7/docs/technotes/tools/windows/javadoc.html .

Appendix D: Glossary

Many of the terms in *italics* in the text can be found in the index, and some of these terms (including abbreviations) can be found here in the glossary. The descriptions of terms in this glossary should not be used in lieu of the complete descriptions in the text, but rather they serve as a quick review. Should a more complete description be needed, the index can guide the reader to the appropriate pages where the terms are discussed in more detail.

Algorithm	A step-by-step sequence of instructions, but not necessarily a program for a computer.
API	Application Programming Interface.
Array	A collection of contiguous memory locations that have the same name and are distinguished from one another by an index.
Assembly language	A low-level language that uses mnemonics and is converted to machine language by an assembler.
Bit-wise	Logical operations performed on the individual bits within a memory location
Bytecode	An intermediate language between Java and machine language.
Class	A definition or blueprint of a set of objects.
Compiler	A translator that converts a high-level language program to a low-level language for subsequent execution.
Computational thinking	Using concepts from computer science to solve problems.
Computer ethics	Ethical issues related to the use and programming of computers such as respondsibility, privacy, and property.
Contour diagram	A visual representation of the state of execution of a program.
CPU	Central Processing Unit.
Data members	The variables and constants that are part of an object.
EOD	End of Data.

J. T. Streib and T. Soma, *Guide to Java*, Undergraduate Topics in Computer Science, https://doi.org/10.1007/978-3-031-22842-1

Exception   An execution error, an error condition, or an unexpected event during execution of a program.

GUI   Graphical User Interface.

High-level language   A more English-like and math-like programming language, such as Java.

HTML   HyperText Markup Language.

IDE   Integrated Development Environment.

Inheritance   The ability of a subclass to reuse methods and data members of a superclass.

Interpreter   A translator that converts and executes a high-level language program one instruction at a time.

IPO   Input Process Output.

Iteration structures   Allows a program to repeat a section of code, often called a loop.

Javadoc   Specialized comments for documenting classes and methods.

LCV   Loop Control Variable.

LIFO   Last In First Out as with a stack.

Low-level language   A language closer to a particular CPU, such as assembly language and machine language.

Machine language   The native language of the processor coded on ones and zeros.

Method   A series of instructions that can be invoked to access and manipulate the data members of an object.

Object   An instance of a class.

OOP   Object-Oriented Programming.

Overloading   A method in the same class that has the same name but a different number of parameters, different types of parameters, or parameters of different types in a different order.

Overriding   A method in a subclass that has the same name and also the same number and type of parameters as the one in the superclass.

Parallel Program	A program written to execute taks at the same time using multiple processors.
Polymorphism	The type of an object referenced by a superclass variable determined at runtime.
Pseudocode	A design tool consisting of a combination of English and a programming language that helps one concentrate on logic instead of syntax when developing a program.
RAM	Random Access Memory.
Recursion	A definition that is defined in terms of itself and includes a base or terminal case.
Selection structures	Allows a program to follow one of more paths, sometimes called decision structures.
Semantics	The meaning of what each instruction does in a programming language.
Shared memory multiprocessor	A system thathas two or more processors that share common memory.
Syntax	The grammar of a programming language.
UML	Unified Modeling Language.
Variables	Named memory locations used to store data in a program.

Appendix E: Answers to Selected Exercises

Chapter 1

1.B. Correct.

1.D. Incorrect, a double number cannot be assigned to a variable of integer type.

2.A. `0`

3.B. `5.34`

4.B. `final double EULER_NUMBER = 2.7182;`

6.
```
System.out.println("** **");

System.out.println("** **");

System.out.println(" ****");

System.out.println(" ****");

System.out.println(" ****");

System.out.println(" ****");

System.out.println("** **");

System.out.println("** **");
```

7. After execution, `value1` is `9`, `value2` is `4`, and `value3` is `9`.

8.B. `s = r * Math.PI * Math.sqrt(Math.pow(r,2) + Math.pow(h,2));`

Chapter 2

1.A. Incorrect, it should be `Circle circle = new Circle();`

1.C. Correct.

4.A.
```
Circle innerCircle;

innerCircle = new Circle();
```

4.C.
```
System.out.println("The value of radius is "
    + innerCircle.getRadius());
```

J. T. Streib and T. Soma, *Guide to Java*, Undergraduate Topics in Computer Science,
https://doi.org/10.1007/978-3-031-22842-1

6.   Answers to A. and D. of the Cone class

```
class Cone {                                    // 6.A.
    // data members
    private double radius, height;              // 6.A.

    // mutator methods
    public void setRadius(double aRadius) {     // 6.D.
        radius = aRadius;                       // 6.D.
    }                                           // 6.D.
    public void setHeight(double aHeight) {     // 6.D.
        height = aHeight;                       // 6.D.
    }                                           // 6.D.
}                                               // 6.A.
```

Chapter 3

1.A. 40
2.B. 50
3.C. 3
5.A. true || false → true
5.C. true || flag1 && flag2 → true || false → true
5.E. (true || false) && false → true && false → false

8.

```
int number;
Scanner scanner;
scanner = new Scanner(System.in);

System.out.print("Enter a number between 1 and 4: ");
number = scanner.nextInt();
switch(number) {
    case 1:     System.out.print("First-year");
                break;
    case 2:     System.out.print("Sophomore");
                break;
    case 3:     System.out.print("Junior");
                break;
    case 4:     System.out.print("Senior");
}
```

9.

```
int number;
Scanner scanner;
scanner = new Scanner(System.in);

System.out.print("Enter a number between 1 and 4: ");
number = scanner.nextInt();
if(number == 1)
    System.out.print("First-year");
else
    if(number == 2)
        System.out.print("Sophomore");
    else
        if(number == 3)
            System.out.print("Junior");
        else
            if(number == 4)
                System.out.print("Senior");
```

Chapter 4

2. the , in the `for` statement

3.
```
sum = 1

count = 2

sum = 3

count = 3

sum = 6

count = 4

sum = 10

count = 5

sum = 10

count = 5
```

6.
```
      **
     ****
    ******
   ********
  **********
```

7.B. `int total, count`

```
total = 0;
count = 1;
do {
    total += count;
    count += 3;
} while (count <= 40);
```

8.A. `int total, count, n;`

```
total = 0;

n = 5;

for(count = 0; count < n; count++) {

    total += count;

}
```

Chapter 5

1. constructor 1 : valid

    constructor 3 : invalid

2. method 2 : invalid

    method 6 : valid

    method 10 : valid

6. answers to A., B., C., and F. of the Cone class

```
class Rectangle {                                        // 6.A.
    // data members
    private static final double DEFAULT_VALUE = 0.0;     // 6.A.
    private double sideX, sideY;                          // 6.B.

    // constructor
    public Rectangle() {                                  // 6.C.
        this(DEFAULT_VALUE, DEFAULT_VALUE);               // 6.C.
    }                                                     // 6.C.

    // methods
    public void setSideX (double sideX) {                 // 6.F.
        this.sideX = sideX;                               // 6.F.
    }                                                     // 6.F.

    public void setSideY (double sideY) {                 // 6.F.
        this.sideY = sideY;                               // 6.F.
    }                                                     // 6.F.
}                                                         // 6.A.
```

Chapter 6

1.B. The second line should be `text2 = new String("Shedding blade");`
2.B. `34`
2.D. `Hose_`

7.

```
class Abbreviation {
    public static void main(String[] args) {
        String org;
        String init1, init2, init3, init4, strTemp;
        org = new String ("American Quarter Horse Association");
        init1 = org.substring(0, 1);
        strTemp = org.substring(sorg.indexOf(" ")+1, org.length());
        init2 = strTemp.substring(0, 1);
        strTemp = strTemp.substring(strTemp.indexOf(" ")+1,
                strTemp.length());
        init3 = strTemp.substring(0, 1);
        strTemp = strTemp.substring(strTemp.indexOf(" ")+1,
                strTemp.length());
        init4 = strTemp.substring(0, 1);
        System.out.println(init1 + init2 + init3 + init4);
    }
}
```

Chapter 7

1.B. Incorrect, the size has to be specified.
1.C. Incorrect, the braces have to be used instead of the square brackets.
1.E. Incorrect, the size should not be specified.
2.

```
int total = 0;
for(int i=0; i<intArray.length; i++)
    if(i%2 == 0)
        total = total + intArray[i];
```

5. 3
   4
   3

7.

```
public class Exercise7 {
    public static void main(String[] args){
        int[][] scores = {{72, 85, 91},
                          {95, 89, 90},
                          {77, 65, 73},
                          {97, 82, 71}};
        double average;
        for(int i=0; i<scores[0].length; i++) {
            average = examAvg(scores, i);
            System.out.printf("average for Exam " + (i+1)
                                    + ": %5.2f", average);
            System.out.println();
        }
    }

    public static double examAvg(int[][] inArray, int col) {
        double total, average;
        total = 0;
        for(int i=0; i<inArray.length; i++)
            total = total + inArray[i][col];
        average = total/inArray.length;
        return average;

    }
}
```

Chapter 8

7.
```
public static String reverseStr(String str) {
    if(str.length() <= 1)
        return str;
    return reverseStr(str.substring(1)) + str.charAt(0);
}
```

9.
```
public static int factorial(int n) {
    if(n == 0)
        return 1;
    else
        return n * factorial(n-1);
}
```

Chapter 9

1.B. Incorrect, a variable of a subclass type cannot reference an object of a superclass type.
1.C. Correct.
2.B. `calcRegPolyArea` and `toString`.
2.D. Yes.

3.

```
class Engineer extends FullTime {
   private String type;

   public Engineer(int id, double salary, String type) {
      super(id, salary);
      this.type = type;
   }

   public String toString() {
      String str;
      str = super.toString()
            + "This employee is a " + type + " engineer.\n";
      return str;
   }
}
```

Chapter 10

1.B. Incorrect, there is no constructor in the File Class which takes the FileReader object as a parameter.
1.D. Correct.

3.

```
import java.util.*;
import java.io.*;

public class ThreeNumbers {
   public static void main(String[] args) throws IOException {

      String file;
      Scanner scanner = new Scanner(System.in);

      System.out.print("Enter the name of the output file: ");
      file = scanner.next();

      PrintWriter outFile =
               new PrintWriter(new FileWriter(file));

      System.out.println();
      System.out.println("Enter three numbers.");
      for(int i=0; i<3; i++) {
         System.out.print("Enter number " + (i+1) + ": ");
         outFile.println(scanner.nextInt());
      }

      outFile.close();
   }
}
```

Chapter 11

1.A. 47
1.C. 118
2.A. 00100001
2.C. 01111000
3.A. 00000000
3.C. 00110101
4.A. 11001010
4.C. 01000010

Chapter 12

1.A. Process 0: myFirstPos = 0 and myLastPos = 375.
   Process 1: myFirstPos = 375 and myLastPos = 750.
   Process 2: myFirstPos = 750 and myLastPos = 1125.
   Process 3: myFirstPos = 1125 and myLastPos = 1500.

5.

Serial Program:

```
public class VectorAdditionSerial {
    public static void main(String[] args) {
        int numThreads, vecSize;
        numThreads = Integer.parseInt(args[0]);
        vecSize = Integer.parseInt(args[1]);
        int[] a, b, c;
        a = new int[vecSize];
        b = new int[vecSize];
        c = new int[vecSize];
        getVec(a);
        getVec(b);

        // addition
        for(int i=0; i<a.length; i++)
            c[i] = a[i] + b[i];
    }

    public static void getVec(int[] array) {
        for(int i=0; i<array.length; i++)
            array[i] = (int)(Math.floor(Math.random() * 1000));
    }
}
```

Parallel program:

```
public class VectorAdditionParallel {
   public static void main(String[] args) {
      int numThreads, vecSize;
      numThreads = Integer.parseInt(args[0]);
      vecSize = Integer.parseInt(args[1]);
      int[] a, b, c;
      a = new int[vecSize];
      b = new int[vecSize];
      c = new int[vecSize];
      getVec(a);
      getVec(b);

      // parallel section
      //#omp parallel num_threads(numThreads)
      shared(numThreads, vecSize, a, b, c)
      {
         int myPart, myID, myFirstPos, myLastPos;
         myPart = vecSize / numThreads;
         myID = Pyjama.omp_get_thread_num();
         myFirstPos = myPart * myID;
         if(myID == numThreads-1)
            myLastPos = vecSize;
         else
            myLastPos = myFirstPos + myPart;

         // addition
         for(int i=myFirstPos; i<myLastPos; i++)
            c[i] = a[i] + b[i];
      } // end of parallel section
   }

   public static void getVec(int[] array) {
      for(int i=0; i<array.length; i++)
         array[i] = (int)(Math.floor(Math.random() * 1000));
   }
}
```

References and Useful Websites

References

1. ACM (2018) ACM Code of Ethics and professional conduct, https://www.acm.org/code-of-ethics.

2. Ghafoor S and Rogers M, Integrating Parallel and Distributed Computing in Introductory Programming Classes, https://www.csc.tntech.edu/pdcincs/

3. IEEE Computer Society/ACM (1999) IEEE-CS/ACM Joint task force on software engineering ethics and professional practices, https://www.computer.org/education/code-of-ethics.

4. Johnson JB (1971) The contour model of block structured processes. SIGPLAN Notices Vol. 6, Issue 2, pp 55–72.

5. Kizza JM (2016) Ethics in computing: a concise module, Springer Nature, Switzerland.

6. OpenMP, https://www.openmp.org/

7. Organick EI, Forsythe AI, Plummer RP (1978) Programming language structures. Academic Press, New York.

8. Streib JT, Soma T (2010) Using contour diagrams and JIVE to illustrate object-oriented semantics in the Java programming language. In: SIGCSE '10: Proceedings of the 41st ACM technical symposium on computer science education, pp 510–514.

9. Streib JT (2015) Critical thinking and debugging software, Journal of Computing Sciences in Colleges, Vol. 31, Issue 1.

10. Streib JT (2020) Guide to assembly language: a concise introduction. 2nd edition, Springer Nature, Switzerland.

11. Vikas, Giacaman N, and Sinnen O (2013) Pyjama: OpenMP-like Implementation for Java, with GUI Extensions. In *PMAM*. ACM, New York, NY, USA.

12. Wing J (2006) Computational thinking, Communication of the ACM, Vol. 49, Issue 3.

© The Editor(s) (if applicable) and The Author(s), under exclusive license
to Springer Nature Switzerland AG 2023
J. T. Streib and T. Soma, *Guide to Java*, Undergraduate Topics in Computer Science,
https://doi.org/10.1007/978-3-031-22842-1

Useful Websites

"Class File," information on File class discussed in Chapter 10:
   http://docs.oracle.com/javase/7/docs/api/java/io/File.html

"Class FileReader," information on FileReader class discussed in Chapter 10:
   http://docs.oracle.com/javase/7/docs/api/java/io/FileReader.html

"Class JOptionPane," information on dialog boxes discussed in Appendix A:
   http://docs.oracle.com/javase/7/docs/api/javax/swing/JOptionPane.html

"Class String," information on String class discussed in Chapter 6:
   http://docs.oracle.com/javase/7/docs/api/java/lang/String.html

"javadoc – The Java API Documentation Generator," information on Javadoc discussed
   in Appendix C:
   http://docs.oracle.com/javase/7/docs/technotes/tools/windows/javadoc.html

"Java™ Platform, Standard Edition 7 API Specification," format of documents created by
   the Javadoc discussed in Appendix C:
   http://docs.oracle.com/javase/7/docs/api/index.html

"Java™ Platform, Standard Edition 7 API Specification," list of classes and packages in
   Java 7: http://docs.oracle.com/javase/7/docs/api/index.html

Index

W
while, 124
While loops, 122-134